"We Are All Leaders"

"We Are All Leaders"

The Alternative Unionism
of the Early 1930s

Edited by

Staughton Lynd

University of Illinois Press
Urbana and Chicago

© 1996 by the Board of Trustees of the University of Illinois
Manufactured in the United States of America

1   2   3   4   5   C   P   5   4   3   2

This book is printed on acid-free paper.

Library of Congress Cataloging-in-Publication Data
"We are all leaders" : the alternative unionism of the early
1930s / edited by Staughton Lynd.
p.   cm. — (The working class in American history)
Includes bibliographical references and index.
ISBN 0-252-02243-2 (cloth:alk. paper). —
ISBN 0-252-06547-6 (pbk.:alk. paper)
1. Trade unions—United States—History—
20th century. 2. Labor movement—United States—
History—20th century.
I. Lynd, Staughton.
II. Series.
HD6508.W344   1996
331.88'0973'09043—dc20
95-50192   CIP

A list of books in the series appears at the end of this book.

The Working Class in American History

Editorial Advisors

David Brody
Alice Kessler-Harris
David Montgomery
Sean Wilentz

This book is dedicated to the late
Michael Kozura

Contents

Introduction

Staughton Lynd

When I was growing up, the CIO was considered the most progressive social force in the United States. There were books in our home about the CIO with such titles as *Labor on the March*. My mother belonged to the executive board of the New York City teachers' union. The first picket line I ever joined was at the General Motors offices in New York City during the 1946 United Automobile Workers (UAW) strike. I remember the happiness in my father's face and voice when he came home after speaking to a UAW educational conference in Milwaukee. He had advocated a labor party. After the speech was delivered, reports of it "circulated through the union with the result" that it was published as a UAW pamphlet.[1]

Even then it was evident that the officers of CIO unions were "new men of power." But centralized national unions were said to be necessary because the corporations with which they struggled were organized nationally and produced goods for national markets.[2] Today corporations have reorganized as *multinationals* and compete in the *international* marketplace. These corporations close plants in the United States and move production overseas at will. National AFL-CIO unions watch helplessly, just as national AFL unions looked on helplessly during the Great Depression. Like the national AFL unions of that period, national AFL-CIO unions today not only are hierarchical and bureaucratic structures, out of touch with the concerns of the rank and file, but also do not perform effectively the protective tasks that might justify their existence. The hopes of men and women who built new industrial unions in the 1930s have been disappointed.

It is very difficult to know what was or was not possible in the past. Most of those who took part in the struggles of the 1930s and had a feel for the possibilities and limitations of that time are dead. What one can say with confidence is that the end product of the process, AFL-CIO business unionism, does not meet the needs of working people at the end of the twentieth century. A qualitatively different unionism is needed.

The essays in this book describe a kind of union qualitatively different from the bureaucratic business unions that came to make up the CIO. We are not speculating about "might-have-beens."[3] We direct attention to facts that have been disregarded.

Recent studies of the labor movement of the 1930s in such communities as Flint, Akron, Chicago, Memphis, and Woonsocket, Rhode Island, offer evidence of an alternative unionism that preceded the CIO. What is lacking in many of these studies is an openness to the possibility that history could have been different. For example, Gary Gerstle, after richly chronicling the success of the Independent Textile Union in Woonsocket, nonetheless concludes, "The only realistic, programmatic option for a radical . . . in 1930s Woonsocket involved . . . building the CIO, and extending the New Deal."[4] But Michael Honey is right in stating that the movement for industrial unionism in the 1930s was much larger than the CIO. In Memphis the most important industrial union organizer was a black business agent for an AFL "federal union" (a local union directly affiliated with the national AFL).[5]

We believe that what happened in communities like Woonsocket and Barberton, Ohio, in the 1930s and beyond represents an alternative to the course followed by the mainstream labor movement. To encounter this alternative, one must be prepared to lay aside the notion that the real labor movement, the labor movement that mattered, began with the formation of the CIO in 1935. One must view the 1930s from the perspective of rank-and-file workers who were active in 1932, 1933, and 1934. Our essays tell the story of what such workers did on their own behalf before the formation of the CIO and, in some cases, continued to do for years and even decades thereafter.

What Is "Alternative Unionism"?

The unionism described in these essays has been called "community-based unionism" or "solidarity unionism." Elizabeth Faue says community-based unionism "emphasized local autonomy and community-level organization" and "opposed bureaucratic unionism."[6] By whatever name, this alternative unionism was democratic, deeply rooted in mutual aid among workers in different crafts and work sites, and politically independent. The key to the value system of alternative unionism was its egalitarianism. The seniority system later negotiated by CIO unions caused some workers to lose their livelihood in a layoff, while others continued to work full-time. In contrast, the Independent Textile Union in Woonsocket, the first industrial unions in rubber, and the anthracite miners of eastern Pennsylvania in the 1930s all favored schemes to share or "equalize" the work among all workers who had completed the probationary period, regardless of seniority.[7] The same attitude was evident in the response of the new, independent local industrial unions in Barberton to the Roosevelt recession of 1937–38. According to John Borsos, until the work available dropped below a certain number of hours (typically twenty-four hours a week), Barberton unions insisted that it be equally shared.[8]

The organizational forms of alternative unionism included federal labor unions, ad hoc factory committees, and improvised central labor bodies.[9] Historians have supposed that the general strikes in Toledo, Minneapolis, and San Francisco in 1934 were isolated events. We suggest that, on the contrary, these local general strikes were characteristic of what Rosemary Feurer and Gary Gerstle call the "mobilization" of working-class communities.[10] In the absence of effective national organizations from which they could seek help, rank and filers were obliged to turn to each other and create horizontal networks that in turn generated a distinctive organizational culture and set of attitudes.

Numerically, the self-organization of the rank and file in the early 1930s was at least as effective as the top-down efforts of the CIO a few years later. In June 1933 the Amalgamated Association of Iron, Steel, and Tin Workers reported less than 5,000 members. By the Amalgamated's national convention in April 1934 its membership had increased to a number variously estimated at 50,000 to 200,000. In a comparable period, from June 1936 to March 1937, the Steel Workers Organizing Committee, using 200 full-time organizers, enrolled about the same number of workers.[11]

The picture was similar in other industries. By June 1935 there were a hundred federal labor unions in Summit County, Ohio (including the city of Akron), with 60,000 members.[12] In Flint the citywide council of federal labor unions said it had 42,000 members in March 1934, and AFL records indicate that there were 14,000 members who paid dues. These numbers are roughly equivalent to the 25,000 UAW members claimed by

the organizer Bob Travis immediately after the Flint sit-down strike of
1937.[13] Similarly, the United Textile Workers union witnessed an extraordinary increase in southern membership, from only a few thousand in July
1933 to between 85,000 and 135,000 (a third to a half of the southern
textile labor force) a year later.[14]

A Wobbly Resemblance

As this book has come together, I have been struck by the resemblance
between the "alternative unionism" of the 1930s and the rank-and-file
militancy of the Industrial Workers of the World (IWW). The following
evidence, for the most part unknown to me before this project began, supports that impression.

In the anthracite coal fields, IWW membership from 1906 to 1916 rivaled that of the United Mine Workers (UMW). Perhaps as a result, Michael Kozura points out, "anthracite miners continued to rely on illegal
wildcat strikes and other forms of direct action, refused on principle to submit grievances to arbitration, tenaciously resisted the contractual regulation of their labor, opposed union dues check-off, habitually rebelled
against the UMW's dictatorial leadership, and sustained this militant syndicalism into the late 1940s."[15]

Individual Wobblies or former Wobblies were often involved in the local industrial unions of the 1930s. Len DeCaux wrote of his fellow CIO
militants that "when the CIO lefts let down their hair, it seemed that only
the youngest had no background of Wobbly associations."[16] Specific examples abound. Tom Klasey, who helped organize AFL members at Chevrolet in Flint, had been an IWW activist in the Pacific Northwest during
World War I. In Austin, Minnesota, organization of the Independent Union
of All Workers (IUAW) was led by Frank Ellis, who was "a Wobbly and
had taken part in the IWW free speech fights out in Everett, Washington,"
and the IUAW itself was remembered by a contemporary as "the old
Wobbly, the old IWW's local." Blackie and Chips, the "1934 men" who
taught Stan Weir the history of the San Francisco general strike, were
among the many older seamen who paid dues to the IWW until 1936. John
W. Anderson jumped up on a car fender to become the chairperson of the
1933 Briggs strike in Detroit, worked as a volunteer IWW organizer for
three years, and later became a dissident local union president in the UAW.
Freeman Thompson, who joined the National Miners Union in the early
1930s and objected when asked to rejoin the United Mine Workers a few
years later, "seemed to have some IWW experience in his background."[17]

A Wobbly style of organizing was sometimes evident even when flesh-and-blood Wobblies were not. David Montgomery has suggested that "in many ways the struggles of 1916–1922 . . . presaged those of at least the early 1930s, that is, before the founding of the Committee for Industrial Organization and the enactment of the Wagner Act."[18] The Westinghouse plant east of Pittsburgh is an example of such continuity. Montgomery describes how just before World War I the Westinghouse workers created an "inplant organization made up of their own elected delegates" that cut across traditional craft lines. The organization "copied the IWW by devoting itself to struggles around demands, rather than negotiating contracts."[19] More than twenty years later, when the CIO established itself in the same plant, bargaining was at first carried on in the same Wobbly manner. According to Ronald Schatz,

> an arrangement existed whereby plant managers would meet with the leaders of UE Local 601 to negotiate about such issues as hours of work or layoff policy, then depart to post the results of their discussions as if management had merely consulted with the union leadership. Although there were few if any Wobblies . . . in the plant, the local had arrived at an IWW-style bargaining relationship. There were no contracts; all agreements could be abrogated by either party at any time; and grievances were settled quickly according to the strength of the workers on the floor of the plant.[20]

As at Westinghouse, the spirit of alternative unionism often carried over into the strongest *local* unions of the emerging CIO. Many CIO locals, not just in anthracite mining and electrical work but also in the automobile, rubber, and steel industries, initially *opposed* "workplace contractualism" in the form of the dues checkoff and written contracts.[21] Sylvia Woods, who belonged to a UAW local in Chicago during World War II, recalled, "We never had a check-off. We didn't want it."[22] In rubber, sit-downs at General Tire, Firestone, and elsewhere convinced workers that "progress did not have to await a formal contract."[23] Goodrich Local 5 in Akron, whose 13,000 members made it the largest local union in the United Rubber Workers, for several years in the 1930s deliberately declined to enter into a collective bargaining agreement.[24] Similarly, John Sargent, the first president of the 18,000-member local union at Inland Steel, recalled, "Without a contract we secured for ourselves agreements on working conditions and wages that we do not have today [1970]. . . . If their wages were low there was no contract to prohibit them from striking, and they struck for better wages. If their conditions were bad, if they didn't like what was going on, if they were being abused, the people in the mills themselves—without a contract or any agreement with the company involved—would shut down a department or even a group of departments to secure for themselves the things they found necessary."[25]

The sit-down strikes in Akron and Flint, far from being planned by the national CIO, arose spontaneously from below and were initially opposed by CIO leaders. David Brody writes, "President Sherman Dalrymple of the Rubber Workers at first opposed the sit-downs. Spontaneous sit-downs within the plants accounted for the initial victories in auto and rubber."[26] Ronald Edsforth confirms that the Flint strike "caught the U.A.W. hierarchy by surprise. They had not planned any action until the first of the year." Although CIO and UAW leaders supported the Flint sit-down once it was under way, their difference with the rank and file over timing was also a disagreement about the authority to start strikes. "It seems to be a custome [sic] for anybody or any group to call a strike at will," Adolf Germer, the CIO representative, complained to John Brophy, the CIO representative, in November 1936.[27] Louis Adamic investigated the sit-downs soon after they occurred and concluded that

> many of the rank-and-file automobile and rubber workers, as well as many of the organizers in the field and some of the people in the offices of the rubber and automobile unions, thought the world of the sitdown when I asked them about it. The top leadership of these unions, however, like the responsible leaders of the C.I.O., seemed to view it with misgivings. Some did not know what to think of the "damned thing," as an Akron leader called it. None went so far as to fight it, but to some of them it looked like "dangerous business" in the long run even if now it helped to organize unions. They at once liked and feared it. Some feared it, perhaps, because it deprived the regular labor official of much of his authority; others because the sitdown was too spontaneous and seemingly haphazard. Too anarchic. It threatened to play the devil with the collective-bargaining idea.[28]

I emphasize that I am talking about the *character* of the alternative unionism of the 1930s, not its *causation*. In many communities, such as the southern textile towns Janet Irons describes, the alternative unionism of the early 1930s developed free of any apparent influence from IWW or other radicals. In some situations, such as the St. Louis nutpickers' strike, the Southern Tenant Farmers' Union, or the first sit-down in the Alabama steel industry, Communists, Trotskyists, Socialists, or Musteites played the role that Wobblies did elsewhere.[29] Much more research would be needed to support any general theory of causation. An essentially localized movement that took form more or less simultaneously in literally dozens of communities is unlikely to show any single dominant pattern of cause and effect.

I think it is clear, however, that a community-based, horizontally bonded "culture of struggle," with roots in such epic battles as the 1916 Westinghouse strike, the Lawrence, Massachusetts, strikes of 1912 and 1919, and community-based strikes in coal mining and cotton textile towns during the 1920s,[30] also pervaded the alternative unionism of the early 1930s and the first years of many CIO local unions.

Because of the affinity between the character of the alternative unions we have uncovered and the tradition of the IWW, we have chosen as a title the words embattled workers in both settings used. When Wobblies approached Everett, Washington, on the steamer *Verona* in November 1916, Walker Smith reported, "Sheriff McRae called out to them: 'Who is your leader?' Immediate and unmistakable was the answer from every I.W.W.: 'We are all leaders.'"[31] Likewise on March 7, 1932, about 3,000 unemployed Ford workers tried to march from Detroit to Ford headquarters in Dearborn, and at the Dearborn city limits, about fifty Dearborn police and private police from the Ford plant blocked the road. "'Who are your leaders?' an officer called out. 'We are all leaders!' someone shouted back."[32] After these words were spoken, the authorities in each situation opened fire, killing five men in Everett and four in Dearborn.

Alternative Unionism and the CIO

There appear to be three basic ways of looking at the CIO in relation to the alternative unionism of the 1930s. The first view is that at the outset of large social movements there is often a period of mass enthusiasm, egalitarianism, and "primitive democracy" (the phrase was coined by Sidney Webb and Beatrice Webb), but as the movement grows and settles down to its serious tasks, an efficient centralized bureaucracy inevitably takes over. In this view the bureaucratized business union movement that the CIO had become by 1950 was natural and inevitable.

A second interpretation of the CIO in its relation to alternative unionism is that everything depends on the ideology of the leadership. Had Communist leadership been able to survive, it is argued, the CIO might have been very different. This way of looking at things tends to lead to campaigns to replace the top personnel of existing AFL-CIO national unions.

While the authors of these essays naturally differ somewhat among themselves, they lean toward a third way of viewing the 1930s. We propose that the CIO *from the beginning* intended a top-down, so-called responsible unionism that would prevent strikes and control the rank and file. It is true that CIO leaders could not get employers to the bargaining table with merely verbal persuasion. For this reason, they were forced to turn the ranks loose against the corporations. Their ultimate objective, however, was succinctly expressed by John L. Lewis, who in effect told the Senate committee sponsoring the Wagner Act, "Allow the workers to organize, establish strong governmental machinery for dealing with labor questions, and industrial peace will result."[33]

Ronald Radosh characterizes Lewis's motivation similarly: "The 'dangerous state of affairs' [of 1935] might very well have led to 'class-consciousness' and 'revolution as well.' Lewis hoped that it could 'be avoided,' and he pledged that his own industrial union was 'doing everything in their power to make the system work and thereby avoid it.'"[34] David Brody also writes about Lewis's interest in taming the new local industrial unions of 1933–35:

> Much of Lewis's sense of urgency in 1935 sprang from his awareness of the pressure mounting in industrial ranks. A local auto union leader told Lewis in May 1935 of talk about craft unions' taking skilled men from the federal unions. "We say like h—— they will and if it is ever ordered and enforced there will be one more independent union." Threats of this kind, Lewis knew, would surely become actions under existing AFL policy, and, as he warned the Executive Council, then "we are facing the merging of these independent unions in some form of national organization." That prophecy, Lewis was determined, should come to pass under his control.[35]

Brody rightly stresses that a CIO led by Lewis, a lifelong Republican who "made no bones about his contempt for democratic processes that he considered injurious to the efficient operation of the union as a 'business proposition,'" was likely to display "a remarkable opportunism . . . . With John L. Lewis as the heroic figure of the 1930s, it is not any wonder that those great days did not transform American trade unionism into a social movement."[36]

Many observers on the scene at the time the Wagner Act was passed predicted with essential accuracy what would eventually happen to the CIO. These observers included spokespersons for the AFL, the American Civil Liberties Union, the IWW, and the Communist Party of the United States, as well as A. J. Muste and many rank-and-file workers. William Forbath writes of the views of the AFL:

As Furuseth, Frey, and the other AFL anti-injunction campaign veterans darkly prophesied, the Act inaugurated a regulatory regime that, in administering the new liberties, might resurrect many of the old restraints. If the old guard grossly underestimated the good that would flow from the new order, they were not wrong about the possibility that within it many of the old common-law restraints on collective action might reassert themselves. The federal courts have interpreted the NLRA [National Labor Relations Act] to prohibit virtually all forms of secondary strikes and boycotts, and the Supreme Court has upheld this bar against constitutional challenges.[37]

Still more incisive were the predictions of Roger Baldwin and Mary Van Kleeck, spokespersons for the American Civil Liberties Union (ACLU). In 1933, three days after the enactment of the National Industrial Recovery Act, Baldwin, the executive secretary of the ACLU, wrote to Secretary of Labor Frances Perkins expressing fear that the bituminous coal code might include the following objectionable features: (1) exclusive representational status for the majority union, (2) the dues checkoff, and (3) the closed shop. Baldwin thought that all three provisions would have the effect of chilling the activity of minorities, such as the Progressive Miners, which was then contesting the hegemony of the United Mine Workers.[38]

In 1934, when the first version of the Wagner Act was proposed, Van Kleeck wrote Senator Robert Wagner advising him that the ACLU would oppose his bill because of the "inevitable trends of its administration." Fundamentally, Van Kleeck stated, "I believe that it is impossible 'to equalize the bargaining power of employers and employees,' since necessarily the decision to produce at all . . . rests with the employer." Under this condition of inequality, Van Kleeck went on,

> the danger is that the effort to regulate industrial relations by requiring of employers certain "fair practices," while appearing to impose those obligations upon them, necessarily brings the whole subject within the scope of governmental regulation. This involves a certain assumption as to a status quo. To prevent or discourage strikes which have for their purpose gradual increase in the workers' power in a period when fundamental economic change in the ownership of industry can clearly be envisaged may only serve to check the rising power of the exponents of human rights, and indeed to protect private property rights in exchange for obligations which are likely to be merely the least common denominator of industrial practice.

Van Kleeck concluded by acknowledging that Senator Wagner's bill explicitly protected the right of workers to strike, but she "insisted that pressures would inevitably be exerted on the National Labor Relations Board to discourage strikes in favor of less disruptive methods of resolving conflicts."[39]

Van Kleeck's analysis of the proposed Wagner Act was echoed by Baldwin. In 1934 Baldwin wrote Senator David Walsh that the machinery proposed in the pending legislation would "impair labor's rights in the long run, however much its authors may intend precisely the contrary." In 1935 he wrote Senator Wagner that the ACLU would oppose creation of the National Labor Relations Board (NLRB) "on the ground that no such federal agency intervening in the conflicts between employers and employees can be expected to fairly determine the issues of labor's rights. We say this from a long experience with the various boards set up in Washington, all of which have tended to take from labor its basic right to strike by substituting mediation, conciliation, or, in some cases, arbitration." Baldwin urged Senator Wagner to consider "the view that the pressures on any governmental agency from employers are so constant and determined that it is far better to have no governmental intervention than to suffer the delusion that it will aid labor in its struggle for the rights to organize, bargain collectively and strike."[40]

Many rank-and-file workers expressed similar views. In the textile industry employers used National Recovery Administration (NRA) boards to impose the hated stretch-out (where workers are required to do extra work for little or no additional pay), while workers boycotted the cotton textile labor board and shifted their struggle to the arena where they had more leverage—on the ground in the South. For textile workers, Janet Irons concludes, "government intervention proved disastrous."[41] Daniel Nelson maintains rubber workers in Akron had concluded by early 1935 "that reliance on the government meant broken promises and endless delays."[42] C. J. Francis, the recording secretary of the National Match Workers' Council, wrote in like spirit to Francis Biddle, chair of the NLRB: "We cannot or at least will not use the agency set up by the Federal Government." Experience had taught these unionists that even a favorable decision would only lead to endless employer appeals. "We are not going to stand for this and as we see it, our only hope is through strike and to battle it out on the picket line," C. J. Francis declared.[43]

From the Beginning

Our view of the relationship between the alternative unionism of the early 1930s and the CIO is exemplified in an incident narrated by Peter Rachleff. In March 1937 at Albert Lea, Minnesota, truck drivers and warehouse workers went on strike. They were joined by Woolworth's clerks and workers at two plants of the American Gas Machine Company, who went on strike and, in the manner of that heroic spring, occupied their places of work. The Independent Union of All Workers coordinated all three actions. Every night the IUAW Drum and Bugle Corps paraded past each of the embattled work sites. The strikes held for two weeks. Then the sheriff and 150 special deputies stormed the offices of the IUAW and arrested sixty-two people. In response, 400 workers at nearby Hormel left their jobs and drove in a caravan to Albert Lea. As Rachleff recounts, "There they marched down the main street to the jail and demanded that all the prisoners be freed. When the brand new Albert Lea police cruiser pulled up, the crowd surrounded it, took the cops out, rolled it over, set it on fire, and then slid the charred remains into the lake across the street. Armed with crowbars, individuals from the crowd began to pry open the bars on the windows of the jail."[44]

Governor Elmer Benson, who had won election on the Farmer-Labor Party ticket, thereupon appeared on the scene as a mediator. The settlement he proposed and eventually negotiated had three elements. First, all imprisoned workers were to be freed. Second, the company was to recognize and bargain with the IUAW. Third, *the IUAW was to affiliate with a national union within sixty days.* As it worked out, different IUAW local bodies joined different national unions, and the "one big union" at a city and regional level that the IUAW had nurtured for four years fell apart.

What did affiliation with a national union represent to the Albert Lea business community and to a governor anxious for social peace? Why was this chosen as the *quid* that would compensate the bosses for the *quo* of emptying the jails and agreeing to bargain?

Corporations like U.S. Steel at first responded to the labor ferment of the 1930s with a localized strategy. They formed local company unions or reasserted their traditional control of local communities through company-owned housing, company stores, and local governments staffed by company supervisors.[45] But the local arena began to slip out of control. When coal miners turned up to picket with the steelworkers at U.S. Steel's Clairton coke works in 1933,[46] when independent federal local unions in Barberton marched on each other's picket lines in strike after strike from 1934 to 1936,[47] and when 170,000 southern textile strikers, many of them organized in local "homegrown unions,"[48] showed that no part of the country was safe from the rank-and-file fever in 1934, then, in Janet Irons's words describing the Cotton Textile Institute, many corporations decided "to elevate the local struggle to [a] national level. They hoped to thereby circumvent the local strategic leverage that mill workers had gained."[49]

Business came to recognize that the national union, whether AFL or CIO, with its vertical structure, its interest in a predictable cash flow from membership dues, and its demonstrated readiness to give away the right to strike and to police the shop floor, offered an alternative strategy of control perhaps more promising than the local company union. U.S. Steel espoused the new strategy in March 1937, in part, it seems, because "union firms had the advantage of avoiding the disruptions incident to conflict over unionization," as at Flint.[50] General Motors followed suit and became, in Ronald Edsforth's words, "a model for other large companies to follow in the 1940s."[51] John Sargent, the first president of the huge Steelworkers' local at Inland Steel, describes how

> the companies became smart. . . . They recognized the national and international leadership of that labor union and took the affairs of that labor union out of the hands of the ordinary elected officials on a local scale. . . . We used to bargain locally with the Inland Steel Company, and we had our own contract with the company. We let a representative of the international union sit in, but we bargained right in Indiana Harbor and settled our differences right there. But soon Inland began to realize that this was not the way, because they were up against a pretty rough bunch of people who had no ambitions to become political leaders and labor representatives on a national scale. They realized that the best way to handle the situation was to work with the international leadership of this union.[52]

Accordingly, in contrast to those who emphasize the *difference* between the original CIO unions and what they became after World War II, we stress those features of national CIO unionism that *from the beginning* (or very shortly thereafter) distinguished CIO unionism at the national level from the horizontal, community-based unionism of the early 1930s.

First, national CIO unions were *from the beginning,* and aspired to be, "semipublic institutions, licensed by the state."[53] As governmental monopolies, they could insulate themselves from competing labor organizations by law instead of proving their superiority in practice or, as in European economies, sharing the representative function with other unions. This surrender of autonomy represented a fundamental departure from labor tradition in the United States.[54]

Second, national CIO unions *from the beginning* practiced top-down decision making. Independent local unions, such as the Independent Textile Union in Woonsocket, were typically led by people who continued to work at least part-time in the shop.[55] In contrast, the national CIO encouraged the proliferation of full-time officers and staff representatives, paid by the national union.

Likewise the national CIO deliberately broke up militant local industrial unions like Local 65 of the Steelworkers in South Chicago and Local 156 of the UAW in Flint. Lizabeth Cohen narrates the disillusionment of George Patterson, who founded the Associated Employees at U.S. Steel South Works in Chicago and led it into the Steel Workers Organizing Committee (SWOC), where it became Local 65 of the United Steelworkers of America:

> Grassroots spontaneity and local concerns often were subordinated to the national CIO agenda. This imposition of "top-down" control happened first and most dramatically in steel, where the national leadership of SWOC began very early to tie the hands of its locals. At the start, district officers were appointed, not elected, and even after elections were held starting in 1944, it became virtually impossible to unseat District 31's director, Joe Germano. Locals also had little fiscal independence. Member dues went directly to the steel union's central office. As early as January 1937, Bittner was telling his organizers in Chicago, "We are dictating policy of all lodges until steel is organized. Democracy is important, but at this time collective bargaining and higher wages are the issues." When Bittner decided to divide South Works Local 65 into four, more controllable locals, . . . George Patterson . . . despaired: "Democracy from the bottom up, that we had practiced in Local 65, was now difficult to pursue. . . ." Steelworkers who had managed to overcome the fragmentation their employers had encouraged now had to contend with a union leadership also bent on dividing them. Similar frustration over lack of autonomy arose when the grievance committeemen elected by the different departments of South Works decided they would rather meet with the company's managers alone: "lo and behold, they found that there was always going to be a [SWOC] staff member coming into the meetings in order to see that the union would be guided." It did not take long for Patterson and other veterans of the grassroots Associated Employees to realize that "what *we* wanted" was not of concern to the men at the top: "They were hand-picking what we would call 'yes-men': anybody that could stand and talk and didn't bow to their thinking was gradually eliminated."[56]

Ronald Edsforth tells a similar tale of the destruction of UAW Local 156 in Flint by the UAW and CIO hierarchies: "By the end of June [1937], Bob Travis and the rest of the local union's radical leadership had been removed from office and transferred to assignments that were deliberately scattered all over the country. Thousands of Flint workers protested this purge, but to no avail. A committee of five was put in charge of Local 156's affairs for the rest of the year. This committee, which contained no one from the union's radical 'Unity' caucus, cracked down on the militants within the auto plants."[57]

Third, whereas the rank-and-file unionism of the early 1930s emerged from and depended on direct action inside and outside the shop, national CIO unions *from the beginning* sought to regulate shop-floor activity from above and to prohibit shop-floor activity not approved at higher levels of the union. "In the next few years following the sit-downs, the main task" of the CIO was "to domesticate the popular insurgency," Steve Fraser writes. Thus, he explains, in Flint "a second conflict that pitted the International Union and GM management against rank-and-file shop-floor organizers supplanted the more celebrated battle between union and corporation. The emerging bureaucracy of the UAW took steps to dismantle the steward system, reduced the authority of local unions while augmenting the power of the International, appended a no-strike and management rights clause to the contract, and perfected the modern grievance procedure and committee system."[58]

Because they were separated from the shop floor and concerned about controlling it, national CIO leaders were insensitive to the shop floor's chief complaint: inhuman working conditions. Irons explains:

> Unions were now tied to an agenda set by the federal government rather than by their own membership. What the government determined to be legitimate grievances the union could fight for; what government policy ignored were inadmissible grievances. . . . [In 1938 the] new CIO-organized Textile Workers Organizing Committee (TWOC) encouraged southern workers to join unions because, thanks to the Wagner Act, the government was now behind them. But southern workers' protests against the stretch-out were ignored by the TWOC as the union fought for goals that jibed more easily with government goals: increased purchasing power and stable unions.[59]

Finally, *from the beginning* the national CIO leadership ardently sought to discourage independent labor politics and to tie the CIO to the Democratic Party. Eric Davin has brought to light the very substantial labor party movement during the early 1930s. In those years local labor parties fielded candidates in at least twenty-three communities and came to control the local government of at least one community, Berlin, New Hampshire. In at least ten other communities central labor unions endorsed the idea of a labor party, as did the state federations of labor in Rhode Island, Connecticut, Vermont, New Jersey, and Wisconsin. At the 1935 AFL convention, where the Committee for Industrial Organization was created, a variety of unions submitted proposals for a labor party and a resolution to that effect failed by only a few votes.[60]

Early in April 1936 John L. Lewis and Sidney Hillman founded Labor's Nonpartisan League, in the words of Steve Fraser, "as a way of circumventing third-party movements."[61] A few weeks later, when the nascent UAW held a convention in South Bend, defeated a resolution to back Roosevelt, and unanimously called for the formation of a farmer-labor party, Lewis directed Adolf Germer, the CIO staff representative, to strong-arm Homer Martin and the delegates into reconsidering.[62] During World War II, when third party enthusiasm revived, the CIO created the Political Action Committee to "discourage every move in that direction."[63]

The Challenge of National Coordination

In presenting this view of the 1930s, we recognize that uncoordinated local disturbances could not have substituted for a national movement.[64] Alternative means were needed to coordinate local efforts on a regional and national scale.

Union activities in the 1930s suggest a variety of ways local unions can coordinate their efforts, without belonging to the same organization and without sacrificing their freedom of action to the heavy-handed, top-down governance that so often has accompanied national unionism. John Sargent's account of bargaining at Inland Steel under his presidency in the late 1930s describes one such mechanism. The local had an agreement with management that the company would match the highest wage rate for a particular line of work that steelworkers established anywhere in the country:

> We made an agreement . . . that the company would not pay less than any of its competitors throughout the country. We never had it so good . . . . All you had to do as a union representative was come into the company and say, "Look, we have a group of people working in the pickle line, and at Youngstown, Ohio or Youngstown Sheet and Tube in East Chicago people are getting more money than we're getting for the same job." And if that was a fact, we were given an increase in wages at Inland. In those departments where we had a strong group of union members, where they were most active, we had the highest rates in the country. We were never able to secure conditions of this kind after we secured contracts.[65]

The experience of Barberton, Ohio, during the half-century following the early 1930s indicates that such mechanisms can function effectively over a long period of time.[66] Barberton workers created industry- or corporation-wide conferences, consisting of members of the same union working for the same company in different locations (the boilermakers), or members of different unions all employed by the same company (the chemical workers), or members of different unions in different companies of the same industry (the insulator workers).

Similar schemes have been projected by paper workers and packinghouse workers in recent years. United Paperworkers Local 20 in Kaukana, Wisconsin, initiated a "coordinated bargaining pool" after losing a bitter eighteen-month strike against International Paper in 1987–88. Locals that joined the pool were to make common demands during their local negotiations, seal their ballots after the final contract vote, and work without a contract rather than take individual action or sign a concessionary agreement. When the pool felt it had sufficient strength, the ballots would be counted. If a majority voted against the local agreements, the union would take nationwide action. The strategy was intended to create a common expiration date and, ideally, one contract for all International Paper locations. By June 1991 the pool included 60 percent of International Paper workers in thirty-five locals. The strategy failed, not because of any substantive defect but because in December 1991 the NLRB declared it illegal.[67]

A Permanent Alternative

The evidence suggests that the horizontal style of unionism described in these essays remains a permanent alternative for the labor movement. Community-based or solidarity unionism is not a transitory phase or epiphenomenon, limited to a particular bygone stage of economic history. Consider Polish Solidarity. It originated in one of the more highly industrialized areas of Poland. It took the form of workplace committees, with elected representatives from all departments, then of regional interfactory committees, and finally, in September 1980, of a national coordinating committee, but *not* a hierarchical national organization. Roman Laba argues persuasively that workers in the northern coastal cities of Gdansk, Gdynia, and Szczecin improvised the first two stages in this process in December 1970 to January 1971, without significant input from intellectuals. Workers built on this experience in the great upheaval of August 1980, challenging each other to recognize that, in the words of Anna Walentynowicz, "if the workers at these other factories were defeated, we wouldn't be safe either." At a meeting of rank-and-file delegates from all over Poland held on September 17, 1980, at the Seaman's Hotel in Wrzeszcz, there was a fierce debate between intellectuals associated with the workers' defense committee (KOR), who wanted a centralized national structure, and workers led by Lech Walesa, who wanted a decentralized structure grounded in many unions. The workers prevailed: Solidarity was to consist of "spreading horizontal structures."[68]

Nor is the alternative unionism described in the following pages limited to the United States and Europe. Of many Latin American episodes of the same kind the following is striking. In 1973 two hundred peasant families in Quebrada Seca, Honduras, occupied idle arable land. Soldiers were called to the site. As Gerald Schlabach recounts:

> The oldest men, the women, and children met the soldiers when they arrived. The military, as usual, first asked to speak with the group's leaders. [The people] replied that everyone was a leader, and whoever would speak would be speaking for all. The military men said they were there to negotiate, but that they wanted to see the leaders so that they could go together to a meeting with INA [the National Agrarian Institute]. The people insisted that this was the place to negotiate, with everyone together. . . . [69]

This book seeks to retrieve the memory of such experiences among workers in the United States. A curious set of union buttons or the stories told by grownups during one's own childhood offer clues to chunks of history forgotten by academia. As Eric Davin points out, historical amnesia can occur even among protagonists if they are never asked to recount their past struggles. He saw this "natural selection process" in action when a veteran of the woman suffrage movement was repeatedly asked by younger feminists to retell *that* past but was never called on to describe her later role in the labor party movement of the 1930s: she remembered the first experience and forgot the second. Stan Weir offers other paradigms. He shows us Blackie and Chips, two veterans of the 1934 San Francisco general strike, systematically instructing younger seamen like Weir about the lessons of their experience. But Weir adds two things. First, he was able to grasp the most important lesson Blackie and Chips taught—that bureaucrats cannot reform themselves—only on the basis of his own experience in another general strike, in Oakland in 1946. Second, student activists in nearby Berkeley did in 1964 what Weir now wishes he had done himself in Oakland eighteen years earlier: they clambered onto a parked car and declared that since official leaders were not leading, a new leadership should be created from below.

Women, whether pecan shellers, textile workers, or garment workers, appear in these accounts as workers perhaps especially inclined to egalitarian, horizontally bonded forms of unionism. Other scholars who wish to explore and test the hypotheses set forth here might take note that several of these essays describe extraordinary instances of black and white workers overcoming their differences in common struggle.

Top-down national union structures patterned on the corporation have failed. Local unions and their rank-and-file members, again prepared to be "all leaders," are needed to develop new forms of alternative unionism. We will not know if it is possible unless we try.

Notes

1. Victor Reuther, Prefatory Note to Robert Lynd, *You Can Do It Better Democratically* (Detroit: UAW-CIO Education Department, [1949]), front matter.

2. Lloyd Ulman, *The Rise of the National Trade Union: The Development and Significance of Its Structure, Governing Institutions, and Economic Policies* (Cambridge, Mass.: Harvard University Press, 1955), 27–32, 37–42. The thesis that union structure follows market development is generally shared by authors of the Commons-Perlman school of labor history. See, for instance, Selig Perlman, *A History of Trade Unionism in the United States* (1922; reprint, New York: Augustus Kelley, 1950), 109–10.

3. Melvyn Dubofsky writes, "In examining the 1930s, how should we go about creating the history of that era? Two convenient models are at hand. In one we can seek lessons for the present in an instrumental view of the past. That approach suggests the might-have-beens of history. If only Communists had behaved differently; if nonsectarian radicals had pursued the proper policies; if the militant rank and file had been aware of its true interests (as distinguished from the false consciousness inculcated by trade-union bureaucrats and New Deal Democrats); then the history of the 1930s would have been different and *better* [citing three works by the present author]. The second approach to our turbulent decade has been suggested by David Brody. 'The interesting questions,' writes Brody, 'are not in the realm of what might have been, but in a closer examination of what did happen.' Brody's approach, I believe, promises greater rewards for scholars and may even be more useful for those who desire to use the past to improve the present and shape the future." Melvyn Dubofsky, "Not So 'Turbulent Years': A New Look at the 1930s," in *Life and Labor: Dimensions of Working Class History,* ed. Charles Stephenson and Robert Asher (Albany: State University of New York Press, 1986), 206. These comments miss the mark with regard to the present book,

which consists precisely of a "closer examination of what did happen." Moreover, Brody himself has called on scholars unhappy with the current labor movement to set forth "the alternative that rivaled the union course that was actually taken." David Brody, "The CIO after 50 Years: A Historical Reckoning," *Dissent* 32 (Fall 1985), 470.

4. Gary Gerstle, *Working-Class Americanism: The Politics of Labor in a Textile City, 1914–1960* (Cambridge: Cambridge University Press, 1989), 165–66.

5. Michael K. Honey, *Southern Labor and Black Civil Rights: Organizing Memphis Workers* (Urbana: University of Illinois Press, 1993), 71, 99–103.

6. Elizabeth Faue, *Community of Suffering and Struggle: Women, Men, and the Labor Movement in Minneapolis, 1915–1945* (Chapel Hill: University of North Carolina Press, 1991), 4. For solidarity unionism, see Staughton Lynd, *Solidarity Unionism: Rebuilding the Labor Movement from Below* (Chicago: Charles H. Kerr, 1992).

7. Gerstle, *Working-Class Americanism,* 143, 145; John Borsos, "Ironing Out Chaos: The CIO-ization of the United Rubber Workers, 1933–1941" (1992 manuscript, in author's possession), 13–14; Michael Kozura, "We Stood Our Ground: Anthracite Miners and the Expropriation of Corporate Property, 1930–41," herein.

8. John Borsos, "'We Make You This Appeal in the Name of Every Union Man and Woman in Barberton': Solidarity Unionism in Barberton, Ohio, 1933–41," herein.

9. See, for example, Daniel Nelson, *American Rubber Workers and Organized Labor, 1900–1941* (Princeton, N.J.: Princeton University Press, 1988), 116–17 (factory council), 117–69 (federal labor unions); and Ronald Edsforth, *Class Conflict and Cultural Consensus: The Making of a Mass Consumer Society in Flint, Michigan* (New Brunswick, N.J.: Rutgers University Press, 1987), 130–36 (strike committee of 120 members), 162 (citywide council of federal labor unions), 181–83 (in the aftermath of the Flint sit-down, the UAW acts as a "general workers union," organizing bus drivers, department store clerks, taxi drivers, etc.).

10. Rosemary Feurer, "The Nutpickers' Union, 1933–34: Crossing the Boundaries of Community and Workplace," herein (in St. Louis the ability to build community mobilizations was the key to working-class strike success); Gerstle, *Working-Class Americanism,* chap. 4 ("Citywide Mobilization, 1934–1936").

11. For estimates of Amalgamated membership in the first part of 1934 of 50,000, 150,000, and 200,000, see Staughton Lynd, "The Possibility of Radicalism in the Early 1930s: The Case of Steel," in *Workers' Struggles, Past and Present: A "Radical America" Reader,* ed. James Green (Philadelphia: Temple University Press, 1983), 191, 205n.6. David J. McDonald, treasurer of the Steel Workers Organizing Committee (SWOC), estimates SWOC membership

at the end of 1936 as a "shaky 82,000" and states that when U.S. Steel signed a contract with SWOC in March 1937, SWOC had signed up only 7 percent of its employees. Ibid., 191–92, 205n.11.

12. Nelson, *American Rubber Workers*, 145. Sidney Hillman told his biographer, Mathew Josephson, that during the NRA period over 40,000 rubber workers had been organized. David Brody, "The Emergence of Mass-Production Unionism," in *Workers in Industrial America: Essays on the Twentieth Century Struggle* (New York: Oxford University Press, 1980), 90.

13. Edsforth, *Class Conflict*, 162, 265n.11, 176.

14. Janet Irons, "The Challenge of National Coordination: Southern Textile Workers and the General Textile Strike of 1934," herein.

15. Kozura, "We Stood Our Ground."

16. Len DeCaux, *The Living Spirit of the Wobblies* (New York: International Publishers, 1978), 143.

17. Edsforth, *Class Conflict*, 159 (Klasey); Shelton Stromquist, *Solidarity and Survival: An Oral History of Iowa Labor in the Twentieth Century* (Iowa City: University of Iowa Press, 1993), 40, 115 (quotes on Ellis and the IUAW); Stan Weir, "Unions with Leaders Who Stay on the Job," herein (Blackie and Chips); John W. Anderson, "How I Became Part of the Labor Movement," in *Rank and File: Personal Histories by Working-Class Organizers,* ed. Staughton Lynd and Alice Lynd (New York: Monthly Review Press, 1988), 27, 47; Steve Nelson, with James R. Barrett and Rob Ruck, *Steve Nelson: American Radical* (Pittsburgh: University of Pittsburgh Press, 1981), 91–92 (quote on Freeman Thompson).

18. David Montgomery, *The Fall of the House of Labor: The Workplace, the State, and American Labor Activism, 1865–1925* (Cambridge: Cambridge University Press, 1987), 457.

19. Ibid., 322 (committee), 319 (IWW).

20. Ronald W. Schatz, *The Electrical Workers: A History of Labor at General Electric and Westinghouse, 1923–60* (Urbana: University of Illinois Press, 1983), 73.

21. *Workplace contractualism* is offered by David Brody to characterize "the essential characteristics of the unionized workplace regime that emerged out of the great New Deal organizing era in the mass-production sector of American industry." David Brody, "Workplace Contractualism in Comparative Perspective," in *Industrial Democracy in America: The Ambiguous Promise,* ed. Nelson Lichtenstein and Howell John Harris (Cambridge: Cambridge University Press, 1993), 176.

22. Woods explains: "We said if you have a closed shop and check-off, everybody sits on their butts and they don't have to worry about organizing and they don't care what happens. We never wanted it." Sylvia Woods, "You Have to Fight for Freedom," in *Rank and File,* ed. Lynd and Lynd, 118. The

organizers my wife and I interviewed for *Rank and File* told us that the advent of the dues check-off was the single most important cause of the bureaucratization of the CIO. Hence our generalization: "Once unions gained recognition and union dues were automatically taken out of the worker's paycheck, unions took on a new character." Ibid., xii.

23. Daniel Nelson, "Origins of the Sit-Down Era: Worker Militancy and Innovation in the Rubber Industry, 1934–1938," in *The Labor History Reader*, ed. Daniel J. Leab (Urbana: University of Illinois Press, 1985), 344.

24. Borsos, "Ironing Out Chaos," 20, 25–26, citing among other sources Donald Anthony, "Rubber Products: With a Specific Reference to the Akron Area," in *How Collective Bargaining Works: A Survey of Experience in Leading American Industries,* ed. Harry A. Millis (New York: Twentieth Century Fund, 1942), 654 ("Although Goodrich was willing by April 1937 to come to an agreement, the first contract was not signed until May 27, 1938. [Local union leaders] felt that unless all demands were won, an agreement would so restrict freedom of action that it would not be worth while").

25. John Sargent, "Your Dog Don't Bark No More," in *Rank and File,* ed. Lynd and Lynd, 99–100. Scholars support Sargent's assessment. Robert R. R. Brooks quotes John Mayo, the subregional director of the Steel Workers Organizing Committee in Youngstown: "In some respects the union was better off [in Little Steel] than in many U.S. Steel plants since it was not bound by a contract to confine its grievance claims to matters covered by the contract. It was able, therefore, to press and sometimes win grievance claims which under the standard contract would be thrown out in the early stages of adjustment." Robert R. R. Brooks, *As Steel Goes . . . : Unionism in Basic Industry* (New Haven, Conn.: Yale University Press, 1940), 146. After examining the grievance committee minutes at Inland Steel during the late 1930s, Lizabeth Cohen states that "at steel mills where the SWOC did not yet have contracts and hence could not control the rank and file, shop floor agitation persisted." Lizabeth Cohen, *Making a New Deal: Industrial Workers in Chicago, 1919– 1939* (New York: Cambridge University Press, 1990), 306, quoting from the accounts of John Sargent and Nick Migas in *Rank and File,* ibid., 306–7.

26. Brody, "The Emergence of Mass-Production Unionism," 103.

27. Edsforth, *Class Conflict,* 171; Germer is quoted in Sidney Fine, *Sitdown: The General Motors Strike of 1936–1937* (Ann Arbor: University of Michigan Press, 1969), 136.

28. Louis Adamic, *My America, 1918–1938* (New York: Harper and Brothers, 1938), 414.

29. See Feurer, "The Nutpickers' Union"; Mark Naison, "The Southern Tenant Farmers' Union and the CIO," herein; and Robin D. G. Kelley, *Hammer and Hoe: Alabama Communists during the Great Depression* (Chapel Hill: University of North Carolina Press, 1990), 143–44 (the Communists Joe

Howard and C. Dave Smith organized a successful sit-down at the American Casting Company in December 1936, only to be fired by the SWOC for acting without authorization).

30. At the Westinghouse plant near Pittsburgh, a key organizer was dismissed and 2,000 men and women walked off the job. By the next morning 13,000 striking workers had linked hands to form a huge human chain around the Westinghouse complex. Giant processions of strikers and supporters gradually closed down the entire Monongahela Valley. On November 1, 1916, a parade, bedecked with red flags and led by a Lithuanian band, invaded steel mills, chain works, and machinery companies, bringing out 36,000 workers. Montgomery, *Fall of the House of Labor*, 322–25. The Lawrence strike is described in *The Essays of A. J. Muste*, ed. Nat Hentoff (New York: Macmillan, 1967), 55–77.

31. Walker C. Smith, "The Voyage of the Verona," in *Rebel Voices: An IWW Anthology*, ed. Joyce Kornbluh (Chicago: Charles H. Kerr, 1988), 108. See also Jack Miller, in *Solidarity Forever: An Oral History of the IWW*, ed. Stewart Bird, Dan Georgakas, and Deborah Shaffer (Chicago: Lake View Press, 1985), 110; and C. Wright Mills, *The New Men of Power: America's Labor Leaders* (New York: Harcourt Brace, 1948), front matter. All accounts agree on the words "We are [or, "We're"] all leaders." Harvey O'Connor writes that this was "the usual Wobbly reply." Harvey O'Connor, *Revolution in Seattle: A Memoir* (New York: Left Bank Books, 1981), 46.

32. Franklin Folsom, *Impatient Armies of the Poor: The Story of Collective Action of the Unemployed, 1808–1942* (Niwot: University of Colorado Press, 1991), 305.

33. Len DeCaux (before he went to work for the CIO) paraphrasing Lewis's testimony, Federated Press Dispatch, Columbia University Oral History Project, April 2, 1935, quoted in Lynd, "The Possibility of Radicalism," 207.

34. Ronald Radosh, "The Myth of the New Deal," in *A New History of Leviathan*, ed. R. Radosh and M. Rothbard (New York: E. P. Dutton, 1972), 152.

35. Brody, "The Emergence of Mass-Production Unionism," 103–4.

36. David Brody, "John L. Lewis," in *Workers in Industrial America*, 169–70.

37. William Forbath, *Law and the Shaping of the American Labor Movement* (Cambridge, Mass.: Harvard University Press, 1991), 165.

38. Baldwin to Perkins, June 2, 1933, in Cletus Daniel, *The American Civil Liberties Union and the Wagner Act: An Inquiry into the Depression-Era Crisis in American Liberalism* (Ithaca, N.Y.: Cornell University Press, 1980), 34.

39. Van Kleeck to Wagner, March 12, 1934, in ibid., 71–73.

40. Baldwin to Walsh, March 20, 1934, in ibid., 75; Baldwin to Wagner, April 1, 1935, in ibid., 101–2.

41. Irons, "The Challenge of National Coordination."

42. Nelson, *American Rubber Workers,* 156.

43. C. J. Francis to Francis Biddle, January 10, 1935, Federal and Mediation Service Files #170–1252, National Archives, Suitland Records Branch, Suitland, Maryland, quoted in Borsos, "'We Make You This Appeal.'"

44. Peter Rachleff, "Organizing 'Wall to Wall': The Independent Union of All Workers, 1933–37," herein.

45. In the spring of 1934, 25 percent of all industrial workers belonged to company unions, with two-thirds of these organized under NRA auspices. Rick Fantasia, *Cultures of Solidarity: Consciousness, Action, and Contemporary American Workers* (Berkeley: University of California Press, 1988), 36–37. For company towns, see Eric Davin, "The Littlest New Deal: SWOC Takes Power in Steeltown" (Paper delivered at the Annual Meeting of the Organization of American Historians, 1992), 17–18 (the sheriff of Allegheny County was the brother of a U.S. Steel plant manager, the president of the Homestead Borough Council was an official in U.S. Steel's Homestead mill, and the burgess of Munhall was the Homestead mill superintendent), 32 (company union at U.S. Steel's Clairton, Pennsylvania, coke works), 33 (John Mullen says of Clairton, "You had to be a mill official to be a public official in this town. They named all the city officials. No one else had a right to run for office"), 34 (Mullen evicted from his home by U.S. Steel, which "owned half this town").

46. Lynd, "Possibility of Radicalism," 192–93.

47. Borsos, "'We Make You This Appeal'" (the Diamond Match strike in 1934, the Columbia Chemical strike in 1934, the Ohio Insulator strike in 1935, the Columbia Chemical sit-down strike in 1936, and the Pittsburgh Valve and Fittings strike in 1936).

48. Irons, "The Challenge of National Coordination."

49. Janet Irons, "A New Deal for Labor? Southern Cotton Mill Workers and the General Strike of 1934" (Paper delivered at the Annual Meeting of the Organization of American Historians, 1989), 6.

50. Brody, "The Emergence of Mass-Production Unionism," 104.

51. Edsforth, *Class Conflict,* 187, 272n.101.

52. Sargent, "Your Dog Don't Bark No More," 101. Sargent believed that the workers at Inland Steel achieved more than workers at the neighboring U.S. Steel mill in Gary, where there was a written contract and the national union was in control: "In those days there were more than twenty assistant grievers and hundreds of stewards. The grievance committee set-up could handle the affairs of the people on every shift and every turn with every group. Where you did have contracts with the companies (at U.S. Steel, for example) you had a limited grievance procedure. The U.S. Steel plant in Gary, the largest steel plant of the largest steel company, had a grievance committee of only eleven. Where union officials did not take over the union through a contract with the

company (as they did with U.S. Steel), you had a broader, bigger, more effective and more militant organization that set an example for unions throughout the country." Ibid., 100.

53. Ronald W. Schatz uses this phrase to describe unions as they were after the passage of the Taft-Hartley Act. Ronald W. Schatz, "Philip Murray," in *Labor Leaders in America,* ed. Melvyn Dubofsky and Warren Van Tine (Urbana: University of Illinois Press, 1948), 250. But the words apply equally well to the status of unions certified by the NLRB as exclusive bargaining representatives at all times after passage of the Wagner Act in 1935. As David Montgomery writes of the work of Secretary of Labor William B. Wilson during World War I: "The consistent theme guiding Wilson's work was that employers should be encouraged to negotiate with legitimate unions and to shun the IWW and other groups deemed 'outlaw' by the AFL. Here was the appearance in embryonic form of the doctrine of a certified bargaining agent, which was to be incorporated into the law of the land in 1935." Montgomery, *The Fall of the House of Labor,* 357.

54. The CIO came into existence just after the passage of the Wagner Act and *from the beginning* cheerfully operated within the parameters of that law. As Christopher Tomlins has most fully explicated, this meant that unions surrendered their autonomy in exchange for government assistance in obtaining employer recognition. In fact, he writes, "the legitimacy of collective activity putatively guaranteed by labor relations law had been conditional almost from the outset. During the debates of the 1930s, proponents of the Wagner Act had stressed, both before and after its passage, that collective bargaining was a means to an end, and that the end was industrial stability and labor peace." The upshot was that "what the state offered workers and their organizations was ultimately no more than the opportunity to participate in the construction of their own subordination." Christopher Tomlins, *The State and the Unions: Labor Relations, Law, and the Organized Labor Movement in America, 1880–1960* (Cambridge: Cambridge University Press, 1986), 318, 327.

55. Not until 1943, twelve years after its founding, did the Independent Textile Union hire its first full-time organizers. Gerstle, *Working-Class Americanism,* 81–2, 269–70. See also Sargent, "Your Dog Don't Bark No More," 99 ("there were no organizers at Inland Steel, and I'm sure there were no organizers at Youngstown Sheet and Tube. The union organizers were essentially workers in the mill who . . . took the union into their own hands").

56. Cohen, *Making a New Deal,* 358. For more on the Associated Employees, see George Patterson, "Your Dog Don't Bark No More," in *Rank and File,* ed. Lynd and Lynd, 84–85.

57. Edsforth, *Class Conflict,* 182–83.

58. Steve Fraser, *Labor Will Rule: Sidney Hillman and the Rise of American Labor* (New York: Free Press, 1991), 403; Steve Fraser, "The 'Labor Question,'" in *The Rise and Fall of the New Deal Order, 1930–1980,* ed. Steve Fras-

er and Gary Gerstle (Princeton, N.J.: Princeton University Press, 1989), 77–78. Ronald Edsforth agrees that in Flint the contract ending the sit-down "established a grievance procedure designed to circumvent the shop steward systems and prevent wildcat strikes," so that after March 13, 1937, "the continued militance of Flint's rank and file violated official union policy." The UAW executive board, company management, and Michigan's Governor Frank Murphy all pressed for an end to shop-floor action. Nonetheless, Edsforth continues, "Meetings were held at the various plants, and the membership dutifully passed resolutions prohibiting unauthorized strikes. But still the disruptions continued. . . . Workers who had won respect and changes in conditions by means of their own shop steward system would not give up that system easily even when their contract and union leaders demanded it. Where they could, workers on the shopfloor continued to pressure their supervisors to correct their grievances directly. The shop steward system was maintained informally at Chevrolet for more than a year after the union's leaders signed it away. At Fisher Body 1 it was still functioning as late as 1940." Edsforth, *Class Conflict,* 177–78.

59. Irons, "The Challenge of National Coordination."

60. Eric Leif Davin and Staughton Lynd, "Picket Line and Ballot Box: The Forgotten Legacy of the Local Labor Party Movement, 1932–1936," *Radical History Review* 22 (Winter 1979–80), 43–63; Eric Leif Davin, "The Very Last Hurrah? The Defeat of the Labor Party Idea, 1934–36," herein; Davin, "The Littlest New Deal."

61. Steve Fraser, "Sidney Hillman: Labor's Machiavelli," in *Labor Leaders in America,* ed. Dubofsky and Van Tine, 221.

62.Fine, *Sitdown,* 90–91; Kevin Boyle, "Building the Vanguard: Walter Reuther and Radical Politics in 1936," *Labor History* 30 (Summer 1989), 433–88. Although Fine characterizes the resolution to support a farmer-labor party as "a Communist party-line resolution" (Fine, *Sitdown,* 90), Reuther's letter reprinted in Boyle's article suggests something very different: "The most amazing thing about the whole convention was the question of the Farm Labor Party. . . . [T]his carried unanimously. What happened was that the two conservitive [*sic*] blocs, South Bend and Wis., came instructed to vote for the FLP and the progressives were obviously for it. The few reactionaries did not dare raise ther [*sic*] voices." Walter Reuther to Victor Reuther and Roy Reuther, April 22, May 2, 1936, reprinted in Boyle, "Building the Vanguard," 442. As a member of the Socialist Party at the time, Reuther was an ardent anti-Communist. Confirming the general thesis of Davin's work, Reuther also writes in this letter of many attempts to set up local farmer-labor parties throughout the country. Boyle, "Building the Vanguard," 446.

63. David Brody, "The Uses of Power II: Political Action," in *Workers in Industrial America,* 220–21, quoting Philip Murray.

64. We agree with a great deal that is said in Frances Fox Piven and Rich-

ard A. Cloward, *Poor People's Movements: Why They Succeed, How They Fail* (New York: Pantheon, 1977), 96–180. However we disagree with the statement, "Factory workers had their greatest influence and were able to extract their most substantial concessions from government during the early years of the Great Depression *before they were organized into unions.*" Ibid., 96. Workers were organized into unions in the early 1930s, as we think the evidence cited throughout this volume proves. They were unions that differed from the CIO unions that succeeded them. Had Piven and Cloward written, "before they were organized into *national bureaucratic* unions," we would agree. Instead of thinking that workers should not be organized or should not belong to unions, we believe that they should organize themselves *in a different way* and should form unions *of a different kind.*

65. Sargent, "Your Dog Don't Bark No More," 100.

66. John Borsos, "Talking Union: The Labor Movement in Barberton, Ohio, 1891–1991" (Ph.D. diss., Indiana University, 1992).

67. Phil Kwik, "Bargaining Pool Collapses at International Paper: 'The Fight Isn't Over,' Activists Declare," *Labor Notes* 159 (June 1992), 1, 14. For a similar plan projected by former activists of United Food and Commercial Workers Local P-9 in Austin, Minnesota, in 1986, see George DeMartino, "Trade-Union Isolation and the Catechism of the Left," *Rethinking Marxism* 4 (Fall 1991), 41, quoting *Industrial Worker* (March 1987), 3.

68. Lynd, *Solidarity Unionism,* 35 (Anna Walentynowicz quote); Roman Laba, *The Roots of Solidarity* (Princeton, N.J.: Princeton University Press, 1991), chap. 2, 3, especially 66–67 (elected workplace committee at Warski Shipyard), 68–69 (interfactory strike committee), and chap. 5, especially 106–12 (Lech Walesa), 112 (horizontal structures).

69. Gerald Schlabach, "The Nonviolence of Desperation: Peasant Land Action in Honduras," in *Relentless Persistence: Nonviolent Action in Latin America,* ed. Philip McManus and Gerald Schlabach (Philadelphia: New Society Publishers, 1991), 66.

1

The Nutpickers' Union, 1933–34

Crossing the Boundaries of Community and Workplace

Rosemary Feurer

This essay tells the story of the St. Louis nutpickers' strike of May 1933 and the building of the nutpickers' union, the Food Workers Industrial Union, into a social movement in the strike's aftermath.[1] This struggle, led by African American women in a marginal industry, clearly marks the beginning of the 1930s union drive in St. Louis. In every facet it seems to go against the grain of established historical thinking on the 1930s. Led by African American women in unskilled positions, it was a successful strike against low pay and race-based pay differentials, even before section 7a of the NIRA was enacted. It runs contrary to current notions that militancy in the workplace during the 1930s was limited to shop-floor enclaves of skilled male workers who composed, as one commentator puts it, the "flotsam and jetsam of sinking radical dreams" in the 1920s.[2] The nutpickers' union was born of and sustained through community struggles that emerged outside the workplace and inaugurated a new style of unionism, one that engaged the imaginations of those who witnessed it in St. Louis. It suggests, in the path Elizabeth Faue has tracked,[3] that the source of labor's revival in the 1930s was in a community-organizing approach and that race, gender, and the Left were critical in building that approach.

The nutpickers' organizing drive grew organically from the relief activities of the Unemployed Councils (UCs), established by the Communist Party shortly after the onset of the Great Depression. Historians of the 1930s recognize that the unemployed movement was often a training ground for labor organizers, noting that it gave activists experience in speaking, training, leaflet writing, and many other skills that were easily transferable to workplace organizing later in the decade. In addition, historians have credited the Left's unemployed movement with "introduc[ing] to vast numbers of workers the concept of organization as a strategic weapon for the solution of economic and social problems."[4]

But the relevance of the unemployed movement activity in St. Louis, I would suggest, was greater than its instrumental effect. The sociologist Rick Fantasia argues that economic and industrial decline "often precipitates political and conceptual links between power relations in the workplace and outside it."[5] Such an understanding, however, needs an organizational impulse to bring it to the surface. The unemployed movement reignited and nurtured a perspective that focused on community organizing as a key component of workplace organization. To see the nutpickers' struggles in context, we must begin with the unemployed movement.

The unemployed movement sought to expose the relationship between the power employers held over the labor market and the power they held in the community. The whole ensemble of local class relations was epitomized in St. Louis's relief system, which was essentially an extension of the Community Fund, a private relief system that businesspeople had helped establish in the 1920s to consolidate and control charity distribution. Relief policies were designed to reinforce the conservative political economy, which structured relations between employers and workers and was based in part on employers' longstanding fears that they might lose control of the labor market. St. Louis's economy was built to a significant extent on seasonal labor, and employers, from 1900 to 1922, had fought a sometimes vicious battle to control the labor market, allowing them to utilize a pool of transient or seasonal labor for everything from manufacturing to processing jobs. In the 1920s, even as some St. Louis businesspeople sought to create a new image for themselves as community leaders (and to advance the idea that capitalism was compatible with compassion), employers still recognized the need to control the labor market. A leading example of the way these dual goals of image and control were played out was the Bureau for Homeless Men, established in 1925. While its publicly announced goal was to care for transients, its actual mission was to remove "drifters" from the streets through arrest and harassment. It should not be surprising that the leading figure on the board of the bureau was also one of the leading antiunion businessmen in St. Louis.[6]

St. Louis's relief system during the early years of the Great Depression was among the most miserly in the country. Contemporary studies showed that it spent less per capita and aided fewer people than any other city of its size and that the amount given was 38 percent less than in any other city. Civic boosters claimed these statistics only demonstrated that St. Louis had fared better during the depression than other areas had. But such claims masked the extreme suffering of many people, particularly African Americans, during these years.[7]

In the first year of the depression, St. Louis continued to rely on the private relief system organized under the Community Fund. In November 1930 the Community Fund was supplanted by the Citizens' Committee for Relief and Employment (CCRE), a special committee to deal with the depression crisis. The CCRE was essentially an extension of the Community Fund, though. Control by St. Louis's business elite resulted in a regressive method of funding the constituent private charities that distributed relief. Major corporations, especially utilities seeking public favor, led the drive for donations. Solicitation of workers who still had jobs in these companies was intense. More of the fund's money was drawn from employees than from any other source. Even when the city began to contribute some of the funding from tax revenue for the CCRE's constituent charities (in large part because of the unemployed movement's agitation), those charities retained control of distribution.[8]

The St. Louis unemployed movement grew out of the vacuum created when the local American Federation of Labor (AFL) central body abandoned any effort to provide leadership for the unemployed. Well before the stock market crash of October 1929, the St. Louis Central Trades and Labor Union (CTLU) recognized the severity of the economic downturn. There were already 75,000 unemployed in St. Louis by April 1929. For a time in 1929 it appeared the CTLU might become a rallying force for a movement of the unemployed. A group of women delegates called for a rally on behalf of the unemployed and sponsored a resolution calling for a government "remedy" to unemployment, a break with the national AFL's voluntaristic policies. But by the beginning of 1930 these weak efforts had been shot down, and the organization quickly retreated to inaction.[9] By failing to provide leadership, the CTLU left the door open for the rebirth of a community-based unionism. From the depths of the depression a style of unionism emerged that embodied community-based struggle and inclusive unionism.

The Unemployed Councils were the first to try to build an institution that could channel discontent about unemployment and relief. Associated with the small, fledgling Communist Party in St. Louis, the UCs challenged the relief system, exposed the degree of neediness, and extracted more relief from the system for their followers. They called for jobs at union wages. They contended that a just relief system should be governed by the unemployed themselves and that money for relief should come from corporations and the rich. They called for federal legislation to fund a national relief system. Most important, they employed a direct action style of protest to obtain relief and concrete reforms.[10]

The unemployed movement was born when a group of mostly black men protested at city hall for jobs and relief. Thereafter, African Americans made up an important component of the UC membership and its leadership. The UCs constituted the first integrated protest movement in St. Louis. Of course, a major tenet of the Communist Party was that work in the African American community was strategic to the development of a revolutionary cadre, which was the basis for this approach. But since African Americans were the hardest hit by the depression in St. Louis—they were one-tenth of the population but one-third of the unemployed, and they received a lower amount when they were granted relief than whites did—they were also a logical source for agitation. Blacks often constituted half the crowd at unemployment demonstrations and sometimes outnumbered whites.[11]

From 1930 to 1933 the UCs agitated in neighborhoods to obtain relief and prevent evictions. This focus on the neighborhood instead of the workplace encouraged the development of more women activists, both black and white. The police designated the diminutive Yetta Becker, a young Jewish garment worker, as the key leader. "Whenever the police would see a leaflet, or some meeting was called, they'd pick her up and put her away!" recalled Fannie Goldberg, who led at least one city hall demonstration herself. But Goldberg added, "There was no major leader in St. Louis, we were just a group of people who believed in the same thing." Goldberg remembered that the UC activists concentrated on mobilizing the community to obtain relief or to prevent evictions: "We would take members of the council and instead of a person going to the relief station alone, we went with them. And on evictions, if we heard someone was being evicted, we would gather a group and get there and put the furniture back in." Roy Rosenzweig has noted that the UCs in various cities "built on a cooperative neighborhood solidarity that emerged in response to the disorganization and inadequacy of local relief." That solidarity was built through agitation, though. In just one example, police complained that a black woman was "submitting quietly" to her eviction until UC activists roused the neighborhood to prevent it. Newspaper accounts indicate that black women played an especially important role in antieviction activities in their neighborhoods. Often UC demonstrations were scheduled to start after school let out so that youth could join the parade to city hall. The parade built on these youth, who cajoled others, including adults, to join them. Scenes from the parades and demonstrations illustrate the diverse composition of the unemployed movement, but the prominence of African American women in chanting and singing is evident.[12]

It was this neighborhood work that occupied the activists and lent the unemployed movement continued strength. One such neighborhood was the swelling "Hooverville" along the Mississippi. Built of ramshackle makeshift housing, it was home to 500 black and white residents by 1931. Little notice was paid to it until the UCs organized its residents to demand relief. The St. Louis delegation to the 1931 National Hunger March took pictures and letters from there to Washington, D.C., to dramatize the residents' condition.[13]

Through these experiences activists revived forms of protest usually associated with labor activism later in the decade. In January 1931, for instance, the St. Louis UCs held what might be considered the first sit-down of the 1930s in St. Louis. Marching in two different contingents, one from the southern section of the city and one from the northern section, around 5,000 people arrived at city hall and made their demands for expanding relief, reducing relief administrators' salaries, and taxing corporations and the wealthy for relief funds. A select delegation of the marchers entered city hall and refused to leave until the board of aldermen heard and acted on these demands. A bloody melee ensued when police were ordered to remove the protesters inside and to disperse the crowd outside. The outcome was predictable—police clubs and tear gas prevailed. The repression these activists met, including repeated long jail sentences for a substantial number, accounts for some of the problems the movement had in sustaining a high level of activity. The repression of leadership was also different for black and white activists. Yetta Becker and other white activists were sentenced to the workhouse, while most black activists were ordered to cease their involvement with the movement.[14]

Nevertheless, the vitality of the movement as a result of community organizing was still evident in July 1932, when the St. Louis relief system reached a crisis point. In June the CCRE started rejecting new relief applicants and announced the cutoff of 15,000 families from the rolls. As one relief worker candidly stated, "All through the Depression we have had the poor sharing with the poor. We have almost come to the limit of that." The UCs began house-to-house canvassing and public hearings, which culminated in two mass demonstrations and resulted in the restoration of relief.[15]

The significance of neighborhood-based activity in reorienting the Communist Party (CP) has recently been underlined by Van Gosse, who argues that through unemployment work rooted in the neighborhood rather than in the workplace, the CP underwent a gendered reorientation in the early 1930s. He argues that UC activists "pioneered a new practice of constant contact around community issues: canvassing and home visits, attending and recruiting for the meanest tasks, embedding themselves in the minutiae of working class life instead of 'going to the workers' with a revolutionary message from afar." This, he argues, represented a "resurgence of a familial-based conception of solidarity" in the Left. Scholars have discovered that personal and familial networks played an important role in black workers' and women workers' organization efforts. The activism of women and African Americans probably gave rise to a propensity to concentrate on neighborhood activities.[16]

The focus on neighborhood organizing and solid community-based work was emphasized by Ralph Shaw, who was the young activists' main contact with the national Communist Party. Shaw was only around thirty years old, but he was already a seasoned organizer. His grounding was in the union battles of the southern Illinois coal fields in the 1920s. In coal towns, Herbert Gutman has observed, conflict between companies and miners usually involved the entire community in the struggle. John Laslett argues convincingly that in United Mine Workers of America Illinois District 12, especially in the southern region where Shaw was active in the 1920s, radical traditions centering on community activism did not die out in the 1920s.[17] Activists such as Shaw, grounded in the struggles of coal mining towns, where there was a strong relationship between work and community and where the community was deeply involved in strikes, carried forward working-class strategies and forms of struggle developed in other areas and in earlier times.

It was through this community-oriented activity that the Left activists came into contact with women who worked for the Funsten Nut Company. Nutpicking, along with chicken cleaning and rag sorting, constituted the very bottom of the submarginal industries in St. Louis in the 1930s, and it was in these industries that African American women found sporadic employment. There were over 1,500 women in St. Louis's nutshelling sweatshops. Processing nuts from all over the Mississippi Valley was centralized in St. Louis, and nuts were shipped across the country from this point. The work force of the shops was made up of mostly women, who picked, sorted, weighed, and packed pecans brought to St. Louis. The Funsten Nut Company was the largest single employer. By 1933 Funsten operated four plants dispersed around the city and three in East St. Louis, Illinois.[18]

The Funsten Nut Company completely segregated women by race. White women were hired for the main plant, which included a storefront visible from the streets, especially in sorting and weighing, but the greatest number—perhaps 80 percent—of its work force was African American women. The turn toward black women as a majority of the work force occurred during the World War I labor shortage, and although nut factories had attempted to replace black women with whites during the depression, they soon retreated to their racially based employment structure. For African American women, this work was one of the few alternatives to jobs in domestic service or the laundries. They were generally hired through family and kinship networks, and often entire families worked in one plant. Irene Bell, who had come to St. Louis from Macon, Mississippi, with her family in the 1920s, got her job through a friend in her neighborhood who belonged to her church. Soon her mother, her grandmother, and her sister were also working at Funsten.[19]

Black women were paid a lower piece rate and worked longer hours than white women. Alice Love, a white girl who was hired in 1931 at age fourteen, at first did not even know that black women worked in the plant where she got a job. Only when the plant manager turned on the lights on a dark day did she discover, through cracks in the floor, that she had co-workers in the basement below—all of them black women. Love quickly deduced who the beneficiary of this division was: "I would read the newspapers, and noticed in the society pages how the Funsten family, oh, his daughters, they were so active in the Veiled Prophet [a local elite festival] and I would think, we're working for nothing for them to go to the ball!"[20] Love's memories show us that class consciousness was a multifaceted development, in which shop-floor grievances were often connected to broader understandings.

Conditions were, Love recalled, "like something out of Dickens" for all workers, but conditions for black workers were worse than for whites. Mary Jefferson remembered that the black women's segregated washroom facilities were "disgusting. . . . I hated to go to the bathroom because it was so filthy. Sometimes I think I hurt myself by not going to the bathroom all day." Jefferson, whose family had come from Little Rock, Arkansas, in the war period, "hated to work there . . . but we had to do it to survive. . . . We were trying to find a better life. But this was all there was for us."[21]

This seasonal work had never provided a living wage, but wages and conditions worsened with the onset of the depression. From 1931 to 1933 Funsten issued five piecework wage cuts. In 1933 average earnings were not above $3–4 a week for blacks, while white women made only $4–6 a week. It is not surprising that over 30 percent of Funsten's employees were able to qualify for relief.[22]

The UC had drawn attention to the plight of the "women workers of the nut factor[ies]" as early as January 1932, and it is likely that some of these women had participated in the relief activities. A black CP member who had two relatives working at Funsten initiated the organizing drive in early 1933, under the aegis of the Food Workers Industrial Union (FWIU), an affiliate of the Trade Union Unity League (TUUL), a federation in competition with the AFL and under the CP's influence. It subscribed to organizing on an industrial rather than a craft basis, especially where the AFL unions were moribund or nonexistent. It also aimed to link the struggles of the employed and unemployed. There was no better place to begin than with the nutpickers, who were poised between employment and unemployment.[23]

Contrary to traditional depictions of the TUUL, which argue that the CP simply took advantage of one spontaneous worker uprising only to move on to others, the FWIU organizing drive was developed methodically and carefully and used experienced organizers. Ralph Shaw initially directed it. In addition to the black CP member who had initiated the drive, young activists of and around the CP aided the drive. One of these, William Sentner, soon took charge of it. Over two months they steadily developed a leadership core of twenty women. They organized the all-black Easton Avenue plant first because the women there were not put off by their radical connections and because a strike in 1927 at the main plant had been unsuccessful, which probably would have made it "hard to penetrate." The drive aimed to unite white and black women, but few white women initially joined the union, while the leftists' attention to the special discrimination against blacks helped attract black women to the organizing drive.[24]

Given the economic situation in early 1933, the nadir of the Great Depression, it seems incredible that the core group of African American women, the most marginal and vulnerable workers in the economy, had the courage to launch and win a drive at Funsten. This confidence came from having reached rock bottom but also from imbuing the struggle with a moral quality on behalf of broader goals. There had been earlier attempts at collective action among the nutpickers. The 1927 strike had been defeated by transferring work to other factory locations, and the memory of that defeat lingered. But meetings galvanized the ranks with the conviction that their struggle constituted a challenge to the political economy of relief and the fight for a living wage for the entire African American community.

It was the leadership of the older black women in the Easton plant that built the ranks. These older women had kinship networks and had developed the allegiance of many of the younger girls by helping them when they started or had trouble with foremen. "They used to lead us in songs as we worked, to help pass the time," Mary Jefferson remembered. She also remembered that "it was the older women who fought those who didn't want to join. Some didn't want to join. . . . They had a fight there to get them to join. I remember one of the older women swung a pan of nuts at another woman who wouldn't join." The key leader of the nutpickers was Carrie Smith, an older religious woman who had worked at Funsten since at least 1918. She helped to build the Easton plant group into a working committee.[25]

The women drew up demands for a 50 percent increase, equal wages for black and white workers, and union recognition. An elected committee of twelve presented the demands to the company on April 24. While they waited for the company to respond, they used personal networks to expand to other Funsten plants in the St. Louis area and gave notice that they might be asked to walk out in solidarity. When the company refused to negotiate, the shop committee at the Easton plant staged a walkout, full of fury, singing, and conviction. They also immediately implemented their prearranged plans for mass action to pull the other plants out.[26]

The nutpickers' strike was St. Louis's first mass mobilization of the 1930s, built around a democratically structured strike committee. The strike used mass picketing, singing and chanting on the picket lines, and roving strike brigades. The women experienced mass arrests but were also determined to gather community support to place the moral issue at the center of their struggle. The CP and the UCs mobilized their forces behind the strikers. On the crucial first day supporters gathered in trucks outside the fully organized plant to await the walkout: "The trucks were loaded and before the boss knew what happened, the women were brought to the doors of the largest plant, two miles away, hailing the other workers and signaling the shop committee inside to call all workers out for a strike." Over 500 workers walked out the first day. Shops pulled out one by one. "Some of us didn't want to go out," recalls Irene Bell, at the time a very young girl at the Washington Avenue plant. "I just wasn't used to it. And that made you draw up, not know whether you should do it or not. That's what you're depending on, and then you can't get a job anywhere because you're black. That's why we didn't rush out. It was slow going out." But, she adds, "we were caught up in the hope." Each plant chose its own shop committee and picket captains. The central strike committee was composed of the heads of the shop committees and held daily strike meetings.[27]

On the second day of the strike 200 white women from the main factory joined the strike, as well as workers from two other Funsten shops. Alice Love remembers coming to work, seeing the black women on strike, and being asked to join with them, although she had no inkling of what was coming. "I thought to myself, it's about time, and if they're ready, I'm ready," she recalls. She took a picket sign and walked every day at the main plant. Many of the white women were hesitant, however, and Fannie Goldberg remembers that white women from the unemployed movement walked the picket line to encourage the white women to join. The key white leader was Marie Nowinski, known as "Blondie," who quickly gained a reputation as a very militant woman. She had been among the small number of white women who had joined in the organizing drive that preceded the strike.[28]

Within six days workers from two other companies, the Liberty Nut Company and the Central Pecan Company, walked out, bringing the total on strike to 1,400 women, almost the entire work force. Picketing began every morning with mass demonstrations around the main plant. The strikers focused on preventing the opening of the plants after the workers walked out. When police brought strikebreakers to and from work in patrol wagons and taxis, the women and their supporters formed a "sandwich parade." One hundred of the most militant formed lines on both sides of the plant entrances and let loose with bricks, bats, and other objects when scabs attempted to go to work. During the course of the strike, a hundred women were arrested. At one of the regular mass meetings, Carrie Smith, according to the Funsten strike chronicler Myra Fichtenbaum, held a brick in one hand and a Bible in the other and vowed, "Girls, we can't lose."[29]

The strikers and their supporters successfully solicited help from the community. Food for the strike commissary was collected from sympathetic workers and businesses, and the strikers secured help from some AFL unions. Shaw recounted that "there was tremendous support and sympathy of the labor movement for these women. The bakery workers sent down a delegation and got them second day old bread. They made a collection at the bakers' hall."[30] The strikers' ranks were also fortified by personal and local networks of support from the African American community. One CP observer commented that the black women involved "were religious and had no experience in the working class movement." But these very attributes encouraged them to solicit support from the African American community, including their churches, to challenge their economic oppression. The women also called on their personal networks for support. "On the picket line men walked side by side with women, husbands and wives were there—young and old," Shaw later recounted.[31]

The strikers sought to build community pressure on Funsten to settle. Shortly after the Funsten strike began, a delegation of two white and two black women appealed for assistance to the Social Justice Commission (SJC), a newly formed self-styled mediation group consisting of white ministers and academics. The women were accompanied by Irving L. Spencer, an attorney for the American Civil Liberties Union in St. Louis, and J. Clark Waldron, a teacher at Beaumont Night High School. (These two were, respectively, an attorney for a legal group associated with the Communist Party, the International Legal Defense, and a Socialist Party member, though this was not reported in the press.) The nutpickers testified about the working conditions they endured. To dramatize their low wages, the strikers brought several unopened pay envelopes for four days' work; at the meeting they opened them, revealing earnings from $1.50 to $2.00. The SJC pledged its support.[32]

Encouraged by the SJC, a delegation of nutpickers asked the new mayor, Bernard Dickman, to arbitrate the strike. Dickman contended the strike was a "private matter" outside his purview. But Sentner countered that it should be considered a "municipal matter," since so many of the workers received relief. In effect, he argued, the local relief system "was subsidizing the Funsten company" and promoting its labor policies. "We think we are entitled to live as other folks live," declared Carrie Smith. The mayor, pressured by the SJC and other groups, agreed to appoint a committee of seven, including four blacks, to negotiate with Funsten. The mayor and the Urban League, however, attempted to get the nutpickers to denounce Sentner and the Communists and to negotiate without them. The women resolutely refused.[33]

The ever-widening circles of support for the Funsten strikers and the strikers' innovative tactics took the company by surprise and rapidly depleted Funsten's initial resolve to defeat the strike. After an all-day hearing and negotiations, Funsten officials agreed to a settlement. The workers won nearly all their demands except union recognition, including equal pay for black workers and a doubling of their pay. The mayor was led by the strike committee to the Labor Lyceum (regarded as CP headquarters) to announce the settlement offer and plead for its acceptance. The strikers applauded him, and the strike leaders thanked him "for his interest and assistance" and afterward voted to accept the settlement.[34]

The Funsten workers' victory, coming just ten days after the beginning of the strike, was electrifying, especially in the African American community. In the aftermath of the strike, the nutpickers became the inspiration and support network for a TUUL organizing drive among the most marginal workers in the St. Louis area. In July 1933, for instance, African American women at rag-making plants successfully waged a strike using all of the same components, including the mayor's committee. At about the same time, the nutpickers successfully struck another nut company by using the same methods. Funsten workers, ragpickers, and Unemployed Council activists converged on each other's picket lines in growing circles of solidarity. By the time of the NRA-inspired union drives, the style of organization that had built the women's union was familiar to other unions in the area. These black women were clearly the most visible actors in the St. Louis urban arena attempting to bring unionization into focus as the key issue of the New Deal era.[35]

Perhaps even more significant than the Funsten strikers' victory and strength in the pre-NRA era is the fact that this community-oriented approach accounts for the union's survival in the year following the strike. During the seasonal downturn 450 laid-off nutpickers secured relief through the union's protests and interventions at neighborhood relief offices. The union was now using the city's resources as institutional building blocks, which it combined with cultural activities (including baseball teams for young workers and picnics and outings for all) that built a social basis to organization. The St. Louis FWIU had become, according to the *Daily Worker,* "one of the best organizations in the U.S."[36]

All of this paid off when in early October the nutpickers faced a challenge just as great as the May strike. Funsten, having found it was unable to break the union, closed its shops with only two hours' notice, idling most of the workers. The union demanded the guarantee of reemployment of those laid off. Building on mass actions, 700 nutpickers and their supporters surrounded the factory. Over sixty policemen pulled up in their wagons and, according to the *St. Louis Argus,* a black-owned newspaper that had deep sympathy for the nutpickers' movement, "arrested the pickets without any cause as there was no disturbance whatever." On October 8 the nutpickers held a "public trial," with a "workers' jury" composed of thirty-five workers from the nut shops, clothing shops (with the support of representatives from the local Amalgamated Clothing Workers), striking miners from southern Illinois, and "many other members of the AFL." The committee visited Mayor Dickman and NRA officials and demanded their presence at the trial. Dean Sweet, one of the original members of the mayor's committee, and "other well known liberals" took part in the trial. The jury found the company "guilty of violating the NRA pledge, misusing the NRA signs, and of deceiving the public."[37]

Meanwhile, protests at relief offices won the guarantee of immediate relief for the laid-off workers. When the relief authorities did not immediately fulfill this pledge, an integrated group of union supporters, led by Sentner, marched on the relief offices, charging that they were complicit in "starv[ing] out the workers." William Parker, a black attorney who had become part of the mayor's inquiry committee, verified that activists had been fired and that Funsten had sped up their work prior to the layoffs. Finally, the union succeeded in pulling the remaining workers out on strike. After a solidly organized four-day strike, the Funsten workers won their demands for reinstatement, partly through the intervention of the newly created local mediation board of the NRA.[38]

Reflecting the emphasis on the intersection of work and community agitation, when the Funsten workers sent their demands to the Pecan Shelling Code of the NRA, they not only demanded wage increases but also called for the establishment of an unemployment fund, with the equivalent of 5 percent of wages to be paid by the employer and administered by an employees' board of trustees, and for the government's immediate creation of unemployment insurance at the "expense of bosses and the state."[39] FWIU activities increasingly became part of the Unemployed Councils. The FWIU hosted a conference in late October 1933 to launch a local drive for national unemployment insurance and a city relief ordinance. The conference elected a committee of action to continue protest around relief issues in conjunction with the Unemployed Council. The conference also resolved to attract more labor unions and churches to the relief work. FWIU members were central to the UCs' agitation in support of the Lundeen bill (strong unemployment insurance legislation then before Congress). This agitation succeeded in getting the St. Louis board of aldermen to approve a resolution supporting the Lundeen bill in 1934.[40]

To understand the nutpickers' community approach, we must take into account the Left's perspectives and experiences. A cursory approach might simply depict the nutpickers' struggle as the playing out of the TUUL's program, which aimed to unite the struggles of the employed with the unemployed. One could point to a similar development in another TUUL union, the Fur and Leather Workers Union, which by mid-1933 had engaged in similar actions and had won its demand for an unemployment fund paid for by employers and administered by workers.[41] But as the outlines of the UC and the Funsten strike suggest, simply to depict this as the playing out of some programmatic agenda set by the national party would be to miss most of the story: the grounding of these developments in local actions and traditions of solidarity.

Much about the nutpickers' story challenges facile assessments of the CP trajectory, including traditional depictions that divide its 1930s history into an extremist "Third Period," in which the CP treated itself as the vanguard of revolutionary practice and eschewed alliances with other radicals and liberals, and the "Popular Front" policy beginning in 1935, which was based on a broad-based alliance. Both policies were supposedly dictated from Moscow and New York.

The solicitation of the SJC and the mayor for arbitration, the involvement of at least one Socialist, and the subsequent inclusion of "liberals" in the October trial challenge the most widespread perspectives on the CP's actions in strikes before the Popular Front era. The nutpickers' actions support the work of scholars who have documented the diverse approaches by CP activists at the local level. The nutpickers' struggle certainly suggests that engagement in community mobilization and struggles altered approaches to organizing. In their attempt to present particular workers' struggles as community concerns, they drew on longer traditions in the labor movement that had been revived by the unemployed movement.[42]

Looking beyond the CP's tangled and confusing chronology but continuing to focus on the local level, we should view the nutpickers' story in the context of parallel developments during the depression era and in a longer-term historical context. The nutpickers were the harbinger of the new kind of alternative unionism of the early 1930s that, as Staughton Lynd describes it, emphasized horizontal bonding of working people at the local level to secure broader, even national, struggles. Such a style of unionism can be seen in the major strikes of 1934, especially the Toledo Auto Lite strike. There the Lucas County Unemployed League played a pivotal role in saving a floundering strike when its members engaged in mass picketing in defiance of an injunction that applied to strikers.[43] Solidarity was being built at the community level, the necessary starting point to any national movement (and, one might add, to any international movement).

That the nutpickers' union integrated the concerns of the community and workplace also owed much to the particular context from which it arose. The nature of the industry and its relation to the political economy of relief constituted the means by which the activists connected their earlier engagements to a broader struggle. Fannie Goldberg, the UC activist whose apartment was the location for the Funsten strike's leaflet writing, credits Sentner with "[coming] up with the idea, we have to prove to the city that the city was supplementing the livelihood of these people" and subsidizing the company and that the city therefore had to side with the strikers, which was a key strategy in the May 1933 strike. If, as Goldberg adds, Sentner's approach moved away from the "raw" approach of the youthful activists of the UC, in many ways it was consistent with the UCs' activities and theoretical approach, which underscored the relationship between the workplace and the community in the local political economy.[44]

The role of race and gender in drawing out those connections between workplace and community was significant too. Given the absence of African American workers from the historiography of the CIO (until recently), it might be surprising that they were central in building this approach, but it does suggest a continuity with other episodes in American history in which African American struggles provided a model for the democratic aspirations of other groups.[45] The nutpickers' story reinforces Alice Kessler-Harris's suggestion that we "lay siege to the central paradigm of labor history, namely that the male-centered workplace is the locus from which the identity, behavior, social relations and consciousness of working people ultimately emanates."[46] To Kessler-Harris's list, we could add strategies.

Race issues made the boundaries of struggle fluid, so much so that the nutpickers became the core group of a nascent working-class-based civil rights movement in St. Louis. The 1933 struggles of black women led the Communists, according to an Urban League study, "to come out with prestige" among black workers. In 1934 the FWIU was one of the major constituent bases for the launching of the local "Bill of Rights for Negroes" campaign in St. Louis, under the aegis of the League of Struggle for Negro Rights, which included attempts to desegregate St. Louis parks. Dennis Brunn, in writing about this, notes the significance:

> Public agitation by large numbers of black workers, characterized by militant demonstrations and determined delegations to city hall, etc. were in themselves relatively recent events in St. Louis. That such black agitation should go beyond the economic grievances of the unemployed and of the low paid food workers to become a broad attack on discrimination and segregation in St. Louis employment and public facilities was even more unusual. And finally, that the social base of such a protest movement should be black women workers was almost certainly without precedent in St. Louis social history.

The solid base in the black community thus led the FWIU to become, for a brief moment, the impetus for a civil rights movement in St. Louis based in the working class, similar to the one that developed in Winston-Salem, North Carolina, under the aegis of the Food, Tobacco, Agricultural and Allied Workers during the World War II era.[47]

The TUUL experienced dramatic success among the black working class of St. Louis in 1933. But the TUUL remained a black workers' movement, a movement that faced overwhelming obstacles in 1934. The marginality of many of the industries in which black workers were dominant, their isolation resulting from racial segregation, and their association with the Communist Party impeded organizational stability and expansion. After 1934 nutpickers' activities dropped off dramatically. A variety of factors apparently combined to spell the end for the nutpickers' union. The intensity of the struggle necessary to sustain the union was overwhelming. Continued relief struggles with singular successes but few sustained gains were debilitating. The multiplant apparatus of Funsten made possible a great degree of leverage. Eventually Funsten closed several plants to evade the union's efforts. Key activists were fired, and other tactics employers used during these years took their toll. The effects of "white chauvinism and Red Scare" were painfully apparent by April 1934 as the TUUL reached the limits of its organizing base.

The TUUL found itself increasingly isolated from the core of newly organized white workers who organized in the aftermath of section 7a. These workers joined the AFL, many forming federal unions, while others affiliated with established unions. The pitfalls of dual unionism were very well exposed in this context. Such antagonisms attenuated the possibility of effective citywide coalition. The inability to connect effectively into a citywide or national movement meant that the formal disbanding of TUUL unions by the Communist Party in 1935 was anticlimactic. Four of the TUUL unions were absorbed into the AFL. The nutpickers' union was not among them. By 1935 mechanization of production had begun, and with mechanization a greater number of employees that were hired were white. Nevertheless, workers who retained their jobs at Funsten testify to the improved conditions that these struggles brought, even after the TUUL ended.[48]

The demise of the nutpickers' union should not blind us to its impact on the local workers' movement, including its great import to the later CIO period.[49] The nutpickers' union had constituted an important chapter in St. Louis labor history, one which drew on the critique of the political economy of control that the unemployed movement had initiated. It had inspired the potential of community-based mobilizations and community appeals. It had demonstrated the possibilities for a vision of unionism grounded in uniting community and workplace concerns. The UCs and the

TUUL, while never composing a strategic section of the white working class, nevertheless influenced the direction of the white working class.

Although the TUUL and the UCs dissolved, their organizational style did not die but was transferred directly to the new federal labor unions and the newly formed American Workers Union (AWU). The AWU, formed in 1934 by left socialists who were friendly with local Communists, modeled itself on the UCs. The AWU sought to organize the unemployed and to aid workers in strike struggles by mobilizing nonstrikers from the community to join the picket lines. The AWU was able to gain a tremendous following, reaching over 80,000 members in St. Louis by 1936. It also succeeded in getting many small grocers, merchants, and businesspeople to endorse it. The AWU maintained the integrated coalition and included many of the women nutpickers in its leadership ranks. Through these activities, a network of activists developed outside of, but not estranged from, the local AFL labor officialdom.

The AWU provided critical assistance to newly organized workers in the AFL in the key federal labor union strikes of 1935–36. The AWU helped collect food from sympathetic merchants and provided assistance in forcing city agencies to give relief to strikers, strategies begun by the nutpickers' union. The AWU also connected with other community organizations, including churches, social workers, professional organizations, and black community groups (even the Urban League) in the 1935–36 period. The well-organized Ministerial Alliance was a moral force behind many of the activities of the AWU; its support for the relief and union activists gave them a degree of legitimacy and moral authority that had eluded the UCs. The alliance between Communists and socialist activists in the AWU, the cooperation between the unemployed and trade unions, churches, black community groups, small merchants, social workers, and professional associations meant that the AWU had become an extremely powerful organization by 1936. Moreover, it was this movement that made the sit-down tactic familiar to St. Louis workers. Workers staged sit-downs in relief offices on a regular basis. In April 1936 a racially integrated group of women and men took over the city's aldermanic chambers. Singing "Solidarity Forever" and "We Shall Not Be Moved," they refused to leave until the city agreed to withdraw the threat to cut off relief to 15,000 families.[50] Essentially, workers' community and workplace struggles had created alternative networks to the AFL that could be effective support coalitions. What distinguished this trade union approach from the AFL in the period before the CIO was not just industrial unionism rather than craft unionism but also the effective linkage with and use of community organizations.

The connection between the nutpickers' struggles and the later CIO era in St. Louis can be seen in the activities of William Sentner. Sentner's involvement with the nutpickers and other black workers in the TUUL was the transformative experience of his life. This movement revealed to him a potential vision of unionism that propelled him into a lifetime commitment to realizing democratic, inclusive possibilities in the labor movement. Although Sentner probably did not join the Communist Party until 1934, these experiences also sealed his commitment to the party. It was the Communist Party's focus on the black working class that had helped the reemergence of radical traditions and models for the labor movement. That the Communist Party was also an organization based on authoritarian and hierarchical principles antithetical to these experiences was a paradox Sentner would never candidly confront or resolve. But the struggle to unite community and workplace concerns as defined by the nutpickers' struggle was one that Sentner worked his entire life to re-create and realize. It was the project he—along with scores of other activists in St. Louis, many of whom had also participated in the earlier campaigns—would later bring to the electrical workers and the CIO. Sentner went on to become president of the St. Louis–based district of the United Electrical Workers Union (UE), which created a distinctive community-based approach to struggle that owed much to the nutpickers. For instance, the local UE survived from 1937 to 1939 through relief campaigns quite similar to those of the nutpickers.[51] Sentner and others recognized that any national framework of unionism required building solidarity at the local level and that the union movement needed to address the local structuring of the political economy to confront effectively the power of capital at a national level. The obstacles these activists faced in building local solidarity from the vertical, hierarchical structure of the CIO, combined with anticommunism, presented roadblocks that continued to frustrate much of their vision. Yet their efforts, like the nutpickers', speak to us now, even as we confront a global international economy.

Notes

1. This essay has benefited from the following studies: Paul Dennis Brunn, "Black Workers and Social Movements of the 1930s in St. Louis" (Ph.D. diss., Washington University, 1974); and Myrna Fichtenbaum, *The Funsten Nut Strike* (New York: International Publishers, 1992).

2. Harvey A. Levenstein, *Communism, Anticommunism, and the CIO*

(Westport, Conn.: Greenwood, 1981), 83. Some notable examples of studies emphasizing skilled male workers include Ronald Schatz, *The Electrical Workers: A History of Labor at General Electric and Westinghouse, 1923–1960* (Urbana: University of Illinois Press, 1983); Gary Gerstle, *Working-Class Americanism: The Politics of Labor in a Textile City, 1914–1960* (Cambridge: Cambridge University Press, 1989); and Steve Babson, *Skilled Workers and Anglo-Gaelic Immigrants in the Rise of the UAW* (New Brunswick, N.J.: Rutgers University Press, 1991).

3. Elizabeth Faue, *Community of Suffering and Struggle: Women, Men, and the Labor Movement in Minneapolis, 1915–1945* (Chapel Hill: University of North Carolina Press, 1991).

4. Bernard Karsh and Phillip L. Garman, "The Impact of the Political Left," in *Labor and the New Deal,* ed. Milton Derber and Edwin Young (Madison: University of Wisconsin Press, 1957), 97.

5. Rick Fantasia, *Cultures of Solidarity: Consciousness, Action, and Contemporary American Workers* (Berkeley: University of California Press, 1988), 218.

6. Judith Levy, "Historical Analysis of the Community Fund" (Master's thesis, Washington University, 1938); Charlotte Ring Fusz, "The Origin and Development of the St. Louis Relief Administration, 1929–1937" (Master's thesis, St. Louis University, 1938); *Greater St. Louis,* October 1919, January 1920, January 1923, March 1923; *St. Louis Labor,* November 22, 1924; Louis Teitlebaum, "The Labor Market in St. Louis" (Master's thesis, Washington University, 1929); Rosemary Feurer, ed., *The St. Louis Labor History Tour* (St. Louis: St. Louis Bread and Roses, 1994), 7.

7. *Post-Dispatch,* November 11, 1930, September 1, 1933, January 14, 1932, April 2, 1935; Neil Primm, *Lion of the Valley: St. Louis, Missouri* (Boulder, Colo.: Pruett, 1981), 467–68. Primm has put to rest the claim that St. Louis fared better than other cities during the depression.

8. Frank J. Bruno, "The Treatment of the Dependent Unemployed in St. Louis in the Winter of 1931–32: A Community Case Study," *Southwestern Social Science Quarterly* 13 (September 1932), 169–76; *Star-Times,* March 9, 1932; *Daily Worker,* October 22, 1931. The CCRE's solicitation of employees was essentially an extension of the Community Fund charity drive methods; however, in the context of the depression—in the midst of lowered wages and irregular work—such solicitations were the source of deep grievance. The Emerson Electric company union in St. Louis, for instance, demanded that such solicitations by foremen cease.

9. *St. Louis Labor,* February 23, 1929; Minutes, Central Trades and Labor Union, February 24, 1929, Western Historical Manuscripts Collection, University of Missouri–St. Louis; *St. Louis Labor,* April 28, 1929; Minutes, Central Trades and Labor Union, February 9 and 23 and April 13, 1930.

10. *Post-Dispatch,* March 3 and 6 and November 11, 1930; "Call for

Meeting" leaflet and "March against Hunger!" leaflet, both in Scrapbook, Bureau for Homeless Men Collection, Western Historical Manuscripts Collection, University of Missouri–St. Louis.

11. *Post-Dispatch,* October 29, 1931; Primm, *Lion of the Valley,* 468–70; Brunn, "Black Workers and Social Movements," 114, 139.

12. On "girl agitators," *Post-Dispatch,* November 14 and 26, 1930, February 20 and 25, 1931; Fannie Goldberg, interview with author, August 1991 (first three quotes); Roy Rosenzweig, "Organizing the Unemployed: The Early Years of the Great Depression, 1929–1933," *Radical America* 10 (July–August 1976), 40 (fourth quote); *Post-Dispatch,* October 10, 1930, November 29, 1931, March 3, 1932, November 21, 1930; Catherine Risch, "The Effects of Communist Propaganda upon the Negroes of St. Louis" (Master's thesis, St. Louis University, 1935), 60 (fifth quote); Antonia Sentner, interview with author, June 1989.

13. Many historians have interpreted the dramatic demonstrations of March 1930 as the high point of UC strength. Such a judgment, Albert Prago has suggested, fails to recognize that the "nature of the movement changed as well as its methods" for locally based agitation and that the movement took a different course in various communities. Albert Prago, "The Organization of the Unemployed and the Role of the Radicals, 1929–1935" (Ph.D. diss., Union Graduate School, 1976), 87. Franklin Folsom's *Impatient Armies of the Poor: The Story of Collective Action of the Unemployed, 1808–1942* (Niwot: University Press of Colorado, 1991) is a rare instance in which the CP's Unemployed Councils are cast in the context of a longer tradition of Left-led unemployed movements. On St. Louis's Hooverville, see *Daily Worker,* November 24, 1931.

14. *Daily Worker,* January 17, 1931; *Post-Dispatch,* January 17, 19, and 20, 1931; *Globe-Democrat,* January 20, 1931; *Post-Dispatch,* October 25, 1931; Brunn, "Black Workers and Social Movements," 178–80. On repression, see *Post-Dispatch,* October 25, 1931. It was through such experiences that the movement also developed strategies to ensure protection and to guard against violence, including the practice of witnessing, and honed arguments about citizenship and civil liberties. *Post-Dispatch,* February 21, 1931; Sentner interview.

15. *Daily Worker,* June 28, 1932; *Star-Times,* June 23 and July 1, 1932; *Post-Dispatch,* July 2 (quote) and 6, 1932; Bill Gebert, "How the St. Louis Unemployed Victory Was Won," *Communist* 11 (September 1932), 786–91; *Post-Dispatch,* July 8 and 11, 1932; *Globe-Democrat,* July 12, 1932.

16. Van Gosse, "'To Organize in Every Neighborhood, in Every Home': The Gender Politics of American Communists between the Wars," *Radical History Review* 50 (Spring 1991), 113. On women's network-based organizing, see, for instance, Vicki Ruiz, *Cannery Women, Cannery Lives: Mexican Women, Unionization, and the California Food Processing Industry, 1930–*

1950 (Albuquerque: University of New Mexico Press, 1987); and Dolores Janiewski, *Sisterhood Denied: Race, Gender, and Class in a New South Community* (Philadelphia: Temple University Press, 1985).

17. Herbert Gutman, "The Workers' Search for Power," in Herbert Gutman, *Power and Culture: Essays on the American Working Class,* ed. Ira Berlin (New York: Pantheon, 1987), 70–92; John Laslett, "Swan Song or New Social Movement? Socialism and Illinois District 12, United Mine Workers of America, 1919–1926," in *Socialism in the Heartland: The Midwestern Experience, 1900–1925,* ed. Donald Critchlow (Notre Dame: University of Notre Dame Press, 1989), 167–214. Antonia Sentner recalled the community-based unionism of the coal mine towns in reference to the sources of her own initiation into the union movement. She also stresses the familial involvement in strikes there, where "the whole family was involved . . . women would wrap up the kids and take them to the picket line." Sentner interview. Note, however, that this was always a politicized and contested issue, rather than one that was inherent in the political economy. The active role of women, long a tradition in mining communities, was rejected by John L. Lewis, for instance, who opposed the establishment of women's auxiliaries. However, the Progressive Miners, the radical union established to contest the United Mine Workers of America in the early 1930s, celebrated and encouraged family involvement, particularly women's involvement, thus suggesting that such issues had become politically charged and lending more evidence to the suggestion that leftists played a role in carrying forth these traditions. See "Minutes of the Social Justice Commission," May 15, 1933, p. 12, Temple Israel, Papers of the Right Reverend William Scarlett, Record Group 107–37–10, Archives of the Episcopal Church USA, Austin, Texas.

18. Fichtenbaum, *The Funsten Nut Strike,* 15–16; Bill Gebert, "The St. Louis Strike and the Chicago Needle Trades Strike," *Communist* 12 (August 1933), 800–809.

19. Gebert, "The St. Louis Strike"; Irene Bell, interview with author, November 1992.

20. *Daily Worker,* January 21, 1932; Gebert, "The St. Louis Strike"; Alice Love, interview with author, November 1992 (quote); *Post-Dispatch,* May 18, 1933; *St. Louis Argus,* May 26, 1933; Bell interview.

21. Love interview (first quote); Mary Jefferson, interview with author, December 1992 (second and third quotes).

22. *St. Louis Argus,* May 26, 1933.

23. *Daily Worker,* January 31, 1932 (quote); Fraser Ottanelli, *The Communist Party in the 1930s* (Brunswick, N.J.: Rutgers University Press, 1991), 21. There were no TUUL unions in St. Louis before the Funsten organization.

24. *Globe-Democrat,* May 2, 1933; Ralph Shaw, "St. Louis' Biggest Strike," *Labor Unity,* August 1933, 8–11 (quote); *American Labor Year Book*

(New York: Rand School Press, 1932); Ralph Shaw, "St. Louis Nutpickers' Strike Sets Example," *Party Organizer* 6 (July 1933), 4. (I thank John Borsos for bringing this last article to my attention.)

25. Jefferson interview (quotes); Shaw, "St. Louis' Biggest Strike," 8; Shaw, "St. Louis Nutpickers' Strike," 4–5.

26. Fichtenbaum, *The Funsten Nut Strike;* Jefferson interview; *Daily Worker,* May 22, 1933; Goldberg interview; Shaw, "St. Louis' Biggest Strike," 9; *St. Louis Star-Times,* May 15, 1933; *St. Louis Argus,* May 19, 1933.

27. Shaw, "St. Louis' Biggest Strike," 9 (first quote); *Daily Worker,* May 17 and 22, 1933; *Star-Times,* May 16, 1933; Bell interview (remaining quotes); Shaw, "St. Louis Nutpickers' Strike."

28. Love interview (quote); Goldberg interview; Sentner interview.

29. Brunn, "Black Workers and Social Movements," 349; Shaw, "St. Louis' Biggest Strike," 9; *Star-Times,* May 15 and 16, 1933; *Post-Dispatch,* May 16, 17, 18, and 19, 1933; *Daily Worker,* May 17 and 22, 1933; Fichtenbaum, *The Funsten Nut Strike,* 29 (quote).

30. Shaw quoted in Fichtenbaum, *The Funsten Nut Strike,* 27.

31. Gebert, "The St. Louis Strike," 800 (first quote); *Daily Worker,* May 22, 1933; Shaw, "St. Louis' Biggest Strike," 9 (second quote).

32. *Globe-Democrat,* May 19, 1933; Fichtenbaum, *The Funsten Nut Strike,* 30–31; *Star-Times,* May 18, 1933; *Daily Worker,* May 23, 1933; editorial, *Modern View* 66 (May 25, 1933), 4–5. Somewhat unique in the country, the SJC was organized in 1931 by Rabbi Ferdinand Isserman of Temple Israel in St. Louis and Bishop William Scarlett of the East Missouri Diocese of the Episcopal church, both social and theological liberals "noted as champions of . . . social and economic justice." In 1933 the SJC included fifteen clergymen and ten professors from Washington University and St. Louis University and boasted that it had "settle[d] a number of industrial difficulties." Rabbi F. I. Isserman to Claude Pearcy, May 9, 1933, Papers of the Right Reverend William Scarlett. Just prior to the Funsten strike, the newly established Progressive Mine Workers Union asked the SJC to investigate what it claimed were abuses of civil liberties by the United Mine Workers in the southern Illinois coal fields. Scarlett and Isserman were accompanied by Clarence Darrow in the coal fields. *Globe-Democrat,* May 1, 1933; *Post-Dispatch,* May 15, 1933.

33. *Globe-Democrat,* May 18 and 20, 1933 (first and second quotes); *Post-Dispatch,* May 23, 1933 (third quote); *St. Louis Argus,* May 26, 1933 (fourth quote). Dickman's committee included Isserman; John T. Clarke, the executive secretary of the Urban League; O. O. Morris, the executive secretary of the "Colored" YMCA; Joseph L. McLemore and William H. Parker, black attorneys; the Reverend Father William Markoe of St. Elizabeth's parish; and Emmett Canty, the chief parole officer for the city. The committee was later expanded to include Dean Sidney Sweet of the Christ Church Cathedral, an-

other figure in the SJC, as well as a few others. *Globe-Democrat,* May 24, 1933.

34. *Post-Dispatch,* May 23 and 24, 1933; *Star-Times,* May 23, 1933; *Daily Worker,* May 23 and 25, 1933; *St. Louis Argus,* May 26, 1933 (quote).

35. Risch, "The Effects of Communist Propaganda"; Brunn, "Black Workers and Social Movements," 356–57; Shaw, "St. Louis' Biggest Strike," 11; Ira Reid, "A Study of the Industrial Status of Negroes in St. Louis, Missouri," series 4, box 9, and "EAC for Negroes, Minutes," series 4, box 11, both in Urban League Papers, Archives, Washington University, St. Louis.

36. Shaw, "St. Louis' Biggest Strike," 11; *Daily World,* June 1, 1933; *Daily Worker,* September 8, 1933 (quote).

37. *Daily Worker,* October 4 and 7, 1933; *St. Louis Argus,* October 13, 1933 (quotes).

38. *St. Louis Argus,* October 13, 1933 (quote); "Re: William Sentner," folder 2, box 5, William Frey Papers, Library of Congress, Washington, D.C.; FBI 100–18332–139 and FBI 100–18332–14, William Sentner Papers, Washington University, St. Louis; *Star-Times,* October 19, 1933; *Post-Dispatch,* October 19, 1933; *Globe-Democrat,* October 20, 1933.

39. *Daily Worker,* November 29, 1933.

40. Ibid., November 6, 1933, June 5, 8, and 12, 1934; *Post-Dispatch,* June 16, 1934.

41. Philip Foner, *The Fur and Leather Workers Union: A Story of Dramatic Struggles and Achievements* (Newark, N.J.: Nordan Press, 1950), 381–87.

42. Harvey Klehr, *The Heyday of American Communism: The Depression Decade* (New York: Basic Books, 1984), is the best source for the traditional depiction, while the latest overview of the literature on this much-debated issue is Maurice Isserman, "Three Generations: Historians View American Communism," *Labor History* 26 (Fall 1985), 517–45. On the traditions of democratic community struggle, see Sara Evans and Harry Boyte, *Free Spaces: The Sources of Democratic Change in America* (New York: Harper and Row, 1986); and Faue, *Community of Suffering and Struggle.*

43. Staughton Lynd, Introduction, herein; Philip A. Korth and Margaret R. Beegle, *I Remember Like Today: The Auto-Lite Strike of 1934* (East Lansing: Michigan State University Press, 1988); Art Preis, *Labor's Giant Step: Twenty Years of the CIO* (New York: Pioneer Publishers, 1964), 34.

44. Goldberg interview.

45. Jacqueline Jones, *Labor of Love, Labor of Sorrow: Black Women, Work, and the Family from Slavery to the Present* (New York: Basic Books, 1985); Janiewski, *Sisterhood Denied*; Robin D. G. Kelley, "'We Are Not What We Seem': Rethinking Black Working-Class Opposition in the Jim Crow South," *Journal of American History* 80 (June 1993), 75–112, expanding on

his work in Robin Kelley, *Hammer and Hoe: Alabama Communists during the Great Depression* (Chapel Hill: University of North Carolina Press, 1990).

46. Alice Kessler-Harris, "Treating the Male as 'Other': Redefining the Parameters of Labor History," *Labor History* 34 (Spring–Summer 1993), 195.

47. *Post-Dispatch,* June 12, 1934; *Daily Worker,* June 8 and 15, 1934; Reid, "A Study of the Industrial Status of Negroes," 55 (first quote); Risch, "The Effects of Communist Propaganda," 60–80; Brunn, "Black Workers and Social Movements," 365, 368–69 (second quote); Robert Korstad and Nelson Lichtenstein, "Opportunities Found and Lost: Labor, Radicals, and the Early Civil Rights Movement," *Journal of American History* 75 (December 1988), 786–812.

48. *Daily Worker,* April 17, 1934; Brunn, "Black Workers and Social Movements," 364–90.

49. Beyond its impact on the workers' movement, the nutpickers' union and other struggles among black workers caused a tremendous change in the local Urban League, reorienting it completely from a pro-business to a pro-worker organization during the 1930s. Involvement with the nutpickers was also one of the factors that prompted the Social Justice Commission to become more involved in community racial issues, with an impact that was significant in the city into the 1940s. The establishment of the New Deal labor boards, with their model of employer and labor representatives, diminished the role of ministers and local academics and lawyers in the settlement of these disputes, however. It is notable that the United Electrical Workers recently decided it would in many cases ignore the NLRB apparatus in union elections and instead set up local community boards made up of prominent citizens, including ministers. See *Economic Notes* 60 (Spring 1992).

50. American Workers Union folders, Socialist Party Papers, Archives, University of Missouri–St. Louis; Rosemary Feurer, *Making History: The Gas House Workers* (video), 1986; *Gas House Workers Bulletin* (1935), Gas Workers Papers, Archives, University of Missouri–St. Louis; *Warehouse Workers Bulletin* (1935–36), Archives, University of Missouri–St. Louis; "Unions—American Workers Union, 1934–1936," series 4, box 11, Urban League Papers; *Post-Dispatch,* April 26, 28, and 30 and May 9 and 11, 1936; Rosemary Feurer, "City Hall and the Unemployed Protests of the 1930s," in *St. Louis Labor History Tour,* ed. Feurer, 21–24.

51. Rosemary Feurer, "William Sentner, the UE, and Civic Unionism in St. Louis," in *The CIO's Left-Led Unions,* ed. Steve Rosswurm (New Brunswick, N.J.: Rutgers University Press, 1992), 95–117.

2

Organizing "Wall to Wall"

The Independent Union of All Workers, 1933–37

Peter Rachleff

When I walked into the Austin Labor Center in the fall of 1984 for a Local P-9 solidarity rally, a wall display of old union buttons caught my eye. At first glance they appeared to be from the Industrial Workers of the World (IWW). There was the familiar globe with the latitude and longitude lines. Upon closer examination, however, I discovered that they read "IUAW" rather than "IWW." They were dues buttons, each a different color, denoting a different month from the summer of 1933 to the spring of 1937.[1]

My historian's curiosity was awakened—what was this organization? I asked around. The first few people I approached could tell me little or nothing. Finally, someone said, "Why, that was the Independent Union of All Workers. They were the first union here in the Hormel plant, before the CIO, and they organized everyone in town." Another person added, "They were started by old Frank Ellis. He was something else. He used to say that if you were any part of the food chain, from a producer to a consumer, you all belonged in the same union."

As I wandered around the Labor Center, I stumbled across another peculiar clue. There was an office for a local of the Oil, Chemical, and Atomic Workers Union. "Say," I asked, "is there some sort of power plant around here? Who does this local represent?" A P-9er matter-of-factly explained to me (as if we college professors tend to be dense) that they represented the waiters, waitresses, and bartenders in town. "Wow!" I exclaimed. "How did that happen?" He didn't know.

I kept asking until I found someone able to explain. It seemed that waiters, waitresses, and bartenders had once been part of the Independent Union of All Workers, too. When that union affiliated with the CIO in 1937 and the bulk of its members joined the Packinghouse Workers Organizing Committee (later to become the United Packinghouse Workers of America), the leftover "miscellaneous workers" had affiliated with District 50 of John L. Lewis's United Mine Workers of America (UMW). The UMW was organized by geographic regions except for District 50, which was a national organization that took in all sorts of workers, as the AFL federal union structure or the British general union did. In 1942 some locals left District 50 and formed the United Gas, Coke, and Chemical Workers' Union (CIO), which merged with the Oil Workers International Union in 1954 to form the Oil, Chemical and Atomic Workers. And that's how they came to represent waiters, waitresses, and bartenders in Austin, Minnesota.[2]

I was so intrigued by the Independent Union of All Workers that I began a major research project to explore its history. I found strategies, tactics, and overall approaches that once worked well and might well work *now*. I also learned that the bureaucratic unionism that has engulfed us was not inevitable. Rather, it was the product of the decisions and activities of hundreds and thousands of men and women, some of whom understood the implications of what they were doing, and many of whom did not. Unpacking this period can help us understand the roots of the fix we find ourselves in today—and how we might get out of it.

Between 1933 and 1937 the IUAW organized locals in Austin, Albert Lea, Faribault, Thief River Falls, Bemidji, Owatonna, Mankato, and South St. Paul, Minnesota; Mitchell and Madison, South Dakota; Fargo, North Dakota; Alma, Wisconsin; and Waterloo, Mason City, Algona, Ottumwa, Fort Dodge, and Estherville, Iowa. The IUAW also influenced activists in Madison, Wisconsin; Cedar Rapids and Sioux City, Iowa; Sioux Falls, South Dakota; Omaha, Nebraska; Kansas City, Kansas; and Oklahoma City, Oklahoma. In many of these cities, the IUAW sought not only to spread industrial unionism among packinghouse workers but also to organize "wall-to-wall." Their efforts—expressed in organizing drives, strikes, strike support, local politics, and various "cultural" activities—threatened entrenched power throughout the region.[3]

Depression-era conditions and employer antiunionism set the context for the emergence of the IUAW. But this union did not explode spontaneously. It was the product of the complex interaction between an energized rank and file and a diverse group of radicals and among the radicals themselves. The lid placed on social mobility by the depression kept bright, capable young men and women from holding onto the family farm or from rising out of the working class. Some of them ended up in the Hormel plant—and became IUAW activists. They found an outlet for their speaking and writing skills, their energy, their imaginations and talents—as well as a vehicle to change society. Depression conditions in the plant—short hours, insecurity, low hourly wages, deteriorating shop-floor conditions, abusive foremen—alienated most workers from plant management. Fear—especially in the face of large numbers of unemployed job-seekers gathered outside the plant daily—had kept them from challenging this situation. But they began to feel empowered by the political climate of 1933, at both a state and national level.[4]

No one had a greater influence on the IUAW than Frank Ellis. The feisty ex-Wobbly not only shaped the union's structure and its emphasis on democracy and solidarity but also imprinted its character with his combative personality. In his late forties, Ellis had a labor record that included the 1904 meat-packing strike in St. Joseph, Missouri; free speech fights from Omaha to Seattle before World War I; the IWW's historic struggles in Centralia, Illinois, and Everett, Washington; a seat on the IWW's executive board in the early 1920s; a lengthy list of arrests, including indictment for criminal syndicalism in Omaha. A skilled "boomer" butcher, he frequently moved around and had little difficulty finding work. By the late 1920s Ellis had worked in packing plants in St. Joseph, Oklahoma City, Omaha, Sioux City, and Albert Lea. Along the way, he had made a lot of contacts. He had also picked up knowledge of a new sausage casing fermentation process. In 1928 Hormel hired him as a foreman to start and run its new casing department.[5]

Though he had only a third grade education, Ellis brought a wealth of experience to the heated labor climate of the 1930s. One of his contemporaries later marveled at how Ellis had "managed to capture workers' restlessness at that time." His reputation as an "agitational speaker" rested on more than his use of words. Another union veteran recalled that "whenever you mentioned the name Amalgamated [Meat-Cutters and Butcher Workmen] or AF of L, he'd spit on the ground."[6]

Ellis kept a low profile after he was hired in 1928, but he did help other experienced (even blacklisted) labor activists get jobs. He later told an interviewer:

> I'd send out and get rebels that I knew from other towns to come in and go to work, and I'd work them during the rush season, see. Then, when it came to lay off time, instead of laying them off, I'd go to some other boss and say, "Here, I've got a good man. And I hate like hell to lay him off. Can you use him? And I'll take him back as soon as business starts up." And I'd place him in the plant and scatter him out. Well, he was an old union man. He knew what to do. I didn't have to tell him.

He knew the idea was to get in there with the gang and to get them emotionally moved so they'd be ready to organize when the time came.[7]

Whether Ellis deserves the credit for having brought them into the plant or not, a diverse group of radical activists did find employment there. As the political climate began to change, they started to organize. In the spring of 1933 a group of young hog-kill workers began meeting for lunch-time bull sessions in the "tank room." Mostly Austin natives, they were angered by the deteriorating working conditions, the tyranny of foremen, and their "second-class" status in the community. Early in the summer they asked Frank Ellis to join their discussions. They also turned to the Minneapolis Trotskyists Carl Skoglund and Ray Dunne, whose reputations as labor activists were on a par with Ellis's.[8]

Over the course of the next four years, these young Trotskyists in the hog kill would provide the IUAW with much of its dynamic drive. They were not alone, however. Together with some independent socialists, they organized the "Socialist Club" caucus. There was also a group of Communists in the plant. Most of them were skilled "boomer" butchers from out of town, having hired in when the beef kill opened in 1931. In addition to these radicals and their allies inside the plant and in the Austin community, there were radicals—again, of all sorts—in most of the cities to which the IUAW spread. Their involvement in other organizations—the Farmer-Labor Party, Farm Holiday Association, Workers' Alliance, the Northwest Labor Unity Conference, even the American Civil Liberties Union—brought additional support to this unusual union.[9]

The IUAW was built solidly from the ground up. The Hormel work force was its initial base. The activists knew the importance of a strong shop-floor presence. "You worked with a group of people who have never belonged to a union, who have never spoken back to a foreman, and a company that didn't want to recognize you," one recalled. They knew that the shop floor itself held the key to dispelling the atmosphere of fear that had held the rank and file back and in demonstrating the potential power of collective action.[10]

In the summer of 1933 Ellis and the hog-kill gang chose a highly symbolic issue to provoke a shop-floor confrontation—and then launch the union. A cornerstone of Hormel paternalism had long been the Austin Community Chest. The company sought 100 percent participation by its workers. When pledge cards were distributed, one veteran recalled, "The foreman just backed you up against the wall and told you you were going to give. If you didn't, it meant your job." Bad enough when times were good, this added insult to injury in a context of layoffs, short weeks, and wage cuts. "This was for the poor people," recalled another old timer. "Hell, *we* were the poor people!" Over the Fourth of July holiday, Hormel announced a $1.20 a week raise—and a new pension plan to be funded by payroll deductions of $1.20 a week. Foremen were to distribute pledge cards for the pension plan along with the pledge cards for the annual Community Chest drive.[11]

On July 13, 1933, pledge cards were distributed to the hog kill. When one worker yielded to the foreman's pressure and signed, the radicals stopped work. The rest of the gang followed suit. They surrounded the foreman and insisted that he tear up the card. For ten minutes no hogs were slaughtered. Then the foreman gave in. That afternoon word of this action spread throughout the plant, together with news of a meeting to be held after work in Sutton Park.[12]

The Hormel workers were electrified by the hog-kill action. One later described the atmosphere surrounding the meeting: "I saw a man walking his way toward the park. His back was bent from the toil of pulling trucks, but he walked with a purpose toward this meeting. I don't know what his thoughts were, possibly better days to come. . . . The speaker spoke about the benefits of organization. You could see the purpose in the eyes of these fellows. I looked at their eyes. New hope was shining in them."[13]

Ellis chaired the meeting. Several speakers—women as well as men—urged the crowd to organize. Ellis laid out his vision of an organization that would reach all workers in Austin and promote the national unionization of the meat-packing industry along industrial lines. The new union was to be open to "all wage earners, no matter where employed." Undaunted by the presence of company stool pigeons, 600 signed up.[14]

Twice in the ensuing months the IUAW relied on visible workplace confrontations to build the union. Each time, they not only demonstrated their strength to the company but also demonstrated the workers' own strength to themselves. Direct action remained the IUAW's preeminent tactic.

It was through mass, direct action that they got union recognition. On September 23, while Ellis was behind closed doors bargaining with Jay Hormel, workers massed at the front gates and refused to go in. Hormel and Ellis came out and addressed the crowd from a hastily assembled platform. Ellis—the veteran soapboxer—stood his ground, as did the crowd. Hormel yielded and signed an agreement in front of everyone right at the gate.[15]

Despite the formal recognition, the wage increase so desperately needed was not forthcoming. When six weeks of negotiations brought no agreement on a raise, the IUAW again turned to mass, direct action. It was the
"hog rush," and the workers felt themselves in a position of power. Some
had recently joined the Farm Holiday Association in picketing roads into
town. Following a tumultuous union meeting on Friday night, November
10, the hog-kill gang went directly to the plant. One of them recalled, "We
rushed to the packinghouse and we took over. We told the sheep kill gang
[which worked the late night shift] to clean the sheep, put them in the
cooler, and get the hell out." For the next three days, in what some labor
historians have considered the first "sit-down" strike of the 1930s, the
IUAW maintained control of the plant. Governor Floyd Olson, a Farmer-
Laborite, rushed to Austin, where he mediated an agreement between Jay
Hormel and the union. A mass meeting at the state armory overwhelmingly approved it.[16]

The IUAW maintained a strong shop-floor presence in the Hormel plant.
Each department elected a three-person committee, and each committee
elected a chairperson. Although the agreement established a formal grievance procedure with arbitration, the union relied largely on direct action—
slowdowns, sit-downs—to resolve grievances on the spot. One union veteran offered this description: "Frank Ellis would sit down in the union hall.
They would call him up and say: 'Come on over, the department is sitting
down. . . .' So over Frank goes. Frank would go over to the hog kill or the
hog cut or one of the departments, and here the people were madder than
hell, sitting against the wall, refusing to work. And then the company would
meet with Frank, and Frank was 175% for the worker. . . . You never had
to worry about Frank seeing the company side of anything. They'd get the
grievance settled right on the job." Ellis himself explained to an interviewer: "Most of our strikes were sitdown, sit down right on the job and not do
a damn bit of work until we got it settled. . . . We had strikes every day. Hell,
if a fellow farted crooked we would strike about it."[17]

From this base in the Hormel plant, the IUAW spread to other workers
in Austin and to community after community. In Austin, where the union
relied on the collective consuming power of the Hormel workers and their
families, it reached its goal of 100 percent unionization. It included "units"
of truckers and warehouse workers, barbers and beauticians, waiters,
waitresses and bartenders, construction tradesmen and laborers, WPA
laborers, automobile mechanics and service station attendants, laundry and
dry-cleaning workers, retail clerks, and municipal employees. From beauty
shops with three employees to the local Montgomery Wards, every retail

and service establishment in Austin came under contract with the IUAW. Many of these "units" were grouped together as the "Uptown Workers Association," which had its own female business agent, the veteran waitress Eva Sauers.[18]

The IUAW built its strength through a variety of tactics. The Austin labor activists frequently led "teams" of rank-and-file "volunteer organizers" on forays into other communities, where they were reviled by the press as "outside agitators." Ellis usually led the way with some inspirational public speaking. He "would set a group of workers on edge for a few weeks, get them to do some thinking." Other activists helped with day-to-day organizing and with publishing newsletters and leaflets. At times they relied on the direct action of workers in these industries. During strikes other IUAW members provided material aid to strikers and their families. Here and there some creative picketing tactics were employed. During a strike against a transfer company, for example, mobile pickets were dispatched to rural roads outside Austin to block delivery trucks. On several occasions, the IUAW hired unemployed workers, who were willing to ignore court injunctions, to put in daily shifts as pickets in front of retail establishments. Solidarity with farmers was a two-way street for the IUAW. At times they secured the cooperation of Farm Holiday Association pickets or collected food donations for union strikers. At other times IUAW members participated in FHA actions, from picketing roads or even packing plants to holding the ranks during a "penny auction."[19]

The IUAW built a rich, active culture for its members and their families, especially in Austin. There was the *Unionist,* delivered free on Friday mornings to every household in Austin. It was edited by Carl Nilson, a Trotskyist from the Twin Cities who had come to Austin under the auspices of the state Bureau of Workers Education. The first issue of the *Unionist,* in October 1935, declared, "In line with the history and tradition of the union, this paper will be radical and militant, dynamic rather than static, alive rather than asleep." It lived up to its own billing. A union veteran, only a teen-ager in the IUAW period, recalled, "The *Unionist* has had a terrific influence in educating our members, tempering the vociferousness of the enemies of organized labor, organizing the unorganized and speaking out for the oppressed and downtrodden people who otherwise could not make their voices or grievances known."[20]

In addition to editing the *Unionist,* Nilson taught classes in public speaking, parliamentary law, labor history, economics, and current events. He also organized classes in band, chorus, and dramatics that played an important part in the culture of the IUAW. The union and its Ladies Auxiliary organized a lively Drum and Bugle Corps, which led many parades, and a drama troupe, which performed several plays. These activities raised funds for the union, educated both participants and audience, and added to the rank-and-file's sense of unity and identity. The IUAW also established a library in the union hall, which featured works by Edward Bellamy, John Reed, and Upton Sinclair. The *Unionist* included a regular book review column, written by Nilson's wife, Marian, whose father had been a Knights of Labor activist in the 1880s.[21]

In the summer of 1937 an IUAW activist looked back over the accomplishments of its four year history:

> Since 1933 the workers in Austin have never let up their efforts to make Austin 100% union. . . . Above all, Austin's unionization is not a shallow thing, but a master organization that penetrates far into the very lives of the workers that live in Austin. . . . It is not merely a matter of wages and more money to spend. Within this program of unionization lies the basis of things that are far reaching and more important. With unionization comes a new freedom—a freedom of the individual that will grow in importance as the organizational experience grows older. A new freedom of thought, of action and knowledge, are products of workers' lives protected through organizations of their own choosing.[22]

The IUAW was structured to maximize participation in running the union. "Units" met on a weekly basis, with all rank and filers able to shape union policy for their industry. "Local 1," which consisted of delegates elected by each Austin unit, met monthly and considered issues of concern to the entire IUAW. Once a week there was an open mass meeting—"the big meeting," one union veteran recalled, "to have a solidarity of the masses, as Frank Ellis used to talk about." These mass meetings did not take formal votes or set specific policy for the union, but they brought together rank and filers and auxiliary members from across the city to hear speakers, debate political issues, and map out solidarity campaigns.[23]

The Ladies Auxiliary brought workers' families directly into the life of the union. Organized in the summer of 1933, it collected dues of ten cents a month and held biweekly meetings in the union hall. Each meeting opened with "Solidarity Forever" and followed with thirty minutes of group songs. The Ladies Auxiliary ran strike kitchens and commissaries, promoted boycotts of companies embroiled in labor conflicts, maintained the popular Drum and Bugle Corps, organized a community lecture series that brought diverse speakers to town, and raised money for union projects by performing plays and holding card parties, dances, and bake sales.[24]

Although the Austin local remained the most fully developed in terms of organizational infrastructure, the entire IUAW was infused with solidarity. Radicals and rank and filers took this spirit from community to community. "Outside agitators" joined in picketing and demonstrations in Faribault, Albert Lea, Owatonna, Mason City, Waterloo, and Estherville. In July 1935, for instance, the IUAW coordinated a series of sympathy strikes by more than 1,000 Wilson packing-plant workers in Faribault and Albert Lea to support the 100 striking Wilson poultry plant workers in Faribault. In January 1935 and April 1937 Austin IUAW'ers responded en masse to an SOS call from Albert Lea. Both times, they joined in street fighting with squads of special deputies. Ellis emphasized the power of solidarity in a speech to a mass meeting of striking Rath Packing Company workers in Waterloo in January 1935: "If you say so, we'll bring in militant workers from other cities who will put this thing over. We'll shut down the packing-houses in Albert Lea and Austin if necessary to get men in here to win this strike."[25]

The IUAW provided a cohesive network for labor activism in these far-flung communities. Annual conventions brought together formal delegates from each "local union," both to handle union business and to picnic and commune together. "Wall-to-wall," 100 percent unionism, may never have been achieved in these other communities, but a powerful foundation was laid for the development of permanent union organization. In some communities IUAW activists entered local and regional politics, usually through "farmer-labor" formations. In Austin and Albert Lea, for instance, they captured seats on the city council, initiated farmer-labor newspapers, and became a force in the congressional district.[26]

Through 1936 the radicals in the IUAW mostly cooperated with each other. Despite some "tug of war" over union offices, one later recalled, they all held "pretty much the same outlook on shop issues." They were anything but shy about presenting their ideas to rank-and-file workers. Ellis, of course, was the most outspoken of all. His advocacy of a "one big union philosophy" was well known. In a letter to the union-supported *American* in March 1935, he wrote:

> Let us unite to make America the place it should be. Our forefathers who rebelled against the iron heel tactics of England were branded as traitors and everything under the sun. They were imprisoned, murdered, and persecuted, but they continued to fight until they won their freedom.
>
> So let us continue the fight to the extent of shouldering arms if need be. Many will go to prison, or perhaps be killed by the powers. But our fight is worth it.[27]

The political climate within the IUAW favored the free expression of ideas. When a crowd organized by the Albert Lea Chamber of Commerce broke up a Communist street meeting, the IUAW responded with a mass meeting "to protest this invasion of the rights of free speech." More than 2,000 attended this hastily called rally. Inside the union, members did not hesitate to express their own views. One wrote to the *American,* "The philosophy of the Communist is that of taking over the means of production and distribution by the workers, for those who work, and on this issue all who toil should concur. I have no use for a system that flaunts its surpluses in the face of starving millions. . . . Capitalism must go, or else we must become reconciled to mass starvation, want, and the carnage of war."[28]

The presence of diverse radicals within the IUAW exposed rank and filers to various critical perspectives on the key issues of the day. In the shop, radicals promoted plantwide seniority, equal pay for equal work for women, and 100 percent union membership. At union meetings and in union publications they debated issues of national and international policy, from the New Deal to the civil war in Spain. The radicals' connections to national movements also enhanced the scope of the IUAW.[29]

The Hormel packinghouse activists who built and extended the Independent Union of All Workers wrestled with a complex problem. Hormel management insisted that raises given to their workers would have to be linked to raises achieved by packinghouse workers throughout the country. This pressure was certainly a factor in efforts to extend the IUAW. It also led Austin activists to meet with packinghouse unionists from around the Midwest to discuss linking up their activities, if not their organizations. After the CIO was formed in 1935, some of the activists contacted John L. Lewis and asked for his help. In these efforts they continued to face a dilemma: how to build a cohesive national organization that would still rest on the local democracy and horizontal solidarity that had been the lifeblood of the IUAW.[30]

These issues were widely debated in the IUAW, at rank-and-file meetings, on the shop floor, and in the pages of the *Unionist.* Virtually all the radicals—Trotskyists, Communists, and Socialists—agreed on the strategy of linking up with the CIO. Each group had its own angle on the issue. The Trotskyists and the Socialists emphasized work inside the major formations within the labor movement, either AFL or CIO, instead of taking up independent positions outside these structures. The Communists were eager to build up the CIO as a counterbalance to the AFL. Even the "straight business unionists" within the IUAW favored affiliation. They concurred with Hormel management's contention that further wage increases would be held back until the rest of the industry moved forward.[31]

Ellis was the strongest voice of skepticism about affiliation with the CIO. He was not opposed to being part of a national network or even a national organization. But he was very concerned that the dynamics of local and regional cross-industry solidarity not be sacrificed. However, at the critical juncture in the road, he was out of the picture, locked away in the state prison on trumped-up charges. Recently discovered evidence suggests that the Communists did what they could to make sure that Ellis stayed in jail. When some of Ellis's supporters sought to involve the American Civil Liberties Union in his case, Nat Ross, the CP district organizer, wrote to Roger Baldwin and urged him to keep his distance from Ellis, whom he described as a "degenerate."[32]

Ironically, the IUAW would not be able to make a reasoned decision on affiliation with the CIO. Instead, in the spring of 1937 the organization found itself in a sudden crisis, in which it had to settle on a course for its future. The unfolding of this crisis allowed for little consideration of the sort of issues that Ellis emphasized. And it sealed the fate of the Independent Union of All Workers.

On March 8, 1937, truck drivers and warehouse workers at two transfer companies in Albert Lea (twenty miles west of Austin) went on strike. Carl Nilson, who had given up the editorship of the *Unionist* to take the lead in organizing truckers in southern Minnesota and northern Iowa into the IUAW, coordinated the Albert Lea strike. In a matter of days, freight began to pile up at the railroad station.[33]

The situation in Albert Lea took on new proportions as other strikes began to break out. On March 18 a dozen young women clerks began a sit-down strike at Woolworth's. They had been in the IUAW for some time, but negotiations for formal recognition, wage increases, and seniority protections had been going nowhere. They knew that the IUAW had successfully organized Montgomery Wards and smaller retail establishments in Austin. Ray Hemenway, the best-known IUAW activist in Albert Lea, was handling the negotiations in their behalf. Described as "part Wobbly, part Trotskyist" by one old timer, Hemenway sat on the executive board of the IUAW as a whole as well as leading "Local Union No. 2" in Albert Lea. After weeks of negotiations, with the full backing of the IUAW, Hemenway and the young clerks had decided the Easter shopping season was an opportune time for them to strike.[34]

The very next day, sit-down strikes also broke out in the two plants of
the American Gas Machine Company. Next to Wilson's packinghouse, they
were Albert Lea's major industrial employer. Since the IUAW had expanded
into Albert Lea, labor conflict had been frequent—and often violent—at
American Gas. In February 1935 a brief strike at the Potter Foundry (a
subcontractor of American Gas) had escalated into a walkout at the main
plant and a physical confrontation between IUAW pickets and sheriff's
deputies that resulted in several injuries and arrests. Half a dozen IUAW
activists were sentenced to sixty days at hard labor as a result of this battle, and a bitter enmity between the union and the sheriff, Helmer Myre,
was established. Over the next two years the IUAW had won a grudging
recognition from the American Gas management. The frequent cyclic and
seasonal ups and downs of American Gas's business, together with the
antiunionism of its management, had kept the IUAW's foothold an inse-
cure one. The *Unionist* called Albert Lea "one of the most vicious and well-
organized anti-labor towns in Minnesota."[35]

On March 18, the day the clerks took control of Woolworth's, American Gas management took a provocative action. They fired four IUAW
activists from the main plant. Though they claimed that a business downturn had necessitated a round of layoffs, the IUAW saw this as an attack
on the union. On March 19 they initiated a sit-down strike at the company's two plants, on Front Street and Clark Street. At the Clark Street location, strikers took up positions in the large street-level display window,
waving to passersby and demonstrating their high spirits to the public.[36]

For two weeks all three strikes held firm. Nilson published a daily strike
bulletin, which answered the rumors and accusations appearing in Albert
Lea's antilabor *Evening Tribune*. Austin IUAW activists visited Albert Lea
regularly, bringing material and moral support to the sit-down strikers.
Every evening the IUAW Drum and Bugle Corps paraded the streets of
Albert Lea, marching from the Clark Street plant (where the occupiers
cheered from the display windows) to the Front Street plant. From there
they marched to Woolworth's. Each night the girls occupying the store
greeted the paraders with a song. Then the parade continued to the Witt-
mer and Thompson & Wulff warehouses, with a side trip by the railroad
depot for a progress report on the accumulating pile of freight.[37]

Nothing endeared the strikers more to the general public than the Woolworth sit-downers' singing. They wrote a "theme song" to the tune of the
"Old Grey Mare," whose chorus became well known throughout Albert Lea
and Austin: "The five and dime / She ain't what she used to be."[38]

The day-to-day atmosphere is suggested by the IUAW's daily bulletin, the *Strike News,* in its description of a parade of hundreds of union members on Friday night, March 26:

> The Girls' Drum and Bugle Corps signalled for stops at both of the American Gas Machine plants and the F. W. Woolworth Store on South Broadway. The girls serenaded the sitdown strikers with a few peppy selections at each of the three stops, outstanding union leaders spoke words of encouragement and the great crowd cheered to the echo.
>
> At the Woolworth store the courageous girl sit-downers grouped themselves together on an improvised platform inside and in front of the swinging doors that have been locked for more than a week. Then they sang their sit-downers' theme song. When the fighting damsels concluded their little ditty it seemed that all Broadway was yelling its approval.[39]

Despite the spirit and unity of the strikers and their supporters, the enemies of the IUAW, organized by the Albert Lea Chamber of Commerce and its "Secret Committee of 500," planned to defeat the union. This network linked Judge J. D. Cooney; the virulently antiunion vice president of Wilson; the local American Gas Machine management; experienced opponents of the IUAW, such as the owner of Burnsmoor Dairies; and enemies of organized labor from the Twin Cities, such as the Minneapolis Citizens Alliance. Their scheme revolved around a citywide company union they had created, the Albert Lea Employees Labor Association (ALELA). Jack Blades, the most notorious sheriff's deputy in town, served as its president. They planned to start a back-to-work movement under the auspices of this "labor" organization, denounce the interference of the "outside agitators" of the IUAW, and, eventually, grant formal union recognition to the ALELA.[40]

Their plan relied on cooperation from several quarters. District court Judge Norman "Injunction" Peterson issued the necessary injunctions to order the evacuation of the plants, the warehouses, and Woolworth's. Sheriff Helmer Myre swore in 150 special deputies, many of them farmers from rural Freeborn County or experienced antiunion private cops from the Twin Cities. The Albert Lea *Evening Tribune* berated the strikers, their "violation" of the "rights" of private property, and published the names of those who were risking arrest by ignoring Peterson's injunctions. The paper pressured the girls in Woolworth's, publishing rumors of "immoral" goings-on among the male and female occupiers. It appealed directly to their parents to pull them out and to the young women themselves, asking them if they intended to miss out on wearing their finery in the traditional Easter parade. Daily, the *Tribune* claimed that back-to-work sentiment was growing. Its claims were further supported by the appearance of a daily ALELA newsheet, the *Labor News,* which red-baited the leadership of the IUAW and reechoed the theme of "outside agitators." The crowning piece of the strategy was provided by the state AFL, which, in the midst of this conflict, granted the ALELA a charter.[41]

A back-to-work movement never materialized, and the pickets held firm. Fearful of increasing penalties, the IUAW and the strikers finally decided to yield to the judge's injunctions. On the morning of April 2 they vacated the plants, warehouses, and department store. They took up positions as mass pickets in each location. Sheriff Myre and his deputies attacked the pickets outside the American Gas Machine plant, dispersing them under a cloud of tear gas and a barrage of rubber hoses. The "forces of order" then laid siege to the IUAW union hall, ultimately destroying it. Sixty-two men were arrested and herded to the county jail. Among them were some IUAW activists from Austin. Ray Hemenway and some others escaped by climbing onto the roof. The scene was a chaotic, pitched battle, reminiscent of the sacking of IWW offices in the Pacific Northwest during the World War I era.[42]

Word quickly reached the Hormel plant in Austin. According to some participants in the events, at least 400 men put aside their tools and walked out. They stopped at their homes to pick up assorted weapons and then drove in a caravan to Albert Lea. There they marched down the main street to the jail and demanded that all the prisoners be freed. When the brand new Albert Lea police cruiser pulled up, the crowd surrounded it, took the cops out, rolled it over, set it on fire, and then slid the charred remains into the lake across the street. Armed with crowbars, individuals from the crowd began to pry open the bars on the windows of the jail. Seated on top of the building, a deputy either could not figure out how to operate the World War I machine gun that Sheriff Myre had obtained or was unwilling to use it. At any rate, the crowd was clearly in command of the situation.[43]

At this dramatic moment, Governor Elmer Benson made his way through the crowd. A Farmer-Laborite, he had won the election of 1936 after the death of popular governor Floyd Olson. Benson had arrived the previous day, eager to mediate a settlement as his predecessor had done in Austin in 1933. So far he had had little luck on that score. When the crowd laid siege to the jail, Benson left the hotel and approached the jail himself. He strode forward and demanded the keys to the jail from Sheriff Myre. He then freed all the prisoners. The crowd carried them away on their shoulders. According to local lore, several prisoners being held for non-strike-related offenses (such as drunk and disorderly) were so jubilant over their liberation that they joined the IUAW on the spot.[44]

The crowd streamed back to the Clark Street plant, eager to avenge that morning's rout. When they surrounded the plant, the deputies fled up to the fourth floor. IUAW leaders negotiated the surrender of the deputies. They were forced to put their badges and weapons in boxes outside the door and then pass through a gauntlet of strikers and supporters. The IUAW was in command of the entire situation, from the plant itself to the very streets of Albert Lea.[45]

That night Governor Benson attempted to work out a negotiated settlement. The union was to call off the strike and return to work immediately. The companies were to rehire all strikers and the four IUAW members fired at American Gas. They would also recognize the IUAW and bargain with them, but on one condition—that the IUAW affiliate with a national union within sixty days. This condition was put forward by the employers, but Benson was encouraged to promote it by his advisers, several of whom were close to the Communist Party and were eager to build the CIO (which is where everyone figured the major pieces of the IUAW would end up). With Ellis behind bars hundreds of miles away and both the Communists and the Trotskyists in favor of CIO affiliation, the IUAW leadership accepted Benson's terms.[46]

The IUAW lost at the bargaining table what it had won in the streets of Albert Lea. A month later the Albert Lea Employees Labor Association actually defeated the SWOC-CIO in an election at American Gas Machine, largely on the votes of several hundred "workers" hired after the strike—and discharged after the election.[47]

Even more important, the IUAW itself began to melt away. City by city, individual units voted over the next several months to affiliate with national unions, the Packinghouse Workers Organizing Committee, the Steel Workers Organizing Committee, or the United Auto Workers. Some connected with the AFL-affiliated Teamsters. Austin's "uptown workers"—largely women retail clerks, waitresses, hotel maids, beauticians, and the like—bounced from the IUAW to the Teamsters to District 50 of the United Mine Workers, losing members each step of the way. Some units never found a home with a national union and faded away altogether.[48]

It was distressingly easy for organizational distinctions to become the basis for hostilities. Nilson's truckers and warehousemen's units in Austin, Albert Lea, Mason City, and Ottumwa left the IUAW to join the Teamsters. The national Teamsters leadership lost no time informing Nilson that since this included a relationship with the AFL, they were to have no ongoing relationship with the units of the IUAW that had affiliated with the CIO. Nilson soon lost his job as a "business agent" for these organizations and also found himself blacklisted from his former position with the state Bureau of Workers Education. The Communists and the Trotskyists turned on each other, letting loose a paroxysm of name-calling and mutual recriminations that soon poisoned the atmosphere in the unions. Letters attacking each other appeared in the local press and the union newspaper alike. An independent socialist recalled, "It's fantastic the way the Communists and the Trotskyists hated each other."[49]

Efforts to maintain the horizontal solidarity of the IUAW fell short. In late 1937 one activist—an independent socialist who had replaced Nilson as editor of the *Unionist*—promoted the formation of an "Austin Central Labor Assembly." It was stillborn, undermined by the centrifugal tendencies of far-flung communities that contended that Austin wanted to dominate them, on the one hand, and by the sectarian squabbles of Communists and Trotskyists, on the other. A year later an effort to link all packinghouse workers in the region in an autonomous organization was scuttled by the CIO itself and its Communist-affiliated regional director.[50]

The Hormel unit affiliated with the CIO, first directly and then with the Packinghouse Workers Organizing Committee, when it was established. Key local leaders joined the regional or national union staff and left Austin. By World War II, a group of "straight trade unionists" had assumed the leadership of the Hormel union. Together, these diverse activists did indeed help build the strong national industrial organization they felt they needed. They also helped ensure excellent wages and working conditions for two generations of Hormel workers.[51]

But something very important was lost in the dissolution of the IUAW. Some of the activists realized what had been lost, but there was no turning back the clock. One, a veteran packinghouse worker from Omaha who described himself as influenced by Ellis's "one big union philosophy," conveyed that sense of loss in a recent interview:

> I thought we were going into an era . . . where we'd tell the leaders of this industrial society how we wanted the country to run. It never came out that way . . . I thought we'd have a case where we'd permanently make a change so that people would have much more to say about the kind of society they lived under. I know we had the foremen off balance. Don't worry, those foremen didn't get away with too much. We had democracy in most of those plants. But I thought there was a possibility that you would make a permanent change in that direction. . . .[52]

The IUAW fell short of making that "permanent change." Under the pressure of external circumstances and hindered by internal conflicts, its leading activists opted for institutional security instead of extending and intensifying the culture of solidarity that they, and the IUAW's rank and filers, had built between 1933 and 1937. The process of rank-and-file empowerment that had accompanied the broadening and deepening of the IUAW shriveled. Ironically—or appropriately—this project would be renewed generations later, by the leaders and members of Local P-9.[53]

Notes

South End Press has granted permission to include in this volume a revised version, with footnotes, of chapter 2 of Peter Rachleff's *Hard-Pressed in the Heartland: The Hormel Strike and the Future of the Labor Movement* (1993).

This essay is part of a larger ongoing study of the Independent Union of All Workers. My research was greatly aided by sabbatical leave support from Macalester College in the fall of 1988 and an ACLS/Ford Foundation Fellowship in 1989. Roger Horowitz and Rick Halpern generously shared their research on meat-packing unionism with me. Shelton Stromquist gained access for me to the Iowa Labor Oral History Project materials at the Iowa State Historical Society. Bud Schulte shared his extensive personal experience in meat-packing with me. Bill Millikan shared documents and his insights on employer antiunionism in the 1930s. David Riehle shared various primary documents with me and helped me puzzle out the dynamics of the Independent Union of All Workers. James Barrett and Dorothy Sue Cobble commented on conference papers that, in part, went into the construction of this essay.

1. On the IWW button, see "One Big Union," in *Rebel Voices: An IWW Anthology,* ed. Joyce Kornbluh (Chicago: Charles H. Kerr, 1988), 1–34. I am indebted to Dan Allen for sharing his collection of his grandfather's IUAW buttons with me.

2. Melvyn Dubofsky and Warren Van Tine, *John L. Lewis: A Biography* (New York: Quadrangle, 1977), 294, 311, 396, 410–11, 413, 446–51, 454, 457, 475; Walter Galenson, *The CIO Challenge to the AFL* (Cambridge, Mass.: Harvard University Press, 1960), 67, 68, 199, 200; Gary Fink, ed., *Labor Unions* (Westport, Conn.: Greenwood, 1977), 76–79, 260–62. I am indebted to Dexter Arnold for calling this last source to my attention.

3. Roger Horowitz and Rick Halpern, "The Austin Orbit" (Paper presented at the Missouri Valley History Conference, Omaha, March 1986).

4. Irving Bernstein, *Turbulent Years: A History of the American Worker,*

1933–1941 (Boston: Houghton Mifflin, 1970); Alice Lynd and Staughton Lynd, eds., *Rank and File: Personal Histories by Working-Class Organizers* (New York: Monthly Review Press, 1988); Richard M. Valelly, *Radicalism in the States: The Minnesota Farmer-Labor Party and the American Political Economy* (Chicago: University of Chicago Press, 1989); Peter Rachleff, "Turning Points in the Labor Movement: Three Key Conflicts," in *A Century of Change: Minnesota since 1900,* ed. Cliff Clark (St. Paul: Minnesota Historical Society, 1989).

5. Frank Ellis, oral history interview, 1977, Minnesota Historical Society, St. Paul (hereafter MHS); *Who's Who in Minnesota* (Minneapolis: Minnesota Editorial Association, 1941), 245.

6. Svend Godfredson, oral history interview, State Historical Society of Wisconsin, Madison (hereafter SHSW) (first quote); Ralph Helstein, interview, SHSW; Ralph Helstein interview, Iowa State Historical Society, Iowa City (hereafter ISHS); Frank Schultz, interview, MHS (second quote); Harry DeBoer, interview, MHS; John Winkels, interview, SHSW.

7. Ellis interview. See also John Winkels interview; Frank Schultz, "History of Our Union," series in the *Unionist,* May–June 1949; Jake Cooper, interview, MHS. The historical record (which, for all practical purposes, consists of oral interviews) is contradictory as to whether Ellis in fact "salted" the plant with union activists between 1928 and 1933.

8. Robert Schultz, interview, SHSW; Frank Schultz, "History of Our Union"; John Winkels interview; Godfredson interview; IUAW elections reported in *Evening Tribune* (Albert Lea, Minn.), July 27, 1933. I treat the background of individual radicals more extensively in my "The Role of Radicals in the Independent Union of All Workers, 1933–1937" (Paper presented at the Conference on "Perspectives on Labor History: The Wisconsin School and Beyond," University of Wisconsin, March 1990). On Skoglund and Dunne, see Jack Maloney, interview, MHS.

9. Joe Voorhees to Governor Floyd Olson, July 25 and August 6, 1935, Vincent Day Papers, MHS; Frank Schultz, "History of Our Union"; Godfredson interview; Cooper interview; Frank Schultz interview; Marian Nilson to Peter Rachleff, February 4 and March 9, 1987, in author's possession; *Herald* (Austin, Minn.), October 16, 1936; *Unionist,* October 1935–February 1937; *Who's Who in Minnesota,* 246; Ellis interview; *Evening Tribune,* July 29, 1935; Matt Kovacic, interviews with author, 1985–89; Marie Casey, interview, SHSW; Casper Winkels, interview, SHSW; Irene Clepper, "Minnesota's Definition of a Sitdown Strike" (Ph.D. diss., University of Minnesota, 1979), 12–25, 43, 60. See also Larry Engelmann, "We Were the Poor People— the Hormel Strike of 1933," *Labor History* 15 (Fall 1972), 483–510; and Peter Rachleff, "The Past Meets the Present: The Hormel Strikes of 1933 and 1985– 86" (Paper presented at the Northern Great Plains History Conference, Eveleth, Minnesota, September 1988).

10. Godfredson interview (quote); Frank Schultz interview.

11. Godfredson interview (first quote); Frank Schultz interview (second quote).

12. Frank Schultz, "History of Our Union," *Unionist*, May 7, 1971 (reprint of 1949 series).

13. Quoted in Fred Blum, *Toward a Democratic Work Process* (New York: Harper, 1953), 8.

14. *Herald*, July 17, 1933; Frank Ellis, "Bits of Labor History," *Unionist*, January 22, 1960 (quote).

15. *Herald*, September 23, 1933; John Winkels interview; Casper Winkels interview; Godfredson interview; Ellis interview; Frank Schultz interview.

16. *Herald*, November 9, 10, and 11, 1933; Frank Schultz interview; Ellis interview; John Winkels interview (quote); Godfredson interview; *American* (Austin, Minn.), January 25, 1935.

17. *Unionist*, November 8 and 15, 1935; Frank Schultz interview (first quote); Ellis interview (second quote); Godfredson interview; John Winkels interview.

18. Godfredson interview; "Proceedings of the Third Convention of the Minnesota State Industrial Union Council," Austin, August 30–31, September 1, 1940, typescript, MHS Archives; *Class Struggle* (Ottumwa, Iowa), September 15, 1937; *Herald*, September 23, 1936; *Northwest Organizer* (Minneapolis, Minn.), November 19, 1936. I explore how the IUAW expanded to women retail workers in "Retail Is No Small Detail: Male Packinghouse Workers Reach Out to Women Retail Workers in Southern Minnesota in the 1930s" (Paper presented at the North American Labor History Conference, Detroit, October 1991).

19. Roger Ostby, editorial, *Freeborn Patriot* (Albert Lea, Minn.), May 27, 1938; Frank Schultz interview (quote); John Winkels interview.

20. *Unionist*, October 1935 (first quote); Frank Schultz, "The History of Our Union," *Unionist*, May 14, 1971 (reprint) (second quote).

21. Rachleff, "Retail Is No Small Detail"; *Unionist*, October 1935–May 1937; Godfredson interview; John Winkels interview; Kovacic interviews; Marian Nilson to Peter Rachleff, February 4 and March 9, 1937.

22. Svend Godfredson, editorial, *Unionist*, August 7, 1937.

23. *Unionist*, October 1935–May 1937; Godfredson interview (quote); Roger Ostby, *Will Minnesota Submit to a Rule by Force and Violence?* (Albert Lea, Minn.: Ostby, 1939).

24. Rachleff, "Retail Is No Small Detail"; *Unionist*, October 24, November 29, and December 20 and 27, 1935; *Herald*, October 16, 1934, January 25 and March 20, 1935; *Mid-West Union News* (Cedar Rapids, Iowa), December 1936; Godfredson interview.

25. Godfredson interview; *Daily News* (Faribault, Minn.), July 26 and 30, 1934; *Daily Courier* (Waterloo, Iowa), January 18, 1935 (quote); *Unionist*,

April 30, 1937; *Herald*, July 31 and August 1, 1934, September 8, 1936, April 2, 1937; *Evening Tribune*, February 5 and March 5, 1935.

26. Frank Schultz, "History of Our Union," *Unionist*, May 7, 1971 (reprint); Frank Schultz interview; IUAW letterhead, June 1934; *Northwest Organizer*, January 29 and August 5, 1936; *Herald*, November 22, 1933, September 27, 1934; Casper Winkels interview; Casey interview; Godfredson interview; Helen Zadrusky, interview, SHSW; Louise Tickel, interview, SHSW; Jenny Shuck, interview, SHSW; Velma Otterman Schrader, interview, SHSW; Jeanette Haymond, interview, SHSW; Louise Townsend, interview, SHSW; Mary Ashlock, interview, ISHS; Abe Meacham, interview, ISHS; Eddie Newman, interview, ISHS; Tobey LoPakko, interview with author, 1989; *American*, 1935; *Freeborn Patriot*, 1937.

27. Rachleff, "The Role of Radicals in the Independent Union of All Workers" (first quote); *American*, March 1, 1935 (second quote).

28. *Mid-West American* (Rochester, Minn.), May 18, 1934 (first quote); Harry Buxton to *American*, February 1, 1935 (second quote); Charles R. Fischer, interview, SHSW; Sidney Wilson, interview, ISHS.

29. *Unionist*, October 1935–August 1937.

30. Ellis interview; Frank Schultz, "History of Our Union," *Unionist*, May–June 1949; *Northwest Organizer*, January 1, 8, 15, and 29 and February 12, 1936.

31. *Unionist*, 1935–36; *Northwest Organizer*, 1935–36; Carl Nilson, "Will We Join the CIO?" (typescript, in author's possession, courtesy of Marian Nilson); Kovacic interviews; "I'm Labor," series in *Herald*, September 1937; Godfredson interview; Paul Rasmussen interview, Oral History of the American Left, Tamiment Library, New York University.

32. Ellis interview; Carl Winn, interviews with author, 1984–85; Nat Ross to Roger Baldwin, March 2, 1937, courtesy of Marda Woodbury, daughter of Walter Liggett (quote).

33. *Evening Tribune*, March 19–April 2, 1937; *Strike News* (IUAW), March–April 1937; Wilson interview; Ostby, *Will Minnesota Submit; Labor News* (Albert Lea Employees Labor Association), March–April 1937.

34. *Freeborn Patriot*, March 26, 1937; Carl Nilson to Robert Wohlforth, U.S. Senate Committee on Labor and Education, n.d., courtesy of Marian Nilson; *Unionist*, March 26, 1937; *Evening Tribune*, April 20, 21, and 22, 1937.

35. *Herald*, April 2, 1937; *Evening Tribune*, April 2, 1937; *Unionist*, April 2, 1937 (quote).

36. *Evening Tribune*, March 18, 19, and 20, 1937.

37. Rachleff, "Retail Is No Small Detail"; *Strike News*, March 23, 1937; *Labor News*, March–April 1937; *Evening Tribune*, March 26, 27, and 28, 1937; *Herald*, April 1, 1937; *Unionist*, March 26, 1937.

38. *Strike News*, March 26, 1937.

39. Ibid.

40. *Herald,* April 2, 1937; *Evening Tribune,* April 2, 1937. I am indebted to Bill Millikan for sharing documents with me that provide evidence of a connection between the Minneapolis Citizens Alliance and the Albert Lea Secret Committee of 500.

41. *Strike News,* March–April 1937; *Labor News,* March–April 1937; *Unionist,* March 26 and April 2, 1937; *Evening Tribune,* March 18–April 2, 1937.

42. Ostby, *Will Minnesota Submit; Evening Tribune,* April 2 and 3, 1937.

43. *Herald,* April 8, 1937; *Evening Tribune,* April 2 and 3, 1937.

44. Ostby, *Will Minnesota Submit; Evening Tribune,* April 3, 1937; John Winkels interview.

45. *Evening Tribune,* April 2 and 3, 1937.

46. Nat Ross to Roger Baldwin, March 2, 1936, courtesy of Marda Woodbury. There is evidence that Ellis would have opposed the dissolution of the IUAW. See Ellis interview; and Winn interviews.

47. Ostby, *Will Minnesota Submit.*

48. Rachleff, "Retail Is No Small Detail"; *Unionist,* August 2, 1937; Godfredson interview.

49. John M. Gillespie, International Brotherhood of Teamsters, to Carl Nilson, August 9, 1937, courtesy of Marian Nilson; "I'm Labor," series in *Herald,* September 1937; John Winkels to *Unionist,* September 3 and 10, 1937; Godfredson interview (quote); *Class Struggle,* September 15, 1937.

50. "I'm Labor," series in *Herald,* September 1937; Godfredson interview; Rasmussen interview.

51. *Unionist,* 1941–80; Blum, *Toward a Democratic Work Process.*

52. George Fletemeyer, interview, SHSW.

53. Peter Rachleff, *Hard-Pressed in the Heartland: The Hormel Strike and the Future of the American Labor Movement* (Boston: South End Press, 1993).

3

The Challenge of National Coordination

Southern Textile Workers and the General Textile Strike of 1934

Janet Irons

The tumultuous and dramatic worker upheavals of the 1930s have for decades provided rich material for accounts of the rise of the modern labor movement in the United States. Recent research, however, has come to focus not on labor's successes but on the limits to its success during those years. One is confronted today with a labor movement that represents only 16 percent of the American working class. After years of monographs detailing the successful efforts of the CIO to organize mass-production workers, historians have returned to this pivotal era to search for possible clues to its long-term failure.

Particularly relevant in this vein are the experiences of workers in the cotton mills of the South. Here, in one of the most antiunion regions of the country, began the massive and unsuccessful general textile strike of 1934. The second largest walkout in the nation's history, the strike embraced 170,000 in the South and nearly 400,000 workers nationwide. How could such a massive mobilization of the collective strength of the workers have failed?

Conventional histories of the strike have stressed its weakness on the ground. These accounts conclude that the walkout failed because the South lacked a strong and deep basis for unions, and they cite as evidence the virulent antiunionism of southern textile employers and the long-term difficulty on the part of the AFL-affiliated union, the United Textile Workers (UTW), to establish locals in the South. The explanations describe a UTW leadership overwhelmed by a "spontaneous" outburst that could not under any circumstances have succeeded.[1]

Such interpretations overlook the strength of textile workers' organizing in the South in the years leading up to the New Deal. These pre–New Deal years witnessed significant southern textile labor protest and organization, strength that has long gone unrecognized because so much of it took place outside the ranks of organized labor. Shunning the New England–based UTW, southern mill hands instead formed "homegrown unions," responsive to local power relations and to the specific characteristics of southern industrial relations.[2]

What changed with the advent of the New Deal in 1933 was the workers' strategic need to coordinate these diverse local activities on a nationwide scale. The passage of federal legislation guaranteeing workers the right to join unions catapulted organized labor into a position of unprecedented legitimacy in the halls of the federal government and attracted thousands of southern mill workers to the UTW. Their enlistment in the ranks of organized labor forced an internal crisis, as the UTW leadership and the new southern UTW membership put forth competing visions of the role that the rank-and-file workers should play in achieving gains for labor at the national level. How would the UTW membership participate in, for example, the ongoing negotiations over the future shape of government labor policy? Would tests of worker power take place in Washington or in the towns and communities where workers lived? In short, how was grass-roots power to be harnessed into a nationwide movement? All this was at stake in the general textile strike. Even at the time, observers understood its importance. The day before it began the *New York Times* called it "the gravest strike threat that has confronted the Roosevelt Administration."[3]

———

Southern cotton textile mill workers of the early twentieth century would at first glance seem unlikely candidates for collective organization and protest. As migrants from tenant farms in the southern upcountry, mill workers had, at least initially, no tradition of factory work. Mill workers also lived and worked in isolation from urban southern society, in privately owned mill villages characterized by company housing, churches, and schools. Unable to function as citizens in the mill village itself, textile workers were also excluded from active participation in civic life in the world beyond the mill villages.[4] As southern poor whites, they were not only politically disfranchised by such measures as the poll tax but also socially ostracized as ignorant, culturally backward, "a different people,

... isolated in their community life, never called into conference with other citizens when matters of interest to all citizens are being acted upon, until the textile workers are not looked upon as other citizens of the State."[5] Their working conditions appeared only to reinforce their inferior status: hot, humid, dusty, and deafening spinning rooms, weaving rooms, and carding rooms; long hours, low wages, and poor sanitation in the mill villages; and the prevalence of disease.[6] In short, southern mill workers occupied a lower rung of a strict class and racial hierarchy, characterized by extreme disparities in wealth and power.

In contrast, mill owners commanded authority and respect as saviors and missionaries of a "new" industrializing South. Active in local politics and holding positions of authority in their local communities, they encouraged an image of themselves as uplifters of the poor, benevolent patriarchs generously providing jobs and shelter for destitute widows and children. Such an image was readily accepted by southern townspeople. As the author Harriet Herring remarked about the beginning of the cotton mill campaign in the South, townspeople would "eulogize" the builders, while the workers "were despised as even cotton mill workers have scarcely been elsewhere."[7]

Under such circumstances, what resources did mill workers have for generating a collective challenge to the power of the mill owner? Southern cotton mill hands were able to retain a measure of control over their lives by drawing on resources from precisely that rural culture townspeople so despised. In their journey from farm to mill, mill workers brought not only themselves and their families but also the customs of mutual help and neighborliness embedded in southern rural society. Mill village residents shared the responsibilities of caring for the sick, growing food to supplement their incomes, and raising children. Bonds of kinship intensified this sense of community and were nurtured by constant reinforcement from the countryside, from which workers came and went as their material and family fortunes changed.[8] These ties among workers were powerful enough to establish customary work practices, whose violation could be cause for an entire work force to leave their jobs in protest.[9] Combined with a constant shortage of factory labor in the South during the first two decades of this century, such community power was something to take into account. Mill supervisors learned there were limits to their authority. As one manufacturer noted, "We find that the overseers and foremen of these plants have been known to their fellow employees since they were children and any orders to do work in a way different from

what they have been accustomed to do would be looked upon as a cur-
tailment of their rights."[10]

Girded by such a collective notion of rights, these early southern textile workers readily engaged in minor flare-ups and on occasion major work
stoppages.[11] With a few notable exceptions, however, such forms of protest were confined within mill village walls.[12] It was not until World War
I that mill workers acquired both the opportunity and the motive to challenge frontally their second-class status in southern society.

Political, cultural, and demographic changes that came about during and
after the war enabled the southern cotton mill hand to break out of the
apparent isolation of the mill village and claim a certain presence in the
larger civic community. Aided by wartime wage increases and by the introduction of trolley cars, automobiles, and highways onto the southern
landscape, textile workers began traveling out of the mill villages into the
booming southern cities of the 1920s to shop and sometimes even to live.
The terrain of contest between workers and owners expanded beyond the
mill village itself to include the population of nearby towns. By 1929, as
one commentator noted, mill workers had an "awareness of the outside
world that did not exist ten or fifteen years ago."[13]

This decade-long development—mill workers' increasing participation
in modern urban life—freed them from an exclusive dependence on the
mill village for their well-being and enabled them to develop new forms
of leverage, which made possible organized resistance to new employer
assaults on their wages and working conditions. In this larger arena textile workers discovered an opening in southern cultural hegemony, that is,
a distancing between the perceived interests of middle-class townspeople
and owners of mills.

Textile worker protest played an important role in altering middle-class
attitudes toward mill owners. During World War I as many as 40,000 southern cotton mill hands successfully struck for higher wages.[14] These wartime
disputes triggered a wave of investigations into living conditions in the mills,
exposing southern mill owners to unusual public scrutiny. From this fresh
perspective, the poverty of mill hands was no longer a consequence of workers' own ignorance but was the result of the mill village system. For the first
time in a generation, journalists and academics openly criticized mill owners for their "isolation and control" of the mill village and for the "creation,
to say nothing of the perpetuation, of a social class."[15]

The industry depression in the late 1920s further eroded public confidence in textile manufacturers' leadership; the mill was no longer an un-

failing source of community prosperity. Such a fracturing of the long-standing alliance between mill owners and the middle classes did not go unobserved by textile workers. Here was a unique opportunity to mold a new cultural order in the South within the crumbling framework of the old.

———

If developments in the 1920s opened up cultural opportunities for southern textile workers, other events severely imperiled workers' economic livelihood. During the years following the war an army of rural migrants, casualties of the failed southern cotton economy, sought jobs in southern industry. Gone was the historic shortage of labor in the South, which for years had prevented mill owners from attempting to interfere with customary work practices. In the wake of these changed economic conditions, manufacturers promptly abandoned the company-sponsored welfare practices that had been designed to attract workers to the mill villages and instead embraced a host of strategies for increasing worker productivity. Owners called them efficiency measures. Workers called it the "stretch-out."

The stretch-out was a wholesale assault on customary work practices. Workers were asked to double up on their work load or to run machines at increased speeds. "You were pushed as a worker," remembered one former mill hand. "More was put on you. More looms. More than you could run." Workers remember the daily insecurity of not knowing if they were to be let go. Even if slower workers were not fired, "exhaustion and nervous stress" would push them out of their jobs. Their work was sped up so fast that "you was always in a hole, trying to catch up." In such a situation, one worker remembered, "I'd think, 'Oh, I just can't take any more.'"[16]

In 1929, however, workers gambled that mill owners' new power could be offset by the power of their own community-based organizing efforts, what one labor leader called "homegrown unions."[17] In the South Carolina piedmont over 10,000 workers in about fifteen mills protested the implementation of the stretch-out in the spring of 1929. Rejecting offers of help from the local AFL representative, striking workers based their entire campaign on the strategy of gaining local public support. They staged their protest not as a narrow economic test of their strength but as a public campaign to make their well-being, not mill owners' profits, the measure of community progress.

The strategy worked. Public sympathy "was very largely with the strikers"; indeed, there had been "a considerable amount of community giving to the strike funds."[18] Even the local press was sympathetic. In a remarkable departure from the usual subservience of the local press to business interests, a Spartanburg, South Carolina, paper defended the striking workers. "Public sentiment in this part of the country supports industrial development," the paper editorialized, but not "oppression or the assignment of tasks that are unreasonable." The workers were "lifelong residents of the region, natives of the South, making their contribution to the South's progress with a pride in their labor and a sense of devotion to the industry."[19] Mill owners were, in the eyes of the public, on the wrong side of the struggle to uplift the mill worker. Manufacturers were put on the defensive to such an extent that they "dared not" evict workers from their homes. In mill after mill owners agreed to abandon the new work loads and return to the customary work arrangements. Indeed, pro-worker sentiment was so widespread that to deflect further criticism, the South Carolina mills agreed as a body to an across-the-board wage increase.[20]

Mill workers continued their resistance to the management offensive even as the full effects of the nationwide depression reached the South.[21] By the summer of 1932 the southern piedmont was the stage for a new wave of strikes, which, once again had as their tactical approach the courting of the sympathy of the surrounding population. In Arcadia Mills, South Carolina, strikers who had been ordered to leave their homes appealed their evictions in court, demanding a different jury for each eviction trial, "so that as many people as possible will see just how the laws of the state are administered."[22] The unions in the Horse Creek Valley mills in South Carolina, just across the border from Augusta, Georgia, were backed not only by 90 percent of the workers but also by local business groups, fraternal organizations, churches, and radio stations. Their appeal for community support had particular cogency because one of the mills had recently been bought by a northern firm. When workers struck over depression-inspired layoffs and wage cuts, they appealed for justice "at the bar of public opinion," asking their community to side with them against the people "into whose hands" the mill had fallen. "Here is our home," they wrote, "here, we and our fathers were born, and our affections for generations have been rooted in this soil; we love our village and its mill. . . ."[23]

Most of these textile worker protests took place without the assistance of the AFL-affiliated United Textile Workers union. In part, workers' rejection of the UTW was a defensive reaction, an acknowledgment of the power of mill owners to portray representatives of organized labor as "outsiders" and the power of local sheriffs to forcibly "escort" union organizers out of town.[24] But southern mill workers also found the north-

ern-based UTW distinctly unprepared to assist them. The UTW was preoccupied with the plight of New England employers who, undercut by
southern competition, were slashing northern workers' wages or even
moving whole plants to the South. Convinced that cutthroat competition
was the cause of northern workers' problems, the UTW sought as its primary goal in the South the achievement of national wage and hour standards.

This set of circumstances severely hampered the UTW when in 1930,
as part of the AFL's southern organizing campaign, it launched a drive to
organize the southern mills. Quite simply, the UTW did not make the local concerns of the southern workers the centerpiece of their campaign.
Concerned more about national wage standards than about the standing
of southern workers in the context of their own local communities, the
union did not oppose the stretch-out at all. To the contrary, as a measure
of its commitment to union-management cooperation, the UTW offered
the assistance of its own efficiency expert to help make mills more competitive. The UTW also preferred back-room deals to a public airing of
grievances. The tone of the UTW campaign was set by William Green, the
head of the AFL, who announced that AFL unions sought to "clear up
misunderstandings" and thus "prevent such strikes as are now harassing
the south."[25]

Southern workers did not universally reject the UTW. In the southwestern piedmont—western Georgia, eastern Tennessee, and northern Alabama—mill hands readily formed UTW locals. Here were newer plants
more likely to be owned by northern interests and supervised by men who
had less of a tradition of personal control over their workers than did the
old-style paternalists in the Carolinas.[26] These owners proved less hyster-
ical about the presence of organized labor in their mills. Here, too, in the
hills of northern Alabama, textile workers benefited from a culture of industrial unionism generated by the steel, iron, and mine workers in the area.

But even where organized labor was more warmly received, southern
cotton mill workers continued to base their organizing on the strategy of
gaining local support. Their unionism was nurtured by the presence of a
growing local merchant class that favored higher wages for its customers,
the mill workers. A store owner from Alabama described in 1930 his opposition to the open shop: "We are sick of the whole business, the open
shop plan has been disastrous; the workers have no money to spend; therefore our goods lie on the shelves and bankruptcy stares us in the
face. . . . Better wages is the answer if we are to have prosperity."[27] In such
towns as Huntsville, Gadsden, and Anniston, Alabama, and Columbus,

Georgia, thousands of workers came to open-air meetings and drew up charters for UTW locals. In Anniston merchants lent organizers their trucks to help transport workers to these meetings.[28] Likewise in Elizabethton, Tennessee, farmers and small merchants supported the women who struck for a pay raise at the German-owned Bemberg and Galanzstoff rayon plants. Local members of the Elizabethton business community even formed a citizens' committee that criticized the plant's owners for misusing local tax dollars and mistreating its employees.[29]

Whether independent of or affiliated with the UTW, then, southern textile unions found their driving force in a creative effort to harness the power of the moral voice of the surrounding population. In this sense they were replicating, on a larger scale, the model of the mill village community as enforcer of a moral order in the workplace. It is no wonder one historian called the year of the 1929 strikes "a watershed, not in the history of the southern industrial movement, but in the development of public opinion."[30]

Evidence of shifting public opinion may be gleaned from the unprecedented criticism of mill owners following the 1929 strike wave. In South Carolina, for example, the state legislature charged "gross negligence on the part of the mill owners [in] maintaining decent and adequate living standards in their villages."[31] Manufacturers lost stature even when they decisively defeated the workers, as occurred in Gastonia and Marion, North Carolina. "Southern middle class opinion about labor matters has been remarkably changed," wrote the contemporary historian George Mitchell. "The harshness of the repression used in the big textile strikes angered many."[32] Meanwhile, labor organization increasingly achieved the status of a positive good. In 1929 415 North Carolinians adopted the "Statement on North Carolina Industry," approving the principle of collective bargaining.[33] Some months later the Southern Council on Women and Children in Industry issued the "Statement by Some North Carolina Citizens," asking for a nationwide investigation into conditions in the textile mills and recognition of collective bargaining rights.[34] Mill owners in the South found themselves on the defensive. At stake was whether the new efficiency measures would be implemented in the southern mills.

―――――

The late 1920s witnessed southern mill owners' searching for a new foundation for the exercise of their power. They found it in their decision to organize on a national level. To be sure, national organization was to prove elusive for an industry historically individualistic and competitive. Manufacturer attempts to act as a unit were limited by the resistance of individual owners—especially southern mill owners—to interference from any source in their business practices. Nevertheless, the effects of overproduction and plummeting prices pushed textile manufacturers to act. They formed trade associations, the most famous of which is the Cotton Textile Institute (CTI), to establish voluntary production limits in hopes of stabilizing the industry.[35]

Then in May 1933 the textile industry found itself in a position to make a compromise with the federal government that would significantly increase its power to coordinate industry activities at a national level. The CTI decided to cooperate with the government's economic recovery program by agreeing to shorter hours and higher wages for textile workers. Higher wages would increase purchasing power, a goal New Dealers considered crucial for economic recovery. In return the government would make the CTI a quasi-government agency, a "Code Authority," empowered to enforce industrywide production levels and labor policies. This compromise was made into law with the enactment of the National Industrial Recovery Act (NIRA) in May 1933 and the approval of the Cotton Textile Code, the first of many such industry codes developed as part of the government's program to bring the country out of depression.[36]

While the eight-hour day and increased minimum wages were unquestionably a benefit for poorly paid textile workers, the code was clearly a triumph for manufacturers. Not only did it make possible industrywide self-regulation, it also served as a tool for circumventing worker power at the plant level. As the southern textile magnate Donald Comer privately noted, "The more nearly we can settle these points in Washington . . . the less need there will be for union labor organization in the plants themselves because if Washington is going to fix the wages and the tasks, that is all organized labor could promise to do and thereby industry will be better off as a result."[37]

Despite manufacturer control over the code-making process, however, the CTI could not prevent widespread public concern over the stretch-out from penetrating the halls of Washington. Many liberals considered the stretch-out a brutal practice that increased unemployment when joblessness had already reached intolerable levels. In a move neither the government nor industry expected, Congressman John C. Taylor from South Carolina introduced a bill into Congress to abolish the stretch-out in the southern mills. Alarmed, NRA administrators siphoned off support for the bill by agreeing to add a new provision to the code that would forbid manufacturers from increasing work loads. This provision was known as section 15.[38]

Section 15 was a provision of the new code that textile manufacturers had not anticipated. Increasing work loads was the heart of industry efforts to "modernize" their operations. Even more to the point, southern manufacturers were counting on a new stretch-out to make up for production lost because of the shorter workday. Characteristically, therefore, on July 17, 1933, the day the new NRA Cotton Textile Code went into effect, southern mill owners implemented speed-up and stretch-out practices with a vengeance. They fired textile workers by the hundreds, doubled up work loads, and sped up machines. Distraught southern mill hands flooded Washington with letters. "Conditions are worse now than Before," wrote one worker from Gadsden, Alabama. "There is more dissatisfaction among labor now than I have ever seen." "Please do something," wrote thirteen workers from Albertville, Alabama. "There is many here that will give you a glad welcome and tell you of the Dirty Deal this eight hour law has give us."[39]

The industry offensive was tantamount to a declaration of war. Southern workers responded in kind, taking advantage of the new section 7a of the National Industrial Recovery Act—giving workers the right to organize free from their employer's interference—to join unions in unprecedented numbers. In this setting the UTW, a union southern textile workers had historically considered irrelevant to their needs, suddenly found itself occupying center stage. Textile workers throughout the country turned to the UTW as their vehicle for expressing dissatisfaction about the code to the federal government. Within a year the UTW witnessed an extraordinary increase in its southern membership, up from a few thousand to somewhere between 85,000 and 135,000 members, or between a third and a half of the southern textile labor force.[40]

But manufacturers' decision to ignore section 15 was simply the opening move in what was to be a year-long campaign by the industry to prevent any government or public interference in its practices. By capturing control of the government agencies overseeing the implementation of the code, the CTI acquired the capacity to design and publicize an illusory reality that rendered invisible both the increase in work loads and workers' resistance to it. The CTI could thus deny the truth of what was really happening in the southern mills and proclaim with impunity that its industry was a model of compliance with NRA codes.

The CTI found an opportunity to assert control over the industry's labor relations in the summer of 1933, when the Roosevelt administration confronted its first major test of the NIRA. In dozens of industries, not just textiles, constant labor unrest threatened the viability of the entire recovery plan.[41] Quickly New Dealers formed the National Labor Board (NLB) to resolve disputes, and they put at its head the pro-labor legislator Robert Wagner. The CTI, however, persuaded the NRA chief, Hugh Johnson, to establish a separate cotton textile labor board for labor problems in the textile industry. This new board was to be entirely independent of the NLB, answerable only to the Cotton Textile Code Authority, the industry-controlled agency overseeing the Cotton Textile Code. Its official name was the National Cotton Textile Industrial Relations Board, but everyone just called it the Bruere Board, after its chairman, Robert Bruere.[42]

This was the industry's most significant achievement. With the Bruere Board in place, the Code Authority now moved to neutralize the hated section 15 of the code with a provision stating that the stretch-out was no longer prohibited but simply a subject of negotiation between workers and their supervisors. If employer and employee could not agree about work loads, the dispute could be brought before the Bruere Board for resolution.

Out from under the supervision of other agencies in the NRA, where labor had sympathetic allies, the Bruere Board was free to operate as a protector of employers' efforts to stretch-out workers. In the name of peaceful resolution of labor disputes, the board ended strikes over the stretch-out, instructing workers to return to their jobs pending further inquiry. Bruere then set up a cumbersome and time-consuming three-tiered appeals process for workers dissatisfied with management actions: an appeal first to a "mill committee" at the plant level, then to the State Textile Industrial Relations Board, and, finally, to the Bruere Board itself. At mill after mill striking workers dutifully ended their walkouts and attempted to submit their complaints to the appropriate bodies and return to their old jobs. Instead, however, manufacturers replaced striking workers. Board hearings were delayed or dispensed with altogether. The Bruere Board's rare actual decisions invariably denied a stretch-out had occurred or claimed the board had no right to require manufacturers to take back striking workers. The effect on worker-management relations in the South was predictable. Upon seeing that mill owners had a friend in government willing to sanction union-busting tactics, mill owners staged an all-out assault on unions in the southern mills.[43]

After ten months of scattered local strikes and thousands of unresolved complaints, southern mill workers had come to understand the forces arrayed against them. The Cotton Textile Code had became the vehicle through which the textile industry could impose its work practices on a resistant labor force. Decisions at the national level had circumvented the local strategic leverage that mill workers had gained. As the Georgia labor leader O. E. Petry described it, "The National Board is being used to deny some of the workers in Georgia their just rights under the law and the code. . . . I begin to understand why the president of the American Cotton Manufacturers' Association believes 'Our National Board has functioned so well.'"[44]

The most severe consequence for the textile workers was their loss of public visibility. By ending strikes and channeling workers' grievances through an appeals' process hidden from public view, the Bruere Board was isolating mill workers from the larger public consciousness, just as if workers had been forced physically to retreat into the former isolation of their mill villages. The public heard about the state of the industry not from workers but from industry leaders like Thomas Marchant, president of the southern-based American Cotton Manufacturers' Association, who in April 1934 wrote officials in Washington that "not in my thirty-odd years of mill experience have I ever seen the textile workers as happy and contented as they are today."[45] Union-busting tactics were further concealed from public view by the CTI's control over the dissemination of government information concerning the experiences of workers under the Cotton Textile Code. Using deceptive statistics, falsifying records, and ignoring the volume of written complaints emanating from southern workers about code violations, the CTI declared the industry to be a model of compliance with the NRA.[46] The Code Authority had built a fortress of silence; workers could petition and complain, and no one would hear them.

By April 1934 southern workers had begun to break the wall of silence and disclose the behavior of the boards to sympathetic members of the New Deal, who up to now had been unaware of cotton mill workers' distress.[47] Building on their earlier bases of community unionism, they organized state textile councils, which, particularly in North Carolina and South Carolina, became hotbeds of unrest. At tumultuous meetings, workers denounced their state boards and announced their intention to return to pre–New Deal strategies for combating the stretch-out. Typical is the statement of the South Carolina UTW organizer John Peel:

> We have been patient and co-operative in our efforts to establish the harmonious relations between employer and employee as has been suggested by President Roosevelt and others of the Federal Administration. Our efforts have been in vain, and daily the manufacturers, or agents of the manufacturers, are giving interviews to reporters of the press of how well the cotton manufacturers are complying with the provisions of the Code. We do not intend to sit quietly by and permit this to continue without letting the public know the facts.[48]

In North Carolina textile workers were even more decisive, launching a statewide petition drive to remove Theodore Johnson, the chair of the State Textile Board, and vowing to boycott the complaint process unless a new chair was appointed. "If Johnson is not removed from office within two weeks," declared the southern labor leader Paul Christopher, "members of the textile workers in this state cannot any longer hold their patience, and will resort to every resource at their command to bring about relief from this abominable condition in North Carolina." "Labor deplores the necessity of a strike," added Peel, but "if this is the attitude of the board set up to handle the complaints, then there is nothing left for the workers to do but strike. . . ."[49]

Through this encounter with deception and delay, textile workers had gained the experience necessary to confront power at increasingly sophisticated levels. By May 1934 they had harnessed their own local resources to build state organizations that brought the membership together and mobilized them for action. Yet the power of the workers had not yet been harnessed at the national level. Organization at this level required the involvement of the UTW national leadership.

———

Pressures on workers not to break the wall of silence were enormous, coming not only from government bureaucrats preaching conciliation and "process" but also from AFL leaders castigating striking workers for "irresponsible" behavior. From the point of view of the AFL leadership, striking workers jeopardized the unprecedented opportunity the NRA created for leaders of organized labor to participate in policymaking at a national level through labor representation on NRA boards and agencies. Eager to present themselves as reliable partners in the administration's bold new recovery effort, AFL leaders found themselves embarrassed by their own workers' apparent unwillingness to cooperate with the New Deal administration.

Among those most embarrassed were leaders of the United Textile Workers. Unprepared for the massive increase in membership that took place after July 1933, UTW leaders expressed dismay at the constant outbreaks of unrest. Flooded by requests that the union authorize strikes, UTW president Thomas McMahon admonished members to use the labor boards and agencies designed to mediate labor disputes and urged them to more fully "appreciate what our government is trying to do for industry."[50] If workers encountered problems with the NRA codes, they should not stir up discord at the bottom but should trust union leaders' efforts to influence policy at the top.

The evolving southern workers' strategy forced a crisis within the UTW, testing the relationship between the UTW southern membership and the national leadership. By criticizing the Bruere Board structure, southern workers engaged in a direct attack on the policy of acquiescence to which national UTW leaders had subscribed to demonstrate their cooperation with the recovery program. The southern workers' tactics revealed with stark clarity that UTW leaders were only nominally the heads of the southern branch of the organization. The union spoke in the name of the southern workers in the halls of Congress and the New Deal administration only because NRA legislation had artificially elevated the union leadership to positions of responsibility inside government, creating the appearance of an authentic national organization before its natural emergence out of local circumstances. The UTW could not even claim to have organized southern workers, since most of the UTW locals established after July 1933 were organized by what veteran strike leaders called "volunteer organizers," that is, workers in the southern mills.[51] Not only tactics but also issues were points of dispute. While southern workers complained of stretch-out, layoffs, and "discrimination" against union members, President McMahon had continued to focus on what the absence of wage and hour standards would mean for the health of the industry in the North, where wages were higher.[52] Here was a supreme challenge: could the existing UTW national leadership become the authentic voice of the southern membership?[53]

Not until the spring of 1934 did the UTW national office recognize the potential for harnessing worker discontent—and the danger of failing to do so. The lead was taken not by President McMahon but by his vice president, Francis Gorman. In March Gorman established an organizing program that increased the number of UTW staff in the South from three to fifteen; his Research Department solicited and documented worker grievances. Complaints now poured into Gorman's office as they had originally poured into the offices of the NRA. For the first time the UTW leadership had a clear picture of the pattern of stretch-out, wage "chiseling," and "discrimination," that is, firing workers for union membership. By the end of April McMahon had toured the South and had begun, however tentatively, to speak the language of the southern workers' grievances. "The load of the textile workers in the south is too great," McMahon said at one meeting, "so much so that it is destroying the physical as well as mental health of the workers."[54]

But while opening their ears to the voices of their southern membership, UTW leaders were not prepared to abandon their tenuous foothold in the halls of power. When in May 1934 an opportunity arose to challenge the

Textile Code Authority's labor policies directly, the UTW revealed itself unprepared to lead. The opportunity was triggered by the Code Authority's announcement that it would require all cotton mill plants to reduce work hours by 25 percent, with a corresponding reduction in pay. For most workers this was the last straw. Aroused by the unrest of its own membership, the UTW threatened a general strike. Intense negotiations, however, convinced McMahon to call off the strike at the last minute in return for—of all things—UTW representation on the Bruere Board. The UTW had secured for itself a seat on a board so discredited that its own membership was boycotting it.[55]

The decision in May not to stage a general strike threw the fragile new union into chaos. Workers immediately took matters into their own hands. By July 20,000 had already walked off their jobs in Alabama. They were joined by 3,000 in South Carolina, perhaps another 1,000 in North Carolina, and, by the first week of August, 2,200 more in a massive and crisis-laden walkout in Columbus, Georgia. So much turbulence beset the southern mills that summer that by the time of the UTW's August convention, as one delegate remarked, 75 percent of cotton textile workers were "practically on strike now."[56]

The actions of the southern cotton mill labor force in the summer of 1934 were significant. Workers had put their leaders on notice in no uncertain terms that if they were to perform the function of leadership, they must follow the lead of the membership. With the union threatening to rage out of control, UTW leaders called a national convention, which voted, by an overwhelming majority, to stage a general strike beginning September 1. The integrity of the union had, for the moment, been reestablished.

———

The general strike put workers in a stronger position than they had been during a year of cooperation with the New Deal administration. It gave southern workers the opportunity to state plainly to the world the actual dimensions of their dissatisfaction, free of misleading interpretations by CTI-controlled government agencies. As UTW vice president Gorman stated, members of the industry could no longer "hide their exploitation behind a cloak of governmental protection. . . ."[57] Clearly worker dissatisfaction was much larger than the CTI had led the public to believe in its public statements.

The walkout also served as a fairly accurate measure of southern workers' power. It was substantial. Not even the deployment of 4,000 national guardsmen in three states could send them back to their jobs. Of the

170,000 workers on strike—a number representing almost two-thirds of the southern cotton mill labor force—only 10,000 to 12,000 defected.[58] As the *New York Times* correspondent Joseph Shapen reported, "The much publicized 'counter-offensive' by the mills has made little progress in persuading desertion from the strike ranks."[59]

Strikers' greatest strengths corresponded to those geographical areas where mill hands had the support of the surrounding population—near major cities, such as Charlotte or Columbus, or in areas with strong industrial unions, such as northern Alabama.[60] Troops sent workers back to their jobs only in those mills where union strength was weak to begin with: in isolated mill villages or in mills where protesting workers had recently experienced a serious failure.[61] Fear kept other workers from leaving their jobs at all; here mill owners used private guards to prevent the spread of the walkout.[62] By the time the strike reached its peak, the South resembled a war zone, in which each side had drawn its battle lines and had settled in for a long siege.

This manifest strength of the strike on the ground has been widely overlooked by historians. In part this is because scholars have been as mystified by this apparently sudden uprising of the workers, as were observers in 1934. The year-long industry concealment of real conditions had reaped a cruel harvest. UTW vice president Gorman was at pains to deny that the strike was "a bolt out of the blue."[63] Even leaders of organized labor were not quite certain what the fuss was all about. AFL president Green had so little understanding of the issues that at the strike's outset he announced its chief slogan was to be "The company union must go."[64] Sidney Hillman, head of the Clothing Workers, reportedly told NRA administrators that the talk about stretch-out was nonsense, that in truth the strike was about instituting a thirty-hour week.[65] Alone among the AFL leadership, UTW leaders understood the sentiment that gave rise to their members' demand for action. The UTW leadership had put itself—belatedly perhaps—squarely behind its workers. McMahon called the stretch-out "the main cause of the strike" and directly indicted the Bruere Board for generating unrest. He continued, "Out of several hundred cases on the stretch-out we have placed before the Board we haven't received one adjustment. On discrimination we can't get adjustments. People are fired and that's the end. Nothing has been done to combat the stretch-out evil. It is worse under the code than it was before."[66]

Yet even UTW leaders were not certain that the union could extract any settlement from industry on its own. Since the union leadership had never been a party to the growth of community-based unionism during the pre–

New Deal years, it was unsure of its own members' resourcefulness. With only a small treasury, the UTW believed from the beginning that a long strike could not endure. Additionally, the leadership was under constant attack by industry for being an illegitimate representative of the workers. At pains to demonstrate the UTW's legitimacy, Gorman made a central objective of the strike a demonstration of his own power to exercise disciplined control over its rank and file. Sealed strike orders, staggered walk-out announcements, and radio broadcasts were all designed to heighten the perception of Gorman's authority as the undisputed representative of the textile workers.

But the workers' own creative tactics tested the limits of Gorman's ability to impose military discipline. Adopting the term *flying squadron,* workers took to the roads and highways of the South in caravans of cars and trucks to monitor the strike's progress. Their claim on public space alarmed southern officials and lent credence to charges that the UTW was an "outlaw" organization. At first supportive, the UTW soon became frightened by the militancy of its own rank and file. Indeed, the UTW national office did not fully trust local leaders, particularly in the South, where volunteer organizers played such a critical role. In Alabama the strike leader Mollie Dowd wrote to a friend, "Gorman and McMahon seem to have forgotten Alabama together, except McMahon writes and bawls us out for the crazy letters our enemies write in about us. . . . We go twenty-four hours a day and still have this other to contend with. . . . it seems to us that with as many as we have had out in Alabama for three months and not even a fist fight the whole time, shows some leadership, and certainly that someone has stayed on the job."[67]

The UTW leadership once again found its goal of taming the insurgency closer to the wishes of the New Deal government than of its own members. The turning point occurred ten days into the strike, when violence erupted in Rhode Island and seven workers were massacred by company guards at the Chiquola Mill in Honea Path, South Carolina. Frightened, Gorman abandoned even the appearance of leveraging concessions from industry and turned to the government for a settlement.[68] After ten days of negotiating with government officials, Gorman called off the strike in exchange for promises from the government that it would investigate and rectify industry abuses in the southern mills.

On the surface the settlement gave reason to believe that the government would act on the workers' behalf. The government abolished the hated Bruere Board and created a new board to resolve labor disputes, the

Textile Labor Relations Board (TLRB). Unlike the Bruere Board, the TLRB would be formally independent of the industry-controlled Code Authority. The settlement also mandated the creation of yet another new board, the Work Assignment Board (WAB), to investigate the stretch-out and recommend measures for regulating it. Until the WAB made its report, no further stretch-out would be permitted.

In fact, government intervention proved disastrous. The settlement replicated with uncanny similarity the terms the Bruere Board itself used to end the hundreds of scattered local strikes that had occurred from July 1933 through July 1934. Based on the government's promise of further action by the newly created boards, the UTW had agreed to end its walkout. Although industry had never agreed to take the workers back to work, the UTW had ordered its members back to their jobs. The results were devastating. Mill owners used the end of the strike as an occasion to push for the total destruction of textile unions in southern mills. Tens of thousands were blacklisted; those who did return to work were required to "humble down" to supervisors before returning to work. The new boards were, if anything, worse than the one they replaced. Southern manufacturers treated TLRB investigators with total contempt, while in Washington the CTI infiltrated and gained control of this ostensibly "independent" board.[69] The Work Assignment Board was so dominated by believers in the value of "efficiency" that within six months it announced that the stretch-out was not even a problem in the southern mills and that therefore no government regulation of work loads was necessary. Southern mills could now freely increase work loads without fear of government investigation.

The 1934 textile strike was effective while it was occurring because, like the strikes during World War I and in 1929, it exposed the illegitimacy of industry claims to moral authority. Mill owners were clearly not benevolent patriarchs providing jobs and housing to a grateful work force. For all who cared to notice, the strike starkly revealed the true basis for industry power: coercion. Owners employed such formidable weapons as armed guards, machine guns, tear gas, and even airplanes to force mill workers back to their jobs. It is a testament to the vision and courage of the southern workers that thousands of them refused to permit the strike to be settled on these terms.

But such a characterization does not apply to the UTW leadership. By participating in a settlement that did not insist on any agreement from industry, the UTW sanctioned the industry's display of raw power as a mechanism for achieving its desired ends. The settlement implicitly recognized coercion, rather than law or morality, as a basis for the industry's legitimate behavior. This moral failure has had lasting consequences. Subsequent efforts to unionize the southern mills became harder, not easier. So contemptuous did southern mill owners become of the force of law that in the years after the strike they routinely ignored the provisions of major government labor legislation.[70]

The aftermath of the 1934 strike had a second consequence: it further linked the UTW to government policy. In abandoning the strikers after three weeks, the UTW effectively threw its lot in with the government as the sole hope for its members. The UTW failed to place its confidence in the part of the organization that was the strongest: on the ground, where workers had built networks of community support. Instead, it centered its efforts on extracting concessions where the union was weakest: inside the offices of the NRA, where the CTI was most entrenched. Here is one of the chief ironies of the strike. It was the failure of government-sponsored mediation machinery that led workers to strike, yet the UTW leadership continued to turn to the government as its chief source of hope for a favorable settlement. To be sure, in the years following the 1934 defeat organized labor strengthened its role in government oversight of labor relations, but the scope of government oversight was now limited to those areas outlined after the 1934 strike was over. Unions were now tied to an agenda set by the federal government rather than by their own membership. What the government determined to be legitimate grievances the union could fight for; what government policy ignored were inadmissible grievances. Crucial areas of union autonomy simply no longer existed.

Stark evidence of the corrosive effects of this new development could be seen in the shape of the union's new organizing drive in the southern mills in 1938. The new CIO-organized Textile Workers Organizing Committee (TWOC) encouraged southern workers to join unions because, thanks to the Wagner Act, the government was now behind them.[71] But southern workers' protests against the stretch-out were ignored by the TWOC as the union fought for goals that jibed more easily with government goals: increased purchasing power and stable unions.[72] Workers "angry about arbitrary management procedures and exhausted by speed-up" were told not to bring up concerns about work loads until a union had been built and a contract negotiated.[73] As the 1934 strike veteran Paul Christopher wrote, "It's hard to try and discipline workers to pursue the policy we have outlined when the company is taking every advantage of our peaceable attitude to impose additional injustices on our members."[74] In fact, the TWOC did not oppose the stretch-out at all, demanding "only that all changes in working conditions be accomplished in full consultation with the union" and that "all savings in production be shared with workers in a manner agreed upon by the union."[75] The TWOC's failure to make the stretch-out a central issue was so infuriating to southern workers that it became the focus of several internal debates between TWOC leaders and southern veterans of the 1934 strike. Southern workers lost. Quietly but decisively, veterans of the 1934 strike were purged from the new southern union leadership. Increased work loads became the order of the day. Bitter and disillusioned, many southern cotton mill workers quietly abandoned unions in any form.[76]

The story of the textile strike contains painful lessons about the dangers of national control of community-based unions. Throughout the period from July 1933 through September 1934, both the federal government and the UTW embraced a highly centralized national unionism that worked against southern textile workers' independent efforts to build solidarity locally and regionally. The labor provisions of the Cotton Textile Code, for example, encouraged workers to shepherd their grievances through a vertically structured bureaucracy, isolating grievants from allies in their communities and from workers in plants with similar problems. The UTW unwittingly abetted this dissipation of "horizontal" worker power by insisting that workers seek to revolve their problems at the national level.

By contrast, southern workers acquired their greatest leverage when, in that tumultuous summer of 1934, they abandoned not only the cotton textile labor board structure but also their own union leadership. So startling is this truth that one wonders whether southern workers would have secured a greater measure of accountability from the government and their own union leadership had they simply continued that fall to stage apparently uncoordinated walkouts throughout the southern piedmont. Ironically, southern unionists' acceptance—at the August 1934 convention—of the UTW's national co-ordination of the strike emerges as a critical turning point, as the UTW proceeded to redirect workers' energies back into a controlled "vertical" structure.

For its part, the UTW eventually learned it had made an enormous error in believing that its strength lay in an alliance with the government. In a poignant speech written for the 1936 UTW convention, Gorman set out the wisdom he had gained from the strike's defeat: "Many of us did not understand what we do now: that the Government protects the strong, not the weak, and that it operates under pressure and yields to that group which is strong enough to assert itself over the other. . . . We know now that we are naive to depend on the forces of government to protect us."[77] From his vantage point Gorman understood, too, the damage caused by too much centralized union control. Attacking "careerism and bureaucracy" in the union, the vice president called for increased "rank and file democracy" and "collective leadership."[78] "The members of the local unions," he declared, "must be made to feel that they are the controlling factor in this union. They must be encouraged to take the initiative in making policies of the organization. This cannot be done unless the local union membership is allowed the widest latitude possible, within the limits of our constitution, to direct and guide their own affairs under leadership of their own choosing."[79]

The conflict between the locally grounded southern textile workers' union and the more centralized UTW leadership might not have been so tragic had they worked out their many points of disagreement under less perilous circumstances. As it was, the mass of southern textile workers joined the UTW at precisely the moment that textile manufacturers had chosen to use the federal government and the UTW to break the back of worker opposition to the stretch-out in the South. The story is not without significance for a broader understanding of the New Deal alliance between government and labor. Not only in textiles but also in other major U.S. industries, management attempts to rationalize the work process had historically encountered powerful worker opposition. Yet as insistently as workers opposed the introduction of "efficiency" measures, industry leaders' obsession with "efficiency" was even more unrelenting. Government policy toward the unionization of the textile industry implicitly suggested a compromise: government would support union organizing if the union did not contest the "modernization" of the industry.

For southern textile workers this deal was unacceptable. Their unwillingness to conform to these unspoken parameters led to their internal battle with the UTW leadership; their subsequent failure to transform the UTW into their agent contributed to the destruction of their indigenous union movement and the humiliating degradation of their work. Whatever benefits other unions may have gained from an alliance with the government, the price textile workers paid was far too high, as Gorman, in the end, understood. "The stretch-out today," he wrote, "is making harried, broken old men and women of the textile workers before they even reach the age of 35."[80]

Notes

1. The classic account of the 1934 textile strike is Irving Bernstein, *The Turbulent Years: A History of the American Worker, 1933–1941* (Boston: Houghton Mifflin, 1970), 298–315. A more recent version of this explanation can be found in James A. Hodges, *New Deal Labor Policy and the Southern Cotton Textile Industry, 1933–1941* (Knoxville: University of Tennessee Press, 1986), particularly chap. 7. An exception to this pattern of explanation is Jacquelyn Dowd Hall, James Leloudis, Robert Korstad, Mary Murphy, LuAnn Jones, and Christopher B. Daly, *Like a Family: The Making of a Southern Cotton Mill World* (Chapel Hill: University of North Carolina Press, 1987). For a neutral account, see Jeremy Brecher, *Strike!* (Boston: South End Press, 1972), 166–67.

2. Southern mill workers' growing strength has been obscured in popular consciousness by a distortion of the historical record because of undue focus on the Gastonia textile strike in 1929. While it is true that Gastonia was a defeat, that same spring witnessed successful walkouts by over 10,000 workers in South Carolina, far more than the number in Gastonia. For a firsthand account of the Gastonia strike, see Fred Beal, *Proletarian Journey* (New York: Hillman, 1937). Other published accounts of early twentieth-century southern textile union organizing include George Mitchell, *Textile Unions and the South* (Chapel Hill: University of North Carolina Press, 1931); Irving Bernstein, *The Lean Years: A History of the American Worker, 1920–1933* (Baltimore: Penguin Books, 1966), 1–43; and Tom Tippett, *When Southern Labor Stirs* (New York: Jonathan Cape and Harrison Smith, 1931).

3. *New York Times,* August 31, 1934.

4. Like most southern poor, the majority of southern textile workers were disfranchised by the poll tax. See George Stoney, "Suffrage in the South, Part I: The Poll Tax," *Survey Graphic* 29 (January 1940), 5–9, 41–43; and V. O. Key, *Southern Politics in State and Nation* (New York: Alfred A. Knopf, 1949). A major exception was in South Carolina, where all white males could vote in the so-called white primary. See David Carlton, *Mill and Town in South Carolina, 1880–1920* (Baton Rouge: Louisiana State University Press, 1982).

5. Part of the text of the resolution the North Carolina Federation of Labor passed at its August 1923 convention in Greensboro, North Carolina, reprinted in the *Labor Herald* (Charlotte, N.C.), August 17, 1923.

6. Edward H. Beardsley, *A History of Neglect: Health Care for Blacks and Mill Workers in the Twentieth-Century South* (Knoxville: University of Tennessee Press, 1987).

7. Harriet Herring, "The Industrial Worker," in *Culture in the South,* ed. W. T. Couch (Chapel Hill: University of North Carolina Press, 1934), 347–48.

8. Hall et al., *Like a Family,* chap. 3, especially 140, 145, 151–52, 169–71; on migration from farm to mill, see ibid., 31–43.

9. Often male relatives intervened in work situations where women or children were being mistreated, but wholesale walkouts also occurred. For examples, see Burns Cox, interview with author and Eula McGill, Gadsden, Alabama, July 1986, in author's possession; Hall et al., *Like a Family,* 103–5, 108–9; and Douglas DeNatale, "Traditional Culture and Community in a Piedmont Textile Mill Village" (M.A. thesis, University of North Carolina at Chapel Hill, 1980), 135–36.

10. *Textile World Journal,* December 16, 1916, 41.

11. Bess Beatty, "Textile Labor in the North Carolina Piedmont: Mill Owner Images and Mill Worker Response, 1830–1900," *Labor History* 25 (Fall 1984), 497.

12. The major exceptions are southern mill workers' participation in the Knights of Labor in the 1880s and in the National Union of Textile Workers at the turn of the century. In both cases southern textile membership numbered in the thousands. See Melton McLaurin, *Paternalism and Protest: Southern Cotton Mill Workers and Organized Labor, 1875–1905* (Westport, Conn.: Greenwood, 1971).

13. Letter from Mary E. Fraser, Division of Home Economic Research, Winthrop College, Rock Hill, South Carolina, to George S. Mitchell, April 20, 1929, Violence, Textiles folder, box 4, G. S. Mitchell Papers, Manuscripts Department, Library, Duke University. For a fuller discussion of this subject, see Gavin Wright, *Old South, New South* (New York: Basic Books, 1986); and Herring, "The Industrial Worker," 352; *Textile Worker,* May 1919, 65.

14. For various estimates of wartime union strength in the southern mills, see Dennis R. Nolan and Donald E. James, "Textile Unionism in the Piedmont, 1910–1932," in *Essays in Southern Labor History: Selected Papers, Southern Labor History Conference, 1976,* ed. Gary M. Fink and Merle E. Reed (Westport, Conn.: Greenwood, 1977), 55, who estimates 40,000; Myra Page, *Southern Cotton Mills and Labor* (New York: Workers' Library Publishers, 1929), 73, who estimates 45,000 in North Carolina alone; and Herbert J. Lahne, *The Cotton Mill Worker* (New York: Farrar and Rinehart, 1944), 204, who estimates 20,000. Unionism emerged in pockets, spreading out from such urban areas as Columbus and Charlotte; many rural mills were left entirely untouched by wartime unionism.

15. Harriet Herring, "Cycles of Cotton Mill Criticism," *South Atlantic Quarterly* 28 (April 1929), 120. See also Frank Tannenbaum, "The South Buries Its Anglo-Saxons," *Century* 106 (June 1923), 205–15; and Paul Blanshard, *Labor in Southern Cotton Mills* (New York: New Republic, 1927), 12. An excellent study of southern reform efforts during the interwar years is Daniel Singel, *The War Within* (Chapel Hill: University of North Carolina Press, 1982).

16. Allen Tullos, interviews with Lora League Wright and Howard K. Glenn, in *Habits of Industry: White Culture and the Transformation of the*

Carolina Piedmont (Chapel Hill: University of North Carolina Press, 1989), 173–204, 285–86 (quotes on 190, 175, 285–86).

17. The labor leader was James F. Barrett, spokesperson for Charlotte, North Carolina, textile workers and president of the North Carolina Federation of Labor in 1923. Barrett's idea of homegrown unions so delighted southern manufacturers intent on keeping the UTW out of the South that his words were reprinted in the industry organ, the *Southern Textile Bulletin,* October 17, 1929, 22–23.

18. James Myers, representative for the Federation of Churches, "Field Notes: Textile Strikes in the South" (1929 typescript), 9; on community giving, see *Knoxville New Sentinel,* May 1, 1929, 18.

19. *Spartanburg Herald,* reprinted in the *Gastonia Gazette,* April 6, 1929.

20. Myers, "Field Notes," 8–11. See also John Garrett Van Osdell, "Cotton Mills, Labor, and the Southern Mind" (Ph.D. diss., Tulane University, 1966), 124–39.

21. One out of every five mill workers was unemployed, and others worked on short time, that is, two or three day weeks. Many mills closed altogether during the summer. John P. Prior, "From Community to National Unionism: North Carolina Textile Labor Organizations, July 1932–September 1934" (M.A. thesis, University of North Carolina at Chapel Hill, 1972), 12; Tess Huff, "A Conference of Southern Workers," *Labor Age,* August 1932, 4; *Textile Worker,* May 1932, 65.

22. *Textile Worker,* July 1932, 126.

23. Ibid., March 1931, 742; April 1931, 11; April 1932, 9.

24. For example, when a UTW organizer appeared in Anderson, South Carolina, in December 1919, he was whipped, robbed of his clothes, and escorted out of town by a gang of thugs. *Charlotte Observer,* December 2, 1919, reprinted in the *Southern Textile Bulletin,* December 4, 1919, 18. For a similar story, see Donna Jean Whitley, "Fuller E. Callaway and Textile Mill Development in LaGrange, 1895–1920" (Ph.D. diss., Emory University, 1984), 295–306.

25. *American Federationist,* June 1929, 658. For a general discussion of the AFL southern organizing campaign, see Nolan and James, "Textile Unionism in the Piedmont, 1910–1932," 48–79.

26. On northern ownership, see George B. Tindall, *Emergence of the New South: 1913–1945* (Baton Rouge: Louisiana State University Press, 1967), 76. Also unlike older mills in the Carolinas, the newer mills contained more modern equipment, so that owners had less economic incentive to institute stretch-out measures. Protests against heavy work loads did not appear in the southwest piedmont in 1929–32.

27. *Textile Worker,* June 1930, 187.

28. *Labor Advocate* (Birmingham), May 31, July 19, July 26, and September 20, 1930; G. S. Mitchell, "Organization of Labor in the South," *Annals*

of the American Academy of Political and Social Science 153 (January 1931), 186; *Labor Advocate,* May 3, 1930; *Textile Worker,* August 1930, 274.

29. Jacquelyn Dowd Hall, "Disorderly Women: Gender and Labor Militancy in the Appalachian South," *Journal of American History* 73 (September 1986), especially 368, 380–81. Not all communities supported mill workers in this way. In the 1930 Marion, North Carolina, strike, for example, not even local store owners supported the workers; the conflict ended in disaster when the sheriff's deputies shot and killed six strikers. See Hall et al., *Like a Family,* 217.

30. Van Osdell, "Cotton Mills, Labor, and the Southern Mind," 110.

31. Robert Grissom Schultz, "A Study of the Reaction of Southern Textile Communities to Strikes" (M.A. thesis, University of North Carolina at Chapel Hill, 1949), xxi, citing *News and Observer* (Raleigh), April 8, 1929.

32. Mitchell, "Organization of Labor in the South," 187.

33. Raymond Marshall, *Labor in the South* (Cambridge, Mass.: Harvard University Press, 1967), 123.

34. Prior, "From Community to National Unionism," 8–10.

35. Louis Galambos, *Competition and Cooperation: The Emergence of a National Trade Association* (Baltimore: Johns Hopkins University Press, 1966).

36. Robert F. Himmelberg, *The Origins of the National Recovery Administration* (New York: Fordham University Press, 1976), chap. 10.

37. Donald Comer to William Anderson, June 23, 1933, in Hodges, *New Deal Labor Policy,* 50.

38. Taylor was a former mill worker from Anderson, South Carolina. The bill was introduced in the Senate by James F. Byrnes. See *Independent* (Anderson, S.C.), May 27 and 30 and June 1, 6, 11, 14, 15, and 21, 1934.

39. Letter from W. L. Hilton of Gadsden, Alabama, September 23, 1933, Dwight Manufacturing Company folder; and letter from thirteen people from Albertville, Alabama, September 25, 1933, Saratoga Victory Mills folder, both in E398, Record Group (hereafter RG) 9, National Archives, Washington, D.C. In general, see Janet Irons, "Testing the New Deal: The General Textile Strike of 1934" (Ph.D. diss., Duke University, 1988), 179–94.

40. There are no extant data on southern membership. The following is one method of obtaining an estimate. In August 1934 Thomas McMahon, the president of the UTW, reported 270,000 members nationwide, representing 600 new locals since July 1933. A minimum of 188 locals existed in the four southern textile states in July 1934, broken down as follows: at least 70 in North Carolina, approximately 60 in South Carolina, 42 in Alabama, and a minimum of 16 in Georgia. UTW southern membership could be roughly estimated to be proportional to the ratio of southern locals to locals nationwide: 188 out of 600 equals 31.6 percent of the total membership of 270,000, which would equal 85,320 southern UTW members. This figure seems a realistic low estimate, since one source estimated 55,000 members in the spring of 1934 in North Carolina

alone, and another cited South Carolina membership at 20,000 at about the same time, making a total of 75,000, without counting membership in Georgia or Alabama. See Prior, "From Community to National Unionism," 55; and *Labor Review* (Augusta), May 18, 1934. On membership nationwide, see Robert R. Brooks, "The United Textile Workers of America" (Ph.D. diss., Yale University, 1935), 350. On the number of locals in each southern state, see Prior, "From Community to National Unionism," 75; *Textile Worker,* July 1934, 291; and *Birmingham Age Herald,* July 13 and 16, 1934.

41. Lewis Lorwin and Arthur Wubnig, *Labor Relations Boards* (Washington, D.C.: Brookings Institute, 1935), 87–89. See also "Labor Strikes and Bombs Punctuate Planning of Codes," *Newsweek,* July 29, 1933, 8.

42. On the creation of the Bruere Board, see "Summary of Findings," submitted to Hugh Johnson by Robert Bruere, Benjamin Geer, and George Berry, July 21, 1933, Summary of Findings folder, E25, RG9, National Archives; minutes of the meeting of the Cotton Textile Industry Committee (CTIC), August 1, 1933, Meetings folder, E25, RG9, National Archives; Hodges, *New Deal Labor Policy,* 68.

43. For examples of this process in the Horse Creek Valley mills of South Carolina, see Aiken Mills folder, E398, RG9, National Archives; *Labor Review,* October–November 1933; and *Textile Worker,* May 1934, 175–76.

44. O. E. Petry to Robert Bruere, June 23, 1934, Berry folder, E397, RG9, National Archives.

45. Quoted in Hodges, *New Deal Labor Policy,* 75. See also Irons, "Testing the New Deal," 216–20.

46. Of the 1,724 allegations that wage and hour provisions had been violated, the Code Authority had investigated only 96 by August 1934. Hodges, *New Deal Labor Policy,* 92. On industry manipulation of statistics, see Galambos, *Competition and Cooperation,* 228–35. In general, see Irons, "Testing the New Deal," 212–20.

47. The effectiveness of this new tactic can be seen in the reaction of L. R. Gilbert, a Bruere Board staff member and a former southern mill supervisor to the involvement of other agencies in textile labor disputes. In early May 1934 Gilbert asked in a memo that all agencies other than the Bruere Board absolutely refuse to respond to worker complaints in the textile industry: "If all original complaint letters from every source throughout the country could be sent directly to this office without any attempt being made to reply or to investigate the charges made, the splendid cooperation of the Cotton Textile Institute would continue with the belief that [the CTI] still had the confidence of the administration and the public." Confidential memo from L. R. Gilbert to Robert Bruere, May 12, 1934, Labor folder, E25, RG9, National Archives.

48. Letter from John Peel to H. H. Willis, chair of the South Carolina State Board, April 11, 1934, South Carolina State Board folder, E397, RG9, National Archives.

49. Christopher made his statement at the North Carolina State Federation of Labor executive meeting, April 14, 1934, cited in Prior, "From Community to National Unionism," 75. Original petitions are in North Carolina State Board folder, E397, RG9, National Archives. The statement by John Peel to the Greenville, South Carolina, press was quoted in a letter from F. S. Blanchard, deputy NRA administrator, to Hugh Johnson, May 28, 1934, Cotton textile folder, E25, RG9, National Archives.

50. *Textile Worker,* December 1933, 340. See also letter from Thomas McMahon to L. R. Gilbert, March 22, 1934, Alabama State Board folder, E397, RG9, National Archives.

51. From July 1933 to March 1934 the UTW placed only three staff people in the South: John Peel, Albert Cox, and C. W. Bolick. Their work was supplemented by the likes of Eula McGill, Alice Berry, John Howard Payne, Paul Christopher, Homer Welch, Lloyd Davis, and Molly Dowd. Many of these people eventually became members of the UTW staff. The expression "volunteer organizers" was used by Eula McGill in her interview with Lou Lipsitz, fall 1975, Southern Oral History Collection, University of North Carolina at Chapel Hill.

52. For example, when criticizing violators of the code, McMahon indicated his fear of a "breakdown of all standards and a return to the fierce cutthroat competition, which brought the industry to the point of destruction." *Textile Worker,* May 1934, 169.

53. There is every reason to believe that similar strains existed between the UTW leadership and the new northern membership as well. See Richard C. Nyman and Elliott Dunlap Smith, *Union-Management Cooperation in the "Stretch Out": Labor Extension at the Pequot Mills* (New Haven, Conn.: Yale University Press, 1934); and Gary Gerstle, *Working-Class Americanism: The Politics of Labor in a Textile City, 1914–1960* (Cambridge: Cambridge University Press, 1989).

54. *Charlotte Observer,* April 24, 1934.

55. Industry spokespersons gleefully noted that the UTW had agreed to sit on a board designed to channel workers' grievances away from industrial action. Henceforth, said one, "they can't pull crazy strikes all over the country. . . ." Transcript of telephone conversation between L. R. Gilbert and Theodore Johnson, June 4, 1934, Telephone Conversations folder, E397, RG9, National Archives.

56. The words the delegate shouted out from the UTW convention floor are cited in the *State* (Columbia, S.C.), August 17, 1934. The Alabama workers struck July 17, 1934. In his *Nation* article, August 29, 1934, 233, Alexander Kendrick estimated 23,000 on strike in Alabama in July. A more conservative estimate of 17,500 can be found in an internal memo to Secretary of Labor Frances Perkins, September 5, 1934, Textile Workers' Strike folder, RG174, National Archives. The preconvention situation in North Carolina is described

in a letter from Paul R. Christopher to Robert Bruere, August 6, 1934, North Carolina State Board folder, E397, RG9, National Archives. For South Carolina statistics, see statement by the state board chair, H. H. Willis, in the transcript of a telephone conversation between Willis and Robert Bruere, July 13, 1934, Piedmont Manufacturing Company folder, E398, RG9, National Archives. For numbers of workers on strike at Eagle and Phenix in Columbus, Georgia, see the telegram from C. L. Richardson and John L. Steelman, commissioners of conciliation, to H. L. Kerwin, director of conciliation, August 30, 1934, Adjustment, Eagle and Phenix Strike case, E398, RG9, National Archives.

57. *New York Times,* August 31, 1934.

58. In Gaston County, North Carolina, for example, workers "held their lines without difficulty," despite a "formidable array" of soldiers and deputies. Report of Van B. Metts, adjutant general, North Carolina, exhibit B: "Resume of Situation by Areas, United Textile Workers' Strike, 1934," North Carolina Division of Archives and History, Raleigh, N.C.; *News and Observer,* September 5, 8, and 12, 1934; *New York Times,* September 18, 1934 (quotes). Sources for estimates of the number of workers on strike include Associated Press reports, September 5, 1934; United Press estimates, September 5, 1934; *Columbia Record,* September 7, 13, and 18, 1934; *New York Times,* September 8, 18, and 19, 1934; and *Newsweek,* September 22, 1934. The total number of strikers nationwide topped 421,000. *New York Times,* September 19, 1934.

59. *New York Times,* September 18, 1934.

60. In Charlotte, Durham, and Belmont, North Carolina, merchants freely aided strikers. The *State* encouraged merchants to support strikers, reminding merchants that "business and workers are in the same boat." All Columbia mills closed by the fourth day of the strike. In Belmont signs in shop windows read "Textile Union We Are Behind You 100%." Robert Grissom Schultz, "A Study of the Reaction of Southern Textile Communities to Strikes" (M.A. thesis, University of North Carolina at Chapel Hill, 1949), 148, 157–60, 174.

61. In Spindale, Henderson, Marion, Laurinburg, and at the Loray Mill in Gastonia, North Carolina, for example, troops easily forced the opening of the mills. In each case the workers had suffered an earlier defeat. For a thorough look at the geography of the strike, see Irons, "Testing the New Deal," 421–77.

62. Such was the case in the Kannapolis Mills in Concord and the Cone Mills in Greensboro, North Carolina; most mills in Greenville, South Carolina; the Springs Mills in South Carolina; and mills in the Chatahoochee Valley in Georgia and Alabama.

63. *New York Times,* August 30, 1934.

64. Ibid., August 17, 1934.

65. Transcript of telephone conversation between Robert Bruere and Benjamin Geer, August 20, 1934, Telephone Conversations folder, E397, RG9, National Archives.

66. *State,* August 20, 1934.

67. Letter from Mollie Dowd to Elizabeth, October 8, 1934, UTW Organizers file, RG9, E397, National Archives.

68. While the CTI publicly refused to negotiate in any way, industry leaders privately conceded the strike was a potential "catastrophe" that could lead to serious embarrassment for the industry and an erosion of public trust in its statements. See letter from O. Max Gardner to O. M. Mull, September 6, 1934, O. Max Gardner Papers, Southern Historical Collection, Wilson Library, University of North Carolina at Chapel Hill.

69. The historian Louis Galambos summarizes how the Code Authority regained control over the new "independent" Textile Labor Relations Board: "If the problem had not been so serious, the government's performance in this interlude would provide fine material for a bureaucratic comedy. Each time the situation was studied, the investigatory process slipped back into the CTI's hands." Galambos, *Competition and Cooperation,* 265–66.

70. For example, in Anderson County, South Carolina, company-hired thugs attempted to run two CIO organizers out of town. When union leaders appealed to the sheriff, he replied that "the Wagner Act did not affect Anderson." Elizabeth Hawes, TWOC director, Greenville, South Carolina, "Organizing a Textile District," in *Let Southern Labor Speak* (Monteagle, Tenn.: Highlander Folk School, 1938), 15. See also Irons, "Testing the New Deal," 484–86.

71. Herman Wolf, "Cotton and the Unions," *Survey Graphic* 27 (March 1938), 149.

72. TWOC president Sidney Hillman described the goal of the organization as "an end to destructive competition which, pervading the industry, had pushed prices and wages ever downward." Paul David Richards, "The History of the Textile Workers Union of America, CIO, in the South, 1937–1945" (Ph.D. diss., University of Wisconsin, 1978), 44. Hillman also called for workers to concentrate on "education, organization, union contract, and responsible collective bargaining." He spoke of a "constructive program" that would have mutual benefits for employer and employee. TWOC leaders also pleaded with workers not to strike. Hodges, *New Deal Labor Policy,* 152.

73. Richards, "The History of the Textile Workers Union of America," 135 (the words are those of Richards).

74. Letter from Paul Christopher to Franz Daniel, quoted in Hodges, *New Deal Labor Policy,* 152.

75. Statement of Sidney Hillman, quoted in Richards, "The History of the Textile Workers Union of America," 135.

76. See in particular the Atlanta Conference in January 1941, described in Richards, "The History of the Textile Workers Union of America," 142. Workers argued that the stretch-out was being, in the words of one, "ignored too much to satisfy a large number of textile workers of the South." Union leaders replied that, like it or not, "stretch-out and time study men were here to stay." Ibid., 142. On the purge of the 1934 strike leadership, see ibid., 140–42.

77. Speeches of Francis J. Gorman, Draft #1, 2, of speech prepared for the 1936 UTWA Convention, n.d., President's Office file, P. R. Christopher Papers, UTWA Records, Southern Labor Archives, Georgia State University, Atlanta, Georgia.

78. Ibid., Draft #1, 10.

79. Ibid., Draft #3, 19.

80. Ibid., Draft #2, 11.

4

The Southern Tenant Farmers'
Union and the CIO

Mark D. Naison

The history of the Southern Tenant Farmers' Union (STFU), an interracial organization of sharecroppers and tenant farmers that rose to national prominence in the depression, illuminates with striking clarity both the potentialities and the limitations of the radical organizing drives in the 1930s. Brought together in 1934 by Socialist Party workers in the Mississippi Delta, this union demonstrated the unique opportunities for radical organization that the depression had opened in the rural South, a section where class conflict had long been suppressed by racial divisions. Beginning as a critic of New Deal agricultural programs, the union grew into a mass movement aimed at the reconstruction of southern agriculture along socialist lines and the elimination of the political and educational disabilities that made poor whites and blacks passive observers of their own exploitation.

To many American radicals, the STFU symbolized the revival of the old populist dream of a black-white alliance that would convert the southern working class into a powerful force for radical change. But as the STFU reached out for aid from other radical groups to magnify its power, the dream turned into a nightmare. An alliance with the labor movement, which the union leaders hoped would provide a new energy and a new independence, imposed a bureaucratic burden on the union's affairs that drained it of its revolutionary spirit. The most powerful mass organizations on the national level, the Communist Party (CP) and the Congress of Industrial Organizations (CIO), possessed a worldview that made them unable to appreciate the union's contribution. Onto a movement that had developed a socialist consciousness with enormous popular appeal, they imposed an organizational strategy that valued sound business practices above political appeal and financial stability above revolutionary militance. In the two years it fell under their influence, the STFU saw its ranks depleted by factional conflict, personality struggles, and racial strife.

Growth of a Movement

To the 8 million sharecroppers and tenant farmers on southern cotton plantations, the depression signaled both unparalleled suffering and a first hope of liberation. The drastic decline in cotton prices that the crisis initiated drove the croppers' already depressed incomes far below subsistence. Starvation, evictions, and foreclosures were a common fate. But the same events dealt a heavy blow to the repressive, paternalistic system of labor control that had dominated the plantation system since the end of Reconstruction. As bankruptcy overtook the planters and farms reverted to the banks, the cohesiveness of the rural social order began to break. The merchant owners and their satellites, preoccupied with their own financial troubles, had little time to supervise the black and white tenants in their purview. Thousands of laborers roamed the highways of the South, seeking shelter, seeking work. For the first time since the 1890s, food riots became a common part of the southern scene.

The New Deal, strongly dependent on southern support for its election, stepped in dramatically to restore order to the demoralized regional economy. By giving planter parity checks to remove acreage from production, it precipitated a rapid jump in cotton prices, which restored the shaken confidence of the landowning class. But the crisis of the tenant was only intensified. The acreage reduction provisions offered a powerful incentive to rid the plantation of its excess labor supply. In the first two years of the Agricultural Adjustment Act (AAA), thousands of tenants were evicted from their homes, reduced in status to casual laborers, or forced to survive on intermittent and grudgingly administered relief grants. One critic doubted if the Civil War had actually produced more suffering and pauperization in proportion to the population than the AAA had done in the few short years of its life.[1] Such was the meaning of New Deal liberalism to the southern sharecropper.

In the midst of this chaotic reorganization of the plantation economy, a movement arose to challenge both the old system of subordination and the rationalizing schemes of the New Deal reformers. In the Cotton Belt of Arkansas, two young Socialists named H. L. Mitchell and Clay East, acting on the advice of the Socialist Party leader Norman Thomas, decided to organize a union of sharecroppers and tenant farmers who had been evicted or reduced in status during the opening year of the Agricultural Adjustment Act. Their political work among the sharecroppers had convinced them that the discontent cut wide and deep and that black and white tenants might be willing to cooperate in the crisis. Socialist Party leaders, anxious to develop a mass base for their critique of the New Deal, promised unlimited aid and support. In the spring of 1934 Mitchell and East organized meetings throughout eastern Arkansas urging sharecroppers to unite and organize. Within a few months they had developed a solid following of 2,000 to 3,000 members and had launched a propaganda attack on the New Deal's cotton program that made government officials very uncomfortable.

The early activities of the union, following Socialist Party traditions, emphasized legal and educational work above mass action. On the advice of their Socialist patrons, the union leaders directed almost all of their organization's energy into a nationwide campaign to expose the brutality of the plantation system and the inequities of the New Deal's agricultural policies. Suits were launched in state and federal courts to test the legality of the cotton contract, speaking tours were arranged to mobilize liberal and radical groups behind the union's effort, and books and pamphlets were written to dramatize the hardships of the sharecropper's life. Socialist in theory, the campaign tended to assume a tone that was paternalistic and reformist in character. Its exposure of injustice, divorced from organization, became an appeal to conscience. The end result of Norman Thomas's speeches, eloquent though they were, was the development of a "sharecropper's lobby" to prosecute the union's cause in Washington.

This incipient paternalism, however, was rapidly destroyed by the enthusiastic, almost violent response to the union's organizing campaigns. The earliest union meetings were organized quietly, often secretly, by the STFU's founder, who feared that a militant posture would bring down the repression of the planters and would divide the croppers by race. Legal, nonviolent methods were stressed. Croppers were advised to organize around existing federal programs and to publicize their grievances through peaceful demonstrations. But at meeting after meeting union leaders were surprised and stirred by the sight of long-humble croppers demanding the seizure of the plantations and the banishment of the owners who had so long oppressed them. Mitchell and East, southerners themselves and the children of farmers, saw the potential for a revolutionary mass movement that could sweep through the South. In the summer and fall of 1934 they brought their organizing into the open and began to prepare the croppers for militant local action.

In this new organizing drive a unique spirit began to emerge, one that had not been seen in the South since the days of the Populists. At mass meetings called throughout eastern Arkansas, white and black organizers, sharing the same platforms, told audiences of thousands of tenants to put aside racial animosities and unite against the plantation owners. Fundamentalist ministers and preachers, the "natural" leaders of the tenant population, became the most dedicated union organizers. When planters moved to arrest black organizers, mobs of white sharecroppers sometimes arrived to liberate them from jail. By the beginning of 1935 the union had a membership of more than 10,000 in eighty local units.

Faced with a range of problems staggering in variety and threatened with reprisals at every point, the union emerged as a "total institution" that absorbed the entire life process of its membership and commanded a loyalty that was passionate and unrestrained. To make an impact on the degradation of the sharecropper's life, the union had to organize against school boards, relief agencies, courts, health programs, and police forces, as well as the planters. With all of these agencies controlled by the same class and administered with the single objective of keeping the sharecropper docile and ignorant, the struggle for public services seemed as fundamental as the battle for control of the plantation system.

Strike!

During the summer of 1935 the union leaders felt confident enough to launch their first mass campaign, a cotton pickers' strike in the fields of eastern Arkansas. Spreading the word by handbills, by articles in the union newspapers, and by the system of underground communication that poor people everywhere seem to develop, the union led tens of thousands of sharecroppers out of their fields in an attempt to raise wages from 50¢ to $1.25 per hundred pounds of cotton and to win written contracts. As a demonstration of worker solidarity and a stimulus to organizations, the strike was remarkably effective—sharecroppers in a vast area of the Delta stayed away from work—but negotiations with the planters did not ensue. For most of the croppers, staying out on strike meant hiding in the swamp or barricading themselves in houses, and the only bargaining that took place was nonverbal and indirect. After a month-long war of nerves, marked by considerable bloodshed, most of the sharecroppers returned to work at considerably higher wages but without written contracts.

Although hardly a paragon of planned and disciplined action, this strike provided the union with an enormous injection of energy on several different fronts. First, it gave a powerful stimulus to the union's organizing drive. The strike brought the union into direct contact with tens of thousands of unorganized sharecroppers, many of whom joined the union when the strike was over. In addition, the economic success of the union's campaign, unprecedented in recent southern history, brought about the organization of union locals in sections of the country that the strike did not even touch. Sharecroppers spontaneously organized chapters in Oklahoma, Missouri, Tennessee, and Mississippi. By the end of 1935 the union claimed a membership of 25,000. On a political level, the strike had an equally important impact. The dramatic quality of the sharecroppers' protest and the brutality of the terror that greeted it focused a harsh beam of light on the New Deal's agricultural programs. Reporters eagerly catalogued the shootings, the burnings, and the whippings that followed the course of the union's campaign, provoking a cathartic display of concern by liberals for the "plight of the sharecropper." The pressures became intense enough to extract at least a symbolic response from the New Deal: when the strike ended, Roosevelt announced that he was initiating a comprehensive review of the problem of tenancy and appointed a federal commission to study it.

During the next year the union continued to grow in size, in militancy, and in political impact. Ten thousand new members were added, another cotton pickers' strike was organized, and a more sophisticated political program was developed. As the union grew in size, it clarified its position as a "movement of emancipation." Union literature railed against the poll tax, the discriminatory administration of federal programs, the denial of unemployment relief; suits, petitions, strikes, and boycotts were employed to make the tenants' power felt. But as the New Deal responded with reforms to this attack on the southern social system, the union leaders began to perceive some of the limitations of their organization's power. Roosevelt's tenancy program was a beautiful example of symbolically gratifying palliatives. Increasing the tenants' share of parity payments from 15 percent to 25 percent and providing that their distribution be direct were open recognitions of the union's attacks on the AAA but had little meaning so long as planters controlled the administration of the program on a federal, state, and county level. The appropriation of $50 million per year to place impoverished tenants on subsistence farms was a nice gesture to the croppers' quest for self-determination but was only a quixotic diversion in a sector of the economy where only large-scale units were profitable. The plantation economy was mechanizing and reducing its need for labor; small-scale gains in income and power won by programs of this kind would be wiped away like dust by the broad sweep of technological change. Roosevelt's "War on Rural Poverty" reaffirmed the union's need to make functional control of the plantation system and its political supports an *immediate goal* of the union's campaign—not just as a philosophic or religious ideal but as a precondition of any final and permanent improvement in the sharecropper's status.

However, the STFU leaders clearly understood that the continuation of the union's growth along current lines would not achieve that goal. No matter how large the union grew, no matter how organized its constituency became, it would continue to be an interest group worthy of only temporary concession so long as its power remained regional. For the success of its program, the union needed to become part of a national radical movement capable of defeating the New Deal coalition and smashing the power of the planter in the national arena. The Socialist Party and the religious groups that had supported the union up to now could not supply such a force. For an alliance to transform U.S. politics, the STFU began to turn to a newly vitalized wing of the labor movement—the CIO.

Thunder on the Left

For most depression-era radicals, the growth of the CIO was an inspirational event that evoked great dreams of political success. Born of a power struggle in a collaborationist labor movement and led by a Republican and a disciple of Samuel Gompers, the movement became, in two short years, the self-conscious advocate of the unorganized and unemployed worker and a sometimes bitter critic of the policies of the New Deal. Fighting lockouts, Pinkerton's agents, and federal troops, the CIO organized 4 million workers into industrial unions and seemed to radicalize everyone connected with it. By 1937 John L. Lewis, a man who had begun his effort with the hope of "winning the American worker from the isms and philosophies of foreign lands,"[2] had begun to espouse a program that seemed anticapitalist. Proclaiming that "it was the responsibility of the state to provide every able bodied worker with employment if the corporations which control American industry fail to provide it," Lewis called for the organization of 25 million workers in a nationwide industrial union and the formation of a farmer-labor alliance to radicalize the Democrats or develop a third political party. This program, limited though it was, seemed to offer the hope of uniting the working class into a conscious political force.

The STFU, with more optimism than the facts would justify, saw itself playing an important role in the "CIO Crusade." If Lewis seriously intend-

ed to create a third party that could break through the New Deal stalemate on questions of unemployment and job security, the union leaders
reasoned, the allegiance of southern workers to their conservative political leadership would have to be broken by intensive organization. The
STFU began to see itself as an "advance guard for the labor movement in
the South," supported by its more affluent and powerful allies in return
for the political appeal it would bring to their organizing drives. It was with
such hopes in mind that the union leaders began to press Lewis for direct
affiliation with the CIO, a relationship they expected would provide much
needed funds to expand and solidify the union organization.

Although the political rhetoric of the CIO seemed to suggest an important place for the STFU, its organizational decisions reflected a different
dynamic. The evident failure of capitalism to rationalize itself had im-
pressed Lewis (who, if an opportunist, was an intelligent one), but his
natural strategic response was to unionize *everybody* in centralized industrial units rather than to transform capitalism politically from above. When
the STFU leaders met Lewis, they were surprised at the kind of questions
he asked: What kind of dues could the union pay? How long would it take
before it could become self-supporting? The political appeal of the union
and the quality of its program seemed less important to Lewis than its
potential financial stability. While praising the union's work, he carefully
avoided committing the CIO to support it.

Lewis's evasion reflected an aspect of the CIO movement that the union
leaders, in their enthusiasm, had totally failed to see: its dependence on
collective bargaining as both an economic and political technique. The CIO
built its organizing drive around the recognition of vast industrial unions
as the sole bargaining agents of workers in U.S. industries; the great majority of its strikes were fought around issues of union recognition rather
than wages or working conditions. These highly centralized units not only
aimed at improving the conditions of life for workers but also sought to
maintain the stability of industries by keeping wage levels uniform in different sectors and by assuring a disciplined response by the work force to
adjustments industries had to make to maintain a competitive position. The
political ideals the CIO articulated—a commitment to full employment,
the defense of the workers' right to organize, the encouragement of political action by organized labor—were important motivating principles, but
they were not what the CIO organized people around. In every instance
in which the CIO had extended funds for organization, its goal was to win
signed contracts and to institutionalize bargaining on an industry-wide
level, a basis on which the CIO could extend its control of wage levels and

productive conditions in the U.S. economy and extract a steady income for new organizing.

The STFU leadership, mistakenly viewing the political rhetoric of the CIO as an indication of a carefully worked out third party program, did not see the contradictions that affiliation would bring. There was no way the standard CIO organizing dynamic could operate in an industry as marginal as cotton agriculture, where an investment in organization would not necessarily yield a return in dues. With the cotton plantation mechanizing and with fluctuations in the international market making for vast variations in plantation income, collective bargaining or any kind of institutionalized relationship between labor and management was impossible to achieve. Any stable improvement in the income of the sharecropper could come about only through political changes that would produce a total reorganization of the plantation system. The STFU could only give a "return" to the CIO if the CIO engineered a mass political reorientation that evoked, as one of its goals, a socialist transformation of cotton agriculture.

But unhappily, radicals within the CIO did not characteristically take an advanced position publicly, partially because of the influence of the Communist Party, the most powerful and disciplined radical grouping in the movement. During the Popular Front period and in its work in the CIO, the CP functioned with a split personality, each side of which was excessively stilted and false. In their public roles Communists took the position of brutal pragmatists, comfortable with the most narrow and pro-capitalist definition of organizing if it succeeded in building unions. In their private roles, however, party members struggled to attain the maximum orthodoxy in what they conceived to be Marxist theory, an enterprise which, if nothing else, could maintain the notion that its participants were revolutionaries. This duality, exceedingly sharp in many CIO Communists, worked against the development of a popular socialist ideology in the great industrial unions. In the case of the Southern Tenant Farmers' Union, for whom the struggle for socialism was a matter of survival, it worked toward the destruction of a movement.

A Disastrous Affiliation

In March of 1937, when the CIO finally entered the field of agricultural organization, it was the CP rather than the STFU that took the initiative, and it did so in a manner that would be acceptable to the most conservative business unionist. Instead of the CIO's granting direct affiliation to the

STFU or forming a national farm workers' federation, CP strategists proposed an international union to organize farm workers and cannery workers simultaneously, arguing that the presence of the cannery workers would give the organization a better chance of becoming self-supporting. Lewis approved the plan and appointed Donald Henderson, a prominent Communist theoretician and the head of the National Rural Workers' Committee, as the international's first president. The STFU, invited to participate in the new organization, called the United Cannery, Agricultural Processing and Allied Workers of America (UCAPAWA), was told this was the only way it could be assured of a connection with the CIO.

To the STFU leaders, frustrated by the (to them) inexplicable reluctance of the CIO to support their organization and its program, the formation of the UCAPAWA was a nightmare whose reality they could never quite accept. Donald Henderson, whose thinking the structure of the international reflected, was a bitter and open critic of the methods and style by which the STFU operated and had openly declared his desire to see the union broken up. In Henderson's view, the STFU's greatest achievement—its development of an independent socialist consciousness based on agrarian and religious symbolism—was a dangerous political deviation. Like many Communists of his time, Henderson believed that a true revolutionary consciousness could stem only from an industrial proletariat and that movements that drew their base from groups other than a strict working class had to be subjected to rigid ideological and organizational control. The STFU leaders knew that if they linked up with the international, their organization would be under constant pressure to adjust its program and tactics to CP directives. But in spite of these doubts, the STFU prepared to affiliate. It really had no choice. By joining the international and working to persuade the CIO of the importance of the union's work, the STFU could at least keep alive the possibility of a political reorientation that could give meaning to its local struggles.

Decline and Fall

The relationship with the international, chosen in the interest of long-term strategy, proved to be even more repressive than the STFU leaders had imagined. The centralized framework of the UCAPAWA, modeled on that of CIO unions in the basic industries, left the STFU leadership with very little control of organizing policies. From the moment the union affiliated (September 1937) its organization was subjected to a discipline that provoked tensions and conflicts it had struggled mightily to repress.

The first serious tensions emerged over the question of dues and accounting procedures—an ideologically neutral question one would think. The international sent every local of the STFU a charter, an accounting book, and a list of requirements for participation in the international. Members were to pay dues of 25¢ per month plus a 5¢ per capita tax to CIO headquarters. Local secretaries were to fill out balance sheets in quadruplicate, keep one, and send one to district headquarters (the STFU office in Memphis), one to international headquarters (in California), and one to CIO headquarters (in Washington). These procedures were the basic organizational cement of the CIO movement, and Henderson applied them without expecting a protest. But the union's organizers rebelled as a unit against those requirements. The southern sharecropper, deprived of education and burdened by debt, was in no position to pay the dues or do the paperwork the CIO demanded of an industrial worker. After seeing the charter materials, Mitchell wrote Henderson that he was convinced the STFU did not have ten local secretaries who could handle them. One organizer's suggestion was that they be kept for the next fifty years, during which time the croppers might be sufficiently educated to handle them.[3]

Henderson's response to the union's complaint was that both the dues and the accounting procedures had to be rigorously applied.[4] When the union leaders went to Lewis to protest this decision, they were told that compliance was a precondition of their participation in the CIO. Helpless, the union leaders instructed their organizers to restructure the local units in line with international directives. At the same time, they revived their campaign to win a separate affiliation from the CIO.

The attempt to apply the international's guidelines, as the union leaders feared, began to undermine the basis of solidarity that the movement had developed. On a local level the STFU held and expanded its membership by two basic techniques: organized action to increase the sharecropper's standard of living and protection in times of crisis; and the cultivation, through rituals, mass gatherings, and demonstrations, of an almost religious belief in the justice of the union's cause and the ultimate success of its program. To force the union members to pay high dues would hinder its efforts in the first dimension, for it would siphon off a major portion of the economic gains that the union was able to win, but to bureaucratize the union's structure would be more deadly yet, for it would draw energy away from the emotional bonds that held the union members together and that were, in the long run, the basis of the union's strength.

By the summer of 1938, nine months after the affiliation had occurred, the STFU was in serious difficulty. A recession of considerable magnitude had complicated the dues-collecting drive by dramatically reducing the effectiveness of the union's economic program. For the first time in its five-year history the STFU was seen by sharecroppers as a burden that drew upon, rather than added to, their tiny cash income. In addition the union leaders' remoteness from activities in the field, imposed by long and fruit-less negotiations with the CIO and the international, brought suspicions of misconduct to a dangerous level. Almost half the union locals went inactive, waiting for the old personalized style of leadership to revive, and serious racial tensions began to develop. In one section of Arkansas, E. B. McKinney, a Garveyite minister who was one of the union's organizers, had become so incensed by the declining effectiveness of the union's pro-gram and the increasing distance of the union's (mostly white) executive board that he began to advocate the formation of an all-black union. McKinney's proposal did little more than get members demoralized, but it warned union leaders that their movement would be destroyed unless they restored the program and the spirit that had been its original basis. It was clear to them the STFU was in no position to rationalize itself along industrial union lines. In August of 1938 the union halted its campaign to collect dues and membership reports for the UCAPAWA.

Henderson, a former Columbia instructor who had never organized in the South, was infuriated by this action. He found it inexplicable that a mass movement could be mobilized around ideology, and he interpreted the union's difficulties as a sign of incompetent leadership. After going to the CIO directors for confirmation, he informed the union leaders that a separate affiliation for the STFU was unthinkable and that its relationship with the CIO was contingent on its conformity to the rules of the interna-tional. At the same time, he mobilized the CP apparatus for a takeover of the union from within.

During the succeeding three months, violent factional conflicts entered the STFU's ranks, paralyzing the union's effort to revive its local program. A popular union organizer, the Reverend Claude Williams, allowed a pa-per describing alleged CP plans to take over the union to fall into the hands of J. R. Butler, the STFU's president. When Williams was suspended from the organization by the STFU executive board, it further confused the de-moralized membership. Then in December the international provoked ad-ditional tensions by cutting union representation on the UCAPAWA execu-tive board to half of its previous level, a "punishment" for its failure to collect dues and membership reports. The STFU retaliated by filing a protest with the CIO and by issuing press releases denouncing Henderson.

The final break came in the early months of 1939, during a severe and unexpected economic crisis. Planters in the "boot heel" region of Missouri, spurred by "reforms" in the AAA that increased tenants' share of parity payments, shifted their labor system from sharecropping to wage labor, evicting 2,000 tenants in the process. When union organizers spontaneously led the evicted families into a "camp in" on the highway between St. Louis and Memphis, a bitter struggle emerged for the loyalty of the demonstrators. UCAPAWA officials organized a relief drive separate from that of the STFU and openly began to seek support for its "strict trade union" position. Owen Whitfield, the leader of the Missouri group, bounced like a shuttlecock between St. Louis and Memphis, alternately wooed by union officials and CP officials. In February the STFU leaders lost their patience. They wrote letters to the CIO executive board declaring that the international had sustained a systematic campaign to destroy its effectiveness and warning that the union would be forced to leave the CIO unless it cleaned up the situation in the international.[5] Soon afterward Henderson announced that he was calling a special convention to reorganize the STFU and expel its leadership.

The CIO directors at this point entered the dispute, and the position they took indicated their preoccupation with the bureaucratic side of union organization and their distance from the problems the sharecropper faced. Although they disapproved of Henderson's plan to call for a dual convention, they would not stop him unless the union leaders agreed to abide by the UCAPAWA's constitution and meet outstanding dues and obligations. The union leaders' complaints that their movement could not survive within such a framework were deemed irrelevant; Henderson's actions all fell within the bounds of standard trade-union practice and had been cleared in advance by CIO headquarters. After ten days of negotiation it became clear that the CIO's approach to organizing was similar to Henderson's and that neither would allow the union to operate on suitable terms. On March 11 Mitchell announced that the union was breaking its ties with the CIO.

During the next few months Mitchell chose to challenge Henderson's drive to reorganize the union. Rounding up whatever loyal members he could find, Mitchell crashed the dual convention, took it over, and led his supporters out.[6] Henderson was left with a handful of croppers, most of them followers of Whitfield and McKinney. With no basis for an interracial movement, he was never to make a serious effort to reorganize in cotton.

But the STFU had been almost as devastated by the dispute. In a survey of the field Mitchell found only 40 active locals out of a total of 200 that the union had at the peak of its strength.[7] The factional fight had been so confusing to people that they had simply shut down and quit for the time being, disgusted with all unions. The racial solidarity upon which the union had based its program, moreover, had been badly shattered by the fight. The best black organizers had left the movement, disillusioned with its declining level of performance, and the whites had gone inactive. But finally, and most important, the almost religious sense of mission from which the union had drawn its strength had been utterly destroyed by the crisis. From the union's earliest days, its members had been sustained by the hope that there were forces within the United States that could shatter the old plantation system and win a decent life for the sharecropper on its ruins. Now, no such hope could be maintained. The most radical mass forces for change in the society, the CIO and the Communist Party, had stood apart from the union's strivings, had smothered it with forms, and had crushed it with obligations. Not even on the distant horizon were there forces of sufficient strength to transform the cotton economy into a free and ordered system of production. From 1939 the STFU confined its work to education and lobbying, serving as a liaison between sharecroppers and federal tenancy programs it had regarded as hopelessly inadequate two years earlier.

The Meaning for the Left

The destruction of the Southern Tenant Farmers' Union epitomized the basic limitation of the most dynamic organizing drive staged by radicals in the thirties—the campaign of the CIO. With few exceptions, radicals in the CIO were willing to live with a definition of union organizing that made it impossible either to organize workers who were outside of an industrial system or to concentrate on political organization that challenged capitalist institutions. In particular, CIO Communists, who should have known better, were so concerned with developing a working-class base that they supported a strategy of unionization that had been consciously designed to rationalize a capitalist economy. And when they came in contact with a movement that could not apply such a strategy and whose economic problems were so severe that not even a temporary solution could be found within capitalism, they allowed and even encouraged its destruction because its supporters were not classic proletarians.

The consequences of these failures have been very serious and very lasting. First of all, they worked against the development of a broadly based radical party and the growth of a popular socialist consciousness. The obsession of many radicals with activities that created powerful, financially stable organizations led them to neglect the very real opportunities to disseminate a cooperative, anticapitalist ideology among the laboring population in the United States. As the growth of the STFU indicates, workers in the most conservative, traditionalistic sections of the society were often receptive to a radical outlook if it was phrased in terms relevant to their experience and was combined with effective organization.

But equally important, the strategic orientation of CIO radicals reinforced the isolation of the black population from the rest of the working class, helping to set the stage for ghettoization and the social crisis of our time. The narrow definition of industrial unionism embodied in the CIO implicitly excluded most of the black working force, which operated in marginal sectors of the economy that could not be rationalized within capitalism. The colonized sharecropper on the southern plantation, living under conditions of dependence radically different from those of a factory worker, could not be organized in a centralized bureaucratic union. When old Left strategists *chose* to avoid a campaign to reorganize the U.S. economy, when they *chose* to neglect the program that the union had advocated, they were postponing the organization of rural black people to some vague and later date. The mistrust of white radicals by insurgents in the ghetto is one painful and indirect consequence of the failure of the union's program.

Notes

This essay, with minor editorial changes, originally appeared in *Radical America* 2 (September–October 1968), 36–56. It is used with permission from the author.

1. Howard Kester, *Revolt among the Sharecroppers* (New York: Civici-Friede, 1936), 27. Most of the material in this essay has been derived from manuscript sources—particularly the very excellent and complete collection at the Southern Historical Collection, University of North Carolina at Chapel Hill. However, the considerable body of secondary literature on the union has been very helpful in guiding the direction of my analysis. Students looking for a more detailed discussion of these events from a different political

perspective should refer to the following books and articles: Jerold Auerbach, "Southern Tenant Farmers: Socialist Critics of the New Deal," *Labor History* 7 (Winter 1966), 3–18; David Eugene Conrad, *The Forgotten Farmers* (Urbana: University of Illinois Press, 1965); Stuart Jamison, *Labor Unionism in American Agriculture,* U.S. Department of Labor, Bureau of Labor Statistics, Bulletin No. 836 (Washington, D.C.: U.S. Government Printing Office); Vera Rony, "Sorrow Song in Black and White," *New South* 22 (Summer 1967), 2–39; M. S. Venkataramani, "Norman Thomas, Arkansas Sharecroppers, and the Roosevelt Agricultural Policies, 1933–1937," *Mississippi Valley Historical Review* 47 (September 1960), 225–46; H. L. Mitchell, *Mean Things Happening in This Land: The Life and Times of H. L. Mitchell, Cofounder of the Southern Tenant Farmers' Union* (Montclair, N.J.: Allanheld, Osmun, 1979); and Donald H. Grubbs, "The Southern Tenant Farmers' Union and the New Deal" (Ph.D. diss., University of Florida, 1963), published as *Cry from the Cotton: The Southern Tenant Farmers' Union and the New Deal* (Chapel Hill: University of North Carolina Press, 1971).

2. CIO publication #10. The literature on the growth and evolution of the CIO is neither very good nor very extensive. However, the following works should be studied before beginning to develop a picture of these complex events: Saul Alinsky, *John L. Lewis: An Unauthorized Biography* (New York: G. P. Putnam's Sons, 1949); Walter Galenson, *The CIO Challenge to the AFL* (Cambridge, Mass.: Harvard University Press, 1960); Sidney Lens, *Left, Right and Center* (Hinsdale, Ill.: Henry Regnery, 1949); Edward Levinson, *Labor on the March* (New York: University Books, 1936); Art Preis, *Labor's Giant Step: Twenty Years of the CIO* (New York: Pioneer Publishers, 1964); and Ronald Radosh, "The Corporate Ideology of American Labor Leaders from Gompers to Hillman," *Studies on the Left* 6 (November–December 1966), 66–88.

3. See H. D. Mitchell to Donald Henderson, October 11, 1937; and Mitchell to Gardner Jackson, October 23, 1937, both in Southern Tenant Farmers' Union Papers (hereafter STFU Papers), Southern Historical Collection, University of North Carolina at Chapel Hill.

4. Henderson to Mitchell, October 27, 1937, STFU Papers.

5. J. R. Butler, "To Members Executive Board, Congress of Industrial Organizations," February 14, 1939, STFU Papers.

6. For a more detailed discussion of radical conflicts in the union, see Mark D. Naison, "The Decline of the Southern Tenant Farmers' Union, 1937–39" (Master's essay, Columbia University, 1967).

7. H. L. Mitchell to Norman Thomas, April 3, 1939, STFU Papers.

5

The Very Last Hurrah?

The Defeat of the Labor Party Idea, 1934–36

Eric Leif Davin

Almost from its birth the labor movement in the United States harbored a strong desire for what came to be called "independent political action." This expression was generally understood to mean a political party separate from all others—a labor party. The first example of this tendency was the Working Men's Party of Philadelphia, founded by that city's Mechanics Union of Trade Associations to contest the municipal elections of 1828. This was the first labor party not only in the United States but also the world, providing inspiration to, for instance, England's soon-to-emerge Chartist movement. A score of the party's candidates was elected that year and again the next. Workingmen in other Pennsylvania cities also began to organize politically, and by 1830 it seemed a statewide Working Men's Party would be formed. Internal dissension, however, tore the incipient movement apart by 1831. Nevertheless, between 1828 and 1834 similar municipal labor parties were organized in sixty-one cities and towns from Burlington, Vermont, to Washington, D.C., and as far west as Pittsburgh and Ohio.[1] From time to time throughout the nineteenth century there were other such municipal and statewide efforts to establish labor parties. By the 1880s a number of these local labor parties had come to power in such localities as Scranton, Pennsylvania, where Terence Powderly, leader of the first truly national labor union in the United States, the Knights of Labor, served as mayor from 1878 to 1884.[2]

The efforts on the part of labor to establish independent political action were not identical with the efforts of socialists to form their own parties friendly to labor. The first of these was probably the Social Party of New York City, formed in 1868 by a merger of two German organizations, the Lassallean German Workingmen's Union and the Marxist Communist Club. In 1874 the Labor Party of Illinois garnered nearly a thousand votes in the Chicago municipal elections, enough to encourage it to continue agitation. In 1876 this party merged with the International Workingmen's Association and the Social Democratic Workingmen's Party to form the Workingmen's Party of the United States. After undergoing various permutations, this party became Daniel DeLeon's Socialist Labor Party, which is still in existence. The failure of this party to win the allegiance of the labor movement, however, gave rise to the Socialist Party of Eugene Debs. Still later came the Communist Party, the Socialist Workers Party, and all the other sectarian grouplets on the Left that appealed for labor's love—and lost.

The rise to dominance of the American Federation of Labor (AFL) under Samuel Gompers meant that the Gompers policy of political neutrality—of "rewarding one's friends and punishing one's enemies" regardless of party—also became the political orientation of a large part of the labor movement. But the Gompers policy was never the sole political tendency in the movement, and labor's desire for a party of its own remained strong in certain quarters.[3] This was especially true following the "Red Scare" of 1919. In the wake of that hysteria and with increasingly hard times for labor as the twenties began, labor party sentiment flared anew. Local Labor and Farmer-Labor parties coalesced across the country, while the Non-Partisan League successfully contended for office as a third party in the upper Great Plains. Some liberals and unionists formed the Workers' Education Bureau, which the AFL executive council supported until 1928, despite the bureau's advocacy of independent political action. Other sources of labor party agitation were the labor colleges that labor activists and progressive intellectuals founded, the most notable being A. J. Muste's Brookwood Labor College in Katonah, New York, launched in 1921.[4]

In 1924 even the AFL halfheartedly surrendered to this tendency when it endorsed (and then abandoned) the presidential candidacy of Robert M. La Follette under the banner of the Progressive Party. With La Follette's defeat, however, the labor party upsurge faltered and most of the local parties faded, leaving only the Minnesota Farmer-Labor Party and La Follette's Wisconsin Progressive Party as viable remnants.[5] Even then, however, the flame was tended by ongoing coalitions of unionists and progressives, such as the League for Independent Political Action, the Conference for Progressive Political Action, and, later, the Farmer Labor Political Federation, which kept the idea alive in hopes of more propitious times ahead.[6] Then, with the coming of the Great Depression in 1929, local labor parties again sprang up all across the United States like mushrooms in a meadow after a warm summer rain.[7]

Even today, some unions, such as the United Electrical Workers (UE), call for the formation of a labor party at every annual convention. On June 26, 1985, Richard Trumka, then president of the United Mine Workers (UMW) and now vice president of the AFL-CIO, called for the formation of an independent labor party at the annual convention of the Newspaper Guild in Pittsburgh. The United States has "one party with two branches," said Trumka, "both apparently subservient to the interests of big money and the power of multinational corporations. All of us in the labor movement must consider the possibility that we are not going to establish a government of the people in this country as long as we remain so closely tied to the Democratic Party."[8]

But the ritualistic convention mandates of such unions as the UE and the rhetoric of leaders like Trumka are mere lip service to the nostalgic dream of an independent labor party, not meant to be seriously acted upon. Even Trumka, while attacking the two-party system, disclaimed any interest in leading a genuine third party effort. Much more indicative of organized labor's attitude today is former AFL-CIO president Lane Kirkland's belief that labor is a "natural constituency" of the Democratic Party and that the Democratic Party is the natural home of the labor movement.[9] Indeed, echoed United Steelworkers (USW) past president Lynn Williams, "If you took the labor movement out of the Democratic Party, what's left? It's the heart and soul of the Democratic Party."[10] So close is this alliance that by the mid-1980s the AFL-CIO had been guaranteed forty voting seats on the Democratic National Committee, the governing body of the Democratic Party. Labor's political neutrality died in the Great Depression of the thirties. So, also, did the old dream of independent political action—the dream of a labor party. For the last half-century, since the great realigning election of 1936, organized labor has been married to the Democratic Party, albeit somewhat shakily.

But before committing itself to the Democrats in that election, a major section of organized labor attempted once more to forge a labor party in the United States. Built on the innumerable local labor party campaigns of 1930–36, which sprang spontaneously and simultaneously into existence and groped toward national coordination, the movement suggests that the loyalty of organized labor could by no means be taken for granted by Franklin D. Roosevelt and the Democratic Party, even as late as the summer of 1936. That loyalty was won only after an intense and wide-ranging struggle in the labor movement—a civil war *within* "labor's civil war" between the AFL and the CIO—which must be seen as the apparent "last hurrah" of the labor party idea in U.S. political history.[11] As such, it was an integral, but historically unacknowledged, factor in the political developments of the thirties and helped shape the political alignments that emerged from that period.

The Urban Demographic Revolution

Another crucial factor in the political developments of the era was an intersecting phenomenon, the urban demographic revolution. The 1920 U.S. Census graphically revealed that the United States finally became an urban nation in the twenties, when the majority of its population for the first time was to be found in the cities. This revolution helps us understand why "labor's millions" were "on the march" in the 1930s. The 1936 presidential election, of course, witnessed the shift of political power at the national level away from the long-dominant Republicans to the Democrats—a trend begun in 1932 (or perhaps 1928, when the Democrat Al Smith carried all of the nation's twelve largest cities by appealing to the "immigrant" vote) but cemented in 1936. What made this shift possible was what Samuel Lubell called "the revolt of the city."[12]

Not only did the industrial cities in the United States contain the bulk of the population after 1920, but also this urban population was primarily an immigrant population. Of course, these cities had contained immigrant majorities for some time. As Lubell pointed out, in 1910, for instance, the great bulk of school-age children in thirty-seven of the nation's largest cities were the children of immigrants. "In cities like Chelsea, Fall River, New Bedford . . . more than *two out of every three* school children were the sons and daughters of immigrants," he reported.[13] By the 1930s these children of the immigrants had at last come of age.[14] Born and reared in the cities, speaking English and thinking of themselves as Americans rather than as strangers in a strange land, and mobilized into the electoral arena as their parents had not been, they not only shifted the demographic gravitational pull decisively away from the countryside but also completed the political power shift from country to city that had been under way.

This political power shift was more than just demographics, since it also changed the long-time *content* of U.S. politics because of *when* it occurred. "The human potential for a revolutionary political change," Lubell noted, "had . . . been brought together in our larger cities when the economic skies caved in."[15] The result was the rise of "class politics."

The reason for this is that the city was not only heavily ethnic but also heavily working class. Indeed, the U.S. working class was primarily an *ethnic* working class. This ethnic diversity may have been a major reason for the lack of "class consciousness" in the United States.[16] The U.S. working class was not "made" at any one time but was constantly being remade as new waves of immigrants entered the work force, bringing with them their "alien" customs, beliefs, and values. This constant demographic churning brought to the fore ethnocultural differences and issues, making them—prohibition, blue laws, religion, and the like—the cleavage lines of U.S. politics. However, World War I and the Johnson Act of 1924 clamped the lid on further European immigration. Without continued injections of foreign elements, both the cities and the work force—the working *class*—grew more "Americanized" as the children of the immigrants grew up and joined the world of urban work.

With the decline of salient ethnocultural conflict and with the economic crisis of the Great Depression, class politics, always present but usually submerged by ethnocultural tensions, became the primary fault line of U.S. political life for the first time. Initially, as Richard Oestreicher points out, the 1932 election of Roosevelt was a rejection of the Great Depression status quo, not a class act. But this quickly changed:

> After 1933 voters' responses to New Deal programs diverged sharply. The unemployed, relief recipients, low-income households, and blue-collar workers registered overwhelming approval in 1936 and 1940, while business people, professionals, white-collar workers, and upper- and middle-income households all expressed increasing disapproval. In 1936 the difference in the percentage voting Democratic between upper- and lower-income households was 34 percentage points; in 1940, 40 percentage points. . . .
> Over the course of the 1930s [class] sentiment did indeed become translated into political consciousness as the class basis of partisanship became successively more marked from election to election. . . .[17]

The new electoral cohort of increasingly class-conscious, urban, working-class immigrant children thus provided the electoral base of FDR's New Deal. Roosevelt never attracted a majority of the WASP vote. His support—like Catholic Al Smith's before him—was in the "ethnic" cities, where he attracted not only cross-ethnic but also *working-class* loyalty.[18] This transformation of the political universe is why Roosevelt attacked "economic royalists" in his 1936 campaign and why the pros and cons of unionization—not the long-time issues of religion, prohibition, or blue laws—dominated the nation's political agenda. The Democratic Party became the majority party in the 1930s by becoming the party of the ethnic working class.[19]

But this development was not automatic or inevitable. Samuel Lubell argued, for example, that this new class-conscious constituency of urban, working-class immigrant children, coming of age and coming into its own in the 1930s (7 million twenty-one-year-old first-time voters in 1936 alone), with its political loyalty still to be won and cemented, was not yet firmly Democratic. If the inchoate political loyalty of the newly arrived, class-conscious, urban working class was up for grabs, it was problematic whether the Democrats would secure and hold it. These newly mobilized voters—overwhelmingly young, disproportionately concentrated in the mass-production industries—were the very ones who were showing an unprecedented interest in independent political action—in a labor party. How, then, was labor won and held for the Democrats?[20]

The Contest for the Class-Conscious Vote

The work of channeling sentiment among the emerging urban, "ethnic," class-conscious voters away from a labor party and toward the Democratic Party was delicate and by no means assured of success. Of course, FDR himself emerged as labor's reluctant champion after a flurry of New Deal social legislation in 1935—the Wagner Act, the Social Security Act, the Works Progress Administration (WPA)—for which he, rather than Senator Robert Wagner and the other urban progressives who pushed these laws through, primarily got the credit. But at the grass-roots level among labor's rank and file, Labor's Non-Partisan League was crucial to securing and hammering home labor's loyalty to Roosevelt and the Democrats.

The 1936 election transformed the role of organized labor. Led by Labor's Non-Partisan League (so-called to distinguish it from the Non-Partisan League of the twenties), the CIO unions contributed $770,000 to Roosevelt's campaign and are credited with carrying Illinois, Indiana, New York, Ohio, and Pennsylvania for the Democrats. The League, with its "energetic, purposeful mobilization of labor behind the Democratic candidates," as Bert Cochran pointed out, "was an innovation; it transformed the old Gompers policy of casual and largely symbolic endorsement of labor's friends."[21] Labor's Non-Partisan League *was* an innovation, for it was designed by its top leaders to be a transitional step toward today's complete alignment of organized labor with the Democrats.

In recording the genesis of Labor's Non-Partisan League, historians have emphasized the perceived threats from the right-wing Liberty League, the organized forces of big business and capital. What is puzzling, however, is that they have tended to ignore the additional reason Labor's Non-Partisan League was formed: to wean organized labor, especially the new CIO unions in the mass-production industries, away from independent political action, away from a labor party for which so many were then clamoring. Committed political action was at last on labor's agenda. The only real question was the form and direction this action would take: into the Democratic Party or into an independent labor party.

It is this resulting civil war *within* "labor's civil war" that has remained unchronicled. Once discerned, however, we get a clearer picture of why John L. Lewis, Sidney Hillman, and other top CIO leaders were so deliberately vague about the eventual political trajectory of Labor's Non-Partisan League—into putative independent political action along the lines of New York's American Labor Party or into an enduring alliance with the Democratic Party. This ambiguity was necessary because of the always smoldering desire in the labor movement for a labor party, which—fanned by the belated arrival of "class politics" on the nation's political agenda—flared and burned hotter at this time. The loyalty of organized labor and the new urban, working-class voter to FDR and the Democrats was therefore *not* a foregone conclusion and had to be won after intense, continuing, and delicate internal struggle. In this struggle the labor party idea lost.

Of course, an authentic political tendency does not die overnight. Labor party sentiment remained powerful at the grass-roots level, even in the U.S. populace at large. An August 1937 Gallup poll, for instance, revealed that 21 percent of the respondents supported the formation of such a party. A series of Gallup polls between December 1936 and January 1938 also discovered that between 14 percent and 16 percent of the respondents would go beyond this and even "would join" such a labor party, if it was formed.[22] The American Labor Party itself maintained an active, though shrinking, political presence for many years. Meanwhile, support for a labor party among union militants across the country continued to be a significant factor even into the late 1940s, as C. Wright Mills and Helen Dinerman have shown. In a 1950 nationwide survey of elected CIO union officers at the national, state, and local levels, Mills discovered that 31 percent of the city-level CIO leaders still favored the formation of a *national* labor party. At the same time, 29 percent of the city-level CIO leaders wanted to see the formation of a *local* labor party, while 10 percent of even the national CIO leadership thought this was a good idea.[23]

Clearly, loyalty to the Democratic Party remained problematic for a sizable minority of CIO activists, even after 1936. In some strongholds of labor party sentiment, such as Akron, Ohio, municipal labor parties continued to challenge local Democrats well into the post–World War II period.[24] In Berlin, New Hampshire, labor party leaders and activists actually *became* the local Democratic Party and continued to dominate local politics with a labor-oriented administration through the 1950s, although they ruled the city as the Farmer-Labor Party through 1943.[25]

What had been lost in 1936, however, was a realistic "window of opportunity" for the establishment of a national labor party. It was the last time significant elements in organized labor struggled hopefully to actualize the idea. Whether such a national party could actually have been created and how successful it might have been—or if it was even politically "appropriate"—is not my subject. There were and are almost insurmountable cultural, psychological, and structural obstacles built into the U.S. political system that argue against the success of *any* third party—labor or otherwise.[26] Still, in the face of these systemic hurdles, in the mid-thirties major sections of both the leadership and the rank and file of organized labor struggled to fulfill the ancient dream of a labor party.

The Idea Takes Shape

As in other times and places, labor in the United States moved toward independent politics after the state intervened to smash strikes in the thirties. The labor party movement was—first and foremost—a product of the injunction, the deputy sheriff, and the National Guard.[27]

Left political parties helped along the growing labor party movement. The Socialist Party debated whether it was opportunistic to support labor parties. The "Old Guard" by and large opposed the idea, while the Norman Thomas wing supported it.[28] In Cambridge, Massachusetts, Alfred Baker Lewis, leader of the local Socialist Party, had advocated a labor party as early as 1924.[29] By 1932 Cambridge trade union members of the Socialist Party, such as Michael Flaherty, secretary of Painters Local 11, were calling for formation of both a union of the unemployed and a labor party.[30] The Cambridge chapter of the Socialist Party later supported the local chapter of the Workers' Alliance of America (WAA), which concentrated on organizing unemployed workers eligible for WPA projects, and the Cambridge People's Labor Party. We also know that Socialist militants were active in local labor party efforts in Philadelphia, Buffalo, Niagara Falls, and Berlin, New Hampshire.[31]

The Communist Party came late to the support of the labor party movement, at both the local and national levels. The party's head, Earl Browder, appears to have come out for the first time in support of a labor party at a National Congress for Social Unemployment Insurance in Washington, D.C., on January 6, 1935.[32] This support of the incipient labor party movement in the United States was later confirmed in Moscow at the Seventh World Congress of the Comintern, July–August 1935. That congress announced the United Front policy in response to the rise of European fascism and declared that the "workers' and farmers' party" was the American version of the United Front.[33]

In keeping with the new policy, the Communist Party withdrew its candidates in two aldermanic districts and one assembly district in New York City in favor of the newly formed United Labor Party ticket based on the affiliation of neighborhood clubs, trade unions, and civic groups in those areas.[34] In early December 1935 Earl Browder and Norman Thomas, only recently blood enemies, appeared together before 20,000 militants in Madison Square Garden, with Browder making a strong plea for joint action to build a farmer-labor party.[35]

Meanwhile, the Workers' Party, founded by A. J. Muste, lent a hand in those places where it had put down roots. One major example was Toledo, where—after helping to lead the 1934 Auto-Lite strike in that city—Workers' Party members joined in a decision in August 1935 to organize a labor party in which all local political groups would merge their identity.[36]

But it was no left political party's propaganda or decision that energized the creation of local labor parties from coast to coast in 1935. It was the strike wave of 1934 and the repression of those strikes. Not since the great railroad strikes of 1877 had there been such widespread labor upheaval. There were 1,856 strikes and over 1,470,000 workers on strike in 1934. In outline, the events of that year are familiar: the big Auto-Lite strike in Toledo; the violent teamster strike in Minneapolis; the general strike in San Francisco; national strikes in auto and steel averted by presidential promises; and then in September a strike of 400,000 textile workers in New England and the South.[37]

Nationally, the United Textile Workers' strike of 1934 was, as Robert Brooks put it, "unquestionably the greatest single industrial conflict in the history of American organized labor."[38] Locally, the strike was a quick course in political education. The hostile actions of the state and the anger of the strikers are suggested by events in Saylesville, Rhode Island, where state troopers and deputy sheriffs turned machine guns and shotguns on 600 pickets, wounding five, while the National Guard finished the job with clubs. That night strikers attacked the National Guard, driving it back behind barbed-wire barricades. The National Guard opened fire on the strikers, wounding three.

At Woonsocket, Rhode Island, strikers and state police battled with stones and tear gas. When the National Guard entered the fray, Guardsmen fired on the strikers, killing one and wounding three. At this, reported a local newspaper correspondent, "the crowd went completely wild with rage. . . . Men and women and boys too, pounded up and down the business district, and where they ran the crash of broken plate glass and tearing splintering wood was heard."[39] Two more companies of National Guardsmen arrived and placed Woonsocket under military rule.

Herbert Gutman viewed the defeat of this strike along the entire Atlantic seaboard as one of "the most tragic" the U.S. labor movement ever suffered:

> The most bitter strike in this country in the 1930s, the longest strike that occurred in this country in the 1930s, was not a strike in the automobile industry. It was not a strike in the mining industry. It was not a strike in the industries that we celebrate for good reason. It was the strike of . . . textile workers seeking to organize themselves.
>
> The failure to organize . . . in the 1930s wasn't because the workers didn't have the will. . . . It has to do with many other factors, including the politics of state government . . . which was so repressive toward that organization phenomenon.[40]

In both the South and New England, the United Textile Workers' strike taught mill workers to distrust the Democratic Party, whose representatives had fought the strike. The Massachusetts Committee for a Labor Party declared in March 1936, "The New Deal was supposed to give us the right to organize. Yet when the textile workers went on strike in 1934 for recognition of their union and to stop the speed-up, Democratic governors in 12 states called out the militia to drive the workers back to work and break the strike. In fact, 14 textile workers were killed by militia called out by Democratic governors."[41]

This distrust of the Democratic Party quickly took the form of agitation among textile workers for a labor party to challenge the Democrats who had betrayed them. Thus, in September 1936 William E. Kuehnel, president of the Hartford, Connecticut, Central Labor Union and chairman of the Connecticut Farmer-Labor Party, described to a meeting of the Cambridge People's Labor Party:

> the stirring story of the state-wide unity for direct political action after the betrayal of the Textile Workers by the friend of the worker, [Demo-

cratic] Governor Cross. His prompt placing not only of the Connecticut State Police at the service of the employers against the picket line but the actual transportation in State Police cars of strike-breakers to the mills, was so flagrant a class alignment against the workers, that not only unions, big and little, responded to the Hartford Central Labor Union's call for a Farmer-Labor Conference, but women's clubs, fraternal groups, YMCA members and other church groups responded and took prompt action. Their fervor was such that the problem of the leaders was to hold them in leash so that their energy could be correctly and effectively used.[42]

The crushing of the United Textile Workers' strike was also experienced by workers across the country. Every major center of industrial unrest in 1934, from Toledo to San Francisco, witnessed labor party activity in 1935. All thinking workers, proclaimed the Labor Party of Chicago and Cook County, "are now realizing that the Republican and Democratic Parties are nothing but political company unions. . . . A Labor Party based upon the unions is required to serve the political interests of Labor and prevent the forces of government from being used consistently against the interests of the workers."[43] This was the declaration not of some closet sect but of 139 official delegates representing sixty local unions.

Events in New England were illustrative of this trend.[44] In July 1935 representatives of 350 union locals of the Connecticut Federation of Labor, meeting under the auspices of the Hartford Central Labor Union, unanimously voted for the formation of a Connecticut labor party, anticapitalist in nature, to be based on trade unions and other mass organizations. A follow-up meeting in New London was attended by representatives of 168 AFL union locals and 21 independent locals representing 68,000 workers. They planned to organize labor party committees in each city and town of Connecticut. The Danbury Central Labor Union was the first to put up a Labor Party slate of candidates for town offices.

In Rhode Island a special August 1935 election in the First Congressional District, which had voted overwhelmingly Democratic in 1934, put a Republican, Charles F. Risk, into office. This district contained thousands of textile workers who felt Roosevelt had betrayed them in the settlement of the United Textile Workers' strike the previous fall. William L. Connelly, president of the Rhode Island Federation of Labor, stated, "Labor is so dissatisfied at this time that there is much real talk of a labor party in Rhode Island for state offices." Reporting on labor party agitation in Rhode Island's Blackstone Valley, the Federated Press declared that "the same discontent which resulted in the election of Congressman Charles F. Risk,

Republican, not because of his party's strength but because of disgust with the Democratic Party, had prompted labor's opposition."[45]

In early October Joseph Sylvia, a New England organizer for the United Textile Workers, told the Woonasquatucket Valley (Rhode Island) Trade Council delegates that the UTW was dissatisfied with the treatment accorded it by the Rhode Island Democratic administration. He said that the General Assembly had failed to keep promises made to labor in the Democratic Party platform of 1934 and that "independent political action" was necessary.[46]

At the convention of the Rhode Island State Federation of Labor on October 5 and 6 organized labor in that state officially went on record as favoring a labor party by an overwhelming vote. The executive council was instructed to call AFL local unions and city central labor unions to a statewide labor party convention within six months to actually launch the Rhode Island Labor Party. The state continued its "anti–New Deal trend" in the important town elections in Westerly and Middletown in late 1935, where Republicans were returned to office. There appeared to be no change in the direction of the anti-Roosevelt tide, and political observers noted, "If the Presidential election were to be held this week . . . there seems to be little doubt that the state would go Republican. There is little doubt . . . that a large part of the change, conservatively estimated at 60 percent, was caused by a growing hostility to the policies of the Roosevelt Administration."[47]

Given the central role of textile workers in the labor party movement as a whole, it was natural that the effort to win national AFL endorsement of an independent labor party should have been led by the United Textile Workers' first vice president, Francis J. Gorman. Frank Gorman was an Englishman, born in 1877 and reared until the age of thirteen in Bradford, Lancashire, the same town that witnessed the birth of Keir Hardie's Independent Labour Party. His father owned a pub frequented by the leaders of the Bradford wool workers' union. The pub failed, however, and in 1890 the family immigrated to the United States. Settling in Providence, Rhode Island, young Frank Gorman joined the Lancashire work force in the textile mills there as a sweeper. In 1910 he became a wool sorter and a member of the National Wool Sorters and Graders Union. Two years later that union merged with the United Textile Workers.

For twelve years Gorman was president of his union local, as well as president of the Providence Central Labor Union and legislative agent for the Rhode Island Federation of Labor. From 1913 on Gorman was an organizer for the UTW and in 1922 became an international representative. In 1923–24 he led an organizing drive in southern textile mills, and in 1928 he became first vice president of the UTW.

In 1929 Gorman was active in the big Marion, North Carolina, textile strike, and when six strikers were killed by the local militia, he delivered the funeral eulogy after local clergy refused to officiate. That same year he organized and led the textile strike in Elizabethton, Tennessee. In 1931 he orchestrated the Danville, Virginia, textile strike, and in 1932 he was back in New England leading the textile strike in Lawrence, Massachusetts. In 1933 Gorman masterminded the successful textile strike in Pawtucket, Rhode Island. Frank Gorman was thus the obvious choice to oversee the giant industrywide textile strike of 1934. In 1937 he became president of the UTW upon the resignation of President Thomas McMahon.

According to Bruce Minton and John Stuart, the Democratic betrayal of the 1934 textile strike "was a revealing lesson for Gorman" and had a traumatic impact on him. It convinced him and many others in the UTW that Democrats could not be relied on to protect the interests of labor. "Many of us did not understand what we do now," Gorman said later, "that the Government protects the strong, not the weak. . . . We know now that we are naive to depend on the forces of government to protect us."[48]

Even more, it convinced him he had witnessed the arrival of European fascism in the United States. As Sinclair Lewis warned, "It *could* happen here," and Gorman felt he had seen the beginning of the end. His answer was the same as that supplied by many others in labor that year: a party of labor's own, a labor party. He became convinced "that a Farmer-Labor Party was as essential to the health of the workers as industrial unionism. 'We have two courses,' Gorman declared. 'First, the building and strengthening of our trade union movement until the millions of workers in mass-production industries are organized; and second, building and strengthening our Labor Party until we have a solid People's Front against the power of industry and wealth which keep us in subjugation at the point of bayonet. . . .'"[49]

Gorman spent the next two years of his life agitating ceaselessly for a union-based labor party. He stepped up his already exhausting speaking schedule until almost every week found him on the road expounding the labor party idea. Under his prodding, every UTW-organized mill town, North and South, made efforts to found a local labor party. "It becomes increasingly apparent," Gorman told his audiences, "that economic organization alone is not sufficient protection for the working class. . . . We feel sure that the only answer is a Labor Party for the United States—a Labor

Party with its roots grimly and solidly embedded in the trade union movement, but inclusive of all the other underprivileged classes in our country."[50]

When the Fifty-Fifth Annual Convention of the AFL began on October
7, 1935, in Atlantic City, intense debate was expected on the deferred question of organizing mass-production workers into industrial unions—indeed,
the CIO would emerge from the conflict of this convention. But Rose Pesotta of the International Ladies Garment Workers Union (ILGWU) tells us,
"Hot debate also was looked for on a resolution to form a Labor Party. The
progressive delegates sponsoring it chose Francis J. Gorman . . . as spokes-
man."[51] Night after night Gorman led the mostly younger delegates—primarily from the mass-production industries—who favored the creation of
a labor party in fevered caucus to plan strategy and to lay plans looking
beyond the convention. These labor party advocates seemed, to some observers, closest to the general spirit of the convention, a convention where
references to President Roosevelt evoked no ovations and where many repeatedly expressed the idea that labor must depend on its own strength rather
than on the promises of "friends" and parties it did not control.[52] Gorman
himself provided the names of some of the key members of the labor party
caucus at that AFL convention.[53] Besides Gorman and William F. Kelley,
second vice president of the UTW, they included Isidore Nagler, International
Ladies Garment Workers Union, New York City; Joseph Schlossberg, Amalgamated Clothing Workers of America, New York City; Paul Rassmussen,
Workers' Alliance, Milwaukee; William Kuehnel, Hartford Central Labor
Union; Wyndham Mortimer, United Automobile Workers, Cleveland; and
N. H. Eagle, Rubber Workers, Akron, who was on the executive committee of the United Rubber Workers and active in the Summit County Farmer-Labor Party, which embraced labor party activists from both Akron and
nearby Barberton, Ohio.

Two-and-a-half years earlier, speaking to the convention of the New
Jersey Federation of Labor, AFL president William Green paid homage to
the perennial desire for independent political action and stated, "The [la-
bor] movement has no constitutional prohibition against the formation of
an independent political party of labor and, in fact, stands ready to undertake such a move if sufficient rank and file support is created."[54] Frank
Gorman and his allies had been laboring without rest to create just that
rank-and-file support for which the AFL leadership claimed it was waiting. Faced with rank-and-file clamor for a labor party, however, Green
denounced the proposals instead of supporting them. Using his opening
speech to red-bait the labor party advocates, Green linked the demand of
American trade unionists for an independent political party with "orders

promulgated at Moscow recently by the Communist International calling on its adherents and sympathizers to pledge labor to independent political action."[55] This new line (the Popular Front) was, he claimed, an attempt by the Communists in Moscow to coerce the AFL into doing something that the rank and file actually opposed.

Gorman rose to challenge President Green and prepared to deliver the principal convention speech in behalf of Resolution No. 135, one of thirteen labor party resolutions introduced at the convention and the one that finally came to the floor. After detailing the disappointments of the New Deal, Gorman turned to his major theme: the "political destruction of the workers' rights." He cataloged incidents of repression by various governmental bodies throughout 1935 as evidence that the labor movement had to organize politically to fight back. He concluded, "It is for this reason that we urge the American Federation of Labor to sanction, through approval of a Labor Party, the people's resistance to tyranny, to the destructive efforts of the bosses, and their agents, the Democratic and Republican parties."[56]

Because of parliamentary maneuverings to stall its introduction, however, it proved impossible to bring the labor party resolution to the floor until just a few hours before the convention adjourned. As Gorman launched into his speech, more objections were raised. His speech was interrupted by the chairman, Gorman's copy was handed over to the convention secretary for recording in the proceedings of the convention, but Gorman himself was not allowed to continue his delivery. Rose Pesotta described the stifling of Gorman by the AFL leadership as "a classic" of such tactics. "Throughout the sessions," she said, "I noticed that whenever some important question was up the steam-roller managed somehow to squash it; by reporting it too early, when those who wished to press the issue were either absent or not prepared, or by leaving it till the last day, when most of the delegates, after two strenuous weeks, were sitting on their suitcases."[57] Thus, when Bill Hutcheson barraged with parliamentary objections a delegate from the Barberton, Ohio, Rubber Workers' union who was introducing the crucial resolution on industrial unionism, is it any wonder a frustrated John L. Lewis punched him out, giving birth to the CIO?

Despite these obstacles, Gorman's labor party resolution almost passed, with a vote of 104 (including a majority of delegates representing central labor unions and state federations of labor) to 108 against the resolution. Encouraged, labor party militants went home confident of victory at the 1936 AFL convention and eager to spread the labor party idea.

In 1935 labor party resolutions had been introduced in twelve state Federation of Labor conventions from New England to Oregon. Favorable action had been taken in five of those conventions.[58] In New England both the Rhode Island and the Vermont Federation of Labor had already endorsed the formation of a labor party. In Berlin, New Hampshire, a strong local Farmer-Labor Party based in the French-Canadian pulp workers was organizing, which would soon elect a mayor and the majority of the city council. Over 150 union locals in Connecticut had endorsed the formation of a labor party, as had the Maine Textile Council and two top Federation of Labor officials in Maine.[59]

After the 1935 AFL convention labor party supporters in Toledo formed the Lucas County Congress for Political Action, endorsed by the Toledo Central Labor Union, among other organizations. In that October's municipal elections, it ran seven labor candidates for the city council and the board of education, four of whom won: two on the council and two on the board of education.[60] After this victory plans were made to launch a statewide Ohio labor party, an action endorsed by the Cleveland District Auto Council and its nine affiliated auto worker locals.[61] Auto worker activities would result in labor political campaigns in the municipal elections of Hamtramck, Port Huron, Dearborn, and Detroit.[62]

For his part, Gorman took to the road on a labor party "propaganda tour" that carried him throughout New England, the South, and the Midwest and lasted nonstop well into the next year. His visit to Gastonia, North Carolina, scene of bloody conflict in the local textile mills, was typical. There, a large audience waited eagerly for two hours past his scheduled time to hear him. When he finally arrived, he predicted the formation of "a huge Labor Party in the United States" and declared that "the opposition was carrying the fight directly into the political area and in order to wage battle effectively, labor, too, must and eventually will do likewise."[63]

The visit of this "famed strike leader" and "one of the half dozen best known labor leaders in the United States" to Kenosha, Wisconsin, was hailed by a mass meeting of workers in the town's Knights of Columbus hall. "Since the 1935 convention of the AFL at Atlantic City," reported a local newspaper, "he has been one of the leading advocates of a labor party. He led the fight for the famed resolution No. 135, presented by the United Textile Workers, which called upon the AFL to mobilize its forces into a Labor Party."[64] Gorman left Kenosha for Chicago, where he was guest of honor at a dinner given by the Labor Party of Chicago and Cook County. The next day he addressed the Chicago Federation of Labor and a mass meeting arranged by the Chicago Labor Party.

At the same time he was rallying trade union members to the banner of a labor party, however, Gorman also made a deliberate effort to reach beyond the ranks of organized labor to find allies among artists, intellectuals, and professionals. For instance, Gorman "was the only representative of a union which did not represent artists" to present a paper at the First American Artists' Congress, held at New York City's Town Hall on February 14–16, 1936. Organized by the Communist Party as part of its Popular Front, antifascist coalition-building effort, the Congress's theme was one that Gorman already preached from labor pulpits across the nation: Fascism had come to the United States. "The first attack upon democracy comes with the destruction of the trade-union movement," declared Gorman in his paper, and for him the attack had been launched:

> Events are swiftly moving in that direction. Our foremost middle-class champions and writers have discarded the outmoded liberal theory of "It can't happen here" in favor of the grim, realistic realization that it not only *can* happen here, but that it *is* happening here. . . .
>
> We are beginning to discover in the trade-union movement that our trade unions, our economic organizations, are no longer sufficient protection for us. We cannot, indeed, even continue with our trade unions if we do not also band together in political unity. Big Business and the controlling financial and industrial interests are making organization harder and harder. They are turning more and more to the use of troops in times of strike; to the hiring of the industrial spy to break up trade unions; to the persecution, framing and murder of trade-union leaders.

Intellectuals and artists, continued Gorman, must organize into their own unions to help prevent this "mass enslavement." But a second, "or simultaneous step," had to be "the organization of the artists, together with the entire mass of underprivileged and dispossessed, into a political front—into a militant, determined Labor Party" to bring about "the destruction of a dictatorship of dying capitalism!"[65]

Gorman's primary audience remained the trade union movement, though. In early May he addressed the National Women's Trade Union League in Washington, D.C., and forecast a new political alignment in the United States resulting in a labor party.[66] Later that month he spoke to a meeting of 700 in New York City who had met to plan a New York City labor party.[67] A few days later Gorman was introduced by the president of the Roanoke, Virginia, Central Labor Union to a crowd of Roanoke "workers, farmers and businessmen" and spoke on the need for a farmer-labor party. "Mr. Gorman is a very interesting and convincing speaker," reported a local labor newspaper, "and is well informed on the subject.

Every person who is interested in knowing more about the movement of the Farmer Labor Party which has been spreading over the country like wild fire during the past few months, should attend this meeting.... As Labor Party movements are being launched in every section of the United States, either on a state or a municipal basis, it was thought wise to have Mr. Gorman come to Roanoke and explain the objectives of such an organization...."[68]

Speaking in New Haven that July at a meeting organized by the Connecticut AFL Committee for a Farmer-Labor Party, Gorman urged an "American People's Front" similar to France's Popular Front. "We can only succeed," he said, "if we take matters into our own hands. In order to take matters into our own hands we must have the same kind of weapons our bosses have. We must have the economic weapon of trade union organization and the political weapon of a Labor Party.... [P]ut the strength of the working class behind the Farmer-Labor Party of Connecticut and the nation-wide movement for independent political action!"[69]

Meanwhile, in Danbury, Connecticut, a railroad signalman, Josephus Van Dyke, was running for city council on the Farmer-Labor Party ticket.[70] In Seattle, unions, homeowners, the unemployed, and taxpayers' leagues placed a coalition workers' ticket in the field. In Detroit Congressman Tom Amlie of Wisconsin addressed progressives and union representatives looking toward a "new party of the producing classes." The Southern Tenant Farmers' Union closed its convention in Little Rock, Arkansas, with a resolution calling for the founding of a farmer-labor party, as did the conventions of the American Newspaper Guild, A. Philip Randolph's Brotherhood of Sleeping Car Porters, and, of course, the United Textile Workers. Studebaker and Bendix auto unionists in South Bend, Indiana, were "determined to organize politically as well as industrially." In Indiana the Gibson County Central Labor Union, the first labor body in the state to endorse the farmer-labor party movement, won the support of nine locals and the Kokomo Central Labor Union to the idea. On March 13 and 14 trade unions and farm organizations in South Dakota met in Mitchell to form a state Farmer-Labor Party. In Texas the Farmer-Labor Club issued an appeal to "prevent the fascist forces of greed, graft, corruption and brutality from gaining a strangle-hold on the lives of the American people. Neither Roosevelt nor the two old parties are an obstacle to the dangerous, dark and evil forces that are threatening the very rights guaranteed by the Declaration of Independence, Bill of Rights, and the liberal traditions of American history."

"Now, more than ever," said an editorial in the *Labor Journal* of Norfolk, Virginia, a paper endorsed by the Norfolk Central Labor Union (CLU), "we need progressive politics that fit the actual needs of the people of the United States and not the practical politics of powerful industrialists, rich farmers, bankers and war-makers. We can protect these fundamental rights guaranteed to us by building a Farmer Labor Party of our own representatives and on a platform which we ourselves decide will benefit us."

On April 30, 1936, a small army of New Jersey unemployed, organized by the Workers' Alliance of America, ended a nine-day occupation of the statehouse, where they had come to demand higher relief appropriations: "Tired, heavy-eyed, but still of lusty voice, the crowd of 200 filed . . . from the State House at 12:45 A.M. after scoring the legislature for its failure to replenish empty state relief coffers and announcing its determination to elect its own legislature through its newly formed [New Jersey] Farmer Labor Party."[71]

That same April, the Brookwood Labor Players of Brookwood Labor College, on a tour of industrial centers, stopped in New Bedford, Massachusetts, to present its play *Picket Line and Ballot Box* to a huge and enthusiastic audience of textile workers at the local high school. The play depicted the struggle of an insurgent group of strikers against a company union and antagonistic local politicians from both major parties, which the bosses controlled. The play ended happily—to lusty cheers from the audience—when the strikers realized the solution to their dilemma and threw their support behind a newly created local labor party.[72]

The Idea at the Grass Roots—Akron and New Bedford

The labor party idea, it seemed, was spreading like a prairie fire across the land. All that was needed was to fan it a little hotter. In heavily unionized towns like New Bedford, that was already being done by local militants. On January 24, 1936, the New Bedford Central Labor Union had voted unanimously to organize a New Bedford labor party and—as such—enter that year's municipal elections held in December. Headed by the CLU's president, George Sanderson, an eleven-person steering committee was elected to oversee development of the Labor Party.[73] All CLU delegates then took on the task of obtaining the support of their unions. A draft party constitution was submitted to every union that was considering the labor party idea. This slow, painstaking, democratic preparation helps explain why, when the Labor Party mayoral and city council candidates were later announced, they were immediately and formally endorsed by every trade union in New Bedford.

The textile workers of New Bedford, however, were not the only ones in Massachusetts who were party-building that year. In the western Massachusetts town of Springfield the United Labor Party was busy running candidates for state representative, as well as for municipal offices. There were no municipal elections in Cambridge that year, so the Cambridge People's Labor Party launched a congressional campaign instead. Besides the active local labor parties in Springfield, Cambridge, and New Bedford, Massachusetts also witnessed labor party agitation in Lynn, where leaders of the seventeen largest unions endorsed the movement, and in Lowell, where the Lowell Textile Council endorsed the Labor Party.[74]

Today Cambridge is viewed primarily as the home of Harvard and MIT. In the thirties, however, Cambridge was the second largest industrial city in Massachusetts, after Boston. The Cambridge People's Labor Party was based in the heavily unionized rubber workers in the working-class neighborhoods of Italian East Cambridge. The president of the People's Labor Party was Salvatore Camelio, who was not only president of the local rubber workers' union but also a United Rubber Workers (URW) district director and a member of the union's general executive board. Sal Camelio was an adamant believer in the idea that "if labor is to survive, we must fight in the political field as well as the economic field. The time has come when we must take independent political action!"[75]

At the URW convention in Akron, Ohio, that year, Camelio led a large contingent of Italian rubber workers from Cambridge who fought for URW endorsement of the labor party movement. He pointed out that the UAW, the ILGWU, the Mine, Mill and Smelter Workers, the Southern Tenant Farmers' Union, Randolph's Brotherhood of Sleeping Car Porters, the United Textile Workers, and the American Newspaper Guild had already endorsed the formation of a national farmer-labor party and that the URW should join the movement. Revealing his concern about the rise of fascism in the United States, Camelio asked the URW convention in Akron, "Who speaks for labor? Is the Black Legion of Michigan for us? Is the resurgent Ku Klux Klan for us? Read the book, *It Can't Happen Here*. It *can* happen here! Only a Farmer Labor Party can defend labor now!"[76]

In fact, the rubber workers of Akron had already begun to act on that very message. Akron was a one-industry town, the site of Goodyear, the biggest rubber factory in the world, with over 14,000 workers, as well as the home of the huge Goodrich and Firestone rubber plants. There were also several smaller rubber factories, such as the General Tire and Rubber Company, with 1,500 workers, and the Mohawk Rubber Company. In February and March of 1936 the gigantic strike of Goodyear workers had energized the rubber workers and brought them into not only the CIO but also electoral politics. They, too, had seen the use of government force against their organizing efforts and had drawn familiar conclusions. "Almost without exception in labor disturbances," URW president Sherman Dalrymple declared, "the rich have looked upon the agencies of government as their private instrument to protect and defend them in their raids upon labor's rights."[77] As far as the rubber workers were concerned, that status quo had to go.

As soon as the Goodyear strike ended, local leaders began working to launch a labor party. On April 6, 1936, 300 men and women representing sixty Akron unions met in the first Summit County Labor Congress for the purpose of founding a labor party. "Organized labor," the Labor Congress declared, "is now convinced that it must work shoulder to shoulder in electing to public office men of character and ability who will defend the rights of the laboring class of America on a basis of equality with that of any other class of people."[78]

Central to the Akron labor party efforts were Wilmer Tate, an AFL machinist and president of the Akron Central Labor Union; James McCartan, president of the Typographical Union; Francis Gerhart, president of the Barberton Central Labor Union; and Luther L. Callahan, president of the Goodrich rubber workers' local. In quick succession following the Labor Congress's convention, the Akron Central Labor Union on April 23 refused to endorse the Democrats for the upcoming primary elections, and Tate began traveling to neighboring towns to stir up support for a labor party. April 26, for instance, found him presenting his message to a group of Youngstown steelworkers.[79]

On Sunday, May 3, Akron workers belatedly celebrated May Day with a mile-and-a-half-long parade of fifty Akron and nearby Barberton unions, as well as a delegation from the Canton Federation of Labor. The parade ended at Akron's Grace Park in what the *Akron Beacon Journal* described as "the largest mass demonstration of labor that Akron has seen." Some estimated that 10,000 workers were massed in the park, while N. H. Eagle, the president of the Mohawk local, a Farmer-Labor Party supporter, and the parade chairman, estimated the crowd at 20,000.[80] "The cry for a Farmer Labor Party rang today in the ears of thousands of working men and women," said the *Akron Beacon Journal*, as "both the Republican and Democratic parties were scored and the Farmer Labor Party was held to be the only refuge for the worker." The four speakers who addressed the crowd that day all used the occasion to champion the idea of a labor party. They included Wilmer Tate; Francis Gerhart; Maurice Sugar, a Detroit labor lawyer active in that city's labor party effort; and Joseph Schlossberg from New York, the Amalgamated Clothing Workers (ACW) executive board member who had championed the labor party with Gorman at the 1935 AFL convention.[81]

Back in Massachusetts, the URW leader Sal Camelio was doing his part in Cambridge with the formation of the People's Labor Party, which he led. The party chose as its congressional candidate Florence Luscomb, who had first come to prominence locally as a suffragist in the woman suffrage movement. The People's Labor Party was also part of the statewide effort to obtain an endorsement of the labor party movement from the Massachusetts Federation of Labor. Under the steady pressure of the labor party militants, the Massachusetts Federation of Labor initiated a statewide referendum of all union locals on the question, "Should the labor movement form a statewide party?" One New Bedford union after another—for example, the Carders and Ring Spinners on March 15, the Weavers on March 21, and the Loomfixers on April 15—voted yes.

The debate that took place in the Worcester Central Labor Union was typical. Those favoring the formation of a labor party were the younger workers, who argued that it was "now or never." They contended the two major parties exhibited little difference in their attitudes toward organized labor. In the South, they said, where the Democratic Party was dominant, workers had been shot down by machine guns when they attempted to organize. One militant declared, "I am a comparatively young man, but in my few years experience in the trade union movement, I have seen enough to satisfy me that labor will never come into its own until it takes control of the machinery of government through representatives of their own choosing."[82]

On August 4 the Massachusetts Federation of Labor met in New Bedford to decide the question. William Baron, the leader of the New Bedford CLU; John Connors, the New Bedford Labor Party's mayoral candidate; and Antonio England, a New Bedford Labor Party candidate for city council, introduced a motion proposing that the executive council of the federation be instructed to cooperate with farmers' organizations in the state to form a Massachusetts farmer-labor party in 1937 to function in state, county, and local elections in 1938. Joseph Salerno, president of the Amalgamated Clothing Workers in Boston and "one of the most accomplished orators of the convention," immediately rose in support of the labor party proposal.

The Committee on Resolutions, however, did not agree and reported "nonconcurrence" with the resolution. On August 6 the convention followed the federation's leadership and voted 119 to 53 against the creation of a Massachusetts labor party. Speakers jumped to their feet to declare in anger that sooner or later, whether the leadership wished it or not, the workers of the state and the nation would organize into an independent labor party.

The leadership ignored the labor party dissidents and presented Walter Considine, a Democratic state senator who was "a friend of labor," to the convention. Considine pleaded with the convention to remember its friends in the upcoming elections. The convention did so by endorsing Roosevelt for president. This was an unprecedented move, for never before had the Massachusetts Federation of Labor endorsed a presidential candidate, not even when the AFL had endorsed La Follette in 1924.

The federation then endorsed three Democrats for state office, two congressmen and Governor James Michael Curley, who was running against Henry Cabot Lodge for the U.S. Senate. Curley's endorsement brought howls of outrage from the third of the delegates who were labor party advocates. Joseph Novo, of the Lawrence UTW, charged that Curley had "fascist tendencies," while Joseph Salerno roared, "We are supposed to be neutral, to be impartial. We appear to be neutral towards the Labor Party, but not to politicians!"[83]

Labor's Non-Partisan League versus the Labor Party

Central to understanding what was happening politically to the labor movement in Massachusetts—and the nation—at this time is realizing 1936 marked the end of the political neutrality that had dominated organized labor for so long. As David Dubinsky, president of the ILGWU, pointed out, "The first re-election campaign of Franklin D. Roosevelt in 1936 was the start of the American labor movement's systematic, year-round involvement in politics."[84] Crucial to this was the formation of the Committee for Industrial Organization (CIO) by John L. Lewis, the president of the United Mine Workers, in November 1935.

Initially, the young workers in auto, rubber, textiles, and steel who poured into the CIO and supported the concept of industrial unionism were the same people who so vocally demanded labor's move toward independent political action.[85] As late as April 1936, with the formation of Labor's Non-Partisan League, or even August, before the AFL-CIO split, the two movements—industrial unionism and independent political action—

appeared as inverse sides of the same coin. Indeed, when the CIO was formed, its leadership included David Dubinsky of the Garment Workers; Thomas McMahon, president of the UTW; and Thomas H. Brown, president of the International Union of Mine, Mill, and Smelter Workers—leaders of unions that had already voted to form a labor party at their national conventions. Another important CIO leader was Sidney Hillman of the Amalgamated Clothing Workers, a union in which labor party sentiment was powerful.

In auto, developments at the United Auto Workers Local 229 in Hamtramck, Michigan, were typical. Throughout this period the local passed a series of "*unanimous* resolutions favoring a labor party."[86] At the April 1936 national convention of the UAW in South Bend, Indiana, a hotbed of local labor party agitation, the delegates voted *unanimously* to form a national farmer-labor party. That UAW convention also voted down a resolution to endorse Roosevelt for reelection. Walter Reuther was there as a labor party militant and wrote to his brothers describing the wild enthusiasm for a labor party, sentiment so strong, he said, that "the few reactionaries" dared not oppose the labor party forces. After urgent pleas from John L. Lewis, however—and private threats by Lewis's lieutenant Adolf Germer to UAW president Homer Martin that Lewis would withdraw $100,000 he had promised the UAW organizing effort unless the union backed down—the convention, with only minutes remaining before adjournment, finally adopted a pro-Roosevelt motion, while not abandoning its labor party support.[87] A number of UAW locals condemned the convention's endorsement of Roosevelt, but their anger was somewhat softened by the labor party resolution that the convention had also passed. This resolution attacked both major parties as "parties of big business" and ordered all UAW locals to form local and statewide labor parties, "exclusive of no worker."[88]

Many UAW locals in Michigan, Ohio, and Indiana proceeded quickly in this direction. In Michigan they backed the Michigan Farmer-Labor Party. In Ohio the Cleveland activists formed the Cuyahoga County Farmer-Labor Progressive Party shortly after the national UAW convention. By summer the State Committee for the Promotion of a Farmer-Labor Party in Ohio was forming locals around the state. The president of this committee was Cleveland's Richard Reisinger, an officer of UAW Local 32 and the UAW's Ohio legislative agent, who would become a member of the UAW executive board in 1937. Another driving force in the organization was the Farmer-Labor Party State Committee's secretary, Jack Kroll. An associate of Sidney Hillman, Kroll was manager of the Joint Board of the

Cincinnati Amalgamated Clothing Workers as well as a member of the ACW's executive board.[89]

An Indiana UAW convention on May 16, 1936, launched the statewide Farmer-Labor Party there, with permanent organizations in three counties and organizing work in several more. This UAW effort shortly garnered the endorsements of the Central Labor Union in South Bend and in Indianapolis, as well as the Indiana State Federation of Labor, the latter in defiance of the AFL. With John Bartee, a South Bend UAW leader, heading the slate, a full Farmer-Labor ticket was announced for statewide offices.[90] Even local leaders and rank-and-file members of Lewis's own United Mine Workers were pressuring the UMW to back a labor party.[91]

This enthusiasm among the rank and file of the CIO's mass-production unions for independent political action— for a labor party—was seen as a serious problem by many in the CIO leadership. John L. Lewis, Sidney Hillman, David Dubinsky, and others thought, of course, that labor should abandon its long-held position of political neutrality. But what they wanted was to align the labor movement with Roosevelt and the Democratic Party. David Dubinsky spoke for them when he said:

> The CIO couldn't stand to have Roosevelt defeated. The NRA had been killed by the Supreme Court; the Wagner Act (giving labor the legal sanction to organize) had just been passed, but nobody could be sure the Court wouldn't kill that too. . . . Labor—and, most of all, the struggling young unions that the CIO was building in the mass-production industries—could not afford to let FDR lose. . . . The venom with which reactionaries were ganging up against him made me decide I had to align myself openly with his re-election campaign.[92]

Dubinsky therefore resigned his long-held membership in the Socialist Party to work for Roosevelt's reelection and to swing his recalcitrant union, the ILGWU, behind the Democratic Party.[93]

The vehicle these CIO leaders developed for combating the labor party tendency within their unions and for swinging them behind Roosevelt was Labor's Non-Partisan League. The League leadership held out the possibility that this was the long-awaited move toward an independent labor party for which many of the rank and file had been clamoring. Indeed, many observers at the time viewed it as such. "Labor League Points to New Third Party," proclaimed headlines in the *New York Times*.[94] Paul Ward, writing the "Washington Weekly" column in the *Nation* declared, "This new organization [Labor's Non-Partisan League] . . . contains the germ of the most promising third party movement the country has yet seen."[95] Even as late as the summer of 1937 many continued to think the League was the fulfillment of labor party hopes. A headline in the *New Republic* proclaimed, "The CIO as Nucleus of a Third Party." Its "Washington Notes" column continued, "All third party talk in Washington now centers around the probable future course of the CIO and its political counterpart, the Labor's Non-Partisan League."[96]

In New York City the Non-Partisan League chapter actually transformed itself into a third party, the American Labor Party (ALP), so much was the tide running in that direction among local elements, and the banners and posters of the ALP proudly proclaimed, "Affiliated with Labor's Non-Partisan League." Indeed, ACW president Sidney Hillman, who headed the ALP, pointed to it as the direction in which the League was headed and vowed that the League was "not supporting the Democratic Party. . . . After November 3, Labor's Non-Partisan League will remain a permanent organization. In this state it is organizing under a separate emblem as a separate party, known as the American Labor Party."[97]

Many, it seems, sincerely thought the ALP was an effort to form an authentic and permanent labor party. David Dubinsky recalls, "All through the 1936 campaign, unions kept asking whether the party was a one-shot affair or whether it was to be a permanent organization. . . . I felt that it should be permanent, and so did Alex Rose. To our surprise, we discovered that Hillman did not seem very eager. He felt that the ALP had served its purpose of helping to re-elect Roosevelt and should disband. At a meeting in Atlantic City, the ALP state executive committee amazed Hillman by demanding in the strongest terms that the party continue."[98]

Hillman was "amazed" that his colleagues demanded the ALP continue because—public declarations to the contrary—he had always seen the ALP simply as a device for obtaining garment workers' votes for Roosevelt, which he might otherwise lose.[99] Moreover, just as Hillman saw the ALP as merely a means for lining up recalcitrant labor votes for Roosevelt, so, too, did he and the League's top leadership view the League. It was never a genuine move toward the formation of a labor party. Rather, it was the instrument they created to defeat labor party sentiment in the CIO and in the labor movement as a whole and to wed labor to the Democratic Party. This is the view, certainly, of Art Preis, who, in his history of the CIO, points out that "Labor's Non-Partisan League was represented, at the time of its formation, as a broad step in the direction of independent political action. Its main purpose, however, was just the opposite. It was created to be a bridge back from independent political action for hundreds of thousands of unionists who then customarily voted Socialist or Communist—or were clamoring at the time for a Labor Party."[100]

The Socialist Party's leader, Norman Thomas, also believed the League was not the step in the direction of independent political action that its leadership claimed it was. At a Socialist Party picnic in Ashland, Massachusetts, Thomas said, "Labor's Non-Partisan committee for Roosevelt, which in New York has taken the form of a so-called labor party, is not even the valid beginning of a labor party. It is frankly a tail to the Democratic kite."[101] This was also the view of the Labor Party's mayoral candidate, John Connors, in New Bedford. "The League," he said, "was merely a dodge to get around people who wanted a Labor Party."[102]

One could see why many labor party adherents would support the League. The increasing vehemence of right-wing attacks on Roosevelt as the presidential election of November neared led many workers who were dissatisfied with him to have second thoughts. In addition, the very ambiguity of the League's labor party intentions held out hope. The quandary of labor party supporters was highlighted in a *New Republic* editorial entitled "Gulliver Stirs":

> For months there has been agitation from numerous sources for a Farmer-Labor Party in 1936. . . . The existing situation has created a dilemma for them. . . . [T]o step out with a Labor Party in this election would probably, in the presence of the reactionary fight against Mr. Roosevelt, and the rallying of the rank and file of the workers behind him, do little more than introduce an old minority—like the Socialists— under a new name. . . . If it became stronger and actually endangered the victory of the President, or was thought to do so, it would split and embitter the rank and file.
>
> Labor's Non-Partisan League is the answer to the dilemma. It is, by its very name, not Democratic, but labor and nonpartisan. . . . Its slogan, "In 1936, Roosevelt for President," is significant of the intention to keep a free hand for 1938 and 1940. . . . There is nothing in this program to prevent Labor Party activists from pushing their own nominees for Congress, governorships or minor offices wherever they are strong enough to do so. And the more strength they are able to develop in such local elections, the better will be the chance that the national movement can be pushed into Labor Party activity in the future.[103]

The Suppression of the Labor Party Movement

While some continued to view the League as movement in the direction of a possible labor party at some future date, its leadership was acting swiftly to cement the League and, through it, the labor movement, to the Democratic Party. Central to this effort was the work of Sidney Hillman, president of the Amalgamated Clothing Workers. John L. Lewis and Sidney Hillman had announced the formation of Labor's Non-Partisan League on April 2, 1936. On April 19 Hillman convened the fifteen-man general executive board of the ACW for a crucial two-day meeting at a hotel in Atlantic City. The sole purpose of this meeting was to reverse the long-standing labor party sentiment in his own union. To do that, Hillman first had to win over his own resistant executive board. His "Address on Political Policy" is an important statement representing not only a break with ancient tradition for his union but also a signal to the rest of the labor movement. His task was delicate, for, as he acknowledged, "the position of our organization is known: that we are for a labor party . . . what is commonly known as independent political action."[104]

But Hillman argued that the experiences of the last four years pointed away from labor party activity. "We know that the NRA meant the revival of our organization," he said, and the Supreme Court's recent decision declaring the NRA unconstitutional made support for Roosevelt imperative, if only to obtain new legislation along similar lines. Moreover, Hillman warned, under a Republican administration, "it would be silly to discuss organization in steel and the automobile industry. There would be no room for the CIO . . . . You talk labor party. But can you have a labor party without an economic labor movement? . . . I say to you that the defeat of Roosevelt and the introduction of a real Fascist administration such as we will have is going to make the work of building a labor movement impossible." Besides, he suggested, out of the new moves into political action might yet emerge a labor party at a later date: "The more progress the CIO makes, the more the logic of the situation drives [our members] into politics."

Those on the executive board who supported the labor party movement—such as Joseph Salerno, head of the Boston ACW; Jack Kroll of Cincinnati, secretary of the Ohio Farmer-Labor Party State Committee; and Joseph Schlossberg—argued against supporting Roosevelt and the Democrats. Hillman ridiculed Schlossberg by saying, "I listened to Brother Schlossberg. . . . I have not heard him give any reason for opposing the policy proposed here other than that he has been a socialist for the last forty years and will not change now."[105]

Hillman's arguments and determination were persuasive, and he eventually brought the executive board, despite Schlossberg's stubborn resistance, around to his position. This victory was followed by the ACW national convention in Cleveland on May 26, where representatives of FDR and the Democratic Party were welcomed and the executive board, now united behind Hillman, stifled the anticipated resolutions by militant rank-and-file advocates for the endorsement of a national farmer-labor party.[106]

The next step in dampening labor party sentiment occurred just four days later in Chicago. Leaders of the labor party movement nationally met on May 30 to coordinate the myriad local labor party efforts and to lay the groundwork for a national farmer-labor party campaign to begin in September.[107] Rank-and-file representatives from twenty-two states attended, most of them leaders of their local unions. Wilmer Tate and Francis Gerhart, for instance, presidents of the Akron Central Labor Union and the Barberton, Ohio, Central Labor Union, respectively, were in attendance as representatives of the Summit County Farmer-Labor Party, which already had candidates in the field.

There were also celebrities. U.S. Representatives Ernest Lundeen and Vito Marcantonio came to urge the creation of a labor party, as did Earl Browder, head of the Communist Party, and David Lasser, head of the Workers' Alliance of America.[108] John Bosh, president of old Milo Reno's National Farm Holiday Association, was unable to attend, but he sent his greetings, as did Meta Berger, widow of Victor Berger, the renowned Wisconsin Socialist Party leader.

Vito Marcantonio voiced the feelings of many in attendance when he urged the conference to go forward with its plans to call a national convention in September formally to launch a national farmer-labor party. Begin now, he said, "and elect a bloc of at least 50 disciplined Farmer Labor Congressmen." Matthew Campbell, leader of the United Labor Party of Springfield, Massachusetts, which also already had candidates in the field, remained fiercely opposed to cooperation with the Democratic Party and stated that the new party must not include members of other parties. Unless they were totally willing to support the Farmer-Labor platform, he said, it would be useless to ask them to go along.

But also in attendance was a large contingent of erstwhile labor party supporters who had since transferred their loyalties to Roosevelt and the Democrats. The leader of this bloc was a Hillman lieutenant, J. B. S. Hardman, representing the Amalgamated Clothing Workers, which had just defeated its labor party advocates internally at its own convention in Cleveland. Hardman introduced a resolution to table the motion to call a national convention, at which a labor party would be launched, and leave the timing of that decision to a committee representing the conservative wing of the Minnesota Farmer-Labor Party. Hardman's resolution passed, and the Labor Party delegates were sent back to their local parties with the encouragement to "try for the election of state and Congressional candidates" this time around. Meanwhile, the Minnesota committee never called a national convention.

This, however, did not discourage the Akron labor party militants. Tate and Gerhart returned from the Chicago convention determined to carry on in Ohio no matter what happened nationally. On June 6–7, Harry Peterson, Minnesota's Farmer-Labor attorney general, was the keynote speaker at a Fourteenth Congressional District convention of the Summit County Farmer-Labor Party in the Akron armory. "Open warfare was declared on both major political parties," the *Akron Beacon Journal* reported, as the 300 delegates from a hundred Akron labor unions nominated Tate to be their congressional candidate against the incumbent, New Deal Democrat Dow Harter.[109]

At a follow-up convention on July 12, 125 delegates filled out the rest of the party's electoral ticket. Rex Murray, president of the General Tire and Rubber Company local, was named to run for Summit County sheriff. For the Ohio senate, the convention nominated James McCartan, president of the AFL-affiliated Typographical Union; Luther L. Callahan, president of the Goodrich local; Harry Kotesky, a Goodyear worker from the Lakemore (Ohio) Council local; and W. R. Govan of the Firestone local, as well as Mae Probst, president of the Women's Union Buyers' Club. For state representative, the convention nominated Redmond Greer of Kent, a Goodrich worker; William E. Boynton of Ashtabula; C. F. MacLennan of Willoughby; and Fred Wells of the Barberton Workers' Alliance.[110]

On July 19 the movement spread to Kent, a town to the northeast of Akron. There, 250 delegates attended a founding convention at the Kent Central Labor Union hall of the Portage County Farmer-Labor Party, presided over by Howard Stokey, executive vice president of the Portage Central Labor Union. The Kent convention also endorsed Tate for Congress and Redmond Greer for state representative, as well as John Eckelberry, a Kent merchant and police officer, for Portage County sheriff. Greer took the opportunity to announce that the members of the Goodrich local in Akron, of which he was a member, had just voted to affiliate formally with the Farmer-Labor Party. The Goodrich workers had always been represented at party conventions and on the executive committee, but formal endorsement by the rank and file had not previously been voted.[111] Thus, despite what happened to the movement nationally, labor party activists in Kent, Akron, and Barberton were confident of the future.

Then came the AFL's decision on August 5 to expel the ten CIO unions in the mass-production industries—including the Rubber Workers, the Auto Workers, the Textile Workers, the ACW, and the ILGWU—unless they dissolved the CIO. The ten unions refused to do so, and the organized labor movement in the United States was at the crossroads in methods and leadership. This splintering (and labor's resulting "civil war") was a further element of confusion for labor party advocates. To begin with, many labor party supporters happened to be members of unions still in the AFL.[112] Still more dismaying, many of those who, with Lewis, snapped the ties of a lifetime to go forth into the wilderness with the CIO were also organizers of local labor parties and expected Lewis to lead them in that crusade also. Increasingly, however, they were doubtful that Lewis would do so.

This confusion among labor party militants was graphically illustrated at an emergency Labor Party conference held in Washington, D.C., on August 8–9, immediately after the expulsion of the CIO, a meeting attended by Luther Callahan, Wilmer Tate, James McCartan, and Redmond Greer from Akron.[113] The historian who reads the minutes of this meeting is ‗rcome with a sense of what might have been. Frank Gorman, opening the meeting, reassured the labor party activists that he still stood firm on Resolution No. 135, introduced at the 1935 AFL convention. However, he wanted to stress the importance of a thorough discussion of Labor's Non-Partisan League and the labor party movement's relationship with it.

Luther L. Callahan, president of the Goodrich United Rubber Workers' local in Akron, followed Gorman and declared that the rubber workers in Akron were still determined to create an ongoing labor party. "Brother Callahan" then introduced Wilmer Tate. Over ninety organizations in Akron had endorsed their Farmer-Labor Party, said Tate, including forty-two trade unions and three Central Labor Unions. Among the local party's strongest supporters were Akron's 25,000 rubber workers in the CIO, but also affiliated were two farm groups, two clubs, twenty-four fraternal organizations, several unemployed organizations, and two members of the Lakemore Village City Council. They would go on with their independent efforts because, said James McCartan, the labor party movement was but the "political reflex of the CIO."

However, representatives from the Promotional Committee for a Massachusetts Farmer-Labor Party, which included representatives from the ACW and the ILGWU, were not quite so sure of themselves. They planned to have a speaker from Labor's Non-Partisan League, Jacob Minkin of New Bedford, at their next meeting "to talk things over."

The Baltimore delegates reported that they had decided to let the Baltimore Labor Party rest until after the November election. The May 26 convention endorsement of Roosevelt by Hillman's ACW had forced them to halt their efforts, since the Amalgamated Clothing Workers formed a large part of the labor movement in Baltimore.

Brother Hellman, from Philadelphia, reported that a successful Pennsylvania-wide Labor Party conference had been held, but that the "announcement of the formation of a Non-Partisan League about two weeks after the conference created confusion." Similarly, the delegate from Allentown, Pennsylvania, reported that all the "leading members of the Pennsylvania Farmer Labor Party in his District are (also members of) Labor's Non-Partisan League."

Brother Brown, from New York City, called attention to the formation of the American Labor Party by Non-Partisan League representatives there. The independent trade union committee and the "peoples committee" set up to organize a New York City labor party had already voted to dissolve themselves into the American Labor Party.

Brother Anderson, of Chicago's Labor Party, stated that the "Labor Party was based on the trade unions. The Non-Partisan League also has a labor base and therefore we should go along with them." Brother Sherman, from New Haven, then spoke for consensus in observing that he "agrees with cooperation with the Non-Partisan League. Says extent to which we win them over to Labor Party depends on our strength throughout the country." The conference ended by "agreeing that the support of the Non-Partisan League in local Labor Party movements would be sought."

For his part, Gorman attempted to be as cooperative with the Non-Partisan League as he could, and he used his influence in this direction. Typical of his actions was his letter directing all UTW locals in Utica, New York, to cooperate with the New York City–based American Labor Party, which they had been reluctant to do until then:

> The International Union expects its affiliated locals to cooperate in every way possible with this movement, which to us means the formation of a real Labor Party in New York state and in the United States.
>
> I have personally taken an active part in the development of the [American] Labor Party in New York for several months. This organization has already joined with the Non-Partisan League for the election of Roosevelt and Lehman, and the promotion of Labor Party activities wherever possible. You know, of course, that our International Union is on record in favor of the formation of a Labor Party and we propose, at the next convention, to recommend a more active campaign in this regard.[114]

Despite such cooperative overtures, however, the League was not about to support local labor party movements, because they might split the Democratic vote. Instead, it resorted to what one Michigan League official described as "Skull Cracking" to keep recalcitrant laborites in line for the Democrats.[115]

Nor were local League chapters liable to be won over to a labor party, since their strength seemed the greater of the two. Rather, local labor party movements tended to be absorbed into the League—as in New York—or simply remained in direct confrontation with the League—as happened in New Bedford. Jacob Minkin, New Bedford's only labor lawyer, had deserted the Labor Party to become head of the New Bedford chapter of the Non-Partisan League. With him went many Labor Party militants. The New Bedford Labor Party campaign itself, however, continued, determined to honor its commitment to run.

Twilight in Akron and New Bedford

The determined labor party campaigns in both Akron and New Bedford soon ran into trouble. On September 1, three days before the deadline for obtaining ballot status, the Akron party ran into a brick wall when the election commission threw all the party's candidates off the ballot. All the party's candidates, including Portage County Sheriff John Eckelberry of Kent, were listed on the same nomination petitions. Voters signing these petitions thus signed for the entire slate of Portage County and Summit County candidates at once, a practice in accordance with long-accepted tradition in placing the Socialist Party on the ballot locally.

Now, however, the Summit County Board of Elections ruled that Portage County nomination papers could not be filed in Summit County and that because the candidates were all on the same petitions, the voters' signatures could not be assigned to individual candidates. The party's nominating petitions, which bore more than the required number of signatures to get on the ballot, were therefore declared invalid. The party immediately appealed to Ohio's Secretary of State George S. Myers, but he ruled against the party.[116] The party next turned to the American Civil Liberties Union (ACLU) for help, and on September 19 the ACLU filed a suit to reinstate the party on the ballot.

Before that, on September 11, the Akron Central Labor Union took two actions that expressed the divided loyalties of the Akron labor movement in the changed circumstances. On the one hand, it voted to protest the actions of the Board of Elections and the secretary of state and financially to assist the Farmer-Labor Party in its court battle. On the other hand, it also endorsed Roosevelt for reelection and approved the formation of an Akron chapter of the Non-Partisan League.[117] The League would quickly move to fill the local electoral vacuum, since the Farmer-Labor Party's suit ultimately failed, with the Ohio Supreme Court ruling unanimously against the party on October 7. The workers of Akron, Barberton, and Kent thus never got the chance to vote for "independent political action" that November. Instead, they faced only two electoral choices: Democrat or Republican. They went Democratic.

But the labor party champions did not entirely abandon the field. Rather, they shifted to a new arena. On September 14 the national convention of the United Rubber Workers opened in Akron, and the struggle within the URW over endorsement of a national labor party was the most fiercely contested battle of that convention.

The battle began on September 17 when the Resolutions Committee recommended 6–4 against endorsement of a national labor party. Cambridge's Salvatore Camelio, a member of that committee, filed a minority report and introduced a motion to endorse the labor party movement.[118] "If labor is to survive," he declared, "we must fight in the political field as well as the economic field. The time has come when we must take independent political action." His sentiment was echoed by N. H. Eagle, president of the Mohawk local; Floyd Holmes of the Firestone local, who was also secretary of the Akron Farmer-Labor Party; and O. H. Fullen and Fred Harold of the Goodrich local.

The labor party advocates were barraged with a constant stream of complex and lengthy parliamentary objections and points of order. Sherman Dalrymple, the URW president; L. S. Buckmaster, chairman of the Committee on Resolutions; and other powerful URW leaders moved to silence and defeat the labor party forces. The decision hung in the balance over several days of intense debate. On September 21 Dalrymple temporarily relinquished chairmanship of the convention, after having held on to it tightly throughout to stifle labor party speakers, in order personally to oppose a labor party. While this had little impact on the Akron unionists, it may well have influenced the out-of-town delegates. Immediately after Dalrymple finished attacking the Akron unionists, the question was moved. The labor party delegates lost by a vote of 61 to 39.

An analysis of the convention vote is revealing. It shows that the battle lines were mainly drawn between Akron and delegates from the rest of the country, because the labor party vote was centered in the large Akron locals, Goodyear and Goodrich in particular. Akron was for a labor party, but the national leadership and the non-Akron locals were not. Thus, the leadership "had to depend upon the small and non-Akron locals . . . to defeat the larger shop militants. The moderates had gained political control of Akron labor by using non-Akron delegates."[119]

Meanwhile, the campaign of the New Bedford Labor Party for mayor and city council had been officially launched on Labor Day, September 7. This fiftieth annual celebration by the local labor movement was a tri-city affair, with labor groups from Fall River and Taunton participating, although all festivities took place in New Bedford's Lincoln Park.[120] The huge picnic began at noon, with recreation, sports, and dancing until after sunset. The highlight of the day, however, was the official unveiling of the Labor Party candidates. In addition to common council candidates, one aldermanic candidate was put up for each of the city's six wards. These aldermanic candidates included three Lancashiremen, as well as an engineer at the Acushnet Textile Mills, the president of Local 241 of the Paper Cutters' union, and the president of the Flint Glass Workers' union, who was also an executive board member of the International Flint Glass Workers' union.

John Connors, the party's mayoral candidate, an English teacher at the local high school, the president of the Teachers' union, and the vice president of the Central Labor Union, declared to the assembled workers and their families that the Labor Party's primary purpose was to put New Bedford's empty mills and unemployed mill operatives back to work—at which the assembled workers cheered enthusiastically. "When we come into office on January 1," he said, "our Labor Party will use every means at its command to get New Bedford capital, management, and labor together to restore activity to New Bedford's mills. In the event capital and management fail to get together, we promise our idle mills will be taken over by the city and will be operated at cost by the city. . . ."

Next to speak, however, was the self-described conservative Robert Watt, secretary-treasurer of the Massachusetts Federation of Labor and an active opponent of the idea of a labor party. Watt spoke to cool the passions of the excited workers, and his words carried added weight because he was also the on-and-off president of the Massachusetts Federation of Labor. Watt told the workers that they would solve no problems in New Bedford by supporting a labor party because their problems were national in scope. "Local labor parties will be helpful and educational," he said, "but I wish the solution of labor's difficulties were as simple as my good friend John Connors explains it. I am afraid you in New Bedford and Fall

River can't of yourselves and by yourselves solve your own industrial problems. The worker needs and must have national legislation and only the
re-election of Mr. Roosevelt can bring that about. . . ."

The debate between independent politics and Democratic Party politics
also surfaced in the meetings of the New Bedford Central Labor Union, a
hitherto solid bastion of the Labor Party. On September 11, for instance—
the same day the Akron CLU approved the formation of a local League
chapter—two speakers from the Non-Partisan League lectured the CLU
delegates on the necessity of backing Roosevelt and the Democratic Party. Rose Sullivan, a Boston member of the Telephone International Union,
told the New Bedford leaders that, of course, she supported a farmer-labor party for 1940—but it was "the duty of labor" to support Roosevelt
and the Democrats this year.[121]

On September 15, at its national convention in New York City—just
as the URW was meeting in Akron—the United Textile Workers abandoned
the AFL and committed itself to the CIO and industrial unionism. The
move was opposed by Emil Rieve of the Hosiery Workers, a vocal supporter
of labor party activity in Philadelphia, and by New Bedford's William E. G.
Batty, a Labor Party stalwart in that town, indicating the larger riptides
tearing at labor party supporters.[122]

However, a sea change of a different nature had also occurred in the
UTW since the beginning of 1936. As was happening in other unions as a
result of the League campaign, the UTW was moving away from its commitment to independent political action. Despite the vociferous objections
of die-hard dissenters—who argued that the New Deal had failed to carry
out its promised social reforms and that the UTW should continue to back
the labor party movement—the convention endorsed Roosevelt and the
Democrats.[123] This reversal of long-standing policy was a crushing blow
to Labor Party activists in such textile towns as New Bedford.

Within the labor party movement in Massachusetts, the former New
Bedford Labor Party champion Jacob Minkin was now arguing strenuous-
ly that the entire effort should be abandoned in favor of the Democrats and
Roosevelt—at least for now. On September 27 he spoke to the statewide
leaders of the Promotional Committee for a Massachusetts Farmer-Labor
Party meeting in Worcester. All Labor Party forces in the state should back
the League's efforts, he argued. There would be time enough later to revive
the labor party idea because "we propose to keep our organizations as living organisms so that in the future we will be in a position to cement the
various forces into one organization which will not be subservient to the
owning classes and which will express the ideals of the working people."[124]

It was a seductive argument. So, too, was the popularity Roosevelt had begun to elicit from the rank and file in the previously cool textile towns of southern New England as the election neared. On October 20 FDR came to New Bedford. It was estimated that 24,000 workers were waiting patiently at the Common for Roosevelt to arrive. The president spoke to this "sea of faces" for a mere two minutes—and then was gone.[125] It was obvious, however, that developments had cut much ground out from under the New Bedford labor party movement.

Nevertheless, the New Bedford stalwarts persevered. Yes, it seemed Roosevelt would be reelected, they acknowledged. But just *because* of that, said the Reverend Allen Keedy, one of the original eleven on the New Bedford Labor Party Steering Committee, the labor movement ought to break away now before becoming tied to the Democrats by "favors, positions, salaries, etc.," as Sidney Hillman and the Non-Partisan League were in danger of becoming. "Francis J. Gorman is right," Keedy said, "in looking beyond 1936 and its sham battle between two 'class parties' to 1940, when, it is hoped, Labor will have its own Party."[126]

On November 3 Roosevelt carried Massachusetts and swept New Bedford. The municipal elections were still almost a month away, on December 1, but now the Labor Party forces were no longer sure of their support. In addition to the renewed popularity of Roosevelt among the city's textile workers, their campaign also faced a popular local Democrat. In a crowded mayoral field, they were up against the Democratic state representative Leo J. Carney, perhaps the most popular man in New Bedford after FDR, a man whose labor credentials were perceived to be impeccable and who was busy attacking the Labor Party as "Red Hot Reds." Moreover, labor's civil war between the AFL and the CIO had locally divided the once united Labor Party supporters into bitterly rival factions. Additionally, Labor's Non-Partisan League had wooed away many top Labor Party activists, such as Minkin, and had convinced others that the time was not yet ripe for independent political activity. Even the once solidly supportive United Textile Workers union—which counted for everything in New Bedford labor circles—had reversed its stand on the Labor Party and was now supporting the Democrats. Finally, the November 3 vote had showed graphically which way the wind was blowing among the workers as a whole.

Still, they had committed themselves to a campaign, and they intended to follow it through to the end. In this decision, Frank Gorman supported them. On November 29 Gorman, described as the "father" of the New Bedford Labor Party, spoke to a rally of 200 enthusiasts at the Labor Temple. While acknowledging that the newly reelected Roosevelt seemed to be pro-labor, he continued to argue that labor's "hopes and aspirations" would remain unfulfilled by the Democrats: "Labor cannot depend on the Democratic or Republican parties and must have its own party. Under either administration we have found ourselves persecuted in times of strikes. . . . Only a Labor Party based on the labor movement and including the white collar workers, the farmers, and the professional groups can obtain for labor economic and employment security."[127]

At the same time, since the November 3 presidential election the Labor Party municipal campaign had been endorsed by a number of local unions, including local unions of Carders and Spinners, Rayon Workers, Weavers, Loomfixers, Carpenters, Street Car Men, Teachers, Typographical Workers, Bricklayers, Barbers, and Maintenance Men, as well as the Electricians', Teamsters', Chauffeurs', Bartenders', Musicians', and Brewery Workers' unions. Additionally, the Central Labor Union had endorsed the Labor Party campaign since the presidential election. Even without the blessing of the national United Textile Workers, it seemed there was still reason to hope.

Nevertheless, on December 1 John Connors did not even bother to stand at the polls and hand out literature. Instead, he taught a normal day at the high school and went home afterward. When all returns were in, Carney led the six-man field with 11,999 votes, or about 32 percent of the 37,072 votes cast. Connors garnered 3,118 votes, or about 8.4 percent of the total. The Labor Party's best returns were from Ward One and Ward Six, the North End and the South End—the heaviest working-class wards in the city.

However, voting was much heavier in the aldermanic races, and in every ward every one of the party's aldermanic candidates did better than Connors. Again, the best wards were the North End and South End, 4,631 and 4,287 votes, respectively, for the party's candidates, with a total of 24,012 votes for the party's aldermanic candidates in the city's six wards.[128] Nevertheless, the campaign was the Labor Party's last hurrah, both in New Bedford and nationally. The League had won.

Labor party sentiment did not evaporate immediately. Almost two weeks after the November 3 presidential election, for instance, representatives of 30,000 workers met in a Farmer-Labor Party organizing convention in Indianapolis to plan for the next Indiana state elections. Their slogan was "A Clean Sweep in 1938!"[129] Although Heywood Broun, president of the American Newspaper Guild, which had endorsed the formation of a labor party in 1936, felt that the Democratic Party had become America's labor party, his followers did not agree.[130] The Guild again endorsed "independent political action" at its 1937 convention.[131] More important, UAW locals also continued to demand the formation of a labor party, and the 1937 UAW convention again endorsed "independent political action."[132] Meanwhile, over Dubinsky's opposition, rank-and-file delegates to the 1937 ILGWU convention once more ordered their leaders to promote a labor party.[133] By 1938, however, labor party advocates were beginning to realize that the Democratic Party had really won, and the ILGWU and UAW conventions both endorsed the New Deal.

The victorious CIO leadership finally signed the death certificate of Labor Party rivals in their constituent unions at the first official convention of the CIO held in Pittsburgh in 1938. After debating the merits and demerits of a labor party, labor's long-held dream of "independent political action" was officially dismissed. With the exception of New York's American Labor Party, the Pittsburgh convention mandated that all CIO political activity was henceforth to take place within the established political system. Labor's fortunes were now firmly wedded to the Democrats.[134]

The Phenomenon of Historical Amnesia

"Most things out of the past disappear," Sal Luria reminds us, and it is most useful to think of history "not as the complete record of past events, but as the incomplete record of the range of possible events that might have occurred."[135] Thus, an evolutionary process of natural selection consigns most human endeavors to oblivion, for, as William J. Goode points out, "our memories, like history books, mostly retain examples of initial successes, or of failed campaigns that ultimately succeeded, such as trial by jury, manhood suffrage, Impressionist painting, the abolition of slavery, women's suffrage. *But that success is why they are remembered.*"[136]

Perhaps indicative of the decisive nature of labor's shift to the Democrats is the fact that most observers have forgotten that significant elements of the labor movement ever looked elsewhere in the thirties. Nevertheless, one would think the defeat of the long-lived labor party idea in the U.S. labor movement and as a perennial possibility in U.S. politics would still evoke considerable historical interest. Curiously enough, that is not the case. For the most part, this last hurrah of the labor party dream has been overlooked by labor and political historians. When I tracked down John Connors, he told me I was the first person in forty years to ask him anything about the New Bedford Labor Party. The same was true when I interviewed the leaders of the Berlin, New Hampshire, Farmer-Labor Party.

When one reads the entry on Francis J. Gorman in the *Biographical Dictionary of American Labor*,[137] nothing is said of his strenuous labor party agitations. The entry leaps from 1934 (the year of the general textile strike) to 1937 (when he became president of the UTW), as if the intervening years did not exist. Irving Bernstein's masterful history of American labor during the depression, *The Turbulent Years*, discusses the role of Gorman in the 1934 strike and guesses at his reasons for returning to the AFL in 1939, but there is no hint that he did anything of interest in the intervening years. When David Gracy conducted his oral history interview with Gorman for the Southern Labor Archives, he never bothered to ask Gorman about the years immediately following the 1934 strike. As far as the Southern Labor Archives are concerned, those years remain blank.[138]

Indeed, they even remain blank to his own family. I spoke with Frank Gorman's daughter, Jo Harechmak, who has been imbued with the idealism of the labor movement and has served as an official for the Textile Workers Union of America (the AFL union her father headed after 1939), at their international headquarters in Lawrence, Massachusetts. It came as a great surprise to her that her father had ever been involved in any labor party efforts, even though his scrapbooks, in her possession, documented these efforts. Similarly, when I contacted the son of Salvatore Camelio, now a union official in Boston, he knew nothing of his father's labor party activities.

Why is the slate so blank? I offer two possibilities. First, labor historians, especially young labor historians coming out of the New Left, have usually been more interested in developments on the shop floor and in working-class communities. Strikes, for instance, have always been considered an important and serious topic for scholarly research. So, too, have working-class life-styles, due to the "New Social History" thrust of recent historiography. Perhaps, also, because of a latent New Left suspicion of electoral politics, most such historians have discounted labor party manifestations as of only peripheral interest.

A second possibility is suggested by my own experience of watching history's natural selection process in action. I had the opportunity to interview Florence Luscomb, the congressional candidate of the Cambridge People's Labor Party in 1936, and to interact with her many times in social situations.[139] Unfortunately, she could remember little about her involvement with the People's Labor Party of the mid-thirties. One reason for this might have been that I was, again, the first person in forty years to ask her anything about the Cambridge labor party movement.

Her memories of her activities in the woman suffrage movement in the years before 1920 were vivid and detailed, though. I observed her repeatedly being asked, especially by younger women, to recount her adventures while fighting for the vote. Luscomb was an honored local heroine in Boston because of that struggle, and the women's center at Salem State College is named for her. After a while, however, I noticed that Luscomb told the very same stories over and over in unvarying detail. I realized that she remembered these colorful stories because her memory was being constantly refreshed by demands that she recount tales of the successful struggle for the vote.

But her memory was never refreshed about her activities in the labor party movement, which was closer to the present, because no one came around to ask her about it. It is the difference between a victorious movement and a failed one. Women won the vote in 1920, and the women active in that struggle left a legacy of victory to hand down to a grateful and curious population of beneficiaries. The trade union activists of the thirties who attempted to create a labor party lost their struggle. Because of this, there has been no similar population of young and curious beneficiaries to value that struggle, to honor them—to even remember them and question them about the struggle. The memory is lost.

Just as Luscomb no longer told tales of her Labor Party experience, neither did other participants. For example, at the 1935 Atlantic City AFL convention, UAW first vice president Wyndham Mortimer fought side by side with Gorman for the passage of the labor party resolution. Later, at the 1936 South Bend convention of the United Auto Workers, Mortimer's parliamentary expertise was crucial in guaranteeing that labor party militants carried the day. When he discussed that pivotal convention in his autobiography, however, he did not mention the UAW labor party struggle, just as he did not bring up his fight for it at the AFL convention.[140] Like Gorman himself in his interview with David Gracy, he preferred to dwell on other matters. Defeat, it appears, is indeed an orphan.

Herbert Gutman once recounted a story similar to that of Frank Gorman's daughter and Sal Camelio's son about an active trade unionist who attended a seminar he taught in Alabama. Gutman assigned a book on southern labor history that revealed unknown worlds of the past to this labor leader, *his own past.* "This is not a man who had run away from his past," Gutman remembered:

This was a man who had built the labor movement in the South. This was a man who had made sacrifices—of a kind that very few of my friends have made—who knew nothing, *nothing* about the world in which his father and grandparents had lived. Absolutely none of that had been passed on to him. Now that raises a really interesting question about historical consciousness. And I suspect the answer to that question rests in the fact that the collapse of popular collective movements is what causes a washing out of historical consciousness. . . .

In other words . . . the only way in which traditions of popular op-positionality can be sustained is through the maintenance of popular oppositional movements. And when you have no such movements, the traditions disappear. You don't expect to see television docudramas on traditions of oppositionality. . . .[141]

The collapse of the "popular collective movement" for a labor party after "Roosevelt's Revolution" caused a similar washing out of historical consciousness. So complete is the amnesia that neither labor and political historians nor even the children of the militants recall that it ever commanded the imagination, loyalty, and dedicated energy of so many working people for so long. The oblivion has been so total that it is as if it had never been. Not only did labor's future belong to the Democrats, but the Democratic tide even claimed labor's past.

Notes

1. See, for example, Gordon Berg, "The Workingmen's Party—A First in Labor Politics," *Worklife* 1 (March 1976), 23–26. An excellent overview of these early efforts can be found in Alden Whitman, *Labor Parties, 1817–1834* (New York: International Publishers, 1943). See also Nathan Fine, *Labor and Farmer Parties in the United States, 1828–1928* (New York: Rand School, 1928).

2. See, for example, "The Workingmen's Party of California, 1877–1882," *California Historical Quarterly,* no. 55 (1976), 58–71; and Neil Larry Shumsky, *The Evolution of Political Protest and the Workingmen's Party of California* (Columbus: Ohio State University Press, 1991). The rise and fall of the local labor parties of the 1880s can be traced in Leon Fink, *Workingmen's Democracy: The Knights of Labor and American Politics* (Urbana: University of Illinois Press, 1983).

3. Indicative of this ongoing struggle is Samuel Gompers's pamphlet published by the AFL, *Should a Political Labor Party Be Formed?* (Washington, D.C.: AFL, 1918).

4. On farmer-labor party movements of the twenties, see, for example, Hamilton Cravens, "The Emergence of the Farmer-Labor Party in Washington Politics, 1919–1920," *Pacific North West Quarterly* 57 (October 1966), 148–57; Wayne Flynt, "Florida Labor and Political 'Radicalism,' 1919–1920,"

Labor History 9 (Winter 1968), 73–90; Stuart A. Rice, *Farmers and Workers in American Politics* (New York: Columbia University Press, 1924); Hayes Robbins, *The Labor Movement and the Farmer* (New York: Harcourt Brace, 1922); Stanley Shapiro, "'Hand and Brain': The Farmer-Labor Party of 1920," *Labor History* 26 (Summer 1985), 405–22; and Murray S. Stedman and Susan W. Stedman, *Discontent at the Polls: A Study of Farmer and Labor Parties, 1827–1948* (New York: Columbia University Press, 1950). An interesting article dealing with the Non-Partisan League is William C. Pratt, "Socialism on the Northern Plains, 1900–1924," *South Dakota History* 18 (Spring/Summer 1988), 1–35.

For an overview of the educational efforts, see Susan I. Wong, "Workers' Education, 1921–1951" (Ph.D. diss., Columbia University, 1976). See also Peter E. Van DeWater, "The Workers' Education Service," *Michigan History* 60 (Spring 1976), 99–113; and Richard Dwyer, "Workers' Education, Labor Education, Labor Studies: An Historical Delineation," *Review of Educational Research* 47 (Winter 1977), 179–207. The Bryn Mawr Summer School for Women Workers, which lasted from 1921 to 1938, was another successful labor college. During its existence 1,700 working-class women were recruited from blue-collar jobs for an intensive two-month program in left-wing trade unionism. See Lucille A. Maddalena, "The Goals of the Bryn Mawr Summer School for Women Workers as Established during Its First Five Years" (Ph.D. diss., Rutgers University, 1979). A fine film on this school is *The Women of Summer*, written, produced, and directed by Suzanne Bauman and distributed by Filmakers Library.

In 1923 the philosopher Will Durant, later famous for *The Story of Philosophy*, was the director of New York's Labor Temple School. Meanwhile, Bertram D. Wolfe directed the Workers School in New York City, which was militantly class-conscious and supportive of a labor party. See its announcement of classes for 1926–27, *Training for the Class Struggle* (New York: Workers School, 1926).

An interesting labor college of the time was Commonwealth College. See William H. Cobb, "From Utopian Isolation to Radical Activism: Commonwealth College, 1925–1935," *Arkansas Historical Quarterly* 32 (Summer 1973), 132–47. On Brookwood Labor College, see Richard Altenbaugh, "Forming the Structure of a New Society within the Shell of the Old: A Study of Three Labor Colleges and Their Contributions to the Labor Movement" (Ph.D. diss., University of Pittsburgh, 1980); Charles F. Howlett, "Brookwood Labor College and Work Commitment to Social Reform," *Mid-America* 61 (January 1979), 47–66; Charles F. Howlett, "Brookwood Labor College: Voice of Support for Black Workers," *Negro History Bulletin* 45 (April–June 1982), 38–39; and James W. Robinson, "The Expulsion of Brookwood Labor College from the Workers' Education Bureau," *Labour History* (Canberra, Australia) 15 (January 1968), 64–69.

The story of Brookwood's decline and fall is told by Jonathan D. Bloom, "Brookwood Labor College: The Final Years, 1933–1937," *Labor's Heritage* 2 (April 1990), 24–43, which is a sequel to his "Brookwood Labor College, 1921–1933: Training Ground for Union Organizers" (M.A. thesis, Rutgers University, 1978). From Bloom's account I gleaned the answer to a puzzling question: Why should Brookwood, the most successful of the labor colleges, collapse in 1937 at the height of labor's insurgency? The answer, I realized, was Brookwood's continued advocacy of a labor party, while the unions providing its major financial support—principally Sidney Hillman's Amalgamated Clothing Workers and David Dubinsky's International Ladies Garment Workers Union—abandoned their long-held support of a labor party in favor of Roosevelt and the Democrats. When these unions pulled the financial plug on Brookwood, it was unable to go on, despite a last desperate attempt to form an alliance with the United Auto Workers, where labor party sentiment remained high. Roy Reuther, brother of Walter and Victor and, like them, a labor party champion, was a Brookwood faculty member during these final years and was seen as a link to the UAW. Bloom does not make these labor party connections, but much becomes clear once they are made.

5. Because Robert La Follette's Progressive Party and the Minnesota Farmer-Labor Party originated in earlier insurgent movements, I do not focus on them in this essay on the 1930s. However, I do recommend two studies on the Minnesota Farmer-Labor Party. The first is Millard L. Gieske, *Minnesota Farmer-Laborism: The Third-Party Alternative* (Minneapolis: University of Minnesota Press, 1979). The other, more provocative in its argument for the viability of localized radical political movements, is Richard M. Valelly, *Radicalism in the States: The Minnesota Farmer-Labor Party and the American Political Economy* (Chicago: University of Chicago Press, 1989).

6. See, for example, Karel Denis Bicha, "Liberalism Frustrated: The League for Independent Political Action, 1928–1933," *Mid-America* 47 (January 1966), 19–28; and Richard J. Brown, "John Dewey and the League for Independent Political Action," *Social Studies* 59 (April 1968), 156–61.

7. For a history of one such local labor party, which dominated the city of Berlin, New Hampshire, from 1934 to 1943, see Eric Leif Davin and Staughton Lynd, "Picket Line and Ballot Box: The Forgotten Legacy of the Local Labor Party Movement, 1932–1936," *Radical History Review* 22 (Winter 1979–80), 43–63. See also David J. Pivar, "The Hosiery Workers and the Philadelphia Third Party Impulse, 1929–1935," *Labor History* 5 (Winter 1964), 18–28. For a study of the United Rubber Workers' efforts to create a labor party, see Richard W. Shrake II, "Working-Class Politics in Akron, Ohio, 1936: The United Rubber Workers and the Failure of the Farmer-Labor Party" (M.A. thesis, University of Akron, 1974). Daniel Nelson treats the United Rubber Workers' labor party efforts superficially in "The CIO at Bay: Labor

Militancy and Politics in Akron, 1936–1938," *Journal of American History* 71 (December 1984), 565–86.

Hugh Lovin has done much work on efforts to form labor or farmer-labor parties in the Midwest and Pacific Northwest during this period. His work includes "The Fall of the Farmer-Labor Parties, 1936–1938," *Pacific North West Quarterly* 62 (January 1971), 16–26; "Toward a Farmer-Labor Party in Oregon, 1933–1938," *Oregon Historical Quarterly* 76 (June 1975), 135–51; "The Persistence of Third Party Dreams in the American Labor Movement, 1930–1938," *Mid-America* 58 (October 1976), 141–57; "The Ohio Farmer-Labor Movement in the 1930s," *Ohio History* 87 (Autumn 1978), 419–37; "The Farmer-Labor Movement in Idaho, 1933–1938," *Journal of the West* 18 (April 1979), 21–29; "The Automobile Workers Union and the Fight for Labor Parties in the 1930s," *Indiana Magazine of History* 77 (1981), 123–49; and "CIO Innovators, Labor Party Ideologues, and Organized Labor's Muddles in the 1937 Detroit Elections," *Old Northwest* 8 (Fall 1982), 223–43.

For a contemporary and fairly comprehensive survey of labor party efforts nationwide, see Harry W. Laidler, "Toward a Farmer-Labor Party," *Industrial Democracy* 11 (February 1938), 3–55.

An additional argument for a labor party and a survey of contemporary efforts to build it may be found in a booklet by a Brookwood Labor College instructor, Joel Seidman, *A Labor Party for America?* (Detroit: Education Department, United Automobile Workers of America, 1937); and the book by the Brookwood instructors Katherine H. Pollak and David J. Saposs, *How Should Labor Vote?* (Katonah, N.Y.: Brookwood Labor College Publications, 1932). Many local labor parties considered the latter an organizational blueprint at the time.

See also Paul H. Douglas, *The Coming of a New Party* (New York: McGraw-Hill, 1932); and Morris Hillquit and Matthew Woll, *Should the American Workers Form a Political Party of Their Own?* (New York: Rand School, 1932). This is a debate on the subject between Hillquit and Woll, with Hillquit (of the Socialist Party) in favor of the idea and Woll representing traditional AFL opposition to it.

8. *Pittsburgh Post-Gazette*, June 27, 1985.

9. *New York Times*, April 29, 1985.

10. Author's notes on Williams's speech at a labor/academic luncheon, Pittsburgh, September 19, 1986.

11. David Brody has argued that the "last hurrah" of the *farmer*-labor party idea was in the 1920s. After that decade the farm element in U.S. society declined too much to make the alliance a viable political possibility. The U.S. Population Census for 1920 supports this thesis. The United States officially ceased to be a rural nation as of 1920, when the urban population of 54 million for the first time exceeded the rural population of 51 million by 51 per-

cent to 49 percent. See David Brody, "On the Failure of United States Radical Politics: A Farmer-Labor Analysis," *Industrial Relations* 22 (Spring 1983), 141–63. This, however, does not conflict with my own argument concerning the *labor* party idea.

12. See his classic description of this trend in chapter 3, "The Revolt of the City," in Samuel Lubell, *The Future of American Politics,* 2d ed. (Garden City, N.Y.: Doubleday, 1961). One can even argue that the trend began earlier than 1928. In the 1924 presidential election, for example, the Progressive Robert M. La Follette garnered 36 percent of the vote in Republican-dominated Pittsburgh running on a local "Socialist-Labor" ticket. Most of his vote was concentrated in heavily immigrant wards.

13. Lubell, *American Politics,* 29.

14. Of the ten largest U.S. cities in 1930 (New York, Chicago, Philadelphia, Detroit, Los Angeles, Cleveland, St. Louis, Baltimore, Boston, and Pittsburgh), only St. Louis and Baltimore had majority native white populations, and that by only 3.4 percent and 3.1 percent, respectively. See Bruce M. Stave, *The New Deal and the Last Hurrah: Pittsburgh Machine Politics* (Pittsburgh: University of Pittsburgh Press, 1970), table 5 on 41.

15. Lubell, *American Politics,* 32.

16. See the useful discussion of this, as well as other possibilities, in Eric Foner, "Why Is There No Socialism in the United States?" *History Workshop* 17 (Spring 1984), 57–80.

17. Richard Oestreicher, "Urban Working-Class Political Behavior and Theories of American Electoral Politics, 1870–1940," *Journal of American History* 74 (March 1988), 1264, 1283.

18. The WASPs continued to vote Republican in the same numbers they always had. For example, in Pittsburgh, 95.3 percent of the voters in 1930 were Republican, while only 4.7 percent were Democrats. In 1936 Republican registration dropped to 43.9 percent, while Democratic registration climbed to 56.1 percent. Numerically, however, the Republican vote was as high as ever. There was, then, no conversion of Republican hearts and minds. Rather, the political universe had been transformed by a tremendous expansion of the electorate—all in favor of the Democrats. See Stave, *The New Deal and the Last Hurrah,* 181.

19. This can be seen graphically in a city like Pittsburgh. In looking at the Democratic Party ward chairmen and committeemen in 1934, we find that *all* were of European origin, with Irish and Germans predominating. Stave, *The New Deal and the Last Hurrah,* table 23 on 180.

20. While I argue that the struggle for the urban working-class vote reached its climax in the 1930s, the roots of the conflict go back to the 1920s and even before World War I. To illustrate, Robert M. La Follette won 36 percent of the Pittsburgh vote in 1924 running on a "Socialist-Labor" ticket. The wards that supported La Follette were the same immigrant, working-class wards

voting for the Socialist Eugene V. Debs in 1912 and the Democrat Franklin D. Roosevelt in 1932. At the same time, John W. Davis, the 1924 Democratic presidential candidate, garnered only 8 percent of the Pittsburgh vote, and it came from wards "poles apart" from the wards that supported Debs, La Follette, and later Roosevelt.

Thus, one sees not only the emergence of an urban electorate made up of the "foreign, lower economic classes" but also the shift of this electorate's loyalty from a progressive "Socialist-Laborite" orientation to a Democratic orientation. Stave, *The New Deal and the Last Hurrah*, 36, 37. How was the Debs–La Follette vote won and held for Roosevelt? This, in a nutshell, is the phenomenon I am exploring.

21. Bert Cochran, *Labor and Communism: The Conflict That Shaped American Unions* (Princeton, N.J.: Princeton University Press, 1977), 107.

22. *Gallup Poll*, 1:104, in George Gallup and Claude Robinson, "American Institute of Public Opinion—Surveys, 1935–1938," *Public Opinion Quarterly* 2 (July 1938), 373–98. See also Donald R. McCoy, "The National Progressives of America, 1938," *Mississippi Valley Historical Review* 44 (June 1957), 76.

23. C. Wright Mills and Helen S. Dinerman, "Leaders of the Unions," in *The House of Labor: Internal Operations of American Unions*, ed. J. B. S. Hardman and Maurice F. Neufeld (New York: Prentice-Hall, 1951), table 24 on 41, 42.

24. See Staughton Lynd, "A Chapter from History: The United Labor Party (of Akron, Ohio), 1946–1952," *Liberation* 18 (December 1973), 38–45.

25. Davin and Lynd, "Picket Line and Ballot Box."

26. See, for instance, the extensive discussion of these obstacles in Oestreicher, "Urban Working-Class Political Behavior."

27. This process in an earlier period can be seen in Lynn, Massachusetts, as Alan Dawley points out: "A certain sequence of events that occurred first in 1860 recurred with uncanny similarity in 1878 and again in 1890. . . . Each time there were three steps in the sequence: (1) a strike occurred, (2) bringing out the police, (3) causing the strikers to mount a political campaign to unseat the incumbent officials and dismiss the police chief." Alan Dawley, *Class and Community: The Industrial Revolution in Lynn* (Cambridge, Mass.: Harvard University Press, 1976), 226.

Such sentiment still exists. When miners went on strike in the winter of 1977–78, the Democratic governor of Kentucky, Julian Carroll, ordered in the state police to protect shipments of scab coal. In protest, the striking miners picketed the Kentucky state capitol. Among the signs they carried was one asking, "Democratic Party—Friend of Labor?" Lois Scott, a prominent militant in the 1973–74 Harlan County strike and a member of the Cumberland UMWA Women's Organization, was quoted as saying, "We've always heard that the Democratic Party was the friend of labor, but from Governor Carroll's tactics he's proven that he's anything but a friend of labor. He's proved to us that he's a friend of the coal operators." The Women's Club president, Goldie Currie, added, "Unless we get together and form our own party, a labor party, well, that's about the only hope that's left for us poor people." *Workers Vanguard,* February 17, 1978.

This same process of strike radicalization leading to labor party sentiment manifested itself among Mexican-American miners and their wives in the Arizona copper mine strike of 1983. The Democratic governor, Bruce Babbitt, crushed the thirteen-month strike in the Ajo-Clifton-Morenci-Bisbee mining towns by ordering in 400 state troopers, armored personnel carriers, and seven units of the Arizona National Guard to protect strike replacements. "Babbitt is with Phelps-Dodge," said Carmina Garcia, one of the women on the picket line. "He owns property, he's in with the banks and the property owners." Rather than vote Democratic again, said another picket, Janie Ramon, they wanted to see a genuine independent labor party. Barbara Kingsolver, *Holding the Line: Women in the Great Arizona Mine Strike of 1983* (Ithaca, N.Y.: ILR Press, 1989), 185.

28. See Lillian Symes and Traverse Clement, *Rebel America: The Story of Social Revolt in the United States* (1934; reprint, Boston: Beacon, 1972), 374; David Shannon, *The Socialist Party of America* (New York: Macmillan, 1955), 221–22; and W. A. Swanberg, *Norman Thomas: The Last Idealist* (New York: Scribners, 1976), 144–45. The Socialist Upton Sinclair's End Poverty in California (EPIC) campaign for governor of California in 1934 on the Democratic Party ticket was an illustration of the dynamics at work within the Socialist Party.

29. Alfred Baker Lewis, "The Socialist Party's Opportunity," *St. Louis Labor,* March 15, 1924.

30. *Cambridge Chronicle,* March 18, 1932.

31. Pivar, "Hosiery Workers"; Davin and Lynd, "Picket Line and Ballot Box."

32. This, at least, is where Otis Hood first heard about the new pro–labor party policy. Hood was head of the Communist Party in Massachusetts and the party's gubernatorial candidate in 1936. He confirmed, however, that the Massachusetts Communist Party did very little to implement the new party line and did not actively take part in the Massachusetts labor party movement then in progress. Interview with Otis Hood, who died in November 1983.

The Central Committee of the Communist Party advocated the creation of a labor party in "On the Main and Immediate Tasks of the C.P.U.S.A.," *Communist* 14 (February 1935), 123–26. But this orientation lasted little more than a year. After the formation of Labor's Non-Partisan League in April 1936, the Communist Party supported it and the Non-Partisan League's adherence to the Democratic Party. See Earl Browder, "The American Communist Party," in *As We Saw The Thirties: Essays on Social and Political Movements of a*

Decade, ed. Rita James Simon (Urbana: University of Illinois Press, 1967), 233, 237; and George Charney, *A Long Journey* (Chicago: Quadrangle, 1968), 75.

33. Georgi Dimitrov, "The Fascist Offensive and the Tasks of the International," in *Abridged Stenographic Report of the Seventh World Congress of the Communist International* (Moscow: n.p., 1939), 151.

34. Federated Press dispatch, August 20, 1935, Special Collections, Columbia University. Within a year, the United Labor Party would submerge itself in the American Labor Party, which was seen as a vehicle for supporting Roosevelt for reelection in 1936.

35. Federated Press dispatch, December 2, 1935.

36. Ibid., August 5, 1935. See also A. J. Muste, "My Experience in Labor and Radical Struggles," in *As We Saw the Thirties,* ed. Simon, 134, 139.

37. See *Radical America* 6 (November–December 1972), a special issue on workers' struggles in the 1930s; Jeremy Brecher, *Strike!* (San Francisco: Straight Arrow Books, 1972), chap. 5; and Irving Bernstein, *Turbulent Years: A History of the American Worker, 1933–1941* (Boston: Houghton Mifflin, 1970).

38. Robert R. Brooks, "The United Textile Workers of America" (Ph.D. diss., Yale University, 1935), 379.

39. Quoted in Brecher, *Strike!* 173.

40. Herbert Gutman, "Herbert Gutman on American Labor History: An Interview with Mimi Rosenberg," *Socialism and Democracy* 6 (Spring/Summer 1990), 60.

41. Letter "To All Local Unions in Massachusetts," in possession of the author. The nine union leaders who signed the letter included John D. Connors, vice president of the New Bedford Central Labor Union and the New Bedford Labor Party's mayoral candidate in 1936.

42. *Cambridge Chronicle,* September 3, 1936.

43. Party program issued by the founding convention of the Labor Party of Chicago and Cook County, August 25, 1935, photocopy in the possession of the author, original in the Florence Luscomb Papers, Schlesinger Library, Radcliffe College.

44. Except where otherwise noted, information in the following paragraphs is drawn from Federated Press dispatches.

45. Undated Federated Press dispatch found in Frank Gorman's scrapbooks belonging to his daughter, Jo Harechmak, on file at the international headquarters of the Textile Workers Union of America (TWUA) in Lawrence, Massachusetts.

46. Joseph Sylvia's speeches and associated events are recorded in unattributed newspaper clippings I discovered in Frank Gorman's scrapbooks.

47. *New York Times,* December 4, 1935.

48. Speeches of Francis J. Gorman, Draft #4, 8, President's Office file, P. R. Christopher Papers, United Textile Workers of America Records, Labor Management Documentation Center, Cornell University, Ithaca, New York.

49. Bruce Minton and John Stuart, *Men Who Lead Labor* (New York: Modern Age Books, 1937), 244.

50. Francis J. Gorman, "Needed: An American Labor Party," *Modern Monthly 9* (March 1936), 460–61.

51. Rose Pesotta, *Bread upon the Waters* (1944; reprint, Ithaca, N.Y.: ILR Press, 1987), 172.

52. Federated Press dispatches for October 1935.

53. The information in the remainder of this paragraph is drawn from Frank Gorman, *A Labor Party for the United States* (New York: Social Economic Foundation, 1936). The booklet includes the text of Resolution No. 135, texts of speeches prepared for the 1935 AFL convention by Gorman and Isidore Nagler of the ILGWU, the platform of the Labor Party of Chicago and Cook County, a sketch of labor party agitation at the convention, and a survey of labor party activity around the country as of May 1936. A copy is in the Rare Book Room of the Bancroft Library at the University of California, Berkeley.

54. Quoted in J. B. S. Hardman, "Is a New Party Possible?" *Common Sense,* May 11, 1933, 3.

55. *New York Times,* October 8, 1935.

56. Gorman's speech is reproduced in *Report of Proceedings of the Fifty-Fifth Annual Convention of the American Federation of Labor* (Washington, D.C.: AFL, 1935), 762–73 (quote on 772). The convention debate on political policy is in ibid., 758–76. Several of the thirteen labor party resolutions were introduced by UAW locals. One such resolution attacked the Democratic and Republican parties because they forced labor to "fight not only the employer, but the police, national guard, courts, and all other agencies of a supposed impartial government." Ibid., 239–40.

57. Pesotta, *Bread upon the Waters,* 180, 181–82.

58. Labor Research Association, *Labor Fact Book III* (New York: International Publishers, 1936), 99.

59. Ibid., 153.

60. *Progressive,* October 12, 1935, 23; January 11, 1936, 46.

61. *Farmer-Labor Challenge* (Detroit), April 1936.

62. For Hamtramck, see Peter Friedlander, *The Emergence of a UAW Local, 1936–1939: A Study of Class and Culture* (Pittsburgh: University of Pittsburgh Press, 1975), 14; for Port Huron and Dearborn, see Arthur E. Suffern, "Brewing a Labor Party," *Current History 47* (September 1936), 37; and for Detroit, see *Farmer-Labor Challenge,* April 1936.

63. *Charlotte Observer,* January 6, 1936.

64. Unidentified newspaper clipping dated February 28, 1936, Gorman scrapbooks.

65. Francis J. Gorman, "Artists and Trade Unions," in *Artists against War and Fascism: Papers of the First American Artists' Congress,* ed. Matthew

Baigell and Julia Williams (New Brunswick: Rutgers University Press, 1986), 22, 95–97.

66. Editorial, "Labor and Politics," *Washington Post,* May 7, 1936.

67. *New York Times,* May 25, 1936.

68. *Roanoke Labor Journal,* May 28, 1936.

69. *New York Herald Tribune,* July 4, 1936.

70. The information in this and the following paragraph comes from the *Railroad Unity News,* March 1936, thought to have been published in South Dakota, Gorman scrapbooks.

71. *Akron Beacon Journal,* April 30, 1936.

72. *New Bedford Standard Times,* April 18, 1936. Many trade union graduates of Brookwood returned to their local unions and communities across the country to proselytize for the creation of local labor parties. Typical in this regard is the story in the *Brookwood Review,* October 1934, about official and vigilante harassment of a Brookwood graduate agitating for a local labor party in Hillsboro, Illinois.

73. *New Bedford Standard Times,* January 25, 1936.

74. Labor Research Association, *Labor Fact Book III,* 153.

75. *Akron Beacon Journal,* September 17, 1936.

76. Ibid., September 21, 1936.

77. Quoted in Ruth McKenny, *Industrial Valley* (1939; reprint, Ithaca, N.Y.: ILR Press, 1992), 334.

78. *Akron Beacon Journal,* April 6, 1936.

79. Ibid., April 24 and 27, 1936.

80. Ibid., May 4, 1936.

81. Ibid. The ACW executive board had voted on April 19, 1936, to abandon the idea of a labor party. Evidently, Schlossberg was not reconciled to that decision.

82. *Labor News* (Worcester, Mass.), May 8, 1936.

83. *New Bedford Standard Times,* August 7 (Novo quote) and 8 (Salerno quote), 1936. Despite the convention's decision to endorse Democratic candidates for national and state office, the statewide bodies of the United Textile Workers, United Rubber Workers, Amalgamated Clothing Workers, International Ladies Garment Workers, Papermakers, and others organized the Promotional Committee for a Labor Party, which endorsed the three local campaigns in New Bedford, Springfield, and Cambridge.

84. David Dubinsky and A. H. Raskin, *David Dubinsky: A Life with Labor* (New York: Simon and Schuster, 1977), 262.

85. The following is an incomplete list of delegates to the 1935 AFL convention who voted for the minority report of the Resolutions Committee calling for industrial unionism and were also labor party advocates: Francis Gorman and William F. Kelley of the UTW; Joseph Schlossberg of the ACW; Isidore Nagler of the ILGWU; Emil Rieve of the Philadelphia Hosiery Workers;

Wyndham Mortimer of the UAW; William Kuehnel of the Hartford CLU; Francis Gerhart of the Barberton, Ohio, Match Workers; A. Philip Randolph of the Pullman Porters; N. H. Eagle of the Akron Rubber Workers; and Paul Rasmussen of the Milwaukee Workers' Alliance.

86. Friedlander, *Emergence of a UAW Local,* 91 (emphasis added).

87. Cochran, *Labor and Communism,* 365n.7; Art Preis, *Labor's Giant Step: Twenty Years of the CIO* (New York: Pioneer Publishers, 1964; New York: Pathfinder Press, 1972), 52; Walter Reuther to Roy and Victor Reuther, April 22 and May 2, 1936, reprinted in Kevin Boyle, "Building the Vanguard: Walter Reuther and Radical Politics in 1936," *Labor History* 30 (Summer 1989), 433–48; Sidney Fine, *The Automobile under the Blue Eagle: Labor, Management, and the Automobile Manufacturing Code* (Ann Arbor: University of Michigan Press, 1963), 425–26; Irving Howe and B. J. Widick, *The UAW and Walter Reuther* (New York: Random House, 1949), 52–53; *United Automobile Worker,* May 1936. Germer was the founder of the Michigan branch of the Non-Partisan League and was also active in dampening labor party activity in the United Rubber Workers, where he ran the union's newspaper, *Rubber Worker.*

88. *News-Week,* August 15, 1936, 9; *United Automobile Worker,* May and September 1936; *Tribune* (South Bend, Ind.), May 1, 1936.

89. *Progressive,* July 25, 1936, 53–55.

90. "Proceedings: Organizing Convention of the St. Joseph County Farmer-Labor Party," mimeograph, July 11–12, 1936, Adolph Germer Papers, State Historical Society of Wisconsin, Madison; *Union News Service* (CIO), September 28, 1936; *United Automobile Worker,* July 7, 1936.

91. Thomas Kennedy, lieutenant governor of Pennsylvania and UMW secretary-treasurer, to John L. Lewis and Philip Murray, January 10, 1936, John Brophy Papers, Library, Catholic University of America, Washington, D.C. In western Pennsylvania's massive Cambria County coal fields, UMW locals had already launched their own local Labor Party. Delegate credentials for one of their conventions are in the author's possession. Labor party agitation was also strong in the UMW locals of the Kenawah Valley, West Virginia.

92. Dubinsky and Raskin, *David Dubinsky,* 262, 265.

93. Samuel Lubell recounted a telling anecdote about Dubinsky from the 1936 campaign. Dubinsky was given a limousine and a police escort to attend a campaign rally for Roosevelt in New Jersey. En route, he reminisced about the days when he had supported the Socialist Meyer London for Congress and had slept for three nights with his wrist strapped to the ballot box so Tammany leaders would not throw the box into the river. "Sinking back into the luxuriously plushed seat, Dubinsky sighed, 'I wonder whether I would do all that over again?' Figuratively that could be asked of the whole labor movement— and merely to raise the question is to suggest the answer. Every Presidential election spurs talk of organization of a labor party. But the simple truth is that,

having enjoyed the confidences of Presidents and ridden behind motorcycle escorts, the nation's labor leaders are not going back to the old soapbox days." Lubell, *American Politics*, 196–97.

94. *New York Times*, April 12, 1936.

95. Paul Ward, "Washington Weekly," *Nation*, April 15, 1936, 10.

96. "Washington Notes," *New Republic*, June 17, 1937, 7.

97. Quoted in Mathew Josephson, *Sidney Hillman: Statesman of Labor* (New York: Doubleday, 1952), 399–400.

98. Dubinsky and Raskin, *David Dubinsky*, 268.

99. In fact, Roosevelt did obtain 300,000 votes for president in New York on the ALP ticket, helping him carry that state.

100. Preis, *Labor's Giant Step*, 47.

101. *New Bedford Standard Times*, August 10, 1936.

102. John Connors, interview with author, October 29, 1977.

103. "Gulliver Stirs," *New Republic*, April 15, 1936, 4.

104. Sidney Hillman, "Address on Political Policy," General Executive Board Meeting, April 19, 1936, Amalgamated Clothing and Textile Workers Union Archives, Labor Management Documentation Center, Cornell University.

105. Hillman comment in *Documentary History of the Amalgamated Clothing Workers of America, 1934–1936* (New York: Amalgamated Clothing Workers, 1936), 402.

106. *Akron Beacon Journal*, May 27, 1936.

107. This crucial meeting is reported in the *Akron Beacon Journal*, June 1, 1936. All quotes from the meeting are from this source.

108. The Workers' Alliance, formed in 1935 by a merger of all Communist- and Socialist-led Unemployed Councils around the nation, endorsed the formation of a labor party in 1936. Its members were often associated with local labor party efforts, as in the case of Fred Wells of the Barberton Workers' Alliance, who was a Farmer-Labor Party candidate for state representative. Alliance members were crucial to the launching of the New Jersey Labor Party.

After the suppression of the labor party movement in 1936, the Workers' Alliance fell back to a dual endorsement of the Communist and Socialist candidates for president. It continued to be bitterly opposed to FDR and his policies right through the 1936 election. On the eve of the election WPA units organized by the Workers' Alliance conducted "folded arms" strikes across the nation, and Lasser himself was arrested leading a protest at the White House.

The one substantial account of the Workers' Alliance is flawed by dealing only with the period after 1937. Frances Fox Piven and Richard A. Cloward, *Poor People's Movements: Why They Succeed, How They Fail* (New York: Vintage Books, 1977), chap. 2. No institutional archives of the Workers' Alliance exist; however, we may be able to learn more about the attitude of the Workers' Alliance regarding the labor party movement when the Federal Bu-

reau of Investigation releases its large, 10,000 document file on the organization. The FBI was ordered to release largely uncensored copies of its WAA file
on August 1, 1995, by the U.S. Court of Appeals for the Third Circuit in *Eric
Davin v. Dept. of Justice, Federal Bureau of Investigation.*

109. *Akron Beacon Journal,* June 6 and 8, 1936.

110. Ibid., July 13, 1936.

111. Ibid., July 20, 1936.

112. In Akron, for instance, Wilmer Tate and James McCartan were leaders of AFL craft unions, but their main support for their labor party activities
came from CIO rubber workers. In New Bedford, William E. G. Batty, vice
president of the Loomfixers, was a leading labor party militant who elected
to stay with the AFL and eventually became president of the Massachusetts
Federation of Labor. Similarly, John Connors, the mayoral candidate, stayed
with the AFL and later established, and for the rest of his life directed, the AFL
Labor Education Bureau at the Federation's headquarters in Washington, D.C.
However, Salvatore Camelio, leader of the Cambridge People's Labor Party,
went with the CIO—and later became Batty's rival as president of the Massachusetts CIO. This splintering of labor party forces into rival labor factions
was duplicated elsewhere.

113. The following account is drawn from the minutes of the Labor Party
Conference held on August 8 and 9, 1936, at the New Colonial Hotel in
Washington, D.C. The author obtained a copy of these minutes from Philip
Glasson, secretary of the Berlin (New Hampshire) Farmer-Labor Party.

114. Gorman letter to all Utica UTW locals, August 20, 1936, American
Labor Party file, Amalgamated Clothing and Textile Workers Union Archives,
Cornell University.

115. Frank Martel to Labor's Non-Partisan League chairman George L.
Berry, December 14, 1936, Open Series 1, Wayne County [Michigan] AFL-
CIO Papers, Archives of Labor and Urban Affairs, Wayne State University,
Detroit.

116. *Akron Beacon Journal,* September 1, 3, 5, and 9, 1936.

117. Ibid., September 11, 1936.

118. Unless otherwise noted, the account of the convention battle comes
from ibid., September 21, 1936.

119. Shrake, "Working-Class Politics in Akron," 100. See figure 1 for a
breakdown of the vote on the labor party question, which verifies his analysis.

120. This account of the Labor Day events is drawn from the *New Bedford Standard Times,* September 8, 1936.

121. Ibid., September 12, 1936.

122. For Emil Rieve's active role at this time in the Philadelphia labor party movement, see Pivar, "Hosiery Workers."

123. *New Bedford Standard Times,* September 16, 1936.

124. Ibid., September 28, 1936.

125. Ibid., October 21, 1936.

126. Letter to the Editor, *New Bedford Standard Times,* October 25, 1936.

127. *New Bedford Standard Times,* November 30, 1936.

128. Arthur Harriman, the Labor Party's highest vote getter for the common council in Ward Six, would later be elected mayor of New Bedford—although as a Democrat.

129. *New Bedford Standard Times,* November 15, 1936.

130. See "Meeting of State Committee Delegates, Labor's NonPartisan League," August 10, 1936, Labor's Non-Partisan League Papers, State Historical Society of Wisconsin, Madison. After Roosevelt's 1936 victory, many top CIO leaders felt that the Democratic Party had become America's "Labor Party." From the vantage point of these CIO leaders, the labor party idea had won. See "Notes on CIO Meeting," November 7–8, 1936, John Brophy Papers.

131. *New York Times,* June 11, 1937.

132. *Detroit Free Press,* March 24, 1937; meeting minutes, Detroit District Council of the United Auto Workers, June 26, 1937, John Zaremba Papers, Labor History Archives, Wayne State University.

133. ILGWU, *Report and Record: Twenty-Third Convention, International Ladies' Garment Workers Union* (Atlantic City, N.J.: ILGWU, 1937), 219, 319–23.

134. Congress of Industrial Organizations, *Proceedings of the First Constitutional Convention of the Congress of Industrial Organizations* (Pittsburgh: CIO, 1938), 230–31.

135. S. E. Luria, *Life: The Unfinished Experiment* (New York: Charles Scribner's Sons, 1973), 9, 10.

136. William J. Goode, *The Celebration of Heroes: Prestige as a Social Control System* (Berkeley: University of California Press, 1978), 233 (emphasis added).

137. Gary M. Fink, ed., *Biographical Dictionary of American Labor* (Westport, Conn.: Greenwood, 1984), 259–61.

138. See Frank Gorman's papers at the Southern Labor Archives, Georgia State University, Atlanta. They include the brief and disappointing transcript of the interview with Gorman conducted by David B. Gracy II on August 8, 1973. Gorman was then ninety-six years old. He died two years later, on June 4, 1975.

139. Florence Luscomb died October 27, 1985, at the age of ninety-eight.

140. Wyndham Mortimer, *Organize! My Life as a Union Man* (Boston: Beacon, 1971), 99–100.

141. Gutman, "Herbert Gutman on American Labor History," 65, 66.

6

Paths of Unionization

Community, Bureaucracy, and Gender in the
Minneapolis Labor Movement of the 1930s

Elizabeth Faue

When Mary Heaton Vorse wrote *Labor's New Millions* in 1938, she was both witness to and advocate of a new unionism that did "not stop at the formal lodge meeting. It [saw] the union as a way of life which [involved] the entire community."[1] Central to this community-based labor movement was the participation of women as both workers and wives. Yet, in the decades that followed, the union movement of which Vorse was an eloquent spokeswoman had disappeared from the scene. Community unionism had been replaced by a vast array of institutions, bureaucrats, and rules that seemed to obscure and suppress, rather than illuminate and express, grass-roots militancy and leadership. Even as it precipitated a decline in the autonomy of local unions, the shift toward a more bureaucratic, workplace-oriented unionism reinforced women's marginality in the labor movement. Labor unions that benefited from the tremendous growth in local activism and in the central involvement of women now reasserted familiar claims of gender and authority.

From the origin of working-class politics in popular protest to the emergence of contemporary bureaucratic unions, workers have chosen the terrain of struggle on which to build a labor movement. They have shifted emphasis toward and away from the community; they have incorporated state strategies and excluded them; they have striven to focus energies in the narrow terrain of craft identity and to broaden them to include all members of the productive class. The roles of women and men have also varied in these configurations of labor. At times workers' definition of labor solidarity required women's inclusion on an equal basis with men, both as workers and as the wives of workers; at other times solidarity was seen as incompatible with gender and ethnic competition.

The relationship between gender and unionism took new forms in the 1930s. In the community-based, grass-roots labor militancy that prevailed through 1937, both men and women played major roles. Further, the labor movement embraced an egalitarian rhetoric that was gender-neutral in its implications. Despite the masculinist tone of press, poster, and prose within the labor movement, it was understood that women as well as men were vital to the movement's survival. By the late 1930s the base of the labor movement had shifted from the community to the workplace. Concomitant with this shift was the marginalization of women within labor unions.[2]

The Minneapolis labor movement of the 1930s provides a case study of these changes. Characterized by a communal vision, local labor activists linked the struggles of truckers, garment workers, ironworkers, and the unemployed in community-level tactics that unified workers across craft and industrial lines. Both women and men were involved in mobilizing workers through union, political, and auxiliary organizations. A central characteristic of these campaigns was the activism and leadership of women in local-level struggles—an activism that did not, however, percolate to the national level.

With the advent of a more bureaucratic unionism, the level and quality of worker participation in the labor movement changed dramatically. As conflict and competition intensified between the AFL and the CIO, unions centralized authority and rigorously repressed factionalism and dissent at the local level. Attempts to create alternative union structures were perceived as threats to the norms of union governance. While men were brought into the union bureaucracy through new channels of promotion, the role of women workers in local union leadership declined, much as it had at the national level. As the decade of the 1930s drew to a close, women's auxiliaries and community organizations waned in importance and in numbers, and grass-roots activists lost the battle for a democratic labor movement.

As a process that marginalized women and finally excluded them from union leadership, bureaucratization was not gender-neutral. The ways in which an organization or a social movement rationalizes procedures, creates and enforces rules, and makes legitimate channels of authority and communication build on societal assumptions about manhood and womanhood. In evaluating both men and women by ostensibly gender-neutral but in fact deeply gendered and male standards of leadership and achievement, bureaucratic labor unions helped to re-create and reinforce gender inequalities in their organizational structures.[3]

Union Bureaucracy and Gender

The emergence of large-scale union bureaucracies in the twentieth century has been the subject of much historical debate.[4] These studies outline the underlying process of co-optation, legitimacy, and consent that created unprecedented power for the labor movement. At issue is the relationship between two very different forms of organizing, one diffuse and stretching beyond the boundaries of the workplace, the other centralized and exclusionary. While fixing organizational forms at its center, however, the literature has been impoverished by the failure to examine gender ideology and the roles and relations of men and women. Centralized bureaucracy and community organizing differ not just in their focus but in the way they are gendered. How the structure of power within the labor movement became gendered and how this process reflected and transformed gender roles are crucial to our understanding of the ways in which labor unions became bureaucratic structures.

The community-based unionism that emerged in the 1930s drew on the configurations of gender and class embedded in local solidarities; it embraced familial and fraternal sanctions of activism for both men and women and legitimated struggle that was expressive of and rooted in the claims of community. It proceeded to unionize workers by recruiting through local networks and institutions and through the culture of solidarity that develops during protest.[5] Championing the brotherly solidarity of men, it gave new and collective meaning to formerly individual violence, aggression, and struggle that in that context defined manhood for the working class. Celebrating a political role for women, it built on their social activism in both neighborhood and workplace. Women had a clear, aggressive role that was legitimized in the context of community and family.

In these ways a community-based labor movement reshaped the role of labor leader and downplayed the importance of ethnic, skill, and gender differences. On a structural level marginalized workers, women in particular, were less disadvantaged in the community arena, where formal rules were kept to a minimum. In the garment unions, for example, women were militant shop-floor leaders and officers at the local level.[6] In the Hotel and Restaurant Employees' union women were disproportionately represented on committees and among officers at the national level. Their national strength was rooted in their visible activism on local and state culinary boards.[7] Finally, through cultural activities, even more than in formal organizational campaigns, unions reconciled labor militancy with femaleness and sisterhood even as they remained expressive of brotherly solidarity.[8]

The development of bureaucratic organization in the labor movement required that leaders control the political skill, information, and means of communication necessary to consolidate power and stabilize the organization.[9] The routinized process of union democracy made the same assumptions as political democracy: that one have a knowledge of the rules, be skilled at coalition building at both local and national levels, possess the ideal characteristics of a leader, and be relatively unconstrained in participation in public life. Unequal levels of education, skills, and resources among men and women restricted women's access to leadership, and contradictory demands of work and family limited their participation.

Further, labor bureaucracies, as the formal voices of tradition in the labor movement, both reflected and constructed gendered expectations of leadership. A labor leader was expected to demonstrate the manly attributes required to confront employers and to exhibit brotherly camaraderie with fellow workers.[10] These characteristics demonstrate the cultural encoding of any political behavior. As one organizing handbook had it, the goal of any union was to win the workers over and to defeat the employer. "The term 'strike' means to hit," the pamphlet explained, and violent struggle was a legitimate way for men to effect change.[11] Thus, in acting militantly and sometimes violently to achieve collective goals, men were not acting improperly. But because violence was proscribed for women in the constricted public sphere of bureaucracy, women's militancy could not be sanctioned.

Moreover, in situations in which the women workers were young, inexperienced in unionism, or reticent, unions posited a male leader as a necessary antidote. In a union's published example of a meeting based on Robert's Rules of Order, the serious, older, and experienced male union leader sets straight the enthusiastic but misguided and often cranky women members.[12] In the garment trades the tension was palpable between men, who dominated positions of skill and leadership, and the "young, pretty, inexperienced girls," who were "NRA babies" in the union movement. "The problem of raising the new locals is as difficult as raising children," wrote Meyer Perlstein, a regional director for the International Ladies Garment Workers Union (ILGWU). Workers, especially women, needed to be "nursed carefully." They suffered from "infantile disorders," such as gossip and jealousy. Perlstein and other union officials agreed that women workers needed to break their individualistic habits. Only if they were "whipped into shape" could they become "trained and loyal members of our great family, the ILGWU."[13]

The ILGWU went to great pains to explain how women could be brought into the union and how the union hall could provide an atmosphere more conducive to women's participation, but it recognized the resentment of men toward the "damned skirts" who dared to "invade the sacred halls of masculinity." Bringing women into the union should not mean that men would be "forced to submit to an atmosphere of rose-tinted femininity." Though a woman organizer for the union "might help to overcome the girls' reluctance to join or to go on the picket line," a "personable man in a predominantly feminine group adds a certain piquancy to the situation."[14]

Within the bureaucratic unionism of the 1930s, activism for men and women was re-formed. Democratic processes defined new and appropriate routines of action, solidarity, and dissent. Taken out of the context of community, women's activism was delegitimized at the same time that normative rules of order and due process translated men's activism and rerouted male aggressive behavior into bureaucratic struggles for dominance. Bureaucratization redefined the very meaning of the political and the public. No longer were the boundaries between workplace and community permeable; the private domain of community existed separate and apart from the public domain of the union. Disagreement and dissent thus took on the aura of private and illegitimate disputes. As the bearers of the private, women were perceived as the most troublesome of unionists, workers who could not understand the rules of collective action and who severely undermined the capacity of leaders to lead.[15]

Organizing the Garment Trade

The ILGWU was one voice of community-based unionism in Minneapolis during the 1930s. Garment workers were the largest group of unorganized women industrial workers in Minneapolis. The labor force of nearly 5,000 was over 75 percent female. Women held a disproportionate number of unskilled and semiskilled jobs, as they did in such industries nationally. Although men held skilled and supervisory positions, women predominated in the skilled positions of cutter and presser regionally.[16] As in other areas, the garment industry was subject to seasonal and fluctuating employment, a situation intensified by the economic crisis. These factors undermined attempts at organization during most of the early twentieth century. From the shop campaigns of the ILGWU to the strike origins of the Hosiery Workers' union and the orchestrated negotiations of the Textile Workers' union, unionization proceeded along various paths to bureaucratization.

Before the 1930s only sporadic attempts had been made to organize the regional garment industry. Labor activists tried to establish unions in garment and textile plants during World War I, and there were a number of short-lived strikes in the 1920s. Labor leaders came to little agreement, if any, on how to organize this vital sector. The United Garment Workers (UGW) unionized shops in workingmen's clothing through union label campaigns, but the effort went no further. As jurisdictional disputes obstructed unionization, garment unions competed with one another for members.

While economic crisis framed the lives of women in the garment industry, the passage of the National Industrial Recovery Act (NIRA) provided the first opportunity to change the conditions of women's work in the trade. Under the legal sanctions of section 7a, workers began to organize in the small but growing cotton and silk dress industry. Despite the ambiguity of its provisions, the NIRA became a powerful tool in the hands of labor organizers. They sought out women who would be willing to testify that their shops violated the NRA's code minimums for wages and hours. Code enforcement soon took the central place in the circulars and pamphlets of organizing campaigns.[17]

In the dress shops of St. Paul women reacted to the new opportunity. Groups of shop workers banded together and asked the state labor federation for aid in unionizing the industry. They wrote to David Dubinsky, head of the newly burgeoning ILGWU, requesting an organizer and admission to the union.[18] In the fall of 1934 Dubinsky hired Sander Genis of the Amalgamated Clothing Workers to organize part-time in the difficult Minneapolis shops. Genis had firsthand experience organizing in the open-shop city of Minneapolis. An immigrant from Russia, Genis worked in the coat trade in St. Paul before World War I and organized the first local of the Amalgamated Clothing Workers in the area. From that time on, Genis devoted himself to union work. His leadership in the 1929 strike of garment workers proved his familiarity with the terrain of antiunion employers, deferential workers, and a hostile police force.[19]

Genis set out to "preach the gospel of unity and unionism" to the garment workers of Minneapolis. He hired Myrtle Harris, an experienced organizer, to assist him in the shops. As "a good loyal union person," Harris had been shop steward and financial secretary of UGW Local 7 for ten years. Her involvement in organizing for the Central Labor Union led to work in the truckers' auxiliary and to the ILGWU job.[20]

From their base in St. Paul dress shops, ILGWU members worked to organize their coworkers in Minneapolis, with Harris and Genis leading the effort. Harris stood outside dress shops when they opened for work in the morning and again when the women left for home. She contacted other women workers by making calls and visiting them in their homes.[21] While Genis worked the office end, Harris and other women who volunteered were responsible for face-to-face contact, the routine process of recruiting workers on the shop floor and in the community. Acutely aware of the obstacles facing the union drive, especially the threat of employer retaliation, they worked to subvert employer sabotage and build worker confidence.

Development of social and educational programs was essential to community organization. The ILGWU's initial drives in Minneapolis involved organization of dress shops with as few as twenty-five workers. Because of the small size of garment shops and their ability to flee union constraints by relocating, along with employers' paternalism and the isolation and poverty of garment workers, the union's success was uneven. Less than a year after workers organized the first locals, the Twin City Joint Board hired an educational director. Aided by the Minneapolis Labor School, the ILGWU organized classes in parliamentary law, public speaking, labor history, and labor journalism. Later, a dance troupe, glee club, and dramatics program developed.[22]

The ILGWU educational program was designed to develop skills in a broad base of the membership. Giving workers knowledge of their history, communication skills, and familiarity with union procedure was one way to overcome the split between organizer and organized. The enrollment figures are sketchy, ranging from 30 to 100 students per term, but impressionistic evidence suggests that women were the target audience. The union was over 75 percent female, and news reports listed women who attended the classes. Rarely if ever are men depicted. Similarly the curriculum between 1935 and 1938 was ostensibly gender-neutral, but in seeking to give members skills in public speaking, parliamentary procedure, and organizing techniques, it laid the basis for a broader distribution of leadership and activism, especially on gender grounds. Many women workers lacked skill in speaking and debate, and union classes such as these enabled them to participate.[23]

The attempt to wed education with organization in the ILGWU was expressed by Betty Hoff, a teacher in the labor school: "The union is more than just an organization to protect your job and working conditions. Your union provides an educational and recreational life." In the first few years the Twin City Joint Board also published the *Twin City Guardian,* a newsletter that first appeared in 1937. The members felt strongly that the *Guardian* ought to "express the opinions and conditions prevailing in [their] own industry before anything else." Union newsletters, workers' theater, and programs that expressed the value of unionism for workers both individually and collectively were vital to the success of the community-building efforts of the local ILGWU.[24]

The Gendering of Craft Unionism

The Strutwear strike of 1935–36 dramatically illustrates the permeability of the boundaries between shop floor and community in the 1930s. For many workers and activities the Strutwear campaign represented a coming of age for the Minneapolis labor movement. As in the truckers' strike of 1934, the forces of community were both vital and visible in the struggle.[25] The culture of solidarity created by the strike promoted interunion cooperation, the coalition of political and workplace organizations, and the support of community and social activists. In this context the community of union workers struggled with the legacy of narrow trade unionism and its privileging of men craftworkers over women and young men on the production line. It organized the unorganized.

When workers at the Strutwear hosiery plant walked out in August 1935, they challenged one of the most viciously antiunion firms in the city. They were ill prepared for the exigencies of a strike. Supported by the American Federation of Hosiery Workers, the union of knitters had organized only skilled male workers in the industry. The majority of the plant labor force—580 women workers engaged in seaming, looping, mating, and mending socks—were not members of the local; neither were the nearly 100 "boys" who worked as toppers on the production line.[26]

Strutwear had been active since World War I in antiunion activities. In 1927 the firm locked out a small union of knitters, and in the aftermath of the strike it forced workers to sign a yellow-dog contract. Under the NRA, Strutwear established a company union to undermine organizing efforts at the plant. Peter Fagerhaugh, a union leader, recalled, "100 men in my department were told to come down stairs for a meeting. We were told to form a union." If the men did not cooperate, they were forced to leave the firm.[27] The firm enrolled only skilled workers in the union. Like the hosiery union they sought to combat, Strutwear officials thought membership in their union should be restricted to men knitters and should not include the production workers.

In the summer of 1935 a group of knitters visited a unionized plant in Milwaukee. On their return, they held a series of mass meetings among their coworkers, where they advertised the higher pay and better working conditions of the union plant. Three-fourths of the 200 male knitters joined the new union, Local 38 of the American Federation of Full Fashioned Hosiery Workers (AFFFHW). But after a dispute over union recognition, managers dismissed eight workers for union activity. The leaders called a strike.[28]

Few workers crossed the picket line the first day. Most amazing, production workers refused to report for work. The knitters who called the strike had made no provision for the participation of the operatives, but their recruitment was essential to the success of the strike. In the earlier strike failure to recruit them had caused the union's defeat, as it had in the Robitshek-Schneider garment strike in 1933.[29] A profile of Strutwear workers showed a labor force divided largely along gender and skill lines, with only the intermediary job category of topper open to both men and women. Moreover, skill lines masked inequality among workers. Knitters started at a wage nearly double that of production-line workers; and while even an experienced woman on the line could get only a few dollars above the NRA code minimum, knitters on average earned twice as much as women and boys training as toppers. Also, the company had a practice of hiring learners below the code minimum (for $6 to $8 a week) and firing them at the end of training.[30]

A strike that began with the grievances of skilled workers eventually had to address the poor pay and working conditions of operatives, both men and women. After the shop committee called the strike, union organizers began to contact them; most operatives knew about the strike from coworkers or public rumor. On the day of the strike the divisions in the labor force seemed to make little difference. Production workers held the line; and knowing that they needed the support of all departments, union leaders urged them to attend union meetings after the strike began and actively sought their participation.[31]

The union went beyond the shop door, into the neighborhoods where workers lived. When the company tried to open the plant on the fourth day, 3,000 workers and union supporters formed a massive picket line. Police clubbed several strikers, driving them from the pavement. Afterward picketers followed the fifty knitters who stayed with the company from the factory to a department store, where the police escort hoped to lose the company workers in the crowd. Pickets confronted disloyal male workers in the aisles of the store; some followed them home. Women who had returned to work, in contrast, were only approached in the store and asked to come to the union meeting.[32]

The labor protests at Strutwear built on layers of meaning in the working-class community. As the funerals of workers had become massive demonstrations of commitment, unity, and mourning, so too did protests that mirrored other rites of passage, of death and rebirth. A funeral for the company union became one such ritual. On the fifth day of the strike union leaders organized a large picket line. At midday hundreds of workers from the plant and the community formed a funeral procession for the company union. They circled the plant with the casket several times and finally held funeral rites in a vacant lot across the street. Evoking the ties among family, community, and workplace, they buried the old union and made way for the new.[33]

Over the eight months of the strike the labor community in Minneapolis supported the Strutwear workers. Unionists organized dances for strike relief, staffed a strike commissary, and donated to the strike fund. In the course of the strike workers at the plant were joined by members of a broad range of labor and political organizations. Emphasizing labor unity, organizations of the unemployed, the Hotel and Restaurant Workers, and the Amalgamated Clothing Workers came to walk the picket line, and at one time nearly a thousand workers could be called upon to support the strike. The Women's League against the High Cost of Living organized a boycott of Strutwear goods, and the Farm Holiday Association sent in truckloads of food from rural communities for the strikers.[34]

The success of the prolonged strike marked a turning point for women workers at the plant. Craft unionism, a strategy that marginalized and excluded both men and women operatives and sanctioned the poor conditions of their labor, was at least temporarily in retreat. In April 1936 Strutwear agreed to most of the strikers' demands, and the strike was won. The eight-month protest had created an opportunity for the union to enlarge and broaden its scope. At the conclusion of the strike, membership had grown to more than 700, including nearly 500 women. The Hosiery Workers' union now rushed to recruit women. By the end of the following year, Strutwear workers signed for a closed shop. New contracts brought both higher wages and hope for greater occupational mobility within the plant.[35]

For many women who sought an active role in the union movement, neither union membership nor its benefits were sufficient to meet all of their needs. Their solution was to form auxiliaries, organizations that directed the

efforts of working women and workers' wives. As the history of the Minneapolis truckers' auxiliary and the Flint Women's Emergency Brigade demonstrates, women's role in strikes proved to be crucial.[36] These organizations
continued to play a political role in the labor movement by serving as a base
of social support and an arena of activism for women workers.

Women workers at Strutwear organized a hosiery workers' auxiliary in
May 1938. At an AFFFHW convention Wanda Pilot, the only woman organizer of the federation, suggested auxiliaries as arenas for women's activism. Sixteen women delegates had intended to form their own division of
the union; but because the constitution did not permit a separate organization, they formed an auxiliary. Membership was open to union members and
to the wives and daughters of members. Though it focused on social events,
it expanded to organize classes in labor history and economics.[37]

The coming of the union to Strutwear had reshaped not only the relation of women to unionism in the plant but also the relation of unionism
to workers generally. James Tibbetts, chair of the Strutwear shop committee, understood that men in the Strutwear union, as a minority of the labor force, feared that women were going to take over the union. Competition between men and women over jobs could soon follow. Tibbetts
argued that "in shops like ours where the majority of members are wom-
en, men are always fearful that the women will try to take control of the
union. This fear is not justified. . . . Women are usually willing to fill the
role that nature put them in, that of being the supposedly weaker sex."
The auxiliary could make a necessary and important contribution to the
union. Recent studies of the auto industry, he claimed, showed that "a
woman on the picket line is worth two men." But in effect, Tibbetts still
envisioned the auxiliary's role as supporting the union: "When shops are
organized and picket lines seem a remote dream, [ladies' auxiliaries] have
a different part to play. Their job is to spread the gospel of unionism into
channels that otherwise wouldn't be penetrated." By support, the shop
chair meant union consumerism and social organization. Finally, Tibbetts
argued that auxiliaries could help women, who lacked a collective spirit
and who traditionally were not good union members, to learn unionism.[38]
The mutuality of the women who had supported a narrowly conceived craft
union strike in 1935 had been forgotten.

Both the auxiliary and the women members of the Strutwear union
helped to create a vital union culture. They organized diamondball and
bowling teams in almost every department. They planned social events—
dances, annual picnics, Christmas parties—to bring the members togeth-

er and raise funds for the local. The union newspaper, *Strutwear Worker,* enabled union members to keep track of union events and meetings, reported the events of workers' lives from marriages and births to deaths and promotions, and included articles on political events and labor history.[39] Both men and women unionists increasingly saw the community's needs for information and education as within the purview of unions.

The Decline of Community-Based Unionism

The high tide of community-based unionism in Minneapolis was reached during the Strutwear strike. Cooperation of the local labor establishment with national unions, political groups, and community activists underscored the importance of local activism for defeating the open shop and organizing the unorganized. In 1937, however, as rivalry between the AFL and the CIO heightened, national unions increasingly began to intervene in the affairs of locals. The recession that year made organizing workers difficult. The National Labor Relations Board's prohibition of sympathy strikes and secondary boycotts defused local union solidarity by denying legitimacy, and jurisdictional battles between unions further undermined the cooperation that was the basis of community unionism.[40]

The consequences for unions—and for their men and women members— were severe. Rank-and-file members of all unions were increasingly isolated from decision making. In the garment and textile unions, where the conflict between men and women members and leaders traditionally had been strong, women lost the fragile gains of the early 1930s. Sexual inequality in labor leadership reasserted itself as national networks, dominated by men with ties to the union movement, replaced local gender-integrated ones at the local level.[41] General Drivers' Local 574, the union that led the drive to make Minneapolis a union town, was increasingly besieged with directives and interference from the international Teamsters' union. With these losses, the promise of an egalitarian, broad-based union movement faded.[42]

In its initial campaigns in the Twin Cities the ILGWU leadership remained largely local, relying on the skills of union veterans from the Twin Cities. By 1936, when the national union began to establish its control over the regional market, the ILGWU replaced Genis with two temporary organizers. These appointments were symbolic of changes in ILGWU policies by which the national office asserted control over local officers.[43]

In the spring of 1936 Loretta DuFour and members of the ILGWU were organizing workers at Boulevard Frocks, the fifth-largest cotton dress shop in the United States, employing from 400 to 600 workers. Originally organizers tried to use NRA code violations as an organizing tactic. Boulevard managers, however, won a vote of confidence from the workers by claiming that they voluntarily accepted the code minimum. With the abolition of the National Recovery Administration in 1935, organizers urged workers to turn to the union to protect recent wage gains and improvements in conditions. Only through collective bargaining could workers "retain in this industry the privileges and security established by the NRA."[44]

Despite slow progress at Boulevard, Sander Genis felt that the groundwork had been laid for a generous contract with the firm. At the same time, Genis slowly withdrew from ILGWU activities and concentrated on his own union, the Amalgamated Clothing Workers. Conflicts with the ILGWU at both local and national levels were at the root of his choice. As a man familiar with the local circumstances and supported by the membership, Genis repeatedly asserted the primacy of community concerns. Cooperation was necessary to unionize the industry in the Twin Cities; expelling unemployed workers would only weaken the local union. In most cases he was overruled by the national office. At one point Genis responded angrily to requests for regular dues payments to the international; work in the cities was scarce, and many members were unemployed. Infighting between the ILGWU and the Amalgamated Clothing Workers was yet another cause for discontent.[45]

The business agents who followed Genis were more attuned to the needs of the national office. The first of these agents, George Glass, told Dubinsky that he had found "a very poor dues-paying institute" in the Twin Cities and that he hoped to set it right. Contract negotiations were similarly mishandled. Glass infuriated the ILGWU organizers by agreeing to a clause making machine operators responsible for the mistakes made by the pressers, unjustly penalizing women workers to the advantage of a group of better-paid men. Resentment began to build. As Genis later reported, "A few mistakes like these and all the good girls will leave the union." Another organizer replaced Glass only months later. He and Genis continued negotiations with Boulevard Frocks to finalize the agreement. The union asked for terms that the ILGWU regional director, Meyer Perlstein, thought unrealistic. Eventually Perlstein took over the contract negotiations himself, convinced that Boulevard Frocks could become "a model union shop in the cotton dress industry naturally if properly handled." He gave no credit to local organizers, nor did he pay attention to local discontent with three successive business agents. Rather, the signing of the union contract, which brought few benefits to the workers at Boulevard Frocks, was portrayed as a victory for the union's efficient bureaucracy.[46]

Genis angrily predicted that the contract would make trouble for the local labor movement, and it did arouse the resentment of workers and local labor organizers. Given the recent Strutwear victory, the agreement was perceived as weak not just by garment workers but by the local labor establishment. The Boulevard Frocks contract and the personal enmity between Perlstein and Genis were recurring themes in union campaigns. They also opened the door for the ILGWU and the Amalgamated Clothing Workers to raid each other. With the understanding that at least the leader would be placed in the union, union officers at a cloak factory tried to swing the workers to the ILGWU. Disloyalty prompted their dismissal. At the same time, Genis was accused of targeting some shops, including the large Munsingwear company, in an effort to keep them away from Perlstein's union. Serious criticisms of the Boulevard agreement led the truckers' union, now known as General Drivers' Local 544, to try to organize those workers who were left out of the contract.[47] Members whose wives worked at the Boulevard factory provided entrée for organizers; the wives' own lack of loyalty to the ILGWU underlined the local resentment toward the international's interference.

While unionists fought for the joint board's autonomy by rejecting one organizer, the New York office intervened by appointing Michael Finkelstein at the end of 1936, but not without complaint; local ILGWU members wanted one of their own appointed.[48] The appointment coincided with other problems at the local level. Continued economic crisis, culminating in the recession of 1937, kept alive fears of unemployment, making union recruitment difficult. Reaction to the new business agent was tainted by resentment over concessions to the crisis and the weak contracts that resulted.[49]

Changes in local union leadership came at the same time the Twin City Joint Board was gearing up for an organizing drive at Munsingwear. Munsingwear, a major hosiery and undergarments firm, was one of the largest employers in Minneapolis, with nearly 2,000 workers. Despite the early depression of the textile and garment industries, the company began to rehire substantial numbers of workers in 1932, and it seems to have made profits during most of the depression years.[50]

Like Strutwear Knitting, Munsingwear had a long history of company paternalism and antiunion activity. Munsingwear officers were prominent members of the Citizens' Alliance, the local employers' association, and they had played a role in the Strutwear strike by agreeing to subcontract some work for the company. To fight unions within the company, it established a company union with the NRA. Further, its management played a key role in the regional labor board of the NRA, where some of its officers were able to circumvent independent actions by the company union.[51]

Munsingwear had long been a target of the ILGWU local leaders. After signing Boulevard Frocks in 1936, they began to make contacts with workers at Munsingwear. In November 1936 Underwear and Lingerie Workers Local 65 of the ILGWU received a charter. Sam Schatz was appointed special organizer. Many women were also involved in the Munsingwear drive, including the educational director, Leah Schneider. By March 1937 officers had been elected, and 30 people had signed up, with the promise of more. At the ILGWU convention that year, 200 members were reported.[52]

On the strength of membership growth, Meyer Perlstein sent a letter to the Munsingwear management stating that the "time is ripe for a collective bargaining agreement. Our union is eager to avoid any interruption of production and cessation of work."[53] Despite Perlstein's optimism, the ILGWU campaign was not successful. It simply could not attract enough members to call for an election. After nine months of organizing, union members had managed to sign only a small fraction of a 1,200-member labor force.

At this time Munsingwear management began negotiating with the Textile Workers Organizing Committee (TWOC-CIO). In two mass meetings the workers voted to sign with the Textile Workers' union and to approve a contract that appears to have gained some wage increases and union recognition for Munsingwear workers.[54] The effort was headed by the new local CIO committee, including the regional director, Sander Genis. He played a central role in persuading workers to join the Textile Workers' Local 66, CIO. The company had been negotiating with TWOC in Chicago, and its reception of union overtures may have encouraged the workers.

Distrust of the ILGWU also played a hand in the organization. A local labor unity meeting demonstrated that memories of the Boulevard Frocks contract remained intact. Despite the ILGWU's advocacy of direct appeal to the workers, "without the help of firm, foreladies, or shop facilities," and the creation of a militant membership, they did not convince the Munsingwear workers. With the signing of the contract, the Munsingwear Employees' Association dissolved, and the ILGWU members were forced to resign from their union (or, it was alleged, from the company).[55]

The failure of the ILGWU to organize Munsingwear was rooted in trends toward a more corporate, industrial unionism that stabilized the labor force and provided a higher standard of living for semiskilled workers. At the same time, the Munsingwear campaign demonstrated the choices workers had between the two models of unionism in the 1930s—the ILGWU, dominated now by nationally appointed officers, and the new CIO union, whose claims were stronger and more immediate because of the participation of a familiar community organizer. Though the company union had been outwardly controlled by management, Munsingwear workers trusted its union officers enough to sign with the CIO.

After the failure of organizing at Munsingwear, there was a noticeable change in the local ILGWU. The business agent and regional director increasingly set the priorities of the union, first and foremost by controlling union meetings. Issues raised in the midst of organizational drives had more to do with employers' demands for wage concessions than with improving working conditions.[56] The nationally appointed director and business agent were concerned largely with contract supervision and industrywide cooperation with management. The needs of the workers as women, as union members, and as workers were downplayed in the struggle to maintain a regional garment industry against national competition. In effect, the national union advised the women to accommodate the employer and proved intolerant of individual dissent. While many workers still experienced some improvement in hours and wages in union shops, the union became a required part of the job, a prerequisite for employment, not a refuge from the demands of management. Moreover, decisions to strike or stay in the shops were directed by the board, the business agent, and the regional director. Complaints against the nationally appointed business agent were dismissed as the work of troublemakers.[57]

At a time when women were the front line for union solidarity, labor education offered not public speaking and labor history but courses in nursing and nutrition. Overall, the ILGWU's educational program backed away from concerns about building community among workers and union democracy into a more instrumental form of union education. Union classes increasingly focused on the training of union officials and time-and-motion study. Taking three classes in union procedure was now a requirement for new union members. In this brief orientation, between thirty and sixty workers were to be introduced to the ILGWU's structure and procedure and its history. These classes promised to turn "card carrying workers into real union members," but they were a poor substitute for the ear-

lier full-term classes in parliamentary law, labor history, and public speaking. More important, the educational program put new emphasis on training union officers, not members.[58]

Classes on time-and-motion study, piecework, and industrial engineering were set up in conjunction with local employers. While these programs
were not gender-specific in their design, they were taught chiefly by men
with the object of reinforcing the role of the specialist, officer, and expert
in labor relations. In one instance the foreladies, class instructors, and
production managers who met as a committee to set prices on piecework
were joined by students in the industrial problems and time-and-motion
study classes. With the goal of "developing methods of improving relations
and eliminating shortcomings that affect earnings and interfere with shop
efficiency," students were expected to cooperate and even emulate industrial engineers. Workers such as Stefannia Petra, a dressmaker, were chosen to supervise time-and-motion study in their own factories and were
sent off to various cities for training.[59] Because women were disadvantaged
in that realm, their training did not bring workers such as Petra into the
national leadership. Finally, during the war, both ILGWU and Minneapolis Labor School classes increasingly incorporated domestic courses into
their curriculum.

By the end of the decade national initiatives had restructured the ILGWU
local joint board. The cutters' local, which had been predominantly female
from its inception, now had men as officers, and these officers participated in the leadership of the joint board. It became, in effect, the men's local. The number of men in the leadership was disproportionate to their
membership generally. Though the staff of the ILGWU local board remained largely female, the decision-making power rested with the business agent and the regional director, whose ties to the international were
stronger than any local solidarities and who were members of the male
leadership of the national ILGWU.

Finally, the dominance of men in the union movement—the product of
closure and of the process by which bureaucracies reproduce themselves—
had an impact on the local market. Finkelstein kept in constant contact
with the national board and the Chicago Joint Board. Through them he
recruited skilled male workers as cutters for local jobs. Elsewhere this move
would not be remarkable, but Minneapolis was one of the few markets in
the country where large numbers of women were employed as cutters.
Bringing in men from the national market helped establish a base for men
on the ILGWU Joint Board, a place effectively maintained through the
cutters' local.[60]

The declining fortunes of the ILGWU at the local level did not immediately reflect those of other CIO unions in the city. The continued growth and vitality of the union at Strutwear Knitting is a case in point. In the aftermath of the strike the Hosiery Workers' union developed a full cultural program. Unionization also provided many women with upward mobility in the firm. In 1939, for instance, women entered the previously all-male ranks of the knitters, a fact that received scant notice in the union newsletter. Several women also served on the shop committee, even outnumbering men in a ratio that reflected the female dominance of the labor force.[61]

Despite their numerical superiority, women workers at Strutwear did not participate equally in the union leadership. There were no women officers of the union; women were noticeably absent from the contract negotiating committee.[62] The auxiliary disbanded in 1939. Given the different needs and conditions of men's and women's work at the firm, a difference paralleled in a fairly rigid division of labor along skill lines, the lack of women's participation in negotiating union contracts seriously undermined their ability to receive equal treatment from the union. It also suggests that despite women's role in establishing and building the labor union at Strutwear, they continued to be marginalized in the local itself. The fate of women workers at Strutwear reveals that women's place in the union— conditioned by its creation under a walkout of skilled workers—did not change.

Conclusion

The 1930s witnessed an upsurge of labor militancy and organization that became a turning point in the history of the U.S. working class. Rooted in a dynamic sense of community, unionism went beyond the boundaries of the workplace to encompass both craft and industrial workers; men and women; immigrants, ethnics, and native-born white and black workers. The inclusive rhetoric of community became a powerful force in giving sanction to configurations of labor organization and protest in which men and women played equal parts.

When the industrial unions in the late 1930s adopted new forms of industrial relations that emphasized national authority over local autonomy and stability over militancy, they alienated many of the rank-and-file members who were the heart of the drive to "organize the unorganized." Centralization and union support for the war changed the nature of both men's and women's labor activism as unions closed down possibilities for grass-roots leadership and direction of union affairs. This bureaucratic transformation regendered the labor movement by limiting the scope and meaning of protest and organization in which women had been involved; it also redirected the activism of men into bureaucratic channels of communication, action, and authority.

The movement away from community issues, organizations, and control toward a more corporate, workplace-oriented unionism took place in an atmosphere of increasing political antagonisms and continued economic crisis. Community-based unions had made possible the rise of labor in Minneapolis, but divisiveness in the distribution of union power and resources at the local level undermined their strength. By the late 1930s unionists at both the local and national levels came to believe that highly centralized, bureaucratic national unions could give locals the stability they needed. What they neglected to see was how this choice altered the nature of unionism and the relationship of women workers to the movement.

Steve Fraser has argued that the bureaucratic trajectory of the union movement in the 1930s absorbed and usurped democratic rhetoric and thus made dissent illegitimate within the union structure.[63] Demands for special treatment of women in the context of an ostensibly gender-neutral union democracy were also delegitimized. For women unionists, the informal assumptions of democracy—that leaders/representatives have certain characteristics that fit the social role of the male—made union participation not merely difficult but culturally and personally risky.

Women in the Minneapolis labor movement of the 1930s experienced the contradictions of being in a social movement that welcomed them with the egalitarian language of labor but wanted to limit the meaning of that language. In the case of the ILGWU, women workers were members of an industrial organization that was predominantly female at both the local and national levels but was controlled and directed by the traditions of male craft union leadership. The shift over the decade from local autonomy to national control demonstrates the erosion of female power in a local arena where union initiative and leadership had come from women. For those women in the Strutwear Hosiery Workers' union, the process was one of exclusion. They composed the substantial majority of members, but the union's origins among skilled workers gave them outsider status. Even militancy on the picket line and majority control of the shop committee did not alter that legacy.

It is important to remember that a substantial portion of union growth and recruitment in the 1930s took place in such organizations as the ILGWU and the Hosiery Workers, which were hybrid organizations.[64]

Created in an era of craft unionism, they were forced by the nature of their mass-production industries to become semi-industrial unions. Historically these unions accommodated the majority of workers who were unskilled or semiskilled and who came from diverse ethnic and racial backgrounds. Despite their extension of membership to these workers, the unions continued to make distinctions between skill levels and to privilege skilled workers.

Unlike the industrial union leaders of another era, the labor leadership in the 1930s had no alternative vision for the movement. Faced with the recruitment of hundreds and thousands of unskilled and semiskilled operatives, unions chose the path of least resistance—incorporating new workers into the membership but creating few opportunities for their input into union organization. End runs around the bureaucratic structure, such as the use of female auxiliaries to involve women operatives, appeared to threaten union structure from this frame of reference. Organized outside the union constitution, the frail attempts at democratic participation were undermined by rhetoric that declared them subversive of true union democracy. Lacking legitimacy, these organizational strategies died, even as they represented genuine attempts at adjusting the labor movement to accommodate new workers.

Notes

This essay is reprinted, with minor editorial changes, from Elizabeth Faue, "Paths of Unionization: Community, Bureaucracy and Gender in the Minneapolis Labor Movement of the 1930s" in *Work Engendered: Toward a New History of American Labor,* edited by Ava Baron. Copyright 1991 by Cornell University. Used by permission of the publisher, Cornell University Press.

I thank Ava Baron, Angel Kwollek-Folland, Sara Evans, Ruth Milkman, and Bonnie Smith for their help in redefining and shaping the arguments here.

1. Mary Heaton Vorse, *Labor's New Millions* (New York: Farrar and Rinehart, 1938), 234.

2. Elizabeth Faue, "The 'Dynamo of Change': Gender and Solidarity in the American Labour Movement, 1935–1939," *Gender and History* 1 (Summer 1989), 192–212; Elizabeth Faue, *Community of Suffering and Struggle: Women, Men, and the Labor Movement in Minneapolis, 1915–1945* (Chapel Hill: University of North Carolina Press, 1991).

3. Jeff Hearn and P. Wendy Parkin, "Gender and Organizations: A Selective Review and a Critique of a Neglected Area," *Organization Studies* 4 (1983), 219–42.

4. See, for example, C. Wright Mills, *The New Men of Power: America's Labor Leaders* (New York: Harcourt Brace, 1948); Joel Seidman, "Democracy in Labor Unions," *Journal of Political Economy* 61 (June 1953), 220–31; Seymour Martin Lipset, *Political Man: The Social Bases of Politics* (New York: Doubleday, 1960), 387–436; Lloyd Ulman, *The Rise of the National Union* (Cambridge, Mass.: Harvard University Press, 1955); Nelson Lichtenstein, *Labor's War at Home: The CIO during World War II* (Cambridge: Cambridge University Press, 1982); Ronald Schatz, *The Electrical Workers: A History of Labor at General Electric and Westinghouse* (Urbana: University of Illinois Press, 1983); John Schacht, *The Making of Telephone Unionism, 1920–1947* (New Brunswick, N.J.: Rutgers University Press, 1985); Steve Fraser, "From the 'New Unionism' to the New Deal," *Labor History* 25 (Summer 1984), 405–30; and Sanford Jacoby, *Employing Bureaucracy: Managers, Unions, and the Transformation of Work in American Industry, 1900–1945* (New York: Columbia University Press, 1985), 207–74.

5. Rick Fantasia, *Cultures of Solidarity: Consciousness, Action, and Contemporary American Workers* (Berkeley: University of California Press, 1988).

6. For an analysis of the reasons men dominate the ILGWU, see Alice Kessler-Harris, "Problems of Coalition-Building: Women and Trade Unions in the 1920s," in *Women, Work, and Protest: A Century of U.S. Women's Labor History*, ed. Ruth Milkman (Boston: Routledge and Kegan Paul, 1985), 110–38.

7. Dorothy Sue Cobble, "Sisters in the Craft: Waitresses and Their Unions in the Twentieth Century" (Ph.D. diss., Stanford University, 1986), 468–525.

8. The most dramatic example may be seen in the Women's Trade Union League. See Nancy Schrom Dye, *As Equals and Sisters: Feminism and Unionism in the Women's Trade Union League of New York* (Columbia: University of Missouri Press, 1979); Susan Wong, "From Soul to Strawberries: The ILGWU and Workers' Education, 1914–1950," in *Sisterhood and Solidarity: Workers' Education for Women, 1914–1984*, ed. J. Kornbluh and M. Frederickson (Philadelphia: Temple University Press, 1984), 38–74; and Colette Hyman, "Labor Organizing and Female Institution-Building: The Chicago Women's Trade Union League, 1904–24," in *Women, Work, and Protest*, ed. Milkman, 22–41.

9. H. J. Gerth and C. W. Mills, eds., *From Max Weber: Essays in Sociology* (New York: Oxford University Press, 1946), 196–244; Robert Michels, *Political Parties* (Glencoe, Ill.: Free Press, 1949); Lipset, *Political Man*, 389–93.

10. These expectations are implicit in the model of shop-floor manliness described in David Montgomery, "Workers' Control of Machines: Production in the Nineteenth Century," in his *Workers' Control in America: Studies in the History of Work, Technology, and Labor Struggles* (New York: Cambridge University Press, 1979), 9–32.

11. International Ladies Garment Workers Union (ILGWU), *Handbook of Trade Union Methods* (New York: ILGWU, 1937), 38. Compare Jeff Hearn's statement that "the whole conceptualization and understanding of the proletariat is male; the model of [class] war waged by the army of laborers led by vanguards and militants with the support of the rank and file. Many words and concepts of potential cooperation and intimacy have been appropriated by particular macho, 'socialist' rhetoric—'solidarity,' 'brotherhood,' 'strength' is forever between vigorous, 'manly' 'brothers,' no soft, gentle ones." Jeff Hearn, *The Gender of Oppression: Men, Masculinity, and the Critique of Marxism* (London: Croom Helm, 1988), 6.

12. ILGWU, *How to Conduct a Union Meeting* (New York: ILGWU, 1934).

13. Meyer Perlstein, "The Human Side," *Justice*, July 1, 1938 (first and second quote); Michael Finkelstein to David Dubinsky, September 2, 1936, copyright ILGWU, folder 4B, box 75, David Dubinsky Papers, ILGWU Records, Labor-Management Documentation Center, New York State School of Industrial and Labor Relations, Cornell University (hereafter NYSSILR) (third quote). Kessler-Harris, "Problems of Coalition-Building," makes some similar points about earlier factional battles in the ILGWU in which women bore the brunt of the attacks. Factionalism, as the expression of private grievances and disagreements, was defined in many unionists' minds as a feminine characteristic.

14. ILGWU, *Handbook of Trade Union Methods*, 25–26. See also Elizabeth Faue, "Public Soldiers, Solitary Warriors: Labor, Sex, and Solidarity on the American Left, 1929–1945" (Paper presented at the Annual Meeting of the Organization of American Historians, St. Louis, Mo., April 8, 1989).

15. Perlstein, "The Human Side."

16. "New Dress Pacts Discussed by Twin Cities," *Justice*, February 15, 1938; "Acute Labor Shortage in Three Markets," *Justice*, June 15, 1939.

17. Affidavits of Jennie Storelie, Sarah Presant, and ten others, October 27, 1934; *To the Workers in the Ladies' Garment Industry* (pamphlet, 1934), both in folder 5B, box 75, Dubinsky Papers.

18. George Lawson to Dubinsky, March 28, 1934, folder 5B, box 75, Dubinsky Papers; "The Union in the Twin Cities," *Justice*, May 1, 1937.

19. Sander Genis, interviews, November 6, 1974, and March 16, 1977, Minnesota Historical Society, St. Paul (hereafter MHS); Dubinsky to Genis, April 19, 1935, folder 5A, box 75, Dubinsky Papers; Hearing before Minnesota Industrial Commission, Division of Mediation and Arbitration, September 10, 1929, Garment Workers file, box 11, Arthur and Marian Le Sueur Papers, MHS.

20. Genis interview, November 6, 1974, 3, 36 (first quote); "Flashes from North, West, and South," *Justice*, February 1, 1935; Genis to Dubinsky, August 15, 1935, folder 5A, box 75, copyright ILGWU, Dubinsky Papers (sec-

ond quote); Myrtle Harris, interview with James Dooley, July 9, 1975, 1–2, MHS.

21. Harris interview, 7.

22. The Minneapolis Labor School was started in 1934 by the Central Labor Union of Minneapolis. During the better part of the decade the school benefited from WPA workers' education project instructors, among them the writer Meridel Le Sueur. In 1941, after the WPA stopped funding the program, local AFL affiliates continued their support. See Minneapolis Union Education Center, Directing Committee, *Workers' Education* (Minneapolis: Minneapolis Union Education Center, 1938); "Labor School Records Four Years of Achievement," *Minneapolis Labor Review,* September 21, 1938; and press release, March 3, 1941, Press file, Central Labor Union of Minneapolis and Hennepin County, Records (hereafter CLU Papers), MHS. On the Educational Department's history, see Wong, "From Soul to Strawberries."

23. See ILGWU, *Handbook of Trade Union Methods;* and ILGWU, *How to Conduct a Union Meeting.*

24. Betty Hoff, "Education and Recreation," *Guardian* 1 (1937), 9 (first quote); Harry Rufer to Leah Schneider, March 11, 1937, folder 3, box 13, copyright ILGWU, Chicago Joint Board Papers, ILGWU Records, NYSSILR (second quote); "Dorothy Rock Gets ILGWU Appointment," *Minneapolis Labor Review,* November 29, 1935; "Amalgamated and ILGWU Progress," *Minneapolis Labor Review,* December 27, 1935; "From Far and Near," *Justice,* January 1, 1936; Dorothy Rock, "Flashes from the Field," *Justice,* February 16, 1936; "ILGWU Opens Worker Classes," *Minneapolis Labor Review,* November 6, 1936; "News and Views," *Justice,* December 1, 1936; *Justice,* February 15, 1937.

25. See Charles Rumford Walker, *American City: A Rank and File History* (New York: Farrar and Rinehart, 1937); George Dimitri Tselos, "The Labor Movement in Minneapolis in the 1930s" (Ph.D. diss., University of Minnesota, 1970), 215–65; and Farrell Dobbs, *Teamster Rebellion* (New York: Monad, 1972).

26. "Strike Ranks Growing Fast at Strutwear," *Northwest Organizer,* August 21, 1935. Newspaper reports estimated as many as 900 women workers in a labor force of 1,200; company figures put the estimate at 581 out of approximately 845 production workers. See "Code Minima and Strutwear Company Averages," October 17, 1935, frames 148–50, roll 20, Citizens Alliance of Minneapolis Records (hereafter CAM), MHS.

27. "McKeown Given Ovation," *Minneapolis Labor Review,* December 13, 1935; "Police, Troops Plan to Open Strutwear," *United Action,* December 13, 1935; "Organizer Shows Up Strutwear Company as Union Smasher," *United Action,* March 27, 1936 (quote).

28. "Swanson Booed by Strikers," *Minneapolis Labor Review,* September 25, 1935; Roy Weir, organizer for Central Labor Union, to Emil Reeves, secre-

tary, American Federation of Hosiery Workers, August 7, 1931, and July 26, 1934; Roy Weir to Alfred Hoffman, secretary, Hosiery Workers' local, Milwaukee, April 20, 1934, all in Hosiery Workers' file, CLU Papers; complaint form 136, Strutwear, June 7, 1935, in Hosiery and Lingerie Code, box 388, Records of the 11th Regional Labor Board, Record Group 25, Administrative Records of the National Labor Relations Board, National Archives, Washington, D.C.

29. Tselos, "The Labor Movement in Minneapolis," 186–88.

30. "Code Minima and Strutwear Company Averages"; Oscar Hawkins to "Dear Folks," August 29, 1935, box 4, Oscar and Madge Hawkins Papers, MHS.

31. "Organizer Shows Up Strutwear Company as Union Smasher."

32. "Strike Ranks Growing Fast at Strutwear"; "Knitters Practically All Members of Union," *Minneapolis Labor Review*, August 23, 1935. See also Farrell Dobbs, *Teamster Power* (New York: Monad, 1973), 91–93.

33. "Strike Ranks Growing Fast at Strutwear"; "Strutwear Mills Stay Closed Two Weeks," *United Action*, September 2, 1935.

34. "Enthusiasm at Strutwear Is Victory Sign," *Minneapolis Labor Review*, September 20, 1935; "Strutwear Blocks Arbitration," ibid., October 11, 1935; "CLU Prepares to Picket Strutwear," ibid., November 15, 1935; "Prepare to Mass Picket at Strutwear," ibid., November 22, 1935; "Employers Attempt Strutwear Opening," *Northwest Organizer*, November 20, 1935; "Strutwear Situation Stirs CLU," *United Action*, February 14, 1936; "Union Officials Tell Strutwear Facts," *Minneapolis Labor Review*, August 30, 1935; "Police, Troops to Open Strutwear"; "Strikers Will Take Decision of Mayor's Group," *Minneapolis Labor Review*, December 13, 1935; "Strutwear Strikers Get Three Tons of Food," *Northwest Organizer*, November 13, 1935; "Congress May Probe Strutwear," *Minneapolis Labor Review*, December 20, 1935. "Miller Strike Enters 9th Week," *Strutwear Worker*, March 1941, mentions the role of Ole Fagerhaugh. For the role of the Communists in the strike, see Carl Ross, "Labor Radicalism in the 1930s" (Paper presented at the Annual Meeting of the Minnesota Historical Society, Minneapolis, 1985); Young Communist League, "Make Strutwear a Union Shop" (handbill, 1935), Strikes, Local, Strutwear file, CAM; and *United Action*, September 16, 1935.

35. "Strutwear Plant Reopens," *Northwest Organizer*, April 8, 1936; "Hosiery Union Moves into Strutwear as Strike Ends," *United Action*, April 10, 1936; "Details Strutwear Settlement," *Minneapolis Labor Review*, April 10, 1936; "Strutwear Not Strutting Like It Used To," *Minneapolis Labor Review*, August 30, 1935; "Bosses Try to Smash Strutwear Strike," *United Action*, September 12, 1935; "Strike Record," Local Strikes file, CAM; "750 Strutwear Employees Sign for Closed Shop," *Northwest Organizer*, May 6, 1937; "Hosiery Workers Sign Strutwear," *Minneapolis Labor Review*, May 7, 1937.

36. Reports on the Emergency Brigade are reprinted in *Rebel Pen: Selected Writings of Mary Heaton Vorse*, ed. Dee Garrison (New York: Monthly

Review Press, 1985), 175–200. On the women's auxiliary in Minneapolis, see Marjorie Penn Lasky, "'Where I was a Person': The Ladies' Auxiliary in the Minneapolis Truckers' Strike of 1934," in *Women, Work, and Protest,* ed. Milkman, 181–205.

37. "Women's Auxiliary," *Strutwear Worker,* October 1938. In October 1938 the auxiliary had a membership of fifty. Its officers were President Marion Carlson, Vice President Laura Mitchell, Secretary Phyllis Mize, Treasurer Hazel Falldin, Trustees Vera Palmquist, Dorothy Hill, and Hazel Cummings. Alice Kessler-Harris has argued that men and women unionists had different goals for unions; in effect, women sought "community, idealism, and spirit," while male trade unionists wanted "unity, discipline, faithfulness." Kessler-Harris, "Problems of Coalition-Building," 129.

38. "Women's Auxiliary" (first two quotes); "Ladies' Auxiliary," *Strutwear Worker,* November 1938 (third quote).

39. "Trade Union Sports Council Conference Held," *Strutwear Worker,* April 1938 (a committee including Alrose Andryski of the Hosiery Workers); "Girls' Diamondball Teams," ibid., April 1938; "Girls' Bowling Averages," ibid., November 1938; "Scenes from Branch 38's 3rd Annual Picnic," ibid., October 1938; "Join the Ladies' Auxiliary," ibid., December 1938; "The Trade Union Woman," ibid., February 1939.

40. Christopher L. Tomlins, *The State and the Unions: Labor Relations, Law, and the Organized Labor Movement in America, 1880–1960* (New York: Cambridge University Press, 1985), 103–96.

41. Barry Leighton and Barry Wellman, "Networks, Neighborhoods, and Communities: Approaches to the Study of the Community Question," *Urban Affairs Quarterly* 14 (March 1979), 363–90, discuss the creation of communities through a variety of network structures.

42. Farrell Dobbs, *Teamster Politics* (New York: Monad, 1979).

43. Michael Finkelstein to Dubinsky, November 30, 1938; Dubinsky to Finkelstein, December 3, 1938, both in folder 2A, box 16, Dubinsky Papers.

44. Sander Genis to Dubinsky, December 12, 1934; "Attention Boulevard Frocks Workers," leaflet, enclosed in Meyer Perlstein to Dubinsky, April 4, 1936, copyright ILGWU (quote), both in folder 4B, box 75, Dubinsky Papers.

45. Sander Genis to Michael Perlstein, February 13, 1936, folder 4B, box 75, Dubinsky Papers.

46. George Glass, St. Louis Joint Board, to Dubinsky, May 9, 1936 (first quote); Genis to Perlstein, March 4, 1936 (second quote); Perlstein to Dubinsky, (telegram), April 17, 1936 (third quote); Genis to Dubinsky, April 29, 1936, copyright ILGWU, all in folder 4B, box 75, Dubinsky Papers. On signing, see "A Company Group Becomes a Real Union," *Justice,* July 15, 1936; "350 Join Union in Boulevard Shop," *United Action,* May 1, 1936; "Boulevard Frocks Signs with Union," *Minneapolis Labor Review,* May 1, 1936; and "Boulevard Frocks, Minneapolis Shop Signs Union Pact," *Justice,* May 1, 1936.

47. Genis to Morris Bialis [April 1936?]; Finkelstein to Dubinsky, September 18, 1936; Genis to Dubinsky, n.d.; Harry Rufer to Dubinsky, June 24, 1936, all in folder 4B, box 75, Dubinsky Papers; Meyer Lewis, AFL, to Dubinsky, March 16, 1935; Finkelstein to Dubinsky, March 30, 1937; Dubinsky to Finkelstein, April 2, 1937; Finkelstein to Dubinsky, April 8, 1937, all in folder 4A, box 75, Dubinsky Papers.

48. On several occasions workers sent letters to Dubinsky asking that Finkelstein be replaced. Finkelstein always responded that the workers were "troublemakers," but persistent complaints suggest that there was some basis for the discontent.

49. Genis to Dubinsky, April 29, 1936, folder 4B, box 75, Dubinsky Papers; "1000 Affiliate to TWOC in Vote at Munsingwear," *Northwest Organizer,* May 6, 1937; "TWOC Continues in Munsingwear," *Northwest Organizer,* May 13, 1937.

50. "Two of City's Industries to Give 600 Jobs," *Minneapolis Times,* January 1, 1932; Munsingwear annual reports in Minnesota Historical Society, St. Paul.

51. Munsingwear Corporation, *Program of the Employment Relationship between Management and Employees of the Munsingwear Corporation* (Minneapolis: Munsingwear Corporation, 1935), in Industrial Relations file, CAM; Tselos, "The Labor Movement in Minneapolis," 183, 189.

52. Unity Committee, "Stenographic Report of the Special Meeting of the Unity Committee of the Central Labor Union on Friday, May 7, 1937, re Munsingwear," Garment Workers folder, box 24, CLU Papers; Leah Schneider to Rufer, March 3, 1937, folder 3, box 13, Chicago Joint Board Papers, NYSSILR; ILGWU, *Report of the Proceedings of the 23rd Convention* (New York: ILGWU, 1937), 215.

53. Perlstein to Munsingwear Corp., April 24, 1937, folder 1B, box 169, copyright ILGWU, Dubinsky Papers.

54. Contract and contact card, dated May 21, 1937, photocopy, courtesy of Keir Jorgenson, research director, Amalgamated Clothing and Textile Workers union.

55. Perlstein to Dubinsky, April 27, 1937 (quote); Charles H. Green to Dubinsky, June 16, 1937, copyright ILGWU, both in folder 1B, box 169, Dubinsky Papers; "1000 Affiliate to TWOC in Vote at Munsingwear"; Unity Committee, "Stenographic Report of the Special Meeting of the Unity Committee of the Central Labor Union on Friday, May 7, 1937, re Munsingwear."

56. This was certainly the case with Cartwright Dress, with which the ILGWU negotiated a work-sharing agreement between its shops in Minneapolis and Cleveland. In the end the company went broke.

57. Members of shop to Dubinsky, May 25, 1939; Perlstein to Dubinsky, June 10, 1939; Finkelstein to Dubinsky, June 6, 1939; Complaints file, all in folder 2G, box 20, Dubinsky Papers. The Finkelstein letter is a lengthy denial

of accusations made by members, whom he assumes worked in the Jane Arden Shop, which went on strike.

58. "Educational Activities," *Justice,* April 1, 1942; clippings file, Minneapolis Labor School, CLU Papers; "Twins Cities to Study Earnings," *Justice,* November 1, 1937; "St. Louis, Kansas City, and Twin Cities Stage Union Classes in Service," ibid., February 1, 1939; "Starting Right," ibid., February 1, 1939; "Minneapolis and Kansas City to Start Time Study Classes," ibid., November 15, 1939; "Compulsory Training," ibid., May 1, 1940; "Arrange Training Institutes for Shop Chairmen, Officers," ibid., September 15, 1940; "They Learn about the ILGWU and Pass It on," ibid., February 15, 1943 (quote).

59. "Industry Meetings Set for All Trades in Several Cities," *Justice,* December 1, 1939 (quote); "Boulevard Frocks Worker off to Kansas City for Training," ibid., February 1, 1940.

60. Finkelstein to Morris Bialis, manager of Chicago Joint Board, March 25, 1940, and May 26, 1941, folder 3, box 13, Chicago Joint Board Papers; *Justice,* May 15, 1940, on the prevalence of women cutters.

61. "Shop Committee," *Strutwear Worker,* October 1938.

62. "Officers Nominated by Branch #38 Saturday," *Strutwear Worker,* November 1938; "Branch 38 Votes to Extend Contract," ibid., April 1939; "Final Results of Election," ibid., January 1941. During the 1935–36 strike Dorothy Trombley was secretary of the union and was important enough to be named in the injunction suit against the local.

63. Steve Fraser, "Industrial Democracy in the 1980s," *Socialist Review* 72 (November–December 1983), 102.

64. Christopher Tomlins, "AFL Unions in the 1930s," *Journal of American History* 65 (March 1979), 1021–42.

7

We Stood Our Ground

Anthracite Miners and the Expropriation of Corporate Property, 1930–41

Michael Kozura

During the 1930s northeastern Pennsylvania's anthracite coal region experienced an extraordinary challenge to corporate power when thousands of unemployed mine workers illegally occupied coal company property and began independent mining operations. At the time, the hard coal region was caught in the throes of economic crisis, precipitated in the late 1920s when the largest anthracite coal producers implemented a strategy of capital concentration and disinvestment. Faced with a stagnant consumer market, a strike-prone labor force, and a heavy burden of capital assets, the anthracite operators set out to downsize and financially restructure the industry.[1] Between 1926 and 1933 the operators cut coal production by one-third and displaced nearly 65,000 workers from the mine labor force.[2] The massive loss of jobs devastated scores of mining communities in the hard coal fields that covered six counties.[3] The southern third of the anthracite region was particularly hard hit, with the jobless rate approaching 50 percent.[4] In many coal towns virtually everyone was without work. Deprived of their livelihood, hard coal miners took matters into their own hands.

In open defiance of the law, the miners—called bootleggers—dug, processed, and distributed "stolen" coal as a means of economic survival. At first, under cover of darkness, small groups of miners exploited surface deposits for coal to exchange in the local barter economy. Within a short time bootleggers were sinking shafts hundreds of feet to recover anthracite, building sophisticated mechanical "breakers" to crack and size it, and establishing interstate trucking operations to haul it to distant markets. The coal region verged on insurrection as 20,000 independent miners and truckers organized and defended their operations against the coal companies and the government of Pennsylvania. The widespread violation of company property overwhelmed the coal and iron police. The state police were powerless in the face of determined resistance. Local sympathies were clear. Grand juries and district attorneys typically failed to prosecute, much as judges and juries refused to convict arrested miners.[5] Whole communities marched, demonstrated, and engaged in mass civil disobedience to advance the bootleggers' cause. Encouraged by this support, the miners held "their ground" in what Pennsylvania's Governor George Earle described as "the greatest conflict between moral and property rights in the history of the state."[6]

The bootleggers' insurgency, although routinely punctuated by violent encounters with police and company guards, did gain a large measure of success. As one bootlegger expressed it, "We battled the companies on the mountain, and we fought them in the courthouse. And we won!"[7] By 1941 bootlegging had evolved into a large-scale enterprise that supplied fully 10 percent of all anthracite production and rivaled the output of the single largest legitimate coal company.[8] In Schuylkill and Northumberland counties, the southern end of the anthracite region where independent mining predominated, bootleg coal production accounted for one in four jobs and provided $40 million in yearly income to the region, surpassing the jobs and income lost to disinvestment.[9]

The bootleg miners' movement has few parallels among U.S. labor's responses to economic dislocation. Unlike most who engaged in twentieth-century industrial conflict, anthracite mine workers occupied corporate property not to wrest concessions but to gain outright possession. Against the coal companies' assertion of the right to dispose of property as they saw fit, bootleggers claimed their right to the region's resources. This exceptional challenge to property rights raises a set of difficult questions. Why, given the massive legal protections afforded private property, did thousands of workers decide to "expropriate the means of production"? What inspired such extreme objectives? Was it radical ideology, pragmatic calculation, sheer desperation, or other motives? How did these militant men and women justify their defiance of corporate power and the law? Finally, what explains the widespread support and marked success of their movement?

Such questions are difficult to answer, partly because historians have largely underestimated or overlooked the story of bootlegging. Those scholars who do take note of illegal mining account for it as a manifestation of depression-born desperation and invariably minimize the extent and significance of the practice.[10] Such interpretations are not satisfactory. While desperation was a common experience during the 1930s, expropriation was not.

The significance of Pennsylvania's bootleg mining industry remains unexplored because the conceptual framework that anthracite historians use to interpret life and work in the hard coal region cannot account for the apparent radicalism of the bootleggers movement.[11] Hard coal miners are renowned for their uncompromising militancy, a reputation earned during a century-long history of violent industrial conflict that could accurately be written in the language of class warfare. Yet, as depicted by most anthracite historians, mine workers were essentially pragmatic in their opposition to the coal companies and, despite their intense militancy, aspired to nothing more radical than secure employment, higher wages, and better working conditions.[12] Purportedly, mine worker pragmatism had its origins in the insecurity of mine labor, in the overwhelming power of the companies, and in the conservatism engendered by obligation to family, church, and community.

Descriptions of life and work in the hard coal region emphasize this pragmatic concern with "bread and butter" issues to explain how mine workers' more militant impulses were held in check and eventually channeled into legitimate labor movement activity under the leadership of the United Mine Workers (UMW). The arrival of the UMW in the anthracite fields in the 1890s offered hard coal miners a practical solution to the problems faced at work and an alternative to the radicalism and violence that had frustrated earlier organizing efforts. As the anthracite scholar Harold Aurand explains, "The union was an instrument of social integration."[13] Continued mine worker combativeness after the establishment of the UMW is interpreted not as a manifestation of radical propensities but as an indication of fervor in the fight to unionize and bargain collectively. According to the historian Joe Gowaskie, coal miners understood that "only formal union recognition could counteract the operators power."[14] Even the mass defection of hard coal miners into the revolutionary syndicalist ranks of the Industrial Workers of the World (from 1906 to 1916 the IWW's anthracite membership rivaled that of the UMW) is described in purely pragmatic terms. An overly cautious UMW leadership was unable to "deliver the goods"; but when the UMW began to deliver, the rank and file returned to the fold.[15] After the nationwide repression of the IWW, anthracite miners continued to rely on illegal wildcat strikes and other forms of direct action, refused on principle to submit grievances to arbitration, tenaciously resisted the contractual regulation of their labor, op-

posed union dues check-off, habitually rebelled against the UMW's dictatorial leadership, and sustained this militant syndicalism into the late 1940s.
The persistence of a syndicalist orientation among the ranks of anthracite
labor remains unexplained.

In the historiography on anthracite, pragmatism and radicalism are
posed as antithetical mental states, as though a concern for the realities of
economic survival were fundamentally incompatible with a commitment
to broad social transformation.[16] Several noted historians draw on the
concept of working-class pragmatism to explain anthracite labor's turbulent reaction to the economic crisis of the 1930s. When the mines closed
and the UMW was either unwilling or unable to respond effectively, coal
miners by the tens of thousands rejected the union and its conservative
leadership, joined the Communist-led Unemployed Councils to demand
relief, formed insurgent unions to fight for their jobs, or turned to bootlegging and took possession of their industry. A leading scholar of anthracite communities, John Bodnar, finds nothing "inherently radical" in these
struggles and instead argues that miners were motivated to rebellion by
"the loving concern which united family and neighborhood." Bodnar in-
sists that "above all else their behavior and perceptions were rooted
in . . . the family economy."[17] Working-class pragmatism, an abiding "realism" grounded in communal obligation, allegedly narrowed mine worker
consciousness to a concern for survival and discouraged any vision of social transformation. According to the historian Ronald M. Benson, the
anthracite insurgency of the 1930s "was unsettling but conservative; that
it appeared 'radical' was the result of collusion between operators and
union bureaucrats, who saw communal action as a disruptive challenge
to . . . their joint control . . . of the coal industry."[18]

Anthracite scholarship tends to emphasize the analysis of community at
the expense of class, and union organization to the neglect of collective action. Although an emphasis on family, community, and union helps explain
the cohesiveness and resourcefulness of the anthracite working class, communal obligation alone cannot account for the complex motivations that
compelled jobless miners to take action. Nor can the objectives of the bootleggers' collective action be derived solely from the culture of the coal towns.
When the mines closed, anthracite's working people waged a struggle that
transcended the bounds of kinship, community, and union, and they raised
demands that challenged the legal and moral foundation of industrial capitalism. The far-reaching aims and radically oppositional practices of the
bootleggers' movement require a conceptual approach that is more sensitive to the transformative potential inherent in collective action.

Recent sociological research on social movements presents an alternative approach for explaining the origins of insurgent perspectives and practices.[19] Defining social movements as the sustained pattern of conflict between authorities and challengers, social movement scholars argue that the experience of struggle strongly influences the consciousness of movement participants.[20] While attentive to the importance of culture and community, these process-oriented sociologists demonstrate that new understandings and new organizational forms arise as people act collectively to challenge authority. With regard to bootlegging, social movement theory does not imply that the communal culture of the coal towns was unimportant for the emergence of the mine workers' struggle. On the contrary, jobless miners initially fashioned their oppositional outlook among family, friends, and neighbors. Moreover, the mining communities provided crucial resources—a communication network, an organizational infrastructure, and a sense of solidarity—all necessary to challenge the power of the coal companies.[21] Yet the miners' resistance would have been sporadic, localized, and short-lived had it been based solely on communal organization. As bootleggers fought back against company repression, they formed a network of social movement organizations to mobilize support for the cause and, in the process, created a new understanding of their rights. Successful mobilization increased the miners' capacity to challenge the companies, attracted more supporters, gained new advantages, and generated more far-reaching demands.[22] The experience of struggle had consequences for mine worker consciousness that cannot be inferred from generalizations about the preexisting culture of the coal towns or the "essential" character of coal miner consciousness.[23] Social movement theory directs attention to this unfolding pattern of conflict to explain the character of the insurgency in anthracite.

The following analysis employs a social movement framework to trace the dynamics of the bootleg miners' struggle from the first tentative acts of resistance to the outbreak of organized insurrection and from the origins of coal theft in the family economy to the establishment of a region-wide independent mining industry. Throughout the account the mine workers' own understanding informs the analysis.[24] The historical interpretation of bootlegging must be consistent with the meanings that the miners themselves assigned to events since their consciousness shaped, and in turn was shaped by, their collective action. Was bootlegging a manifestation of radical opposition to the coal companies or a pragmatic response to desperate times? Perhaps scholars who have posed the question as a choice between radical or pragmatic polarities are mistaken. Perhaps working-class pragmatism and radicalism do not necessarily represent two mutually exclusive states of awareness. It may be that communal loyalty is not necessarily inconsistent with a commitment to fundamental social change. Such questions are best answered by the bootleggers themselves.

The Moral Economy of Bootlegging

Illegal mining originated in traditional practices that skirted the gray area between custom and crime. For as long as anyone could remember, mine worker families scavenged waste coal from the culm banks—mountainous banks of discarded dirt, rocks, and coal—that surrounded their communities.[25] They used the reclaimed coal as a source of fuel in their homes, and if they had any extra, they sold it or bartered it, with their neighbors. The task of recovering coal typically fell to the younger children in the household. Joe Padelsky began his lifelong career in anthracite on the culm bank at the Lytle Colliery picking coal with the neighbor kids: "We used to pick coal there for the house and we'd sell coal if we had extra . . . . We would crack it, and screen it, and wheel it home with a wheel barrow. . . . That's the way we used to make our money."[26] As the people saw it, the waste coal was their due since the company deducted "waste" from the miners' tonnage. The coal companies generally tolerated the insignificant pilfering. In slack times and during strikes, jobless miners joined their families on the culm banks and managed to endure the hard times with income from reclaimed coal.

Pressed to the limits of endurance during the six-month industrywide strike in the fall and winter of 1925–26, mine workers again resorted to picking coal. The culm banks were soon picked clean.[27] As supplies of coal became scarce, some of the more enterprising strikers opened makeshift mines on company property and dug coal from outcroppings and breaches, where coal veins were exposed and in easy reach.[28]

Mike Lucas, a sixteen-year-old slate picker at the Otto Colliery, naturally joined in the general strike. To outlast the company, Mike and several buddies from the Otto Colliery followed the lead of an experienced miner: "he dug a hole . . . so we dug one, and went down 'til we hit coal. . . . We'd crack it, and screen it. We'd sell most of it in Minersville and Pottsville to business persons."[29] Younger children who were experienced at picking coal provided indispensable labor in their families' workings. At the age of eleven, Bill Heitzman was among those who received an initiation in illegal mining after school and on weekends in his father's coal hole: "we went down the mine and we worked . . . just to survive!" Kids like

Bill learned that "miners had to fight to survive. . . . Many a time we were routed by coal and iron policemen."[30] It was a short step from picking coal on the surface to digging primitive free-lance mines, but, in taking that step, jobless miners and their families crossed the line that separated customary practice from criminal activity. Of course, the companies did not tolerate strikers' opening their own mines and dispatched patrols of coal and iron police to arrest trespassers. The "Coal and Irons" never did catch Heitzman or Lucas, and the two youthful miners continued working in the illegal coal trade until the strike ended.

The strike was finally settled out of exhaustion. Neither side won any significant gains. Essentially, the agreement extended the terms of the old contract for another four years, until 1930. Nevertheless, the hard coal miners returned to work with a sense of relief, secure in the knowledge that they had held the line against the companies' demand for a 25 percent cut in pay. They had no way to anticipate the crisis that was about to present itself.

The first signs of trouble came on the heels of the strike settlement with reductions in working days and increases in part-time operations. By 1928 the coal companies began to concentrate operations and close mines. As dozens of mines shut down, union locals disputed the need to close mines permanently and demanded that the companies instead spread, or "equalize," available work among the collieries.[31] The call for work equalization found wide support among the anthracite rank and file, who looked to the UMW to negotiate a work-sharing agreement with the operators in the upcoming 1930 contract talks. However, the union leadership failed to wrest any concession on work-sharing and, with minor revisions, agreed to an extension of the 1926 contract for another six years, to 1936. Local newspapers reported that the union's negotiators raised the work equalization demand for the sake of appearances but gave it no real support at the table.[32] After much dissension, the contact was ratified. With the UMW pledged to support the agreement, the coal operators were free to complete the consolidation of operations. Shortly, tens of thousands of miners were left jobless.

Union leaders counseled patience and promised better days ahead as rank-and-file unrest surged. Convinced that their union had abandoned them, jobless miners in the southern district again turned to bootlegging, while the miners of UMW's District 1 in the northern field carried the equalization fight to their union locals. Dissension soon split the northern district down the middle. Union loyalists lined up behind the UMW to protect their jobs; dissidents formed the United Anthracite Miners of Pennsylvania (UAMP) to fight for equalization. The UAMP staged a series of violent strikes, pitting worker against worker in bloody encounters that left a hundred dead and many more injured before the insurgents were finally exhausted. Occupied with rebellion in District 1, the UMW was unable to attend to matters in the southern field. In the Panther Creek Valley, at the eastern end of the southern field, solidarity held among the UMW locals at the Lehigh Navigation Coal Company's mines, and the rank and file wrested a de facto work-sharing arrangement by means of mass illegal strikes. Elsewhere in the southern field, with more than half the collieries permanently closed, the equalization fight held little attraction for the district's miners.[33] Instead, displaced miners resorted to illegal mining, while those still employed in working collieries relied on illegal strikes to challenge company power.

By the summer of 1932 the crisis in the southern anthracite region had become inescapable. In Schuylkill County alone, with a population of 235,000 and a labor force of 82,000, there were 39,000 displaced workers (including 16,000 miners) with no prospect of employment.[34] The County Poor Board was unprepared to assist the vast number of destitute families. Four million dollars in emergency relief provided meager support for less than a third of the county's jobless. Churches and union locals responded with soup kitchens and collected contributions. Yet these relief efforts were truly paltry when measured against an estimated $40 million in lost aggregate yearly income.[35] Moreover, such charitable efforts could not begin to address the anguish of a once-proud miner, whose masculine identity depended on his ability to provide for his family.

The full force of disinvestment struck the smaller coal towns that had sprung up around a single colliery. In these company-dominated towns, housing, water, sanitation, and policing were all provided by the company. Branchdale, a prototypic company town, was home to the Philadelphia and Reading Coal and Iron Company's (P&RC&I) Otto Colliery, which employed 650 mine workers.[36] When the P&RC&I announced its plan to suspend operations at the Otto Colliery permanently, Branchdale was reduced to a state of shock and denial. Mike Lucas, then a miner at the colliery, recalls that the initial disbelief was quickly dispelled when the company "shut the thing down altogether. They shut the boiler house . . . there was no steam to run the generator or pumps. They shut everything down. . . . We thought the end of the world was coming."[37] To survive, Lucas fell back on his experience as a bootlegger and provided an example that friends and neighbors soon followed.

Just a few miles from Branchdale, the Hecksherville Valley, with six P&RC&I mines and as many company towns, was devastated. Jack Campion grew up in Greenbury at the eastern end of the valley and remembers the temper of the people as the last mine was closed: "There was hate for the company. . . . We couldn't understand why all the mines were shut down. The companies came in, they raped the land and pulled out. . . . It was their way of punishing the people [after the strike]. We were very bitter. That's when the bootlegging started. . . . Since the coal was in the ground and we all knew where it was at . . . people started digging their own coal holes."[38]

Charles Komarosky, a bootlegger from Thomaston, at the other end of the Hecksherville Valley, shares Campion's perspective: "At that time, the coal companies kept a pretty heavy thumb on the workers. . . . They controlled everything. . . . They kept the people down." When the people of the valley "started to bootleg coal the Reading Company did try to stop it, but then it got out of hand."[39] Hundreds of illegal mines were dug from one end of the valley to the other. Komarosky recalls that "one lad down the street said 'If they [the company] have it and I need it I'm going to get it too, whether they like it or not, whether I get it by stealing it or what.' That's the feeling that people had. We're going to make a living regardless. . . ."[40]

The mine closings sparked a deeply felt anger, a class anger fueled by a history of struggle that reached back a century, to when the first coal was cracked. The memory of past struggles—of the Molly Maguires, twenty labor activists framed and hung by the P&RC&I in 1877; of the victims of the Lattimer Massacre, fifty-one strikers shot down in cold blood by the coal and iron police in 1897; of pitched battles fought by women and children against the Pennsylvania militia; of six-month strikes won by unbreakable solidarity—was preserved and passed on in the oral traditions of the mining communities. Each community had its own particular legacy. Jack Campion recalls the traditions he learned growing up in the Hecksherville Valley: "You've heard of the Molly Maguires? . . . Black Jack Kehoe was a leader of the Molly Maguires in this area. The people swear he was innocent. He was a martyr. . . . The miners were always very mistreated. . . . They were known to knock bosses off who mistreated them. It's legendary in our area. I've learned it since I was a boy. They always said the Mollies were good. They were actually the first union."[41] The culture of the coal towns was thus enriched by a legacy of class struggle. Drawing inspiration from this heritage, jobless miners reacted to the economic crisis not from desperation so much as from anger, and they directed that anger toward the company.

Yet, at the same time, bootleggers saw the situation pragmatically: "We 'stole' coal, but. . . ."; "We had no choice"; "It was survival"; "It was something we had to do, there was no other way"; "We had to feed our kids"; "It was our bread and butter"; "We had to take care of our families."[42] While jobless miners had every reason to despise the coal companies, illegal mining was no less rooted in a deep concern for family. Moreover, bootleg mines began as family affairs, with the economic practices of mine worker households providing the initial structure around which mining operations were organized.

The self-reliant household economy was the norm among anthracite mine worker families, and women were at the center of the household's economic activity. Elena Kozak grew up in a large and quite resourceful anthracite household, with three sisters, three brothers, and two boarders. Elena's father was among the fortunate. He worked as a skilled miner at the Lytle Colliery, and it remained open. Elena's mother managed the household. The house, a small barn, and three-and-a-half acres of land sustained the family through countless strikes and layoffs:

> We had . . . apple trees, a peach tree, plums, grapes. . . . We had a garden . . . vegetables, potatoes, cabbage, corn. We grew hay for the cow. We raised chickens and pigs. We had a goat. . . . We picked berries and mushrooms. . . . We all had to help. . . . We worked hard. We felt bad to see our parents work so hard. . . . My mother had it hard. She had to raise seven kids . . . take care of my father, and the boarders. She canned and dried things for the winter. She cooked and baked bread. . . . She married my father when she was thirteen. . . . That's how it was back then.[43]

When Elena was fourteen, in October of 1925, she started working in a local garment factory for seventy-five cents a day. Her pay was the household's only income during the long strike. Anna P., another of anthracite's working women, also started work in the same factory when she was fourteen. When Anna's mother died in childbirth, she took responsibility for managing the household. As Anna explains, "It was something we had to do. We took care of each other."[44] According to a 1925 Department of Labor survey, 31 percent of all women in anthracite mine worker families and 57 percent of all "adult" daughters of mine workers were employed outside the home in silk mills, garment factories, and commercial establishments.[45] The typical anthracite woman also managed a household of at least five individuals.[46] In the hard coal region, anthracite women were "working women," and the household economy depended on women's wages as much as their homemaking skills.

Moved by this powerful sense of responsibility, many women worked alongside their men in the illegal mines. Mary W. proudly recollects her experience as a bootleg miner: "I know a little bit about bootleg coal. . . . In those days . . . that was the only thing . . . to survive. Even my mother and my sisters and I used to go into the drift. We used to scoop the coal after my father would fire. We'd scoop it on a wheel barrow and wheel it out and . . . scoop it on a truck and my brothers would haul it home. . . . We used to scoop it on different screens to size it . . . stove coal, nut coal, pea coal, buckwheat. I know a little bit about coal!"[47]

Women working in bootleg mines represented a sharp break with the gendered nature of mine labor, a potential source of ill-will from men whose sense of self-worth rested on their ability as miners. However, by all accounts, men who worked in bootleg operations felt encouraged rather than threatened by the presence of women in the mines since women and men were already accustomed to sharing responsibility for the economic well-being of their families.[48] Significantly, a not-so-subtle shift in roles also occurred in bootlegger homes; after a day of sharing the risks in their coal holes, wives and husbands also shared the housework. As the bootlegger William Adams explains, "They'd both chip in when they'd get home and get [it] done."[49] Apparently, economic necessity prompted a rethinking of gender roles, and the organization of mining operations within the household economy eased the process. This much is certain: as bootleggers, women and men stood united.

As managers of their household's finances, women were also involved with the traffic in coal. John Onushco worked as a helper on Mick Kozak's coal truck and always turned over his pay to his mother. Eventually, he decided to buy a truck and start his own business. As Onushco explains, "I talked to my mom. I told her it might be better if we kept our own truck and I could start hauling coal myself."[50] John's mother agreed and gave him the money for a down payment. Similarly, Joe Padelsky describes his mother's influence the time he decided to quit working at his neighbor's coal hole: "She sent me right back." On payday, as Joe recalls, "I put the money on the table. I got a quarter out of it on Saturday. Sunday, if I asked for another quarter I got a kick in the rear end . . . and I'm a workin' man already!"[51]

The involvement of women in the illegal coal industry should not be overstated. Mining remained predominantly "men's work." Very few daughters actually followed in their father's footsteps to become skilled miners. Women rarely involved themselves with the management of mining operations. Yet women did have a direct stake in the bootleg industry, and they made their presence felt. At work, "they could handle a pick and shovel just like a man."[52] And, in defense of their livelihoods, women stood their ground. In fact, women often held the front line in the struggles to defend bootlegging. However, women made their greatest contribution as "community organizers," fostering a moral climate that legitimized the expropriation of coal. In countless conversations over backyard fences, after church on Sunday, and during the round of daily activity, women exchanged, analyzed, and spread the news among their friends and neighbors. Anna P. reports the gist of the interchange: "We were pro-bootlegger, and we weren't afraid to say so!"[53] As active members of their communities, women mobilized pro-bootlegger sentiment and created a supportive environment in which the efforts of individual bootlegging families could coalesce into a regionwide economic force.

Self-reliant anthracite households did not stand entirely on their own. Individual families were joined through a web of interdependency within a larger community economy, where goods and services were exchanged on the basis of obligations that existed independent of the cash economy. As the collieries closed and the cash economy collapsed, it was this exchange economy, rather than charity or relief, that sustained the coal towns. When the P&RC&I abandoned the Hecksherville Valley, as Jack Campion relates, "it was people helping people. People who had cows, they shared their milk. People who had pigs, shared their meat."[54] In Branchdale, when the Otto Colliery closed, "there was no such thing as money," as Pat Sanza explains, "we bartered."[55] Barter could stretch the resources of the anthracite communities, but many necessary goods and supplies were not produced locally. For such necessities, people relied on the local storekeeper and the long established practice of buying "on the book." Local merchants, accustomed to extending credit to mine worker families during strikes and layoffs, naturally continued the practice when the collieries shut down. At the time of the closings, Mick Kozak drove the delivery truck for his father's grocery store. His route wound through the Hecksherville Valley, over the mountain to Forestville, and then on to Branchdale before returning back to Minersville. As Mick remembers, "Everyone was on the book." Often, he traded groceries for garden produce, eggs, or berries to sell in the store in Minersville. Bootleg coal found its way into these exchanges. "I traded flour or potatoes for coal . . . and I sold the coal in town," Mick explains.[56] The exchange economy thus presented an initial network for the illegal coal trade, and, in turn, bootleg coal provided cash to supplement barter.

The traffic in bootleg coal rapidly expanded as enterprising individuals like Mick Kozak lined up miners with markets beyond their own communities. By 1931 Kozak had saved enough for a down payment on a short-wheel-base dump truck, one of the first in the region. Soon Mick was hauling coal directly from the coal holes to sell in Baltimore and Philadelphia. Finding buyers for bootleg anthracite was easy since it was cheaper than the exorbitantly priced coal sold by "legitimate" coal dealers in the cities. Getting the coal off the mountain and to the city proved more difficult, since the coal and iron police combed the mountains and the state police patrolled the highways in search of bootleggers. Elena Kozak often accompanied her husband to "watch for the police." To evade the police, Mick and Elena drove through the mountains to the coal holes at night, with headlights dimmed, guided by the signals of lookouts posted to monitor police activity. According to Elena, "Mick flew down the mountain. The police couldn't catch us."[57] "Once he made it off the mountain," as Mick explains, "the trucker was home free."[58] In the early 1930s truckers were not required to possess paperwork that documented the origin of their coal. Consequently, unless a bootleg trucker was caught in the act of loading coal or hauling it off company property, the police lacked evidence to prosecute. The highways of the Northeast thus presented freewheeling truckers with an open road to huge anthracite consumer markets in Maryland, New Jersey, New York, and New England. Before long, more than 2,000 bootleg truckers were at work hauling anthracite to those distant markets.[59]

Almost overnight, depressed coal towns revived with income from the traffic in bootleg coal, and local economies that had survived on barter and credit grew increasingly dependent on expropriation. The economic impact of the bootlegger, as Joe Padelsky reports, was simple and direct: "The money you made, you spent. You didn't hoard it . . . like the rich guy hoards it. . . . You had to spend it. You kept the wheels turning in this county."[60] "The towns in this region," Mick Kozak concludes, "owed their survival to the bootlegger."[61] Bootlegger cash supplanted barter, but the ethics that governed the exchange economy—mutual obligation, sharing, solidarity—remained deeply ingrained in the practices of the illegal industry.

As independent mining became larger and more sophisticated, it outgrew the bounds of the family economy. To coordinate large-scale mining operations, family members, friends, and neighbors formed partnerships. Partners worked together, shared the risks and dangers, decided matters collectively, and divided profits equally. Mutuality also governed relations between bootleg operations. Mines were laid out to allow everyone access to the coal seams, and air shafts were dug between adjoining mines to provide ventilation as well as an alternate means of escape if there was any trouble. As Jack Campion describes it, "The bootleggers . . . we were all neighbors, so to speak. We all had a lot in common. No one resented the other person. Everybody tried to help each other. We shared equipment, new ideas . . . a new technique in mining."[62] This sense of community was shared by bootleggers throughout the coal region. Bill Heitzman describes it as "a feeling of oneness. . . . We were all one."[63]

Bootleg miners also shared strong bonds of solidarity with miners employed at "legitimate" company mines. Most independent miners had worked in company mines until they lost their jobs, most had been members of the UMW, nearly half were veterans of the strike of 1925–26, and many had brothers, uncles, or fathers who still worked for the company.[64] Often, "legitimate" miners helped out in their family's bootleg coal hole after work and during slack times. Tony Russian worked as a miner in the Oak Hill Colliery near Minersville, where he was a respected local union leader. After a day's work at Oak Hill, Russian helped out at his brother Frank's bootleg hole. As Tony remembers, his union local "sided with the bootleggers" and on one occasion staged an illegal strike in solidarity with Minersville's bootleggers who were being harassed by the company. As he puts it, "We took care of our own." In the southern field, which had by far the largest concentration of bootleg operations, mine worker solidarity was particularly strong. This, according to Tony, despite the bitter opposition of UMW president John L. Lewis, who reviled the independent mines as "dangerous dog holes unfit for a man."[65] The coal companies demanded that the UWM take an even stronger stand against illegal mining and discipline members who supported bootleggers. However, Lewis and the international leadership, already hard-pressed by the rebellion in the northern field, were unwilling to test the loyalties of miners in the southern field.[66]

The Organization of Insurgency

Early on, bootleggers camouflaged their mines, covered their tracks, and traveled at night to avoid detection by the coal and iron police. Their activity resembled guerrilla warfare as much as coal mining. Pat Sanza recalls an incident that occurred when he was posted to keep watch on the mountain near Forestville, his hometown. Pat heard another lookout call, "Hey, the coal and iron cop is coming up." The bootleggers responded in an instant: "They got the windlass, and they got the buckets, and they covered them with brush. They got limbs and covered up so you wouldn't know there was a hole there." Pat remembers that "the Coal and Iron came around looking [and he thought to himself]: 'Nobody workin' here.' He wasn't gone twenty feet down the road; . . . we were [back in the mine] working. . . . We had no respect for them."[67] Joe Hudock bootlegged on the other side of the mountain near Branchdale, where "the coal and iron police didn't really have that much authority. The authority was there with a club or a gun."[68]

If an unlucky group of bootleggers got caught in the act, the coal and iron police were required to take them to a magistrate to press charges. However, local magistrates typically sympathized with the miners. Jack Reilly remembers the day he and a dozen of his buddies were apprehended and taken before Squire Flynn. Flynn demanded that the Coal and Irons prove that the miners were trespassing by producing the maps and deeds to the land. The cops were unable to produce the evidence, and the miners were released.[69] Pat Sanza remembers that when people heard what happened at the magistrate's office, "everybody jumped right in" to the illegal industry.[70]

When bootleggers grew more numerous and "got a little braver," as Joe Padelsky explains, open resistance erupted on the mountainsides. In Forestville, he says:

> when the coal and iron cops tried to put the people off, [we] sort of lived up there . . . in the mountain. [We] wouldn't give in to nobody. . . . My brother had a coal hole . . . on the Reading ground. . . . They blew his hole shut. That was it! . . . Things got rough then. . . . They had to let the people make a living or there would have been a civil war. The Reading bought that ground for four dollars an acre. . . . How in the hell? . . . Four dollars an acre! . . . It was the people's ground. That's the way we figured. We were digging our own coal. We owned the land! Land of the free![71]

As bootleggers held their ground in confrontations with armed company police, a decidedly more defiant attitude toward the company and its property emerged: "Nobody was entitled to all that land that the Reading company had"; "They stole the land in the first place"; "The company was the oppressor"; "It was a battle between the landowner and the worker"; "The company didn't own it. Show me the deed"; "They didn't pay taxes, they had no right"; "We weren't criminals. The companies were the criminals."[72] The attempts to forcibly suppress illegal mining radicalized miner-worker sentiments. Although illegal mining might have originated as a pragmatic response to desperate circumstances, it became, as

Charles Komarosky describes, "a rebellion of the people against the coal companies."[73] When miners first resorted to bootlegging, they might have understood their actions to be criminal, though justifiable as a matter of survival. Encounters with company police convinced them otherwise. Through the experience of struggle, bootleggers came to recognize the illegitimacy of company claims on the land and instead asserted their own right to the mineral resources of the region. The struggle to defend the bootleg coal holes became, in Jack Campion's words, "a fight for what people rightfully believed was theirs."[74]

In Branchdale, when the Coal and Irons showed up to put the independents off the mountain, the whole town was ready to fight to defend their rights. Some of the older women of the community sounded the alarm and assembled to block the road while others alerted the miners. Mike Lucas recalls that the confrontation had just started as he and his buddies arrived on the scene: "My mother and the other women were there . . . standing up to the cops. . . . People were mad. . . . What could you do? They were like God, the coal company. They put people out of their homes, those who would stand up and fight. They kept us down, and we just wouldn't . . . knuckle down to them to be like slaves."[75] That day, the people of Branchdale faced down the Coal and Irons without a fight. Such encounters became ever more frequent as the companies attempted to reassert their control.

The mountain between Forestville and Branchdale was covered with bootleg operations, and the miners from both communities realized they had to coordinate their resistance to hold "their ground." Local miners credit a few of the more experienced bootleggers with the initial organizing. Mike Lucas was prominent among the activists. Pat Sanza describes Lucas as "a fighter, a leader. . . . [The coal and iron cops] were afraid of him."[76] Mike bootlegged during the long strike, and his experience, self-confidence, and combativeness made him a natural leader. He and his brother John had no trouble convincing people to stick together and stand up against the cops. Lucas himself describes the first confrontations quite matter-of-factly: "At that time they only had, maybe four or five policemen . . . they'd try to blow your holes. . . . Well they'd blow a couple of holes and we . . . put up a fight. . . . You would get together [bootleggers from] twenty different coal holes, and what's four or five company police? We all got together and went up there and chased them the hell off the mountain."[77]

In the early 1930s bootleggers in dozens of coal towns organized informal groups to advance the struggle. They called their organizations "bootleg unions." Neighboring units communicated, supported each other, and engaged in concerted actions when necessary. Although the bootleg unions functioned primarily as self-defense groups, they also provided a setting where miners met to regulate and promote their industry. Bootleg unions arbitrated disputes, set coal prices, organized rescue teams, taught first aid, and hired lawyers for legal defense. The unions were community-based and operated democratically. Weekly meetings were held at the local fire company or union hall, elected officers served at the pleasure of the group, and all decisions had to be put to a vote. Organization gave bootleggers a decisive advantage, as Pat Sanza explains: "As soon as we got a union everything was going our way. All the men stuck together. We had a guy going from coal hole to coal hole with buttons, 'independent miners' buttons. . . . Everybody that was in a coal mine got a button. If you were in trouble and you had a button, you were okay. We fought for you! . . . If you went to jail or were told to get off the ground, we were right there fighting for you."[78]

The bootleg unions fought scores of legal battles in the courthouse and almost always successfully defended arrested miners and truckers. At first arrested bootleggers pleaded guilty to trespass before local judges who, in sympathy with the miners' dire situation, dismissed the cases with dollar fines. When the bootleg unions organized, arrested miners pleaded not guilty and demanded jury trials. Juries composed of friends and neighbors found the miners not guilty, and the charges for prosecuting were levied against the coal company. This tactic made the cost of legal repression prohibitive for the coal companies.[79] As Pat Sanza describes it, "We outsmarted them."[80]

Local unions also presented their case to the public. The Minersville unit, for example, organized street meetings that attracted large crowds from Branchdale, Heckssherville, Forestville, and the other neighboring coal towns. People came to hear prominent activists speak on the issues of the day. Al Akulauckas, a bootlegger from Minersville, recounts the message delivered by the widely respected local socialist Con Foley: "Where did the company get the deeds? Did God give them the deeds? Go and mine the coal! They don't own the land. Don't run. Let them take you to jail. Send your wife and children to the courthouse and let them feed them." According to Akulauckas, speakers like Foley "put nerve in the people."[81]

In both the courthouse and the coal fields, the coal companies found themselves outnumbered and outmaneuvered by organized units of determined bootleggers. Intent on a show of force, the companies requested assistance from the state police for an all-out offensive to eradicate bootlegging. The offensive was launched in Schuylkill County during the summer of 1934. Detachments of coal and iron police, reinforced by the state police, staged a series of predawn raids against bootleg operations and blasted shut every illegal mine they could find. The raiding parties encountered stubborn resistance as they moved against the coal holes, but bootleggers gave way before the force of arms.[82]

The apparently successful campaign reached a climax in a raid on a pit near New Philadelphia. State police Corporal Pepple's "special duty" report for July 23, 1934, describes the encounter: "The entire detail of [twenty-five] State Police [and a dozen coal and iron police] . . . proceeded to the mountainside near River Run Colliery. . . . After the fifth hole was blasted . . . approximately (250) Men, Women and children appeared on the scene. . . ."[83] Led by a grandmother carrying an American flag, the march gathered at the pit just as a charge of dynamite was set off. The blast showered the crowd and wounded one of the women. The elderly woman with the flag surged forward followed by a small group of girls. According to Corporal Pepple, "Just as the last hole was about to be blasted, and [sic] elderly woman and several girls marched to the hole with the american [sic] flag. Just before the blast was put off the State Police ordered the crowd back, all responded and the blast was put off. Everything was quiet and orderly."[84]

News of the confrontation electrified the coal fields. The bootleggers of Branchdale and the other communities in Schuylkill County's "West End" grew all the more determined to defend their operations. Delegations from the district's bootleg unions met and devised a joint strategy. On Tuesday, July 31 at 4:00 A.M., the Philadelphia and Reading Company's raiding party invaded the West End and began blasting coal holes, but the bootleggers were ready for them. The evening edition of the *Pottsville Republican* reports, "Sirens and fire whistles awakened the miners in the districts affected and soon more than a thousand were on their way . . . to protect their workings." The blasting was halted by the press of the crowd. The "intruders" were "escorted" the six miles back to the Coal and Iron Building in Pottsville by a caravan of coal trucks loaded with miners. Afterward, the caravan of a thousand triumphant bootleggers paraded through the streets of the city, encouraged by the cheers of its citizens. Local newspapers noted that "no violence or disorder marked the assembly."[85] The campaign against illegal mining in Schuylkill County ended in a rout. Although isolated groups of bootleggers were easily put down by police raids, the bootleg unions in the West End were organizationally prepared to mobilize a coordinated districtwide resistance and successfully defended their right to mine coal.

Company officials were enraged by the "breakdown of law and order" in the coal fields and demanded that Governor Gifford Pinchot intervene. But, guided by his progressive sensibilities and his political instincts, Gifford Pinchot refused to get involved and instead suggested that the coal operators could "put an end to the production of 'bootleg' coal by re-employing the men. . . ."[86] Delegations of bootleggers accompanied by their local legislators had already convinced Governor Pinchot that it would be politically costly to harass bootleggers.

Although the companies failed in their drive against bootlegging in Schuylkill County and neighboring Northumberland County, they were more successful in the counties of the northern and middle anthracite fields, where jobless miners were routinely convicted for trespass and theft and illegal mining was quickly suppressed. A distinct pattern of industrial development distinguished southern anthracite from the rest of the coal region and accounts for both the companies' failure and the bootleggers' success in the southern field.[87] Back in the 1880s the absentee owners of the P&RC&I gained control of 90 percent of the coal measures in the southern field and displaced the local coal elite.[88] By contrast, in the northern and middle fields local capitalists remained preeminent in local affairs. The absence of an indigenous capitalist class in southern anthracite meant that the local power structure was composed largely of petty entrepreneurs, professionals, politicians, and P&RC&I officials, with the company men predominating. When the mines closed, the P&RC&I's system of influence and patronage collapsed. The balance of power shifted in the southern field as bootleggers translated their broad-based community support into political power at the polling booth and elected sympathetic judges, county commissioners, and legislators. No such shift in power occurred in the northern and middle fields, where the power of local capitalists more than offset the political influence of unemployed miners. What the companies branded "a breakdown of law and order" was actually a shift in power that put local government in the hands of the people.

Unable to rely on southern anthracite law and order, the companies devised a new strategy: they sent strip-mining equipment onto bootlegger tracts to disrupt the surface and make mining impossible. One of the first big power shovels arrived near Minersville to open stripping operations on the outskirts of town. Steve Nelson, one of the Communist Party's most effective organizers, was in town that day to meet with some of the local party members who were among the leadership of Minersville's bootleg union. Nelson attended the union meeting that night, where the men and women discussed what to do about the shovel. Karl Herman, a local Communist Party activist insisted, "We're not going to let them strip. We've got to go down and stop it." Later that night, Herman and some of the other miners met and planned their strategy. "The next day," as Nelson recalls, "I heard a fire whistle blow and drove out to observe the situation. . . . State police were protecting the shovel. . . . Hundreds of miners had gathered and got into arguments with the police to divert their attention. In the mean time, Karl Herman came up and said to me, 'There is going to be trouble. You'd better leave.' While all this was going on, someone put dynamite under the shovel . . . and blew it up."[89] Such confrontations became commonplace. Between 1934 and 1941 dozens of the huge power shovels, drag lines, and bulldozers were dynamited, burned, or otherwise sabotaged by bootleggers. Yet, as Mike Semanchick, a member of the Minersville union, explains, "Nobody had the idea that he was doing something illegal. . . . When things get rough you've got to do something."[90] The ethics of class warfare demanded intense militancy.

It should not be assumed that the class-war mentality of hard coal miners was simply a product of leftist agitators. Quite the contrary, under pressure from the company, bootleggers in such conservative-minded Pennsylvania Dutch communities as Donaldson in Schuylkill County's West End resorted to the same militant tactics, felt the same antagonism, and shared the same objectives as their more left-leaning counterparts.[91] Leon Richter worked with his uncle in a coal hole near Donaldson and recalls the sentiment in his area: "People had the idea that the coal here in the county belonged to everybody, same as the water. . . . Yes we stole coal. We didn't think about it; we didn't categorize it; we were bootleggers, and we were proud of it. . . . It was our right to take the coal. . . . This was the entire talk of the mining community: they are bringing in shovels; there is going to be a showdown. In my youth I was going to defend this industry in which my father worked and my uncles worked. . . . The anger was there."[92]

The coal region's leftists cannot take much credit for the spread of oppositional sentiments; the antagonism was already there. However, they did take an active part in organizing the insurgency. Many southern anthracite coal towns had well-established left-wing groups, and local activists were widely regarded as respected members of their communities. Harry Charowsky remembers, "Bolsheviks, we called them; there were a half-dozen families in Forestville. We went to school and grew up together. . . . They had affairs and everybody went to them . . . . You had Democrats, and Republicans, and Communists."[93] Left-wing politics, Leon Richter explains, "was certainly more or less accepted at the time." In Minersville, according to Mike Semanchick, "most of the members of the Communists were miners, working men. My brother was in it and . . . Karl Herman. He was a good man. He gave speeches. He organized a Hunger March on the Court House. He organized the factory workers in town."[94] One of the most renowned local Communists, Herman served as treasurer for the Minersville bootleg union. Pat Sanza describes Herman as "a leader. . . . If the coal and iron cops came around to chase you, he was right there to fight."[95] Communists like Karl Herman were taken seriously because they stood shoulder to shoulder with their friends and neighbors and because what they had to say "made sense." Even staunch anti-Communists like Mike Lucas admit, "Herman . . . had good ideas, but I didn't agree with everything he had to say."[96] The region's leftists were perhaps better prepared by their anticapitalist worldview to voice sentiments that fellow bootleggers felt in their hearts but were less able to articulate. In anthracite, radical objectives had become consistent with pragmatic common sense, and knowledge of radical ideology was not required.

The Institutionalization of Expropriation

By 1935 the coal companies had lost control of the situation in the southern field. Bootleg miners operated with impunity, and there was not much that could be done to stop them. Bootleg truckers were more vulnerable, however. Once outside the coal region, truckers were fair game for prosecution. The only problem was proving that a trucker was actually hauling stolen coal. The solution to that problem was presented to the state assembly in the form of a series of legislative bills designed to eliminate the production and transportation of illegally mined coal. The first bill, introduced by Charles Baldi, a Republican from Philadelphia, was rushed through the general assembly and passed on February 20. The "Baldi Bill" required coal truckers to possess receipts from state-licensed weigh-masters certifying the weight of their loads, and it specified fines and imprisonment for violators. Four additional bills that stipulated harsh punishment for mining or processing bootleg coal were scheduled for debate in early May. Even more ominous, the legislature established a special committee charged with "investigating" the permanent removal of "illegally mined anthracite from the markets."[97]

The coal region's press sounded the warning with front-page headlines: "Anthracite Mine Bills Aimed at Bootleggers";[98] "Bill Would Drive Coal Trucks Off Highways Of The State."[99] Realizing that the threat from Harrisburg could only be answered with regionwide concerted action, bootleggers established an "executive committee" to unite the region's truckers and miners in one big association. Activists circulated petitions and gathered statements of support from members of the clergy, civic groups, and town councils. Delegations of miners and truckers traveled to Harrisburg and lobbied sympathetic lawmakers. Organizers visited coal holes and enlisted the unorganized. On April 7, sixty delegates representing 10,000 miners and truckers assembled in Shamokin for the first regionwide convention of bootleg unions. The convention demanded a public hearing on the proposed legislation and called for a march on the capital.[100]

The public hearing on the proposed legislation was held on April 30, and the bootleggers showed up in force. The local headlines tell the story: "Truckers and Miners Storm Capital."[101] Ten thousand miners streamed into Harrisburg in the backs of coal trucks and marched through the streets to the Capitol Building. Men and women in grimy work clothes surged through the capitol and left its white marble blackened with coal dust. To accommodate the huge demonstration, the public hearing was moved to the farm-show arena. Seven thousand demonstrators packed into the arena, and thousands more stood outside. The newspapers reported that "thousands of wildly enthusiastic independent miners and truckers . . . booed and cheered and stamped their feet" until the coal company officials who had come to advocate for the legislation were driven from the speakers platform and the bootleggers took over the proceedings.[102] The independents created a powerful impression that day in Harrisburg. As Joe Padelsky remembers, "We raised hell!"[103]

When the coal dust settled in the capitol, it was clear that bootlegging could not be legislated away. The Baldi Bill stood as law, but the remaining antibootlegging legislation was soundly defeated. Consequently, the regulation of coal trucking encoded in the Baldi Bill—without the full legislative package designed to criminalize bootlegging—actually worked to legitimize rather than eliminate the independent coal industry. Bootleg breaker operators simply had their scales licensed by the state and then proceeded to issue weight slips to truckers hauling bootleg coal. Among bootleggers, the victory in Harrisburg confirmed the righteousness of their challenge to the coal companies. Moreover, this successful mobilization demonstrated to skeptics that ordinary working people could band together and influence the political process. Although a unified association of all independent miners and truckers proved elusive, the organizational capacity for united action was created and sustained. The Independent Miners, as they now called themselves, had arrived as a force in the politics of Pennsylvania's New Deal. The Independents became active participants in the political process. They lobbied, petitioned, endorsed candidates, mobilized votes, and, when necessary, marched on the capital to "raise a little hell."

The years between 1935 and 1939 were particularly good ones for the independent mining industry. The companies continued in their efforts to regain control over the coal fields, but the balance of power had shifted decidedly in favor of the bootleggers. The administration of George Earle, a New Deal Democrat, gave tacit support to the miners' cause. Governor Earle routinely consulted with the leadership of the Independent Miners on matters that affected their industry. The state police were instructed not to intervene in conflicts between bootleggers and the companies unless they turned violent, and then to remain strictly neutral. Earle himself pushed for legislation to form a state corporation that would employ bootleggers to produce coal on idle coal tracts. However, when political power shifted back to the Right in 1938 with the election of Arthur James, a pro-business Republican, the bootleggers' fortunes quickly changed.

Governor James campaigned as the "red-haired breaker boy from the coal region" who could solve the problems of the anthracite industry. Once James took office, however, he proved to be no friend to the bootleg miner. James was the force behind a series of nine bills introduced in the state legislature in the spring of 1939 that were designed to "rehabilitate" the hard coal industry. The measures called for the regulation of the industry as a public utility: coal producers were to be licensed; licensing would require proof of coal ownership; and the sale of bootleg coal would be strictly prohibited. Once again, the Independent Miners mobilized their forces and marched on the capital, and the bills were narrowly defeated. Failing in the legislature, James created the Anthracite Emergency Committee and brought together representatives of the coal operators and the United Mine Workers to create a "voluntary" plan to regulate the anthracite industry.[104] The Independent Miners were noticeably excluded from the committee's proceedings.

The economic terrain in the coal fields also began to shift. Since 1937 the P&RC&I had been tangled up in bankruptcy proceedings and had fallen millions of dollars in arrears on its property taxes in Schuylkill and Northumberland counties. To escape its tax burden, the company formally divested itself of over 100,000 acres of coal lands, most of which were located in Schuylkill County's West End. The coal lands were vested in dummy corporations and then leased to stripping contractors. It was no coincidence that most of the land in question was controlled by bootleggers.[105]

The Correale Construction Company was one of the first to move a strip shovel into the West End. It initially met no resistance since its stripping did not threaten the local bootleg mines. In early January 1941, however, Correale brought a "Bucyrus"—a monstrous strip shovel, so huge that it "walked" rather than rolled—onto the operation. The Independents recognized the Bucyrus shovel for what it was and readied their defenses. On January 23, when the shovel began to move toward the mountain west of Donaldson, local miners massed to blockade it. On January 27 Independent Miners from the West End held a mass meeting in Minersville, where they composed a telegram to Governor James requesting that he "refrain from sending police assistance . . . to the vicinity of Donaldson." The miners, as reported in the press, "have been told the company plans to bring thirty more [shovels] in to do the stripping."[106] The Independents' fears were confirmed the next morning when six more strip shovels approached the Donaldson area. Miners, the press recounted, "congregated there from nearly every town in the West End of the county. They said they are going to continue in their efforts to block the shovels."[107]

While the stripping contractors laid siege to the West End, the Anthracite Emergency Committee opened its assault on bootlegging in Harrisburg. On February 6 the committee unveiled its plan to regulate the coal industry: production quotas would be fixed, and prices would be set by a committee of legitimate operators; all bootleg breakers would be closed, and bootleg coal would be sold only to legitimate operators; bootleg holes would eventually be blasted shut as miners were hired by the legitimate operators. Bootleggers were given a May 1, 1941, deadline to comply with the plan.[108]

The Independent Miners called a holiday for Monday, February 10, and thousands of bootleggers poured into Minersville for an emergency meeting. The meeting was "originally scheduled to be held in Union Hall, but so large was the turnout that . . . [it] was held outdoors . . . in the bitter cold." A motion to defy the Anthracite Emergency Committee "was passed unanimously with a rousing shout that could be heard for several blocks." Next, miners voiced their outrage at the arrest of Mike Lucas and nine other leaders, who had been picked up off the street by detectives a few days earlier and charged with riot and destruction of property. The assembly then adjourned to organize round-the-clock pickets to maintain the blockade of stripping in the West End.[109]

With the stripping contractors outmaneuvered, the Independents concentrated on the situation in Harrisburg. Along with the deadline imposed by the Emergency Committee, they had to contend with a new legislative initiative aimed at bootleg truckers and breakers. The Independents, already well schooled in the political process in Harrisburg, applied their expertise to these new threats. On April 16, 10,000 miners and truckers rode en masse into the capital, crowded into the public hearings, and got their point across. As a result, the legislation was amended to the satisfaction of the truckers, and the Anthracite Emergency Committee extended the deadline for compliance with its plan.[110]

In Schuylkill County's West End, the Independent Miners maintained their blockade into the summer, and the contractors grew desperate for a means to break the six-month stalemate. In early July Correale brought in armed guards from outside the area to force a showdown. On July 8 a company of twenty-one guards was stationed at the stripping, and the shovel was prepared to begin operations. That evening several of the guards visited a local tavern, where they drank heavily and bragged about how they were going to "teach the locals a lesson" the next day. News spread fast in the coal region, and by the next morning word of the threat had traveled to every bootleg community in the area.

Before dawn a crowd of nearly a thousand men and women had already assembled on the road that led to the stripping pit, with more arriving every minute. Leon Richter was there to protect his mine and "defend the bootleg industry."[111] Joe Padelsky arrived with a group from Forestville "to make a stand."[112] Mick Kozak and Elena Kozak came with a dozen miners from Minersville loaded in the back of their truck, all "ready for a fight."[113] At dawn Mike Lucas and John Lucas led a formation of 400 bootleggers through the brush toward the stripping. When the contingent reached the shovel, the guards "vainly attempted to halt the miners' advance with riot clubs and when this failed, two of the special police, armed with shot guns, fired six shots into the crowd. . . ."[114] Two company guards emptied their revolvers point blank. Thirteen miners were wounded by the gunfire. The miners regrouped, armed themselves with clubs and rocks, and charged the guards, who then retreated onto the shovel and called for a truce. Mike Lucas disarmed the guards and promised them safe passage to their cars. As the guards walked toward their cars, several thousand more bootleggers arrived at the stripping pit. When the crowd saw their wounded comrades, they tore into the guards and "beat them all to hell." At that moment, a company of state police arrived and took the badly mauled guards into custody.

The crowd then turned its rage on the shovel and set it ablaze. Next, as Leon Richter describes, "one of the miners said, 'Hey, there is a shovel moving in at Good Spring.' Hundreds of cars drove up to Good Spring." The shovel operator and guards were chased, and, according to Richter, "somebody took the oil plug out and left the diesel engine run until it froze up. Then somebody said, 'There are shovels in the Bear Valley,' and [we] stopped those." As Richter remembers, "We thought we had them on the run."[115] During the rest of the day contingents of miners surged through the countryside, dynamiting and burning several more shovels before the state police were deployed at the stripping sites to deter further violence. The next day "order" was restored by a force of 150 state troopers stationed in the area.[116]

For the Independents the battle at Donaldson was both a tactical victory and a strategic defeat. The violence achieved the operators' intended results. The state police maintained a presence in the West End through the fall and deterred any further attempts to disrupt stripping operations. Bootleg miners were compelled to coexist alongside the stripping operations as best they could. Demoralized by the debacle, the Independent Miners fractured into three locally based organizations. However, the conflict in the coal fields was soon eclipsed by the U.S. entry into World War II. The war effort drained away a fourth of the region's labor force and all but eliminated joblessness.[117] Nearly every bootlegger who was of age went into the military service or found employment in the defense industry. Some were moved by patriotism, others by draft notices. Local draft boards filled southern anthracite's induction quotas with bootleggers since miners employed by "legitimate" companies were considered necessary to the war effort and therefore exempt. The older men, the women, and the children were left to hold their ground as best as they could. And hold it they did.

On October 15, 1943, the State Anthracite Committee issued its twentieth "final ultimatum" to the Independents to close down all bootleg operations immediately. In a press release for the Anthracite Committee Richard Maize insisted, "November 30 is the final deadline. There are plenty of jobs in legitimate mines. . . ." Representing the West End Independent Miners, Clyde Machamer answered, "We don't think the committee can go against the people and tell us to stop operating. The committee has far exceeded its authority . . . and we are going to continue operating."[118] The Independent Mine Workers defied the ultimatum, just as they had defied every previous deadline. From their point of view they were engaged in legitimate independent mining. The claim had some basis in law. Township supervisors and county commissioners confiscated substantial tracts of land from the P&RC&I in lieu of unpaid taxes and leased them to bootleg miners. At the same time, the P&RC&I's dummy holding companies sold large coal tracts to local investors, who then leased parcels to miners.[119] In this way, most bootleggers got to be "on the up-and-up."

Conclusion

Jobless miners resorted to illegal mining as a matter of economic survival. When the collieries closed, the prospect of starving families provided a strong motivation to skilled miners, who literally held the means of production in their hands and saw no alternative except to employ those means. Historians who emphasize obligation to kin and community have identified a powerful motivating force. Yet, in calling attention to the importance of communal solidarity, many scholars assume that such attachments predispose workers to strike a pragmatic accommodation with industrial capitalism. The example of bootlegging demonstrates that concern for family and community does not necessarily work to narrow working-class consciousness. Reference to communal obligation, however useful for understanding the cohesiveness of anthracite's working-class communities, does not answer why jobless miners concluded that they had a right to the coal, nor does it explain how they successfully defended that right. To understand how bootleggers achieved the capacity to expropriate coal, historians must take into account human agency in the form of a community-based, working-class social movement.

This does not imply that communal solidarity was inconsequential for the emergence of the bootleggers' insurgency. On the contrary, the self-reliant households and exchange economies of the coal towns enabled bootleggers to mobilize the commitments and resources essential to sustain their struggle. The close bonds shared by anthracite's working people provided a supportive moral climate in which expropriation was legitimized and defended. Without such community-based solidarity, illegal mining would have remained no more than that: isolated criminal behavior. The anthracite communities not only sustained the bootleggers' claim to legitimacy but also presented a ready consumer market and an established exchange network that stimulated illegal coal production. Further, many towns in the region were wholly dependent on income from bootlegging. From 1930 through 1941 bootleg mining infused an estimated $250 million into the local economy. The southern anthracite region's working-class communities lined up behind the bootleggers to protect economic interests no less than to defend friends and neighbors. In the coal towns social obligation and economic interest were tightly intertwined.

Economic necessity pitted jobless miners against the coal companies in an elemental fight to survive, a struggle that quickly escalated into a battle for control of the coal fields. At first bootleggers justified coal theft by referring to their lost jobs and hungry families. Yet the mine closings gave rise to a deeply felt anger—a class anger—which roused anthracite's working people to question the authority of the companies and the legitimacy of their claimed property rights. As company pressure on illegal mining increased, what had been an amorphous class anger crystallized into an intensely oppositional consciousness that inspired defiance. This intense class antagonism provoked bootleggers to challenge the legitimacy of corporate power and assert their own right to the region's resources. Thus, when the companies attempted to suppress illegal mining by force, they confronted a populace unified by a powerful set of motivations: communal solidarity, economic interest, and class antagonism. Repressive force worked to harden the bootleggers' resolve and transform their concern over lost jobs into a class-conscious challenge to corporate property rights.

Repression also spurred bootleggers to organize in defense of their operations. Local groups of independent miners and truckers worked out elaborate systems of communication that permitted them to evade the coal and iron police. Encouraged by supportive communities and reinforced with increasing numbers, miners banded together and drove off the company police. When the companies called on the state police for assistance, local groups of bootleggers coordinated their opposition and successfully defended their mines. When the state assembly initiated legislation to eliminate the transportation of illegally mined coal, the independents organized, lobbied, petitioned, marched on the capital, and transformed the initiative into law that legitimized the sale of bootleg coal. At every turn, mine workers responded to repression with increasingly sophisticated forms of organized opposition. The creation of the regionwide Independent Miners' union enabled bootleggers to hold their ground in the coal fields, assert their rights in the political process, and operate their industry democratically. Moreover, organizational success reinforced and legitimized the bootleggers' claim that the land rightfully belonged to the people.

Historians who endeavor to explain the reaction of anthracite's working class to the crisis of the Great Depression must be cognizant of the transformative potential inherent in social conflict. It was through the experience of struggle that bootleggers became aware of the illegitimacy of corporate control over the resources of their region. Their outlook was not shared by miners who worked only in "legitimate" company mines or by those freelance miners who operated on property leased from private owners. Although many legitimate mine workers sympathized with the bootleggers' cause, they did not have the illegal miners' perspective on coal company property unless they happened to be drawn directly into the movement.[120]

To be sure, anthracite miners generally were intensely militant opponents of the coal companies and possessed a cultural legacy of class consciousness that had been enriched by generations of militant struggle. But their consciousness fell short of the independents' full-blown defiance. The bootleg miners' outlook was shaped by the experience of struggle. On a more theoretical level the insurgency in anthracite thus exemplifies a core argument of process-oriented social movement theory: collective action has the potential of transforming the consciousness of participants.

On a more practical level bootlegging demonstrates the capacity of community-based movements to challenge the hegemony of industrial capitalism. Hard coal miners took possession of the land and created a system of industrial self-governance in defiance of labor leaders, capitalists, and the law. Were the bootleggers radicals? Yes, but only if our conception of radical is expanded to include staunch Democrats and Republicans as well as Socialists and Communists. Bootleg mining was not inspired by political ideology; the independents were just doing what came naturally. Was bootlegging simply a manifestation of working-class pragmatism? Yes, but only if our definition of pragmatism is stretched to include expropriation of the means of production. Such concepts cloud rather than clarify our understanding of working-class consciousness. If the bootleg miners' consciousness must be categorized, it is more aptly defined as a homegrown, community-based version of working-class syndicalism, an impulse that emerged as mine workers achieved the capacity to control the means of production. But perhaps the bootleggers' own words best express their outlook: "We were defiant. We stood our ground."

Notes

My thanks to Linda Blum, Eric Davin, Howard Kimeldorf, Carol Landry, Peter Rachleff, and Bob Rivera for their valuable comments on earlier versions of this essay. I would also like to extend special appreciation to fellow workers John Borsos, Ingrid Kock, Alice Lynd, and Staughton Lynd, whose solidarity made this essay possible. I owe my deepest gratitude to anthracite's bootleg miners; may their courage, determination, and vision continue to inspire defiance.

1. *Report of the Anthracite Coal Industry Commission* (Harrisburg: Murelle Printing, 1938), 67 (hereafter cited as *ACIC Report*). The Anthracite Coal Industry Commission was established by the Pennsylvania legislature in 1937 to investigate bootlegging. The commission's report includes a field survey of

illegal mining, processing, and trucking operations as well as a detailed investigation of the organization and operations of the legitimate coal companies. The *ACIC Report* provides the best single source of information on the crisis in the anthracite industry.

2.   Anthracite Production and Employment for Selected Years

	Production	Employment
1926	83,875,000 tons	169,000
1930	65,166,000 tons	140,000
1933	49,507,000 tons	102,000

Source: Pennsylvania Department of Mines, Annual Reports.

3. An integral component of Pennsylvania's economy, the hard coal region produced over $500 million worth of mining and manufactured goods annually. *ACIC Report,* 22, 155. In 1930 the anthracite counties constituted 14 percent of the state's population, 15 percent of its industrial labor force, and 54 percent of its mine workers. Works Progress Administration, *The Employment Situation in the Pennsylvania Anthracite Region* (Washington, D.C.: n.p., 1935) (hereafter cited as *WPA Report*), 4. The hard coal region's size and economic importance meant that the impact of the mine closings was felt far beyond the coal fields.

4. Ibid., A-1 through A-6. See also the report of the administrator of the Pennsylvania Emergency Relief Administration, quoted in the *Pottsville Republican,* December 27, 1933.

5. *ACIC Report,* 50–51.

6. *Pennsylvania in Review,* September 11, 1937. This magazine is included in the "Bootleg Scrapbooks," a collection of news clippings and memorabilia produced by local WPA Writers Project writers and held at the Pottsville Public Library.

7. Mick Kozak, interview with author, January 5, 1989.

8. U.S. Bureau of Mines, *Minerals Yearbook* (Washington, D.C.: Government Printing Office, 1949), 24. The Bureau of Mines reports 6,200,000 tons of bootleg coal were produced in 1941 by 10,762 workers employed in bootleg mines, compared with 53,942,177 tons produced by 88,840 miners employed in the legitimate anthracite industry.

9. Estimates for bootleg coal production and employment vary widely. The Anthracite Institute, the lobbying and propaganda arm of the coal companies, conducted a survey of bootleg mines in March of 1937. The results of the survey were submitted to the Anthracite Coal Industry Commission and support a claim that approximately 20,000 workers were employed in the mining, transporting, and processing of 4.0 million tons of bootleg coal. Report of the Anthracite Institute, March 29, 1937, box 225, Collection 4742, W. Jett Lauck Papers, Alderman Library, University of Virginia. The Anthracite Commission conducted its own survey during the summer of 1937 and found

11,000 men and women employed in the production of 2.4 million tons of illegally mined coal. *ACIC Report,* 43. Commission members were aware that the survey, conducted during the slack summer season, would provide an undercount of bootleg production and employment totals; however, no effort was made to adjust the estimates. See, for example, the letter from James W. Angell to Anthracite Commission chairman Jett Lauck, April 2, 1937, box 221, Lauck Papers. An estimate, based on the Bureau of Mines report of 1941 bootleg production at 6,200,000 tons and the ACIC's calculation of labor ratios and sales receipts, suggests that well over 30,000 workers were employed in the bootleg industry and accounted for gross annual receipts of $47,000,000 by 1941. There were approximately 28,000 miners employed in company mines in the southern anthracite field, with average per capita income under $1,500.

    10. Bootlegging is mentioned in Irving Bernstein, *The Turbulent Years: A History of the American Worker, 1933–1941* (Boston: Houghton Mifflin, 1970), 423–25; Jeremy Brecher, *Strike!* (Boston: South End Press, 1972), 184–86; Steve Nelson, with James R. Barrett and Rob Ruck, *Steve Nelson: American Radical* (Pittsburgh: University of Pittsburgh Press, 1981), 163–65; Donald L. Miller and Richard E. Sharpless, *The Kingdom of Coal: Work, Enterprise, and Ethnic Communities in the Mine Fields* (Philadelphia: University of Pennsylvania Press, 1985), 319–20; and Douglas Monroe, "A Decade of Turmoil: John L. Lewis and the Anthracite Miners, 1926–1936" (Ph.D. diss., Georgetown University, 1977), 31–32. For a contemporary report, see Louis Adamic, *My America, 1918–1938* (New York: Harper and Brothers, 1938), 316–28. The only extensive scholarly examination of the subject is Rodney Lechleitner, *Bootlegging in Schuylkill County: 1930–1936* (Master's thesis, Bloomsburg University, 1986).

    11. For a representative sampling of anthracite historiography, see David L. Salay , ed., *Hard Coal, Hard Times: Ethnicity and Labor in the Anthracite Region* (Scranton: Anthracite Museum Press, 1984). Miller and Sharpless present a finely textured and fairly comprehensive social history of the anthracite region in *The Kingdom of Coal.* Harold Aurand's *From the Molly Maguires to the United Mine Workers* (Philadelphia: Temple University Press, 1971) remains the single best anthracite labor history.

    12. For one example of recent anthracite scholarship that breaks with the received wisdom on pragmatism, see Grace Palladino, *Another Civil War: Labor, Capital and the State in the Anthracite Regions of Pennsylvania, 1840–68* (Urbana: University of Illinois Press, 1990). See also Victor R. Greene's penetrating analysis of the combustible mixture of class and ethnicity in the coal region, *The Slavic Community on Strike: Immigrant Labor in Pennsylvania Anthracite* (Notre Dame: University of Notre Dame Press, 1968). Against "the generalization of the Slav in America as thoroughly conservative and tradition oriented," Greene persuasively demonstrates the "militant potential"

of the immigrant miner: "In a strike, change was his goal, and his methods were radical . . . ." (213).

13. Aurand, *From the Molly Maguires,* 166.

14. Joe Gowaskie, "John Mitchell and the Anthracite Mine Workers: Leadership Conservatism and Rank-and-File Militancy," *Labor History* 27 (Winter 1985), 83.

15. Historical accounts that cover some of the most intense episodes of rank-and-file insurgency cite "pragmatism" to account for insurgent motivations and objectives. See, for example, Gowaskie, "John Mitchell and the Anthracite Mine Workers," 83; Perry K. Blatz, "Ever-Shifting Ground: Work and Labor Relations in the Anthracite Coal Industry, 1863–1903" (Ph.D. diss., Princeton University, 1986), 662; and Patrick M. Lynch, *Pennsylvania Anthracite: A Forgotten IWW Venture, 1906–1916* (Master's thesis, Bloomsburg State College, 1974).

16. In a comment on the pragmatic character of hard coal miners, the historian Ronald M. Benson authoritatively recites the received wisdom: "American workers were essentially *conservative;* family was often more important than job, religious values more important than secular dogma, and social linkages more attractive than political ideology." Ronald M. Benson, "Commentary: The Family Economy and Labor Protest in Industrial America and the Coal and Iron Police in Anthracite Country," in *Hard Coal, Hard Times,* ed. Salay, 121.

The tendency to reduce the variety of complex motivations operating in the psyche of every American worker into an "essential" characteristic is rooted deep in the historiographic traditions of U.S. labor history. Equally deep rooted is the tendency to reduce workers' ideas on a wide array of political, economic, and social issues to the radical-conservative dichotomy. From such reductionist reasoning, Selig Perlman crafted his highly influential theory of job-consciousness. According to Perlman, American workers are job-conscious not class-conscious, naturally predisposed to a narrow concern with economic interests and job rights and away from any radical propensities by a "universal" psychology of scarcity. Bouts of radicalism originate from the influence of leftist agitators. Selig Perlman, *A Theory of the Labor Movement* (New York: Macmillan, 1928).

Perlman's theory continues to have influential advocates. The preeminent labor historian David Brody, for one, has consistently sung Perlman's praises. Reacting to the alternative unionism thesis advanced by the contributors to *"We Are All Leaders,"* Brody countered with the theory of job-conscious unionism, arguing that Perlman "still serves us well" in two respects: "first, by insisting on some organic link between labor movements and the particular working classes they serve . . . and, second, by identifying the basic characteristics of the American movement. Perlman uses the term 'job-consciousness,' and I am content with it." David Brody, "The Enduring Labor Movement: What the 1930s

Suggest about the Future Prospects of Organized Labor in America" (Paper presented at the North American Labor History Conference, Wayne State University, Detroit, October 1992), 15. Brody has argued for Perlman's theory of job-consciousness in, among other places, "The CIO after 50 Years: A Historical Reckoning," *Dissent* 32 (Fall 1985), 457–71; and "Reinterpreting the Labor History of the 1930s," in *Workers in Industrial America: Essays on the Twentieth Century Struggle* (New York: Oxford University Press, 1980), especially 128–29.

17. John Bodnar, *Anthracite People: Families, Unions, and Work, 1900–1940* (Harrisburg: Pennsylvania Historical and Museum Commission, 1983), 14–15. Donald Miller and Richard Sharpless present much the same interpretation of the hard coal miners' response to the depression, arguing that "the union [UMW] . . . gave them nothing in time of crisis. . . . Once again the workers had to fall back on their own resources, on their families, friends, and kinship networks." Miller and Sharpless, *The Kingdom of Coal*, 311.

Bodnar presents a more fully developed version of his theory of "working-class pragmatism" in "Immigration, Kinship, and the Rise of Working-Class Realism in Industrial America," *Journal of Social History* 14 (Fall 1980), 45–65. See also John Bodnar, *Workers' World: Kinship, Community, and Protest in an Industrial Society, 1900–1940* (Baltimore: Johns Hopkins University Press, 1982).

18. Benson, "Commentary," 121.

19. Howard Kimeldorf and Judith Stepan-Norris present a strong case for the relevance of social movement theory for labor history research in "Historical Studies of Labor Movements in the United States," *Annual Review of Sociology* 18 (1992), 495–517. For a brief critical review of the social movement literature, see Aldon Morris and Cedric Herring, "Theory and Research in Social Movements: A Critical Review," *Annual Review of Political Science* 2 (1987), 137–98; for a more comprehensive review of the literature, see Doug McAdam, John D. McCarthy, and Mayer N. Zald, "Social Movements," in *Handbook of Sociology,* ed. Neil J. Smelser (Beverly Hills, Calif.: Sage Publications, 1988), 695–737. For a sampling of recent theorizing on social movements, see Aldon D. Morris and Carol McClurg Mueller, eds., *Frontiers in Social Movement Theory* (New Haven, Conn.: Yale University Press, 1992).

20. On the definition of social movement as a sustained pattern of conflict, see Charles Tilly, "Social Movements and National Politics," in *Statemaking and Social Movements,* ed. Charles Bright and Susan Harding (Ann Arbor: University of Michigan Press, 1975), 297–317; and Doug McAdam, *Political Process and the Development of Black Insurgency, 1930–1970* (Chicago: University of Chicago Press, 1982), 36–64.

21. McAdam presents a seminal discussion of "indigenous" (community-based) organization and its significance during the course of insurgency in *Political Process and the Development of Black Insurgency,* 43–51.

22. For a critical appraisal of the impact of organization on social movements, see Frances Fox Piven and Richard A. Cloward, *Poor People's Movements: Why They Succeed, How They Fail* (New York: Vintage Books, 1977). Piven and Cloward argue that poor people do not have the resources to sustain movement organizations, and, as a consequence, activists intent on building organizations among the poor must rely on elites for resources. This dependency on elite sponsorship tends to co-opt the activists and dampen the insurgency. This dynamic was largely absent in the bootleg miners' movement since the practice of illegal mining provided the insurgents with the resources needed to sustain their struggle.

23. For an incisive analysis of the transformative consequences of collective action, see Howard Kimeldorf's discussion of the 1934 West Coast longshore strike in *Reds or Rackets: The Making of Radical and Conservative Unions on the Waterfront* (Berkeley: University of California Press, 1988), 100–110; and Rick Fantasia, *Cultures of Solidarity: Consciousness, Action, and Contemporary American Workers* (Berkeley: University of California Press, 1988).

24. In addition to the standard historical sources, this research relies on information gathered from over fifty oral histories (and countless less structured conversations) conducted with people who participated in the events.

25. *ACIC Report*, 43; Greene, *The Slavic Community on Strike*, 185.

26. Joseph Padelsky, interview with author, August 7, 1990.

27. For an account of the long strike, see Miller and Sharpless, *The Kingdom of Coal*, 286–96.

28. The "Bootleg Scrapbook" contains a brief description of coal theft during the long strike.

29. Mike Lucas, interview with author, July 27, 1990.

30. Bill Heitzman, interview with author, August 12, 1991.

31. Monroe's finely crafted history of the equalization movement, "A Decade of Turmoil," is far and away the most balanced and comprehensive treatment of the subject. Steve Nelson, one of the Communist Party's most effective organizers, was assigned to the anthracite region during the 1930s. Nelson's autobiography presents a firsthand account of the anthracite mine workers' struggles and is must reading for any serious student of anthracite. Nelson, *Steve Nelson*, 163–80.

32. Monroe, "A Decade of Turmoil," 137–38.

33. "Final Report of the Anthracite Committee of the Secretary of Labor," April 6, 1934, Secretary Perkins General Subject file, 1933–41, box 132, Office of Secretary, Department of Labor, Record Group 174, National Archives, Washington, D.C.

34. *WPA Report*, A-1; *Pottsville Republican*, December 27, 1933.

35. Estimate based on WPA estimates of unemployment and average yearly wages. *WPA Report*, 19.

36. Pennsylvania Department of Mines and Mineral Resources, *Annual Report* (Harrisburg: Pennsylvania Department of Mines and Mineral Resources, 1931), 22.

37. Lucas interview.

38. Jack Campion, interview with author, July 29, 1990.

39. Charles Komarosky, interview with author, August 2, 1990.

40. Ibid.

41. Campion interview. Remarkably, the Mollies were mentioned without any prompting by almost every bootlegger interviewed. While doing field work in Minersville, I was approached by a woman who looked to be in her nineties. She heard that I was doing research on independent mining and insistently offered this advice: "If you want to learn about bootlegging you'd better find out about the Molly Maguires first."

42. In conversations with nearly a hundred bootleg miners, these were the typical initial responses to the question "Why did you start bootlegging?"

43. Elena Kozak, interview with author, January 5, 1989.

44. Anna P., interview with author, August 12, 1990. Anna chose to remain anonymous, as did a number of other participants in this study.

45. U.S. Department of Labor, Women's Bureau, *Home Environment and Employment Opportunities of Women in Coal-Mine Workers' Families,* Bulletin No. 45 (Washington, D.C.: U.S. Department of Labor, Women's Bureau, 1925), 5.

46. Ibid., 45.

47. Mary W., interview with author, August 3, 1990.

48. The male hard coal miner's acceptance of women in bootleg mines contrasts with the male antagonism typically observed in such male-identified occupations. For an informed analysis of gender identity and class consciousness among coal miners, see Michael Yarrow, "The Gender Specific Nature of Class Consciousness of Appalachian Coal Miners: Structure and Change," in *Bringing Class Back In: Contemporary and Historical Perspectives,* ed. Scott G. McNall, Rhonda F. Levine, and Rick Fantasia (Boulder, Colo.: Westview, 1991), 285–310. Yarrow points out that mine workers' gender consciousness impedes working-class solidarity by excluding women from the "brotherhood of miners" and by maintaining a sense of male superiority over women. Sally Ward Maggard's description of the strike at the Brookside Mine during 1973 captures the volatile mix created by gender and class identities. The presence of women in the strike "did not do much to build [male] self esteem. The men not only were unable to fulfill their roles as family breadwinners, but also were unable to win their strike without the aid of women. This symbolic double emasculation ensured trouble." With women heavily involved in the strike, "household duties did get tended to, however, . . . almost always by the women. No new household division of labor occurred because of the strike." The strike was won largely because of women's participation; however, the relationships

between men and women were deeply strained. Sally Ward Maggard, "Gender Contested: Women's Participation in the Brookside Coal Strike," in *Women and Social Protest,* ed. Guida West and Rhoda Lois Blumberg (New York: Oxford University Press, 1990), 88.

49. William H. Adams, interview with George Korson, September 6, 1957, George Korson Folklore Archive, D. Leonard Corgan Library, Kings College, Wilkes Barre, Pennsylvania. What makes this remark so compelling is that it was made in 1957, long before the contemporary women's movement influenced our sense of fairness about housework. Although many bootleggers claimed they shared the housework, I was somewhat skeptical until I came across the Korson interviews.

50. John Onushco, interview with author, January 2, 1991.

51. Padelsky interview.

52. Pat Sanza, interview with author, July 26, 1990. The same sentiments were often expressed in other interviews.

53. Anna P. interview.

54. Campion interview.

55. Sanza interview.

56. Mick Kozak interview.

57. Elena Kozak interview.

58. Mick Kozak interview.

59. *ACIC Report,* 109–11.

60. Padelsky interview.

61. Mick Kozak interview.

62. Campion interview.

63. Heitzman interview.

64. The ACIC survey indicates that 63 percent of bootleg miners had been previously employed in company mines and nearly half had worked for at least seven years. *ACIC Report,* 91.

65. Tony Russian, interview with author, January 3, 1989.

66. When put to the test, the solidarity of rank-and-file miners in the southern field was undoubtedly stronger than their loyalty to Lewis and the UMW leadership. The debates over contract negotiations at the UMW Tri-District Anthracite Convention in 1935 convey the southern field miners' dissatisfaction with the leadership. John L. Lewis, in his opening report to the convention, implied that the UMW would aid in wiping out bootlegging if the companies "cooperated" with the union. In response, southern district delegates argued heatedly for the bootleggers' cause, while middle and northern district delegates (from the areas where bootlegging never took hold) condemned illegal mining. Although the contract presented for ratification in June 1936 made no mention of bootlegging, a majority of southern district delegates voted against ratification (many argued that it failed to help the jobless situation),

while northern and middle field delegates overwhelmingly voted to ratify. UMW, *Proceedings of the Tri-District Convention* (Hazleton: UMW, 1936).

67. Sanza interview.

68. Joe Hudock, interview with author, August 28, 1990.

69. Jack Reilly, interview with author, July 25, 1990.

70. Sanza interview.

71. Padelsky interview.

72. Such rationales were often reported by bootleggers during these interviews. Miners employed in "legitimate" mines did not express such sentiments toward the legitimacy of the coal companies' property rights.

73. Komarosky interview.

74. Campion interview.

75. Lucas interview.

76. Sanza interview.

77. Lucas interview.

78. Sanza interview.

79. *ACIC Report,* 50–51.

80. Sanza interview.

81. Al Akulauckas, interview with author, August 24, 1990.

82. *Pottsville Republican,* July 9 and 19, 1934.

83. Special Duty Report, July 23, 1934, Bootleg Coal file, box 2249, Gifford Pinchot Papers, Manuscript Division, Library of Congress, Washington, D.C.

84. Ibid.

85. *Pottsville Republican,* July 31, 1934.

86. Open letter from Gifford Pinchot to State Senator Charles W. Staudenmeier, August 9, 1934, Bootleg Coal file, box 2249, Gifford Pinchot Papers.

87. For a somewhat more complete description of the divergent patterns of development, see Miller and Sharpless, *The Kingdom of Coal,* 52–82.

88. The disappearance of local coal capitalists from the southern field is discussed in Edward J. Davies, *The Anthracite Aristocracy: Leadership and Social Change in the Hard Coal Regions of Northeastern Pennsylvania* (DeKalb, Ill.: Northern Illinois University Press, 1985).

89. Steve Nelson, interview with author, August 17, 1990.

90. Mike Semanchick, interview with author, July 29, 1990.

91. In the interviews bootleggers from the Minersville area insisted that the Donaldson-area miners were the "radicals." The Donaldson bootleggers identified the Shamokin group as the "radical ones." The Shamokin miners said that bootleggers from Minersville were the "most radical."

92. Leon Richter, interview with author, August 29, 1990.

93. Harry Charowsky, interview with author, July 28, 1990.

94. Richter interview; Semanchick interview.

95. Sanza interview.

96. Lucas interview.

97. *Pottsville Republican,* April 1, 1935.

98. Ibid., February 19, 1935.

99. Ibid., March 12, 1935.

100. *Shamokin News-Dispatch,* April 3 and 8, 1935.

101. Ibid., May 1, 1935.

102. *Pottsville Republican,* May 1, 1935.

103. Padelsky interview.

104. By 1939, with the insurgency in District 1 long suppressed and the southern field membership in a clear minority, the UMW leadership took a more openly hostile stance toward bootlegging and worked together with the companies to suppress it. At the same time, southern field locals grew increasingly dissatisfied with the UMW and routinely engaged in illegal strikes rather than submit grievances to arbitration. Several locals jumped to an AFL-sponsored miners' union. During World War II southern anthracite locals struck in protest over an increase in union dues and refused to support the nationwide coal strike of 1943.

105. This brief outline of the rather complex period from 1934 to 1940 was drawn from local newspapers, the papers of Governor Earle and Governor James, the Jett Lauck Papers (notes on these sources appear elsewhere in the endnotes), and the records of the U.S. District Court, Eastern District of Pennsylvania, and the U.S. Court of Appeals for the Third Circuit.

106. *Pottsville Republican,* January 27, 1941.

107. Ibid., January 30, 1941.

108. "Anthracite Emergency Program," Governor's file, Governor James Records, Manuscript Group 160, Carton 11, Pennsylvania State Archives, Harrisburg; *Pottsville Republican,* February 6, 1941.

109. *Pottsville Republican,* February 11, 1941.

110. *Shamokin News-Dispatch,* April 16, 1941.

111. Richter interview.

112. Padelsky interview.

113. Mick Kozak interview.

114. *Pottsville Republican,* July 9, 1941.

115. Richter interview.

116. Detailed reporting of the events at Donaldson can be found in the local press. A thick file of state police reports, depositions from each of the company guards and the wounded miners, reports of state police informants, and much more are contained in "Strike Reports File, 1941," Reports of the State Police, Record Group 30, Pennsylvania State Archives.

117. U.S. War Manpower Commission, *Labor Market Problems in the Anthracite Coal Industry* (Washington, D.C.: Government Printing Office, 1943); U.S. Forest Service, *The Population and Employment Outlook for the*

Anthracite Region of Pennsylvania, Anthracite Survey Paper 16 (Washington, D.C.: U.S. Forest Service, May 1, 1945).

118. *Miners' Journal,* November 17, 1943.

119. This piece of the story remains shrouded in mystery, deception, and innuendo. The local papers contain only a hint of the facts. The records of the P&RC&I have "disappeared," and the land transfers are difficult to trace from court records.

120. Not one of the more than twenty-five "legitimate" miners interviewed questioned the coal companies' right to the land or coal, not even when pointedly questioned. Nearly every bootlegger interviewed contested company legitimacy.

8

"We Make You This Appeal in the Name of Every Union Man and Woman in Barberton"

Solidarity Unionism in Barberton, Ohio, 1933–41

John Borsos

Not since the 1920s has the organized labor movement in the United States been in such a weakened position as it is today. Union membership continues to slip from a mid-1950s peak by most estimates of over 33 percent to approximately 12 percent today. Bureaucratic structures, concessionary bargaining, and apathetic rank-and-file members are, with few exceptions, the state of the unions. Assessing the historiography of the Congress of Industrial Organizations, David Brody has chastised those who have argued, "It could have been otherwise." "Rich though the scholarly findings have been," Brody writes, "they have not brought forth one essential for historical reformulation: they have not revealed the alternative that rivaled the union course that was actually taken."[1]

A major reason why Brody could justifiably offer such an assessment has been the paucity of community studies that concentrate on labor in the 1930s. This study challenges Brody's (and others') assertion that the direction the bureaucratic CIO in particular and organized labor in general followed in the 1930s and beyond was the only one possible. In the 1930s in Barberton, Ohio, rank-and-file workers, with virtually no outside leadership, created a broadly inclusive, citywide labor movement based on the notion of community. As such, the Barberton labor movement posed an alternative to the framework of the centralized CIO by making the local movement, rather than the international union, the fundamental basis for its union activity.[2] Certainly bureaucratic unions are the major story of organized labor in the United States from the 1930s to the present, but they are not the only tale.

The Making of an Industrial City, 1891–1929

Barberton is a planned, industrial city located on the outskirts of Akron, Ohio. It was founded in 1891 by Ohio Columbus Barber, a man as obstreperous and vain as his name. Barber was the driving force behind the Diamond Match Company, one of the world's first multinational corporations. In the 1890 census Barber proudly recorded his occupation as "capitalist," and clearly he envisioned the founding of a city as a way to make even more money. Like his Chicago poker-playing buddy George Pullman, Barber was captivated by the idea of a town bearing his own name. But Barber also saw firsthand that Pullman's model city required reciprocity from the founding father; unlike Pullman, Barber was not a paternalist.[3]

In many ways Barberton was the stepchild of corporate capitalism and the bastard child of O. C. Barber. Three of the city's four largest factories in its formative decades—the Diamond Match Company, Pittsburgh Valve and Fittings, and the Columbia Chemical Company—were among the most modern facilities in their respective industries. Unskilled and semiskilled workers formed the corps of the hourly employees. In the fourth, the Babcock and Wilcox Company, the world's largest manufacturer of marine boilers, skilled craftsworkers, particularly iron molders and boilermakers, retained significant control of the shop floor. Yet even at Babcock and Wilcox, this power was usurped after a vicious strike in 1906. By 1910 only a few organized building trades even hinted at the existence of workers' organized power at the point of production.[4]

In the following decades two additional mass-production factories opened in Barberton: the Ohio Insulator Company, a large-volume producer of high-intensity porcelain electrical insulators, and the Seiberling Tire Company, begun by the rubber magnates Charles Seiberling and Frank Seiberling after they were ousted from control of Goodyear Tire and Rubber in 1921. Never growing to the size of the major rubber companies, Seiberling Tire nevertheless became, in the words of one scholar, "the king of small fry" rubber shops.[5]

A city of mass-production industries as the factories expanded, Barberton grew exponentially. It grew so fast (from 1,800 in 1892 to 19,000 in 1920) that the city soon began to call itself the "Magic City." After a period of years the local high school adopted the term for its nickname, and even today, after two decades of deindustrialization, the hometown fans still cheer for the Barberton "Magics."[6]

To fill the ever-increasing number of industrial jobs, local managers recruited European immigrants. In a rough, descending order, Slovaks, Hungarians, Poles, Croatians, and Serbians were the most heavily represented groups. By 1920 at least 50 percent of the population was of immigrant stock. As the local industrial economy stoked up in the years preceding and during World War I, a small number of African Americans came to Barberton. More numerous than the African Americans were the thousands of white Protestants from coal mining and farming backgrounds who migrated from western Pennsylvania, southern Ohio, and West Virginia in the late 1910s and especially the 1920s. The native white migration was enhanced after the passage of restrictive national immigration laws in 1921 and 1924. Gerald "Joe" Palmer, later an activist at the Seiberling tire plant, related:

> An individual came down to [Marion, Ohio] looking for workers at the Seiberling Rubber Company. And we came up here March 25, 1925. There was four of us that came up here. At that time, there was a shortage of help in Akron. They even had men out, they went to West Virginia and places where there was a surplus of labor and brought men, and women as well to Akron and Barberton to work in their rubber shop. I guess they brought some up to work in the foundry as well. A far cry from today when you can't buy a job; then they were soliciting workers.[7]

With rare exceptions, Barberton workers found little success organizing collectively as a class in the first three decades of the twentieth century. Sporadic outbreaks of labor militancy did certainly occur prior to the 1930s: iron molders struck unsuccessfully in 1906, match girls struck in sympathy with the Industrial Workers of the World–led general strike among rubber workers in Akron in 1913, and there were other walkouts, but they were typically unorganized. The city did boast a relatively strong Socialist Party local that consistently drew 25 percent of the vote throughout the 1910s, but it never mustered the votes to capture a single municipal office. On the whole, labor-left traditions were rather tenuous, and by 1919 a lethal combination of repression and welfare capitalism eradicated even those weak tendencies.[8]

With a union option largely unavailable, Barberton's immigrants and later its African American citizens compensated by forming resilient social communities. Between 1903 and 1917 Slovaks, Slovenians, Hungarians, Poles, and African Americans each built churches, many accompanied by parochial schools. Fraternal and benefit societies also proliferated; many, including the Sokol Club, the Jednota Club, the Liedertafel, and the First workers to unionize. Much has been made of the NIRA's section 7a, which purportedly gave workers the right to organize. In reality, as millions of workers found out, section 7a was worth little more than the piece of paper on which it was written. At least in Barberton, however, section 7a gave workers enough confidence to go out and organize. Unions had not had a strong public presence in Barberton since 1906. Yet in the summer of 1933 talk of union was in the streets, in shops, and in the homes of Barberton workers.[13]

The push to unionize Barberton workers grew out of the first attempts to organize the tens of thousands of rubber workers in Summit County, especially Akron, in the summer of 1933. For the first time in decades the Akron Central Labor Union, energized by its dynamic secretary, Wilmer Tate, began to leaflet the huge Akron rubber shops, telling workers they had the right to organize and criticizing the brutal speedup. On June 30, 1933, Tate held the first public union meeting for rubber workers in Summit County, which was open shop, and drew a crowd of several thousand. The impact was electrifying.[14]

Within weeks workers in a variety of industries began to apply to the American Federation of Labor (AFL) for charters as federal labor unions (FLUs), that is, quasi-industrial unions directly affiliated with the AFL rather than an international union. The AFL considered the FLUs temporary structures. The AFL still was resistant to organizing unskilled, mass-production workers, but it hoped it could shove those workers who wanted to be organized into an FLU, from where they could be parceled out into the appropriate craft unions. At a rank-and-file level, workers were unconcerned with the AFL's craft jurisdictional hang-ups. They just wanted to unionize.[15]

Characteristically, rubber workers were the first in Barberton to receive FLU charters. Workers at Seiberling Tire organized FLU 18616 in September 1933, preceding the organization of smaller locals at Seiberling Latex and Sun Rubber. Other Barberton workers soon followed: workers at Diamond Match organized FLU 18928 in October, and those at Columbia Chemical formed FLU 19019 in November 1933. Also in November the insulator workers at the Ohio Insulator plant organized Local 149 of the National Brotherhood of Operative Potters. By late December workers from across the city felt sufficiently empowered to establish the Barberton Central Labor Union (CLU), an umbrella organization that included not only those unions listed above but also craft locals of machinists, bricklayers, and carpenters. Writing to the AFL to request a central labor union charter, one Barberton unionist observed in January 1934, "For the past

Hungarian Society, still exist today. These ethnic social institution:
vided a safety net in an otherwise hostile, capitalistic world and reinf
family ties. Adella Rabith remembered, "We went to dances at our cl
They had dances, almost every Saturday night one lodge or another v
have a dance. And the mother and the father and the children all
You went as a family to the dances. And they had a curfew. Live r
polka bands, they had dances down there all the time."[9]

The development of ethnic communities in Barberton heighten
pervasive spirit of mutual aid and protection—of solidarity—that
characterize the labor movement there when it was launched in the
Though modest spatial groupings did occur, Barberton never devel
Little Poland, a Little Slovakia, or a Little Hungary. One man wh
up on the city's predominantly ethnic West Side recalled, "Our gang v
to Highland Junior High School, there was a Black boy, a Jewish
couple of Slovaks, and a hillbilly, who all walked to school tog
Workers from various ethnic groups often lived side by side on th
working-class West and South sides; they ran into each other on the
and shopped together in the same local stores; most important, the
together in the factories.[10]

At least through the 1920s there were few institutions that attem
meld these various cultures into a class-based movement. But the c
experience of being workers in industrial America would lay the foun
for the emergence of a powerful labor movement. "There were a lot
ple like my parents who lived in neighborhoods," one second-ger
immigrant offered, "and they left Europe because of the oppressio
felt the oppression was in the plant, so it didn't take too much cor
them to join when these guys started the labor movement."[11]

The Formative Era, 1929–35

The Great Depression, beginning in the winter of 1929–30, roc
Magic City especially hard. Nearly all of the city's economy was l
the manufacturing sector. With factory workers laid off in 1930–:
the ethnic Catholic churches teetered on the brink of financial i
1931–32, despite the attempts of local factories to maintain the f:
welfare capitalism by continuing to sponsor company picnics an
leagues, laid-off men who once worked in these factories were se
ples in the streets while their families dined in soup kitchens.[12]

Indirectly it was the inauguration of Franklin Roosevelt and
sage of the National Industrial Recovery Act (NIRA) in 1933 that p

two months, delegates from the Barberton locals have been meeting as the Barberton Labor Council. They have been functioning effectively and have drawn locals close together. Beginning January 1934 all locals are meeting under one roof in what we choose to call our Labor Temple. Here all union activities of this community are centered."[16]

A considerable portion of the close cooperation between the locals stemmed from the fact that Barberton workers largely organized themselves in 1933. Only one AFL organizer was assigned to Summit County in these early, heady days of organizing, which was not enough. But workers were too impatient and determined to wait for the official organizer to launch an organizing drive; they simply organized themselves. Among the first standing committees created by the Barberton CLU was the organizing committee. When one factory established a viable organization, Barberton unionists moved on to the next one. From the outset, therefore, they were not beholden to either the AFL or an international union for their existence.

Like the AFL in general, however, the Barberton CLU in its earliest years was dominated by craft unionists. The CLU president was Harry F. Buffington, a machinist at the Babcock and Wilcox Company and a member of the International Association of Machinists Local 607; its vice president was Russell A. Lisk, a bricklayer. Three of the remaining six officers were also craft unionists. The other three were rubber workers from Seiberling Tire and Sun Rubber.[17]

The leadership was diverse in the new locals. Several were former coal miners from western Pennsylvania and southern Ohio. Many other new leaders, such as Joe Palmer at Seiberling and Forrest Brackett at Ohio Insulator, were from farming backgrounds. There was also, at least initially, a coterie of aspiring businesspeople, such as James "Chick" Evans, who had a B.A. in business from the College of Wooster and dreams of a career as a Republican politician. Immigrants too became active in leadership roles in the new unions: Frank Debevec (a Slovenian) at Diamond Match and Steven Randolph (a Slovak) at Ohio Insulator, for instance. Several women were also involved in organizing the new unions: Jennie Lentol and Leona Morgan at Diamond Match, Mary Randolph and Anna Jastraub at Seiberling Tire, Goldie Robichaud at Seiberling Latex.[18]

The dominant personalities behind the city's early unionization efforts were radicals, especially A. P. Lee of the chemical workers and Francis Gerhart of the match workers. Notably absent among union activists in Barberton in the 1930s were identifiable members of the Communist Party (CP). While Gerhart and Lee were willing to work in conjunction with the CP, they were indigenous non-CP radicals with roots in the Barberton community. This made local rank and filers more receptive to their radicalism. Lee was a young firebrand with a flair for publicity. A socialist, Gerhart first began working at the Diamond Match Company in 1914. According to one profile, he was "a deep student and heavy reader [who] developed certain socialistic tendencies during his boyhood." Already in his fifties when the 1930s began, Gerhart, with a "heavy booming voice," would do more than any single person to shape the Barberton labor movement in its first two decades.[19]

In general, early Barberton labor leaders were native-born Americans, many of whom had resided in the Magic City for a number of years, if not decades. Though ideological differences existed, a certain ecumenical spirit was created as workers united behind a desire to build a strong labor movement, a common goal that overrode the potential conflict between the conservatism of an Evans and the radicalism of a Gerhart. The emerging labor movement in the 1930s provided a vehicle to institutionalize this cooperation—this class solidarity—into structures that would challenge the corporate order.

Like their predecessors in the fraternal organizations, Barberton labor leaders projected a vision of unions as social institutions. Beginning in the winter of 1933–34 the various locals and the Barberton CLU sponsored dances, Christmas dinners, and other social events to draw people into unions. At the meeting of FLU 18616 in December 1933, speeches by the AFL organizer Coleman Claherty and Jacob Coxey, national leader of the hunger marches in the 1890s, were followed by an evening of musical entertainment. In the same month, the local at Diamond Match, FLU 18928, sponsored a "kiddies' party" for all match workers (and their children) who had recently been laid off. Other locals staged round and square dances, often featuring the orchestra of Ray Potts, the pro-labor Summit County sheriff workers helped elect in 1932. In March 1934 the CLU even opened a bar and grill at the Barberton Labor Temple to accommodate workers on their lunch hour and to encourage further class camaraderie. CLU president Buffington made it clear in February 1934 that creating a culture of solidarity was a conscious policy of Barberton organizers: "The social program if properly carried out will weld the members of local labor organizations more closely together and pave the way for even closer cooperation. . . . By attending these affairs, the various members would become better acquainted and probably would understand more fully the viewpoints of the other crafts."[20]

Barberton workers were breaking new ground in building a socially oriented, inclusive labor movement, but they were also doing so with out-moded tools. As Buffington's observation suggests, local labor leaders sought to preserve, at least initially, craft jurisdiction in the union struc-ture. The labor movement that emerged in Barberton in the 1930s was not born as an industrial movement. It was a hybrid, an amalgamation of national AFL structures translated into the real experiences of workers in a small midwestern industrial city. The need and demand for industrial unions would develop out of experience, not ideology. It was organic. In the earliest months of unionization, few perceived the inadequacy of the AFL's approach to unionization.[21]

Through 1934 the AFL did surprisingly well in Barberton, if only be-cause it was inadequately staffed, giving workers at the rank-and-file lev-el enough space to create their own movement. The AFL conceived of fed-eral labor unions as temporary, but the influx of mass-production workers, such as the rubber workers at Seiberling Tire and the match workers at Diamond Match—those seemingly devoid of craft status (at least in the eyes of the AFL)—gave the new FLUs in Barberton a more permanent sta-tus.[22]

According to prevailing stereotypes, Barberton workers should have been difficult to organize because many were immigrants themselves or of foreign extraction. The docility of immigrants was something management counted on and unions hedged against, but the actual nuts and bolts of organizing workers into unions in Barberton were screwed into place with relative ease. Many of the immigrants, as well as the native-born migrants, had been members of the United Mine Workers during their years in the coal fields of western Pennsylvania, West Virginia, and southern Ohio. At least initially, only a small number of immigrants became union leaders, but as one union activist noted, they "were very active. You'd go to meet-ings and they were there and they were saying what they thought. I'd say they were very active, not holding union jobs, but supportive of the offic-ers. When you needed them, they were there."[23]

It seemed to local activists who volunteered as organizers that few Bar-berton workers needed much convincing to join the union. One early member of FLU 18928 at Diamond Match recalled, "They had to have a union, they needed it. They joined easy." Reasons cited for joining included the need for water fountains, restrooms for women, and longer relief pe-riods. A Columbia Chemical worker remembered, "I joined right away. It was a rough place to work and it was hard to keep people because the conditions were so bad. And when conditions are bad it's hard to satisfy a worker no matter who he is—he's gotta take so much. That was one of the first things I did. Nobody asked me. When I saw people get pushed around in the Chemical I said, 'That's for me!'" A depression-era Ohio Insulator employee explained that one day he heard that people were trying to organize a union, and the next day he was asked to join: "They asked me to join one night, and I did. There wasn't much to it."[24]

Others did, in fact, have to be convinced to join. Joe Voros of Diamond Match recalled, "I never wanted to join a union when I first started working [1924]. Then I came to realize that a workingman would be foolish not to join a union." While they were sympathetic, many workers were not going to stick their necks out. Marie Starn, later a long-time officer of FLU 18928 at Diamond Match, explained that she "held back from joining right away" because she was not sure that the union was going to last. Even for those who "held back," however, most were not opposed to unions. Rather, practical concerns delayed their signing up. On the whole, Joe Palmer, an early leader in FLU 18616, recalled, convincing people about the benefits of unionization was not a problem: "We had little trouble organizing the Seiberling. Of course, there were always a few who didn't want to, but we didn't have to encourage too many."[25]

Barberton's Catholic priests also aided local organizational efforts. Father Edward Stanko, the son of a Youngstown steelworker and pastor of SS Cyril and Methodius, was a strong advocate of organized labor; Joseph Medin, the pastor of Sacred Heart, was militantly pro-labor and was frequently identified as Barberton's "labor priest." While many Catholic theologians stopped short of embracing the class struggle, Medin became a familiar sight on Barberton picket lines. According to George Marinich, one of Medin's altar boys who became a leader in the Seiberling Tire local, Father Medin came to Barberton from the Minnesota copper mining areas. Prior to that, he had been involved in labor struggles in Croatia: "He supported the unions. He used to talk to the younger people: 'That's the only way you're going to survive—sticking together.' He'd buy hams and take them down to the soup kitchen."[26]

One additional factor also aided the organizational drives of the early 1930s in a few of the factories: management itself. Brought under the jurisdiction of the National Recovery Administration (NRA), some Barberton corporations actually adhered to the NRA codes and section 7a. At Columbia Chemical, the plant manager, Hugh Galt, used his position on the local NRA board to battle the union, but others were more conscientious in following the law of the land. Diamond Match and Seiberling Tire, in particular, were less inclined to use extralegal means to thwart unionization efforts.[27]

Although managers at Seiberling Tire and Diamond Match continued to resist unionization—they refused to bargain collectively and withheld union recognition—they did refrain from attempting totally to repress the union movement. As one unionist put it, "I think Seiberling was all right, once they got used to the ideas of unions—it was like the South didn't want to give up the slaves—they hated to give up power to poor workers." Developing their movement horizontally, reinforcing the notion of class solidarity, workers at these two plants used this breathing space to aid organizers in other plants, where the going was more difficult.[28]

Workers at Babcock and Wilcox (B&W), Ohio Insulator, and Columbia Chemical were less fortunate than their brothers and sisters at Seiberling Tire and Diamond Match. B&W had earned the nickname locally as the "Butcher Shop," a loaded phrase capturing the atmosphere of low pay, dangerous work conditions, and adversarial labor-management relations prevailing in the company. Employees at B&W had been among the first in Barberton to begin organizing, staging a protest against wage cuts after the adoption of the NRA code in the boiler industry in August 1933. But the organization was never able to get off the ground. B&W responded to the protest by forming a company union. Few participated in it, but it did dissipate interest in an independent union.[29]

Disinterest in an independent union at B&W also was a product of the craft bias of Barberton CLU president Harry Buffington. One of the limited number of B&W employees eligible for membership in an AFL craft union, Buffington was a proud member of Machinists Local 607. Buffington was so proud, in fact, that he publicly distanced himself from the fledgling organizational drive that developed among the plant's unskilled work force. Organizers among the unskilled took great pains to attract the predominantly immigrant B&W rank and file into the union. For example, they brought in foreign-language organizers to speak to aspiring members. But organizers were unsuccessful in bridging the gap between the skilled and unskilled workers.[30]

In the spring of 1934 B&W workers threatened to strike to force company adherence to the NRA, only to be undermined by Buffington's insistence on craft autonomy. Disheartened, workers at B&W generally lost faith in the union. Though union activists continued to try to nurture the fragile organization and Buffington would soon resign as head of the Barberton CLU, at B&W the damage was done. Renewed employer resistance choked the rank-and-file union that had sprouted briefly in 1933–34 and delayed unionization of that company for another two years.[31]

Employer opposition to unions also flourished at Columbia Chemical and Ohio Insulator, but at these workplaces unionism was not hindered by internal tensions. Extant records are sparse for determining how workers built a cohesive union in a hostile environment at Columbia Chemical, but the survival of the local union minute book helps explain how that process occurred at Ohio Insulator.

As the minute book of Potters' Local 149 reveals, the unions that Barberton workers created were both labor (i.e., trade unions) and social organizations. Local union meetings were deeply ritualized affairs, with passwords, membership inductions, singing, guest speakers, and recurrent exhortations on the benefits of labor. In many ways they paralleled a church service. The president of Local 149 opened the weekly Friday night meetings, quickly moving into the organizational and business matters at hand. Since Ohio Insulator was not yet fully organized at this stage, part of the meeting was devoted to bringing in members. New members were fully initiated into the organization when a union member in good standing vouched for their veracity. Once accepted, the new members earned full union status: they received full voting rights, were made responsible for paying union dues, and were given the password that enabled entry into the next union meeting. As one Barberton worker who was sworn into the B&W local union in similar fashion recalled, the oath "really made you feel like you were a member of the union, with an obligation too."[32]

Following the initiations, Local 149 turned to committee reports, after which the president of the union would offer comments. Members frequently discussed local strike situations and labor unrest in general. When these matters were concluded, the floor was opened for comments under the heading of "Benefit of Labor." After all had spoken their fill, the meeting might end in song, typically one of the labor standards like "Solidarity Forever." Joe Palmer of the Seiberling local noted that members sang "more at the meetings, not at the picket line. They'd have union meetings and sing at them to stir up enthusiasm."[33]

The union often became the vehicle for working-class leisure activities. Union-sponsored dances were common. The Barberton CLU and several other local unions also encouraged the spouses of male members to participate in women's auxiliaries and union buyers' clubs. At factories that directly employed women, such as Diamond Match and Seiberling Latex, women fully participated in the affairs and management of the union. Women replicated prevailing gender norms concerning the role of females in the movement by assuming responsibility for food preparation and record keeping, two traditionally female-classified tasks. Nevertheless, some women also assumed leadership positions in the unions, albeit secondary ones. Two out of three of the officers of FLU 18928 at Diamond Match, for example, were women. As Jennie Lentol, the twenty-five-year-old secretary of FLU 18928, put it at the time, "I am glad organized labor is giving the women of today something to say about their working conditions and the general conduct of industry."[34]

The Friday night Local 149 meetings included a postmeeting social hour, with refreshments and a raffle. Often there was music, performed by a hired band. Like the ethnic fraternal organizations, the locals and the Barberton CLU also frequently sponsored dances that the entire family—kids and all—was encouraged to attend. Unions developed as family organizations; joining a union in Barberton became similar to joining a church.

In the initial months of organizing, Barberton workers were laying a foundation for a community-based movement bonded together by class solidarity. But solidarity is not simply achieved at a union dance, or at a union picnic, or even at a union meeting. Solidarity is a product of struggle, a precipitate of conflict, a feeling that develops when one group of workers is willing to undertake direct action at great risk, often physical, for the benefit of others. The organizational acumen of Barberton's labor leaders brought rank-and-file workers into the social world of the union by way of dances and other social activities, but the collective development of these workers formed only under fire—in struggle. The development and maturation of solidarity unionism in Barberton was the product of class conflict.

Striking for Union

Prior to the 1930s the city of Barberton had last experienced a strike in 1913, when the workers at Diamond Match walked out in sympathy with the rubber workers engaged in a general strike in Akron. It was therefore fitting that the workers of Diamond Match were the first to puncture the air of labor tranquility in the 1930s. On its face, the walkout at Diamond Match, which began March 17, 1934, was uneventful. Workers walked out for a relatively mundane reason—compliance with the NRA match code—which would significantly raise the wages of the approximately 50 percent of the labor force that was female. Though the employees were represented by three separate unions—FLU 18928, Machinists Local 607, and a union of Maintenance Mechanics—the unions worked "in coordination," including joint negotiations with the company. While they were out, the match workers also railed against the hated piece-rate system known as the Bedaux system.

For five weeks the workers held out before winning, in the words of local president Francis Gerhart, "all points asked for." The match workers won a signed, six month written agreement from the company that included provisions for seniority by crafts within departments. The workers at Diamond Match drove the newborn Barberton labor movement into new territory, the world of picket lines, mutual aid, victory, and solidarity. Community support was broad. Non–Diamond Match workers contributed money, food, and picket line support. Barbers and dentists even offered free services to the strikers. Summarizing the victory for the *Akron Times-Press,* Francis Gerhart explained the importance of the Diamond Match strike and his union's relation to other workers: "This plant is now 100 per cent organized. It is the first match plant in America to reach that goal. I have ordered the piles of ashes, stoves, fallen trees and other obstructions and piles of bricks removed at once from the old picket line. We have put them safely away because someone may need them." His assessment was correct; they were needed, and almost immediately.[35]

Workers at Diamond Match had been fortunate in that their picket line was largely unobstructed. The members of FLU 19019 at Columbia Chemical were afforded no such luxury. Management at Columbia Chemical, a subsidiary of Pittsburgh Plate Glass, consistently opposed union organization. In March 1934 the company fired seven union activists, including A. P. Lee, in an attempt to chop the head off the organizing campaign. Rank-and-file opposition to the firings was still simmering when Columbia Chemical announced the implementation of a company union on April 22, 1934. The day the company union plan was announced, workers spontaneously walked out. The strikers made no wage demands.

Hugh Galt, Columbia Chemical's plant manager, viewed the strike as a personal affront and ordered strikebreakers into the plant to maintain operations. A speeding car tried to crash through the picket line and injured three workers. The Summit County sheriff, Ray Potts, displayed his loyalty to the Barberton workers by having the driver of the vehicle arrested for criminal endangerment. Unable to pierce the picket line by automobile, Columbia Chemical then attempted to sneak scabs into the plant by railcar. Sentries of workers discovered the ploy, blocked the train, and forcibly removed the special force of strikebreakers from the railcar. For a short while a hand-to-hand battle ensued. The picket line held. Two days later the company was willing to settle.[36]

The victorious Diamond Match strike generated wide community support and contributed to a growing class consciousness among Barberton workers, but the strike at Columbia Chemical had an even greater impact. Both men and women figured dramatically in the strike activity. As one West Side resident remembered, women physically attacked one particular boss who was "anti-union, anti-religion, and anti-Hunky." During the strike he tried to climb a fence to get into the plant, but "those Hunky women grabbed him off the fence and pulled his pants off." In a U.S. Senate investigation of the strike, a professional strikebreaker responded affirmatively to Senator Robert La Follette's question whether mass picketing inhibited the use of scabs: "The women would lay down in front of the cars. The executives would start to go in, and they would lay down right in front of the car."[37]

The strike's settlement was anticlimactic. Columbia Chemical agreed to submit the employees' discharge case to the National Labor Board (NLB), the weak forerunner of the National Labor Relations Board. Eventually, the NLB upheld the company's firings. But as a goodwill gesture, and in an attempt to reassert paternalistic control of the company, Columbia Chemical agreed to rehire the men. In two successive strikes, one marred by violence, Barberton workers had tasted victory. More important, they had generated and experienced solidarity.[38]

The NLB's decision in the Columbia Chemical discharge case provided a rude awakening to local unionists regarding the role of the federal government in protecting union activity. One year later as another strike loomed at Diamond Match, the National Match Workers' Council, under Francis Gerhart's control, refused to allow the Regional Labor Board to intervene. According to the match workers, their reluctance to use the board was

> not motivated by disrespect but solely because the activities of Employers has made it unwise or inadvisable for us to avail ourselves of the services of the Board. . . .
>
> In other words, we know from experience of other Unions in this district, and also by the veiled threat from our own Match Employers, that if we submit our case to the Regional Board and the Board's decision was in favor of the Union, (as it undoubtedly would be) they would appeal the case to the National Labor Relations Board and if the National Board's decision sustained that of the Regional Board, (which undoubtedly they would in this clear case of law violation) then the Employer would resort to the Courts and this whole procedure would

take months and it is just this time that the Employers are playing for in the hope that somehow in the interim, the members of the union will become disgusted and discouraged with the result that the Union will break up.

We are not going to stand for this and as we see it, our only hope is through strike and to battle it out on the picket line, which procedure they cannot take to Court. This, of course, is a ridiculous situation in that the Government's idea and purpose was to prevent and make unnecessary the vicious weapon of strike, but when the Employers of this country are permitted to violate the laws of the land and defeat the purpose of Government and organized labor in their efforts to establish a peaceful and controlled society, the Match Workers are ready to take up the instruments of industrial warfare and prosecute that warfare with every ounce of energy that they possess.

That is, we'll take care of ourselves.[39]

Columbia Chemical's resort to violence also had a sobering effect on local union activists. The company's use of strikebreakers and thugs and their willingness to attack peaceful picketers seared into workers' consciousness the stakes for which they were fighting. Rather than weaken the Barberton labor movement, however, the Columbia Chemical strike empowered it. The Columbia Chemical strike converted the primarily financial and spiritual support generated during the Diamond Match strike into solidarity. At Columbia Chemical strikers and their supporters were cornered into putting their ideals into reality, fusing theory and practice. Columbia Chemical transformed an intellectual ideal—solidarity, an injury to one is an injury to all—into a way of life, sealed by the very real possibility of physical injury. As the daughter of one union activist involved in the Columbia Chemical strike captured it, "Not only did they risk their jobs, they risked their lives."[40]

It was more than just Columbia Chemical strikers and their families who were taking these risks; it was the entire working-class community of Barberton. To Barberton workers, it was becoming evident that their cause was becoming the struggle of the community against the corporations, a fusion that had the potential of transcending class boundaries. For the first time the Magic City was beginning to polarize between pro-union and anti-union sectors, with little room for equivocation. One member of the Sacred Heart parish described the aftermath of the Columbia Chemical strike: "I remember some families in our church, Sacred Heart, who were leaders in the church, who scabbed. They were no longer pillars in that church. The people wanted nothing to do with them. For a long time they weren't treated very good."[41]

Several factors contributed to class polarization in Barberton and heightened Barberton workers' suspicions of the federal government and the national labor movement. The Supreme Court's nullification of the NIRA in the so-called Sick Chicken case confirmed what the local labor movement already knew: the right to organize, under section 7a, was only as good as the Barberton working class, not the Roosevelt Administration, had the power to make it.

Cynicism concerning Washington as a friend of labor deepened in 1935. Rubber workers in Akron and Barberton were on the verge of a national strike in April, only to be undercut by a sellout agreement negotiated between William Green, president of the AFL, and the various rubber company executives. In Akron this agreement diffused the popularly mobilized strike sentiment among rubber workers and precipitated the rapid decline in membership among rubber workers in the FLUs.

But the effect in Barberton was a little different. The labor movement in Barberton was less tied to the rubber industry than in Akron, and it was also less tied to the AFL structure. For some of the smaller Barberton rubber worker locals, such as Sun Rubber FLU 18557 and Seiberling Latex FLU 18491, the rubber agreement did in fact spell an end to early union efforts. But in the larger, better organized local, Seiberling Tire FLU 18616, the impact was less damaging. In a city largely forsaken by outside union organizers, the rubber agreement seemed to strengthen local unionists' resolve.[42]

The AFL's role in the rubber agreement also encouraged Barberton unionists to work horizontally and independently. Local labor leaders began to interpret ambiguous AFL policy in their own way, for their own ends. At its annual convention in San Francisco in November 1934, the AFL gave a lukewarm endorsement of industrial unionization. To Barberton workers, this was translated as open advocacy of industrial unionism: coordinating bodies were organized in plants where craft unions had a presence, while workers elsewhere were channeled exclusively into the FLUs. When the United Rubber Workers' international union was organized in September 1935, the Seiberling local was among the first to join. At about the same time, Francis Gerhart encouraged the formation of the National Match Workers' Council, in effect a national coordinating organization of match workers' locals from across the country. Within the Diamond Match local, the maintenance mechanics had moved beyond functioning "in coordination" with FLU 18928 to outright affiliation. In the words of the boiler mechanic Joe Voros:

> When they first started the union they had to be part of the AF of L. And they found out that it just didn't work right. For instance, the power

house, the entire power house was under the engineers in Akron. And it seemed like Gerhart did all the negotiating and as far as the engineers were concerned a fellow by the name of Jones just sat there. Jones got involved in a bombing, and he ended up in the state penitentiary and after that we broke away from the engineers and became a part of the match workers. And that's when I became active in it. I thought, "We've got to have somebody speak up for us," so I became active in the organization. The match workers did all the negotiating. We had no representation. We said, "Hey, let's get into the one that's doing the work for us."[43]

FLU 19019 at Columbia Chemical closely coordinated with the craft unions in the plant, and Potters' Local 149 at Ohio Insulator made no distinction by way of craft. By the winter of 1934–35, though they were not always officially sanctioned or recognized as such, Barberton locals were functioning as industrial unions. Furthermore, individuals who advocated industrial unionism gained control of the Barberton Central Labor Union. The Harry Buffingtons, who insisted on craft autonomy, had been brushed aside by the Francis Gerharts, who demanded class solidarity.[44]

The Barberton labor movement dared to project this vision nationally. At the 1935 AFL convention in Atlantic City, twenty-one resolutions were introduced advocating industrial unionism. Among these twenty-one were two resolutions from Barberton locals: FLU 19019 at Columbia Chemical and FLU 18616 at Seiberling Tire. The resolution from FLU 19019 asserted that "every man can see the crying need of enlisting together not only as workers in a particular shop or factory but as a class of workers. . . ." Appropriately and symbolically, it was debate on the resolution from Seiberling FLU 18616 advocating industrial unionism that inspired John L. Lewis to sock William Hutcheson of the Carpenters' union in the jaw, delivering the blow that launched the Committee for Industrial Organization.[45]

Washington indifference and AFL ambivalence reinforced the notion among Barberton unionists that meaningful social change would occur by first focusing energy in the community, by building solidarity at the grass roots. In doing so, workers themselves contributed to the intensification of class relations in Barberton in 1934–35. Among their most provocative acts was to sponsor the mayoral candidacy of Fred Marvin in the 1935 municipal elections. Marvin was a machinist and activist in International Association of Machinists Local 607. A former secretary of the Barberton CLU, Marvin ran as a Republican.

Marvin's opponent, Earl Davis, had a credible past with the labor movement. His father, George Davis, had been a moving force in the Barberton labor movement at the turn of the century and a towering figure in local Democratic politics. Elected mayor of Barberton in 1933 at age thirty-three (the youngest mayor ever), Davis carried the city in that year by the largest percentage in Barberton history. When labor began to organize as his term was beginning, Davis preached a doctrine of labor-management neutrality—he did not want to take sides. By 1935, as relations between management and labor strained to the breaking point, neutrality was no longer appropriate. In the words of John McNamara, then-president of the Barberton city council, "For some reason, labor got anti-Davis, and they took it out on me too." As Davis retold it, "It was labor's time, and they were on the move. It was a ground swell. And I got beat."[46]

Marvin's victory was indicative of organized labor's rapid accumulation of power in Barberton. Just as local unionists progressed toward an industrial unionism within the dilapidated structure of the AFL, so too did Barberton organized labor's initial success in politics emerge within the shell of the traditional local political structure. The fact that Marvin ran and won as a Republican should not obscure the importance of his victory. Nationally by 1934 workers were beginning to identify almost exclusively as Democrats, but locally the political climate was more personalized and less bound to party labels. Like John L. Lewis himself, many Barberton workers, especially those with pasts as coal miners and farmers, had remained faithful to the Republican Party. Local business dominance of the Barberton Democratic Party also stimulated a willingness for workers to vote for a Republican labor candidate.

Labor's victory at the polls in November 1935 was set in bold relief by a strike by Potters' Local 149 at the Ohio Insulator plant. Local 149 struck over several demands: a wage hike, improved ventilation, an end to the Bedaux incentive pay system, and termination of employees' forced contributions to the Community Fund (a forerunner of the United Way). The Bedaux system especially outraged workers. The son of an Ohio Insulator union activist recalled that his father "would be very unhappy when the time study men would try to redo the rate in what they called the Bedaux system. I don't know why I remember that so well, but I'll never forget how he talked about that Bedaux system and how unfair it was." The strike began September 19, 1935, and for nine weeks the picket lines were peaceful and free from incident. The *Akron Times-Press* described the strike as "one of the most peaceful labor demonstrations ever held in the Midwest."[47]

On the night of November 22, however, a group of strikebreakers led by the infamous commander of Goodyear's Flying Squadron, Colonel

Joseph Johnston, crashed through the picket line, firing tear gas at the peaceful picketers. Johnston's charge came unexpectedly and without provocation. Unarmed, the picketers and their supporters retaliated by throwing rocks. In the confusion a pitched battle broke out. Several innocent bystanders were injured by the wanton release of tear gas. Gassing victims ranged from a seven-year-old girl to a grandmother. To this day, eyewitnesses will describe the heavy clouds of tear gas that descended over the city.[48]

In the melee the strikebreakers were able to force entry into the plant, but they then became trapped inside. After several hours the battle simmered. With the situation relatively pacified, the lame duck mayor, Earl Davis, along with the new Summit County sheriff, James Flowers, read the riot act to the pickets, ordering them to disperse. By then the members of Local 149 were flanked by brothers and sisters from each of the Barberton local unions, as well as supporters from Cleveland and Akron. They defied the order, which provoked more violence—a street battle lasting for nearly ten hours. The *Akron Times-Press* described the scene as a "street war," and included in its coverage a map of the "battlefield," complete with arrows pointing out the parries and thrusts of the opposing sides. One participant later explained, "It was sort of like a war with two units clashing like that." Remarkably, no one was killed.[49]

Solidarity unionism was on the verge of maturity in Barberton. Responding to the unprovoked violence and the action of the mayor and sheriff, the Barberton CLU sanctioned a general strike in Barberton to begin the following day, unless a suitable solution could be worked out. Francis Gerhart justified the general strike "in view of the fact that Sheriff Flowers and Mayor Davis won't listen to reason." "A city-wide strike," he continued, "seems to be our only hope. I move that we ask the Chamber of Commerce to try to call a halt to the gassing. If they refuse or are unable to stop this warfare, then we'll all strike. The final decision on this move rests with the members of the potters' local. If they approve, we'll support them with all the strength we have." A pottery worker told the gathered crowd, "Twenty-four hours ago I wouldn't have even thought to consent to such a move. Now I am. I see no other way out." James Evans, president of the Seiberling rubber workers' local told Sheriff Flowers, "Probably the most unpopular man in the country tonight is you. And Mayor Davis is probably next." A. P. Lee, president of the chemical workers' local, told the strikers, "Your battle is our battle and if necessary we will quit work to help picket the Ohio Insulator. If our own forces are inadequate there are plenty of reserves in Akron and Cleveland."[50]

With a general strike imminent, civic leaders from outside the mayor's office rushed into the fray, organizing a forty-eight-hour truce between Ohio Insulator and the unions. Few were optimistic. Forest Brackett, president of Potters' Local 149, warned, "It looks very much like a general strike will follow if no agreement is reached." On November 23, 1935, Francis Gerhart, speaking on behalf of the entire Barberton labor movement, announced a massive labor rally to be held in two nights. If the strikebreakers were removed from the plant, Gerhart declared, the gathering would be a celebration. If they were not removed, however, the rally would ring in a general strike. While on his soap box, Gerhart also threw in the need "in this city for an organized labor party" to transform Barberton into a "Utopia" of unionism.[51]

On November 25, when the truce was due to expire, the Barberton CLU formally approved a general strike. A committee of seven, headed by Francis Gerhart, representing various locals in the city was empowered to call the strike when "all other reasonable means of settling the strike are exhausted." In a statement released to the press, H. D. Hanna, the secretary of the committee of seven, warned, "After 6 P.M. today the CLU will not be responsible for any violence perpetrated by any person or persons connected with the strike. The CLU does not indorse any further extension of the truce after 6 P.M. today and the CLU will not be satisfied unless labor be removed from the plant after 6 P.M."[52]

If the plant managers of Ohio Insulator were inclined to test the limits of working-class solidarity in Barberton, the rest of the business community and local government were not. Catering to the demands of the labor unions, as well as to civic pressure and the threat of federal intervention, Sheriff Flowers, with the support of Mayor Davis, officially closed the Ohio Insulator factory on November 25. Ignoring the protest of the Ohio Insulator plant manager, William Marr, who decried this abridgement of corporate rights, Flowers justified his decision with the contention that "human property supersedes private property." In spite of Flowers's rhetoric (which seemed more indicative of the beliefs of the workers of Barberton than his own feelings), Gerhart for one remained unimpressed with the sheriff's change of heart: "It doesn't change my attitude. Sheriffs, as officers, are representatives of the capitalist class."[53]

The official decision to close the plant spelled victory for the Barberton labor movement. Though the strike would continue for another four weeks and would conclude with no apparent gains for the potters, solidarity unionism prevailed in the Magic City. As one Barbertonian, who as a young boy had "helped to break a few windows there" during the strike, expressed it, "That was one time when this community was really together. The people of Barberton really stood behind the workers."[54] Local unions in Barberton had proven under fire their willingness to act in sympathy with other unions in trouble. They were willing to engage in battle if necessary. They were willing to defy authority if necessary. They were willing to carry out a general strike if necessary. They proved to themselves in practice that solidarity unionism worked.

That evening, November 25, 1935, union members and their families from all over the area gathered in Barberton for a victory parade. Among those who spoke to the assemblage were Sherman Dalrymple and John House of the United Rubber Workers, who in a few short weeks were to lead a monumental struggle against the Goodyear Tire and Rubber Company. The Ohio Insulator victory energized the entire region. Francis Gerhart also spoke and publicly warned the company and anyone else who was interested that bad-faith bargaining could still trigger a general strike: "I want to instruct all local union presidents to be in readiness at any moment to call a meeting to decide on a general strike as we have outlined." Mayor-elect Marvin reaffirmed to the labor crowd that they had done well in selecting him as their candidate. "I'm with you," he told them, "I'm one of you." Men, women, and children marched defiantly through the Magic City. They sang labor songs as they paraded. Most popular was the local adaptation, "Tie Jim Flowers to the Sour Apple Tree." A revolution of sorts had occurred, indicated most dramatically by the vehicle that led the paraders—a Barberton police cruiser adorned with banners and singing strikers. Solidarity unionism, in short, had arrived in the Magic City, and with a police escort no less.[55]

Solidarity Unionism in Barberton, 1936–41

By November 1935, in the very month John L. Lewis formed the Committee for (later Congress of) Industrial Organization, solidarity unionism was already firmly entrenched in the city of Barberton. It is more than ironic that a Barberton local introduced the resolution that precipitated John L. Lewis's famous punch, for the solidarity unionism and the CIO unionism that connected historically were related, but alternative visions, of a new labor movement. As Mike Davis has commented concerning the period of 1933–34, the new unionism confronted the AFL old guard with two subversive forms: "mass industrial unions, or their functional homologues, broadly inclusive and independent city labor movements."[56]

CIO unionism was business unionism. As Staughton Lynd has suggested, "The CIO *from the beginning* intended a top-down, so-called responsible unionism that would prevent strikes and control the rank and file."[57] The CIO, with its origins in Lewis's autocratic United Mine Workers, was a centralized, tightly controlled movement from its very inception. It was preoccupied with top-level negotiations, signed contracts, a no-strike provision, dues check-off, and a closed shop. It was greatly concerned about checking a militant, democratic rank and file, except in a local union's struggle to win its first signed agreement.

Solidarity unionism in Barberton was one of the second subversive forms: "broadly inclusive and independent city labor movements." It developed organically; it grew out of the experience of Barberton workers in class conflict with their employers. Solidarity unionism originated within the outmoded structure of the AFL and transformed it. Direct action, sympathy strikes, general strikes, and social organizations were its essence.

In recent years historians have fatalistically accepted the development of industrial unionism of the CIO variety as a fait accompli, as if there were no other possibilities. The Barberton experience suggests otherwise. The development of a militant labor union culture was not dependent on the CIO. In fact the CIO was more a product of the growth of solidarity unionism in Barberton and other places like it than vice versa.

John L. Lewis tasted the flavor of the Barberton labor movement in an appearance on January 19, 1936, at the Akron Armory on behalf of the rubber workers. Braving the cold and snowy weather, Barberton workers turned out in droves to see Lewis but also to cheer their mayor, Fred Marvin, who shared the platform with the Mine Workers' leader. Within weeks of the Lewis rally, Barberton workers were back in the streets.[58]

In early February members of Barberton's Workers' Alliance, a left-wing organization of local Works Progress Administration (WPA) workers, led a demonstration against proposed WPA cuts. The CLU supported the protest, significant for its expressed dissatisfaction with the local WPA as well as for its display that the community's unemployed were also a vital part of the local labor movement. By working together, the city's WPA and unemployed strengthened the hand of unionists in the factories by eliminating this potential source of strikebreakers. They further contributed to a spirit of working-class solidarity.[59]

Inspired by the victory at Ohio Insulator in November 1935 and the wave of sit-down strikes that electrified the Akron rubber shops in early 1936, Barberton unionists took the offensive in February 1936. The strikes at Columbia Chemical in 1934 and Ohio Insulator in 1935 had been largely defensive; 1936 was different. Barberton workers sought to create not just a union presence but also, more poignantly, a union town.

On February 18, 1936, with sit-downs spreading throughout area rubber shops, eleven pipe fitters at Columbia Chemical sat down, demanding a four-cent raise to bring them to parity with fellow workers in the chloride department. Columbia Chemical became the first nonrubber shop to sit down. Management refused to consider the pipe fitters' demand, which led to the sit-down of the full first shift. The strike of the first shift shut down the entire plant. Interestingly, even a job action focusing on the shop floor could involve wider community and family support. "I remember when we was a kid," one man whose father was involved in the Columbia Chemical sit-down recalled, "they had a sitin and we used to take his lunch and hand it over the fence." Workers stayed inside for four days, before pulling out of the plant and commencing a more standardized strike. By this time, the great Goodyear strike in Akron was in full bloom.[60]

Once the strikers came outside, both sides dug in. Columbia Chemical was not, however, prepared to sponsor a repeat of its picket-crashing performance, which could very likely turn into a general strike; once workers hit the bricks, FLU 19019 was not content merely to press the pipe fitters' demand for a small wage increase. Along with the pay raise for pipe fitters, A. P. Lee added the demand for outright union recognition. As in the past, the Barberton labor community rallied to the strikers' cause.

The stalemate dragged on for nearly six more weeks. Facing again a formidable show of community solidarity, Columbia Chemical indicated its willingness to negotiate. The company offered a written agreement that withheld formal recognition of the union but did give a slight pay increase. The contract also contained a binding arbitration clause, in exchange for the union's relinquishing the right to strike. Hoping to circumvent the rank-and-file militants, Columbia Chemical drew up the contract in consultation with the AFL regional organizer, H. A. Bradley. The agreement awaited only FLU 19019's approval.

To the horror of the company and Bradley, A. P. Lee denounced the settlement. Lee described the agreement as "35 points and 27 pages with nothing in it" and recommended that the membership vote it down. Bradley was incensed and exerted great pressure on FLU 19019 to accept the offer. But the rank and file voted to hold out.[61]

Bradley had erred badly by trying to settle the strike without FLU 19019 input. In response FLU 19019 offered its own contract as a basis of negotiations, a process that dragged on for two more weeks. Severely damaged by the strike because of the peculiar nature of the chemical manufacturing process that required around-the-clock maintenance (which also made management desirous of a no-strike clause), Columbia Chemical sued for peace on April 8, 1936. FLU 19019 became, after FLU 18928 at Diamond Match, the second Barberton local to sign a union contract.[62]

As a fitting epilogue to the strike, FLU 19019 remained in the AFL long enough to receive the several thousand dollars in strike benefits that had been delayed by the union bureaucracy. But once the benefits' check was received, they bolted to the Flat Glass Workers, CIO, becoming Local 32. Lee and other FLU delegates first met the Flat Glass Workers' international president, Glen McCabe, at the AFL Atlantic City convention in 1935. McCabe urged the local to affiliate with the Flat Workers at that time to solidify the effort to organize the Pittsburgh Plate Glass Corporation (Columbia Chemical's parent company). At the time, Lee and others favored the independence of being a directly affiliated federal labor union. Bradley's intervention in negotiating the agreement, however, made it clear that an FLU's autonomy had its limits.[63]

Although conflict with an international union would grow more common as the decades progressed, in 1936 local unions were most concerned about their relationship with their employers. By the summer of 1936 workers at all of the remaining major Barberton factories except Ohio Insulator—Seiberling Tire, Pittsburgh Valve and Fittings, and Babcock and Wilcox—had gained official union recognition.

Seiberling Tire was one of the best organized locals in the city, both when it was independent and after it affiliated with the United Rubber Workers' international union. Originating as FLU 18616, the union became URW Local 18 in 1935. The local had functioned more or less formally as the collective bargaining agent, without being officially recognized, since 1934. In June 1936 Local 18 demanded and won official union recognition when the predominantly male union sat down to prevent the dismissal of a female employee. The entire incident took a total of two hours. Like many of the most militant and best organized locals in the United Rubber Workers (particularly Local 5 at Goodrich and Local 9 at General Tire, both in Akron), URW Local 18 initially refrained from signing a union contract. These locals saw no need to be locked into collective bargaining agreements when their demands could be enforced on the shop floor without one. Local 18 would not formally sign an agreement with management until 1939.[64]

At B&W, FLU 20186 won union recognition only five months after the local was first organized. The union was forced to strike two-and-a-half weeks to gain recognition, but in the context of the Barberton labor movement the work stoppage was peaceful and uneventful.[65]

Like B&W Local 20186, the local union at Pittsburgh Valve and Fittings, FLU 20183, was chartered in March 1936. Yet where FLU 20186 acted virtually without impediment in establishing collective bargaining at B&W in 1936, FLU 20183 faced heavy resistance from management at Pittsburgh Valve and Fittings. As in the Columbia Chemical strike in 1934 and the Ohio Insulator strike in 1935, Pittsburgh Valve and Fittings' oppression in 1936 would force the local labor movement to develop the bonds of solidarity further.

FLU 20183 differed from the city's other locals in one significant way: between one-third to one-half of its members were African Americans. Attempts by the International Association of Machinists (IAM) to organize the plant were crippled by that union's constitutional barrier to blacks as union members. Forsaken by the IAM, Pittsburgh Valve and Fittings' African American workers, both skilled and unskilled, were welcomed into FLU 20183.[66]

Like other Barberton locals, FLU 20183 decided in the spring of 1936 to press for union recognition. On May 8, 1936, FLU 20183 struck. As usual, the entire labor community rallied to FLU 20183's aid. In a circular letter, the Barberton Central Labor Union Strike Committee, consisting of workers from several Barberton locals, solicited donations, while informing supporters, "The members of this union, Federal Labor Union No. 20183 are one of the poorest paid in this town. Women have been employed in the Foundry of the Pittsburgh Valve and Fittings Co., doing the work that is considered heavy work for men, and have been paid wages not fit for a child. We have won every strike in town for the past two years and we cannot go down to defeat this time." Writing to William Green in an effort to solicit AFL aid on behalf of striking FLU 20183, H. D. Hanna, secretary of the CLU, summed up the situation:

This Valve strike MUST not be lost. It is the only Mixed local in town. about 50% being collored. and they have so far pulled together like one race. Should this strike be broken, the employer will at once use the one race against the other as he has in the past. It took us two years of constant effort to override race prejudice and get this a 100% organization as it now is and we CANT see it fail. We make you this appeal in the name of every union man and woman in Barberton. "Do all in your power to aid this local 20183 finacialy with a donation and help us keep the race prejudice licked in Barberton."

P.S. This is not alone the problems of local 20183 but is of vital importance to every organized man and woman in Barberton.

Even Green, who normally kept miserly control of the AFL's funds and typically dismissed such requests with a reminder to the local that they had not been in the AFL the necessary year required to earn strike benefits, was touched. He sent a check for $500.[67]

Solidarity crippled the company. As a Federal Mediation and Conciliation Service investigator reported in late August, "The plant is closed tight, and not even a watchman or fireman are permitted to enter. The company seems helpless." The AFL organizer H. A. Bradley offered his assessment of the situation: "The local unions of Barberton and Akron have been very generous in their financial support of the strikers added to which is the five hundred dollar contribution of the A.F. of L. As a result thereof, most of these people are living as well or better than they did prior to the strike as long as adequate financial assistance is obtainable, it is my opinion that they will not enter into any kind of agreement because by doing so it would simply mean that they have to return to their daily toil." Three months after they had walked out, on September 1, 1936, FLU 20183 and the company signed a contract. Solidarity in Barberton transcended the imposing barrier of race.[68]

It should not be surprising that the vanguard of the city's local unions joined the strike wave in the summer of 1936. FLU 18928 had won union recognition in the strike of March–April 1934 and had since worked to extend its influence on the shop floor and to build the labor movement locally in Barberton and nationally in the match industry. In his editorials in *The National Match Worker* and *Summit County Labor News* Francis Gerhart, president of FLU 18928, continually put shop-floor rights at the forefront of the demands of match workers and Barberton workers in general. Even after most Barberton factories had eliminated the Bedaux system in the wave of strikes during the spring and summer of 1936, Gerhart continued to rail about "parasitic" industrial engineers and incentive systems that operated "the same as an old tread power mill where the carrot is just beyond reach of the animal operating it so it will continue working . . . ."[69]

In the summer of 1936 FLU 18928 struck for the closed shop. Despite its strength, however, FLU 18928 was not powerful enough to enforce this demand, and it would not be until 1941. But in demanding it and striking for it, the local union was pressing the limits of what was possible.

According to the AFL organizer H. A. Bradley, Francis Gerhart dominated "practically all union affairs in Barberton." Working in an industry that employed less than 6,000 nationally, Gerhart and the match workers attracted little attention from the CIO, and they themselves did not seem interested in the CIO. Before the CIO had been created the match workers of Barberton had successfully created the National Match Workers' Council.[70]

In fact, most Barberton unions had their origins prior to the formation of the CIO. Those that did not—FLU 20186 at Babcock and Wilcox and FLU 20183 at Pittsburgh Valve and Fittings, which most likely would have been steelworker locals—were formed prior to the creation of the Steel Workers Organizing Committee in June 1936. Much of this stemmed from the Barberton Central Labor Union functioning as a community-based union, coordinating organizing activity and strike support—matters typically overseen by an international union. Of all the Barberton local unions organized in the 1930s, not one was organized by an international union; they were organized by fellow workers in the city operating under the auspices of the Barberton Central Labor Union Organizing Committee.[71]

Horizontal organization of this kind encouraged community-based solidarity and put Barberton union leaders in a position to exploit the rivalry that developed nationally between the AFL and the CIO. In 1941, for example, when FLU 18928 successfully struck Diamond Match for the closed shop over AFL objections, the AFL considered revoking the militant union's charter but then balked, fearing that the match workers would go to the CIO. Offering his thoughts on the Barberton situation in 1936, H. A. Bradley observed that "Gerhart's slogan is 'if we don't get what we want from the A.F. of L. we will get it from the CIO' and he has this philosophy pretty well sold in Barberton." Archetypical of the old guard AFL organizers sent to work in mass-production industries, Bradley (like his boss William Green) viewed the CIO as a threat to the very survival of the AFL. The AFL therefore took all measures to fight the CIO's influence when it could. A. P. Lee had used the AFL-CIO rivalry to win strike benefits for his membership in FLU 19019's strike against Columbia Chemical in 1936; Francis Gerhart and FLU 18928 used the internecine conflict to conduct strikes that the AFL was reluctantly forced to support. Barberton workers quickly recognized that particularly after William Green declared "Labor's Civil War" in 1937–38, nothing elicited faster support from the AFL than the threat of a shop's going CIO. Aware of the AFL's knee-jerk, reactionary policy, Barberton workers manipulated this AFL hysteria to push forward increasingly militant demands. In the fall of 1936 locals began to demand the closed shop, increased shop-floor rights, and even in the case of the FLU 18928 at Diamond Match (reflecting the gender composition of the labor force) equal pay for equal work, if necessary claiming that the strikes were required to keep the CIO out.[72]

Duplicitous and exaggerated reports to the AFL notwithstanding, the comity among Barberton's unions—the AFL, CIO, and Workers' Alliance—was incredible, considering the splits that racked the rival unions in other cities. Joe Palmer remembered that the CLU was "where all the organizations met. They all participated to help each other out. They sent pickets and food. There was no AFL-CIO ill feelings. No animosity to my knowledge. It might have showed in some areas, but we never noticed anything like that."[73]

Cooperation extended beyond simple trade union demands. Beginning with the Marvin campaign in 1935 (and his two reelections in 1937 and 1939), Barberton workers became increasingly active in political affairs, and the activity extended beyond simple two-party politics. Many in the Barberton labor movement were interested in the Farmer-Labor Party that emerged in the summer of 1936. Francis Gerhart was on the party's executive committee and was the party's second vice president, and Fred Wells of the Barberton Workers' Alliance was slated to be that party's candidate for the state house of representatives in the fall of 1936. A legal snafu barred the party from the ballot in the general election, while the landslide election of Franklin Roosevelt and the creation of Labor's Non-Partisan League spelled the movement's ultimate doom. Even with the collapse of the Farmer-Labor Party in Summit County in 1936, the labor party idea continued to resonate in Barberton. In 1937 a group of union activists laid what they hoped would be the groundwork for launching their own local labor party by forming a party "nucleus," though their plans never came to fruition.[74]

Barberton unionists perpetuated their community-based solidarity movement in other ways, despite the fragmentation of the labor movement nationally. After AFL president William Green ordered the purge of all CIO local unions from the Barberton CLU, organized labor continued to hold AFL and CIO interunion meetings. The Barberton Women's Union Buyers' Club also continued to seat delegates from both the AFL and the CIO. In 1938 Barberton organized labor went so far as to create the Joint Labor Legislative Committee, which included representatives from all Barberton unions—AFL, CIO, and Workers' Alliance. The ubiquitous Francis Gerhart was the group's president.[75]

In several instances following the emergence of the CIO, Barberton unionists indicated their desire to advance their movement of interunion cooperation. In October 1937 workers at Ohio Insulator, then Local 149

of the Potters' union, passed a resolution urging the national union to make
some effort to settle the dispute between the AFL and CIO. In April 1938
the Barberton CLU circulated "a petition to end the civil war in labor's
ranks." When local CIO unions, ordered out of the CLU, formed their own
local central labor body, unionists on both sides promised cooperation.[76]

Indeed, activists in the Barberton CLU, the AFL umbrella organization,
willingly aided local CIO unions in establishing their own central labor
body, the Barberton Industrial Union Council (BIUC). Writing to the CIO
in support of granting a charter to the BIUC, Paul Smoyer, an AFL activist, explained to CIO national secretary John Brophy that

> we are here where organization is moving forward very rapidly and each
> week I sit as a delegate from this local in the Barberton Central Labor
> Union, where a number of CIO organizations are represented and their
> delegates are my close personal friends. I want to be sure to be informed
> so that if something comes up in the meeting to make it difficult for these
> organizations to carry out the wishes of the workers in this district, I may
> be in a position to assist their worthy purposes, also to inform other
> groups who are trying to better their conditions.

So much for hostility.[77]

Barberton workers after 1936 also continued the trend of making their
unions both economic and social institutions. Seeking to eliminate the last
vestiges of corporate paternalism, organized labor began to sponsor its own
baseball, bowling, and basketball teams and to pay for its own summer
picnics and Christmas dinners. It organized its own industrial sports
leagues. The culmination of the social impulse came on July 10, 1937, when
the city's factories closed for the day at the behest of labor and Mayor
Marvin to allow all of Barberton's workers to enjoy a summer labor holiday, sponsored by organized labor. Afterward, the labor-sponsored summer holiday became an annual event on the Magic City's social calendar.[78]

Joined under fire, both literally and figuratively, Barberton workers began to think in class terms as the labor movement became an extension of
the familial world from which the workers had emerged. Besides the experience and violence of the picket lines, two factors especially reinforced that
familial ethos. The first was the widespread participation of all family members in the labor movement, particularly during strikes, a product of organized labor's efforts to cultivate the image of unions as social institutions.
For those plants where women did not compose a significant portion of the
work force, the Women's Union Buyers' Club and the women's auxiliaries
brought nonwage working women into the thick of labor activity.[79]

Second, Barberton unions were quite literally a family affair, since various family members found employment in different Barberton shops. Consider, for example, the Williams brothers, Everett and William. Everett became president of the Pittsburgh Valve and Fittings local in 1941 at about the same time his brother William became vice president of the Columbia Chemical workers. Or Bill Oyler, who during the 1930s was the vice president of the Diamond Match local, while his uncle was an officer in United Electrical Workers' Local 747 at Ohio Insulator, and his brothers and father worked at Columbia Chemical. Or Jasper Morgan, who was an officer in the Columbia Chemical local, while his wife, Leona, served as a trustee in the Diamond Match FLU 18928. Barberton was, and remains, a city with intertwined family connections. There is a rule of thumb in Barberton that one should not speak ill of another Barbertonian, because the listener is probably a cousin to the person in question.[80]

Because Barberton unions were so centrally based in the family structure, they ensured the secondary status of women in organized labor; even among activist women in Barberton, a feminist critique had not yet emerged. Nevertheless, the males who dominated the local union structure were relatively sensitive to the demands of female workers. Deriding the "Match Barons," Francis Gerhart reminded his readers in the *National Match Worker* in 1937 that "women work harder than men in this industry because of the speed and conditions they faced." One woman recalled that in the mid-1930s when she and her husband, an activist in the Ohio Brass union, were forced to decide which one of them would stay home from work, he willingly agreed to allow her to continue to work at Seiberling. At Diamond Match the union continued to fight for the right of married women to work during the depression, even in the face of opposition.[81]

Barberton organized labor was also willing to breach the institutional divide between the AFL and the CIO, even beyond the corporation limits of the Magic City. The members of B&W FLU 20186, AFL, were active supporters of the United Electrical Workers' attempt to organize the B&W plant in Bayonne, New Jersey. FLU 20186's generosity drew praise from the *UE News* in 1941. The UE newspaper quoted appreciatively the comments of a rank and filer at a local membership meeting supporting a motion to aid the Bayonne workers: "AFL or CIO—unless we all stick together we'll both lose out."[82]

The broadening of a class consciousness even penetrated to concern for the proper slogans on the local union letterhead. Under the craft union influence of the AFL, early letterheads urged the recipient to "BUY UNION." By 1935–36, after the genesis of the community-based solidarity movement, "BUY UNION" was replaced with "UNITED WE STAND—DIVIDED WE FALL."[83]

Throughout the 1930s the Barberton CLU remained the operative labor movement institution in the Magic City. Nationally, the CIO sponsored the Steel Workers Organizing Committee, the Packinghouse Workers Organizing Committee, even the Public Workers Project Organizing Committee—centralized bureaucracies created to foster industrial unionism. But in Barberton organization was carried out under the auspices of the CLU. From 1936 through 1939 the Barberton CLU, working in conjunction with rank-and-file workers at each of the various work sites, was responsible for creating United Rubber Workers Local 58 (Sun Rubber), United Rubber Workers Local 77 (Midwest Rubber), American Federation of State, County and Municipal Employees Local 265 (the City of Barberton), FLU 20246 (Yoder Brothers Greenhouse), and FLU 22153 (Babcock and Wilcox office workers). As H. D. Hanna observed in January 1937, "The field is growing smaller and smaller for new locals in Barberton."[84]

With the coordination of the Barberton CLU and the Women's Union Buyers' Club, Barberton workers also began to carry their union identity into the consumer market. Local unions organized boycotts of gas stations with nonunion attendants, stores with nonunion sales clerks, and nonunion products, such as Zenith electronic goods. When it became public knowledge that the movie star Buck Jones had the audacity to build his Hollywood mansion with nonunion labor, they organized a boycott of Buck Jones movies. More than challenging recalcitrant nonunion manufacturers, gas stations, and Hollywood actors, boycotts and consumer activism strengthened the power of organized labor by incorporating women who were not wage laborers into the movement structure.[85]

In a related development unionists at B&W, Ohio Insulator, Seiberling, and Columbia Chemical organized credit unions as a way to pool resources and curb reliance on commercial banks. Credit unions in Barberton reflected the family-oriented nature of local society—they encouraged thrift, not consumption. Credit unions were designed to allow members to borrow in times of need, when they were out of work, when calamity hit, when that rainy day finally came.[86]

When relief was necessary, organized labor in Barberton gave full support to the unemployed. The Barberton CLU had been a long supporter of the Workers' Alliance local and gave it the full use of the CLU hall. The CLU seconded the demands of the Workers' Alliance for more WPA programs and better working conditions. They also went beyond simply supporting the Workers' Alliance. In January 1938, for example, twenty-four local unions signed a petition to urge that local government machinery take steps to speed relief to unmarried men and women. Fifteen months later the Barberton CLU sponsored a drive "to ensure that all eligible receive their unemployment benefits—union members or not." These were not humiliated and degraded workers graciously accepting relief scraps from Washington; these were politicized organized workers, employed and unemployed, demanding their rightful share of the nation's wealth.[87]

Solidarity Unionism Institutionalized

In spite of the Barberton labor movement's impressive gains beginning in 1933, the five years between 1936 and 1941 were filled with peaks and valleys for the movement. There were several setbacks along the way. The most damaging symbolically and ideologically was the defection of Columbia Chemical's A. P. Lee to management in the aftermath of the 1936 sit-down strike. Offered a truck-driving job in his native Tennessee, Lee accepted it. For a time his defection sapped the morale of the Columbia Chemical local. Lee was a young, brave, articulate, radical local labor leader, and he had bolted the movement. Lee's actions also led to suspicions about the motivations of other Barberton labor leaders. Rushing a response into print, Francis Gerhart wrote a letter to the editor in the *Akron Beacon Journal,* assuring Barberton rank and filers that he and others were not for sale and that they were sticking to the union. In the fall of 1936 Gerhart would get a chance to prove it after being fired by Diamond Match for leaving work to attend the AFL convention in Tampa. Like others, he had to fight to keep his job.[88]

More damaging than Lee's defection materially was the Roosevelt recession of 1937–38. By 1937 a large number of Barberton unions had signed union contracts, but many contractual provisions had never been tested, particularly layoff rights. Heavy layoffs also forced local unions to consider the problems of unemployed workers who sought relief work.

In general Barberton local unions responded to the crisis by continuing to operate their organizations as social institutions. When possible they shared the work, and if work dropped below a certain number of hours, typically twenty-four hours per week, they insisted on strict applicability of seniority. The unions themselves concentrated considerable energy in meeting the daily needs of their members on layoff. They relaxed collection of dues, negotiated the ambiguous gray area of membership on an ad hoc basis, and devoted a generous portion of their locals' finances to general welfare work among needy members and their families. FLU 20186 at B&W, for example, sent along cartons of cigarettes to financially ailing members as a gesture that the union was still concerned about their situations. At other times, if a member was especially hard-pressed, the union might offer a direct financial contribution. These efforts showed unemployed brothers and sisters that the union was concerned about their situations, even if they could not afford union dues. When the economy began to revive in 1939, the unemployed looked favorably on the union, instead of viewing it as an institution that was concerned with only its own interests and the interests of its dues-paying membership.[89]

The social foundation of solidarity unionism was firmly entrenched by the end of the 1930s. By the summer of 1939 even the Barberton Chamber of Commerce sought amicable relations with the Barberton labor movement. In 1936 the chamber had appealed directly to Secretary of Labor Frances Perkins for aid in quelling labor militancy. The business organization urged the Labor Department "to eradicate" what it termed "undesirable leaders" (for example, Francis Gerhart). In July 1939 the chamber made one last effort to initiate an open shop drive in Barberton. They invited a Dr. Haacke to speak at the chamber-sponsored "Civic Unity" drive. The Barberton labor movement immediately denounced the drive for "Civic Unity" as a plot to destroy organized labor and exposed Haacke as a representative of the American Liberty League. Haacke answered the charges by urging non–working class Barbertonians to drop any plans of trying to rid the city of organized labor. The movement is too strong, Haacke advised. "After all," he added, "labor, important as it is, is only one of the problems."[90]

The aborted "Civic Unity" forced the Chamber of Commerce to reassess its position on the labor movement. From 1939 through the 1970s the chamber more or less coexisted with the Barberton labor movement. Giving up trying to destroy organized labor, the chamber tried to solicit the support of the labor movement for the community's well-being, though on the movement's terms. Among the joint initiatives was the Community Fund, headed by James Evans, the former president of the Seiberling Tire local. Another was a labor-inspired proposal to create a municipal hospital that would operate on an at-cost basis to make possible affordable health care for all. As Gerhart noted at the time of the "Civic Unity" threat, "Our Labor Unions have and always will continue to participate and cooperate in any worth while cause or civic minded movement." Labor's cooperation with the Chamber of Commerce and similar organizations could have carried the risk of co-optation. But unenlightened management in a few of the factories constantly reminded unionists that there were distinct class differences in Barberton.[91]

At Sun Rubber in the summer of 1939 the members of URW Local 58 struck for sixteen weeks in an effort to win a contract. The following year, workers successfully struck Babcock and Wilcox for higher wages. In the winter of 1940–41 unionists at Seiberling Tire and Columbia Chemical averted walkouts only when management gave in to their wage demands. In January 1941 FLU 20183 struck Pittsburgh Valve and Fittings for three days, "the first strike in the area along defense lines."[92]

From 1939 through 1941, even as labor relations purportedly cooled down nationally while the United States made preparations in anticipation of its entry into World War II, class conflict continued to rage in Barberton. This was nowhere more apparent than at Ohio Insulator, where a general strike had nearly occurred in 1935. By 1941 Ohio Insulator remained the last antiunion citadel, resistant to union recognition and collective bargaining. Although the 1935 strike had been a victory for Potters' Local 149 and even more so for the workers in Barberton in general, that win did not translate into immediate gains for Ohio Insulator workers.

Relations between labor and management had hardly improved since the 1935 strike. During a strike in the summer of 1936 the company agreed to recognize the union's existence and legitimacy but refused to sign a contract. For several weeks Local 149 held out, acquiescing only when Ohio Insulator threatened to close its factory.[93]

Two years later, in the midst of the Roosevelt recession of 1937–38, Ohio Insulator's management provoked another dispute when it slashed piece rates and refused to abide by seniority when laying off. Local 149 asked the national office of the National Brotherhood of Operative Potters (located in nearby East Liverpool) for a strike sanction, which the national refused. The denial forced Local 149 to accept the pay cut without a fight.

Going down without a fight was not the way in Barberton, and from the moment the potters' national union refused to back them, workers at Ohio Insulator sought a more militant national organization. With the encouragement of the Barberton rubber worker locals, they decided to affiliate with the United Electrical Workers in May 1938, becoming UE Local 747. The UE had a stronger reputation for carrying on rank-and-file struggles, a characteristic that fit snugly with the pervasive Barberton union culture. The company fought UE Local 747's certification with the National Labor Relations Board and refused to negotiate through 1939.[94]

By 1941 UE Local 747 felt sufficiently strong to challenge the company openly. In the wake of the military-expenditure boom, most Barberton locals engaged in strike action in 1940–41, and UE Local 747 soon joined the strike wave. In May 1941 Local 747 decided to "take strike action," in the words of local president Edwin S. Fout, "to end the Fordism of this company. We feel that our demands of a union contract, job security, and 10 cents per hour are just." True to its past, the company took a hard-headed approach and refused to negotiate. According to a Federal Mediation and Conciliation Service (FMCS) investigator, the union was quite "cooperative," while the company was "stiffnecked." Another neutral observer, a representative of the Standard Oil Company, reported to the FMCS field representative "that he would report to the O.P.M. [Office of Price Management] that the company was entirely in the wrong." The strike continued into the summer.[95]

In late August the company was successful in obtaining a court injunction against mass demonstrations. Several days later ten picketers were arrested for violating the injunction. Two of the ten arrested were members of the chemical workers' union, reflecting community-based solidarity. Once again the scene was set for a class showdown in the Magic City.[96]

On Labor Day Barberton workers staged a massive parade, with both AFL and CIO unions in full regalia. Nonunion groups, including the Barberton High School marching band, joined in the festivities to express community support for the UE strikers. Like the parade in the midst of the 1935 strike at Ohio Insulator, the Barberton Labor Day parade in 1941 served notice to management that the labor community was united and prepared to take further action if necessary to force Ohio Insulator to conform to the standards of decency prevalent throughout the city. "Labor here," the *UE News* observed in the middle of the strike, "is giving its support to the UE strikers and there is a distinct feeling in this community that the company is being very unAmerican in its bullheaded refusal to meet the union's just demands." As Local 747 president Fout phrased it in a letter to the UE national office in July, "This strike must be won. . . . We must see to it that this anti-labor management is brought into line and the demands of the men met." By the fall of 1941 citywide norms demanded union recognition, bona fide collective bargaining, and signed contracts. On the eve of victory the *OB Striker,* Local 747's strike publication, crystallized the ideology of the local's struggle, and that of Barberton workers in general, in this epoch: "Why should we feel the necessity of battling with our fellow men, for glory, position or wealth, when by intelligent cooperation, which really means working together, we can create two or three many times as benefits for everyone concerned instead of a smaller amount apportioned to only the victors of battle?" As working-class pressure boiled, Ohio Insulator finally gave in. It became, in September 1941, the last of the city's major factories to sign a union contract, just as the United States was finalizing preparations to enter World War II.[97]

The Legacy of Solidarity Unionism

Barberton workers, like most U.S. industrial workers in this period, concentrated their efforts on the relatively mundane, job-conscious goals of union recognition, signed contracts, and seniority rights. Still, a closer look finds something more progressive than a simple quest for security among Barberton workers, both on the shop floor and in the community at large. Neither pie-in-the-sky idealists nor calculating businesspeople in working folks' attire, Barberton workers established a foundation of security and then tested the limits of what was possible.

Francis Gerhart, in particular, frequently urged Barberton workers to fight corporations that "think property rights are superior to human rights." At other times he would "offer orchids to the woman who slapped the foreman" and ask, "Why don't some of you men try it?" as he reminded Barbertonians that "workers are the sole source of profit and if there were no workers there would be no profits." He demanded that workers "take their share of the commonwealth." And when red-baited by the company, he responded, "Being Red is only a matter of opinion."[98]

Nor was Gerhart alone among labor leaders in such orations. Joe Palmer of URW Local 18 derided the "Barons of Finance," while he advocated the organization of "all workers" and called for a stronger labor "political arm for greater distribution of wealth." The outbreak of war in Europe in 1939 precipitated the sponsorship of a huge antiwar rally and the CLU's passage of a resolution stating, "The reacting big business forces which are trying to involve our country in the war are interested in greater profit for themselves at the expense of the working man and women and the consuming public . . . [and] the drive to drag us into war is being combined with a campaign to deny labor its hard earned civil rights." In short, Barberton labor leaders did not soft-peddle their radicalism; they balanced the material incentives of trade union membership with the language of class.[99]

This blending of a larger vision with bread-and-butter concerns is best captured in an unsigned piece published in the *National Match Worker* in 1937. Most likely written by Francis Gerhart, the article is entitled "Why

Labor Should Be Organized." It enumerates several of the job-conscious demands sober-minded historians would rightfully point to as expressions of working-class realism: wage benefits, job security, seniority rights, vacations, and so on. But, at least according to the article, labor should organize not just for these limited goals but also "because of the enemies it has made. When you see people outside the wage class fighting trade unions, put it down that trade unions are desirable"; "because it is your class organization. Your interests as a seller of labor are the interests of your class"; and, finally, "because it teaches cooperation. When laborers cooperate they will own the earth."[100]

In the process of fighting for these basic demands, workers were forging a new ethic based on solidarity. In the words of one Columbia Chemical worker, this meant that "the bosses had to get used to the fact that they were no longer dictators. They had to treat people like human beings and not like animals." Dick Lowry, a union activist at Columbia Chemical, noted that this quest to be treated as humans entailed looking out for one another both at work and in the community: "I think it's because of the ethnic people that's in there. I suppose, coming from the old country they had to band together to survive and I think that just carried on into the workplace. They were all very folksy people. Your problem's my problem, and my problem's yours. All the people there. If someone had a problem in town they all turned out to help. It's like your neighbors."[101]

If there was a radical component to the Barberton labor movement in the 1930s, it was that it taught cooperation—solidarity, a solidarity based on direct action. The widespread community support for the labor movement dictated that an injury to one was indeed an injury to all. While the CIO shifted the labor movement along a terrain of centralized, top-down, decision making that favored contracts with no-strike pledges, Barberton labor continued on its path of rank-and-file control and sympathetic collective action. The local movement, rather than the international union, remained the operative union structure.

Initially inspired to preserve what was familiar, Barberton unionists first guaranteed the survival of the workers' world before taking tentative steps toward the workers' nirvana. Although these steps were few, their significance should not be discounted. Faced in later years by the forceful reemergence of the employer class and the fratricidal war and ensuing climate of business unionism at the national level of the labor movement, Barberton's community-based local labor movement continued to produce results and retain its militancy.

Based on a community form of organization that was social as well as economic in character, Barberton's labor movement inculcated a class-based culture that formed a foundation for class-based activity. In this way class and community became one. If this were a study of Barberton in the nineteenth century, this fusion of class and community would hardly seem extraordinary, particularly to historians nurtured by Herbert Gutman. But solidarity unionism did develop and flourish in Barberton in the twentieth century, departing significantly from Gutman's studies. Barberton's labor movement was not a struggle of modernization, that is, precapitalist versus capitalist. Rather Barberton unionists were modern workers waging modern class warfare on the shop floor and in the community.[102]

At its base, this movement was predicated on the belief, forged in the volunteeristic ethos of the early 1930s, that rank-and-file workers should control the destinies of the unions that they had built, a vision that clashed with the top-down model of most CIO unions. This sentiment was reflected, for example, in the decisions of workers at Ohio Insulator to change their affiliation from the National Brotherhood of Operative Potters to the United Electrical Workers and those at Columbia Chemical to transform from AFL FLU 19019 (1933–36) to Flat Glass Workers Local 32 (1936–37) and to the United Mine Workers District 50, Local 13013, when their interests were not being met in their existing national organizations.[103]

This culture of solidarity did not wither away in subsequent decades. Barberton, to the joy of union militants and chagrin of town boomers, earned a reputation as a strong labor town to the extent that even today, after a decade of deindustrialization, the Chamber of Commerce and city planners are still fighting the image. Wildcat strikes in the postwar period became rather common, particularly at the Babcock and Wilcox, where during one ten-year period (1965–75) there were over fifty illegal work stoppages, and the Seiberling plant, which in the 1950s earned the reputation as the "king of the wildcats."

Barberton unions also fought bureaucratization in their own unions. Even in city locals where membership climbed into the thousands (4,500 was the largest), locals were staffed by at most one full-time union official and an office secretary. The union president in all locals received only a modest salary, which, considering rank-and-file workers received compensation for overtime and officers did not, meant that they actually often made less than the men and women in the shop. At the Columbia Chemical local the membership voted every year by secret ballot whether their union president would be full-time or part-time. At Diamond Match and

Pittsburgh Valve, the union president always worked in the shop. Furthermore, as they had in the 1930s, when locals thought their needs were not being met, they had no compunction about switching unions: UE Local 747 switched to the International Association of Machinists in 1957 and back to the UE in 1961; FLU 20183 affiliated with UMW District 50 in 1945 and then the Boilermakers in 1969; and, most dramatically, the peripatetic UMW District 50 Local 13013 at Columbia Chemical founded its own independent union, Allied Chemical and Alkali Workers of America, Local 1, after a decade of chafing under the UMW's centralized structure. When B&W's FLU 20186 became ripe for international affiliation after the merger of the AFL-CIO in 1955–56, it elected to join the Boilermakers over the Steelworkers because the Boilermakers promised it local autonomy. In the mid-1980s, when the Boilermakers began reneging on this promise, there was a concerted effort in the local to go independent.[104]

Interunion cooperation continued as well. Most noteworthy, unionists, in addition to participating actively in the Barberton Central Labor Union and the Barberton Industrial Union Council (which merged in 1957, becoming the Barberton Council of Labor), created the Joint Labor League, open to all delegates from all Barberton unions, "AFL, CIO and Independent." The Joint Labor League grew out of local opposition to the Taft-Hartley Act in 1947 and continued to sponsor an annual Labor Day parade for over three decades. By the 1960s, after the tradition had died in such cities as Flint and Akron, the event would draw crowds of 100,000 to the Magic City, population 33,000. Describing the extent of labor unity in Barberton, John Knight, president of Local 747, told the 1951 UE convention, "The Joint Labor League in Barberton puts on a mammoth [parade] in the city of Barberton, where all labor unites . . . . All the shops in Barberton, both AFL and CIO . . . take each other's membership in on transfer from one local. That's forbidden by top officials, but we get away with it. Another situation where I want to prove that labor does want unity down amongst the rank and file, they would like to have it on top, but the rank and file make it down below, and that is what we are doing." They did indeed.[105]

Barberton workers created an alternative model of labor mobilization, one that stood in contrast to the bureaucratic path of most twentieth-century labor organizations in the United States. The degree of interunion and intraunion cooperation in Barberton dictated that an injury to one was truly an injury to all. As one activist phrased the pervasive Barberton union attitude, "When the B&W was on strike, we all were on strike. The PPG, the Ohio Brass, it didn't matter. We were like a family. We had our strikes in Barberton before Akron. The strikes in Barberton showed that if people stick together they could win. And not only workers, but the community as a whole, sticking together, and backing up the people at odds with their company."[106] As international business unions continue to ossify and crumble, such a model of community organizing might be worth pursuing.

Notes

This essay is dedicated to the memory of my father, George Borsos, a Barberton rubber worker. I would like to thank Gene Borsos and Rita Hart for their sustained support and Clare, Elizabeth, Charlie, and Anna Borsos for making it possible. Special thanks goes to Staughton Lynd, who has been a real comrade and from whom I borrowed the expression "solidarity unionism."

1. David Brody, "The CIO after 50 Years: A Historical Reckoning," *Dissent* 32 (Fall 1985), 470. For essential overviews of the period, see Irving Bernstein, *Turbulent Years: A History of the American Worker, 1933–1941* (Boston: Houghton Mifflin, 1970); Melvyn Dubofsky, "Not So 'Turbulent Years': Another Look at America in the 1930s," *Amerikastudien/American Studies* 24 (January 1979), 5–20; Art Preis, *Labor's Giant Step: Twenty Years of the CIO* (New York: Pioneer Publishers, 1964; New York: Pathfinder Press, 1972); James Green, *The World of the Worker: Labor in Twentieth-Century America* (New York: Hill and Wang, 1980); David Montgomery, *Workers' Control in America: Studies in the History of Work, Technology, and Labor Struggles* (New York: Cambridge University Press, 1979), chap. 7; David Brody, *Workers in Industrial America: Essays on the Twentieth-Century Struggle* (New York: Oxford University Press, 1980), chap. 3; and Alan Dawley, "Workers, Capital and the State in the Twentieth Century," in *Perspectives in American Labor History: The Problem of Synthesis,* ed. J. Carroll Moody and Alice Kessler-Harris (DeKalb: Northern Illinois University Press, 1989), 152–202.

2. For some studies that do deal with the 1930s from union-oriented, rather than community-oriented, perspectives, see Peter Friedlander, *The Emergence of a UAW Local, 1936–1939: A Study of Class and Culture* (Pittsburgh: University of Pittsburgh Press, 1975); Ronald Schatz, *The Electrical Workers: A History of Labor at General Electric and Westinghouse, 1923–60* (Urbana: University of Illinois Press, 1983); Daniel Nelson, *American Rubber Workers and Organized Labor, 1900–1941* (Princeton, N.J.: Princeton University Press, 1989); Joshua Freeman, *In Transit: The Transport Workers Union in New York City, 1933–1966* (New York: Oxford University Press, 1989); Steven Fraser, "Dress Rehearsal for the New Deal: Shop Floor Insurgents, Political Elites, and Industrial Democracy in the Amalgamated Clothing Workers," in *Working-Class America: Essays on Labor, Community, and American Society,* ed.

Michael Frisch and David Walkowitz (Urbana: University of Illinois Press, 1983), 212–55; and Bruce Nelson, *Workers on the Waterfront: Seamen, Longshoremen, and Unionism in the 1930s* (Urbana: University of Illinois Press, 1989). For exceptions as community studies, see Gary Gerstle, *Working-Class Americanism: The Politics of Labor in a Textile City, 1916–1960* (New York: Cambridge University Press, 1989); Ronald Edsforth, *Class Conflict and Cultural Consensus: The Making of Mass Consumer Society in Flint, Michigan* (New Brunswick, N.J.: Rutgers University Press, 1986); and Elizabeth Faue, *Community of Suffering and Struggle: Women, Men, and the Labor Movement in Minneapolis, 1915–1945* (Chapel Hill: University of North Carolina Press, 1991). On the paucity of community studies for the twentieth century, see Dawley, "Workers, Capital and the State in the Twentieth Century"; and Leon Fink, "Looking Backward: Reflections on Workers' Culture and Certain Conceptual Dilemmas with Labor History," in *Perspectives in American Labor History*, ed. Moody and Kessler-Harris, 5–29. For examples of lumping all labor developments in the 1930s under the rubric of the CIO, see Robert Zieger, "The CIO: A Bibliographical Update and Archival Guide," *Labor History* 31 (Fall 1990), 413–40; and Gerstle, *Working-Class Americanism*. Gerstle's work is a solid treatment of local labor politics in the 1930s, but he fails to recognize that a great deal of Woonsocket workers' militancy was because they were an independent union rather than part of the CIO. Similar criticisms could be made of Edsforth's *Class Conflict and Cultural Consensus* and Daniel Nelson's *American Rubber Workers and Organized Labor*, both of which seem to overlook the pre-CIO and extra-CIO organizing efforts that took place in Flint and Akron in the 1930s.

3. Basic background material on the founding of Barberton and O. C. Barber can be gleaned from William Fleming, *America's Match King: O. C. Barber* (Barberton, Ohio: Barberton Historical Society, 1980), but this source should be used with caution. See also John Borsos, "Talking Union: The Labor Movement in Barberton, Ohio, 1891–1991" (Ph.D. diss., Indiana University, 1992), chap. 1.

4. On the Diamond Match Company, see Alfred Chandler, *The Visible Hand: The Managerial Revolution in American Business* (Cambridge: Cambridge University Press, 1977), 250, 292–93, 350, 374; and Herbert Manchester, *The Diamond Match Company* (New York: Diamond Match Company, 1935). On Columbia Chemical, see David F. Noble, *America by Design: Science, Technology, and the Rise of Corporate Capitalism* (New York: Oxford University Press, 1977), 14–15. Some insight into the early labor movement in Barberton was derived from Earl Davis, interview with author, December 27, 1988, Barberton, Ohio. Some pertinent information on the Babcock and Wilcox Company can be gleaned from John Douglas Forbes, *Stettinius, Sr.: Portrait of a Morgan Partner* (Charlottesville: University of Virginia Press, 1974).

5. Ohio Insulator began under the name of the Akron High Potential in 1906 as the exclusive supplier to the Ohio Brass Company of Mansfield. In 1910 Ohio Brass bought the plant outright and changed the name to Ohio Insulator. In 1937 the plant's name changed again to the Ohio Brass. On the Seiberlings' ouster, see Daniel Nelson, *American Rubber Workers and Organized Labor,* 78, 80; and Michael D. French, "Structural Change and Competition in the United States Tire Industry, 1920–1937," *Business History Review* 60 (Spring 1986), 28–54. The quote is from Alfred Winslow Jones, *Life, Liberty, and Property: A Story of Conflict and the Measurement of Conflicting Rights* (Philadelphia: J. P. Lippincott, 1941), 33. For context of the development of the rubber industry and Seiberling's place in it, see Howard Wolf and Ralph Wolf, *Rubber: A Story of Glory and Greed* (New York: Corici, Friede, 1936); and Harold S. Roberts, *The Rubber Workers: Labor Organization and Collective Bargaining in the Rubber Industry* (New York: Harper and Sons, 1944).

6. Figures are from the 1930 and 1940 censuses. According to the 1935 and 1939 manufacturing censuses Barberton employed 5,944 and 5,723 production workers, respectively. For a superlative treatment of semiskilled operatives and unskilled laborers in this period, see David Montgomery, *The Fall of the House of Labor: The Workplace, the State, and American Labor Activism, 1865–1925* (New York: Cambridge University Press, 1987), especially 58–170.

7. Estimates are roughly computed from the 1910 manuscript census and "Barberton City Schools, Census of Foreign-Born Parents, 1923," Barberton History Vertical Files, Barberton Public Library, Barberton, Ohio. In these migrations Barberton resembles its nearby neighbor Akron, though Barberton maintained a larger foreign-born population. Some personal memories of this migration can be found in Gerald "Joe" Palmer, interview with author, March 13, 1990, Barberton, Ohio (quote); and Dale Ray Sr., interview with author, March 15, 1990, Barberton, Ohio.

8. On the iron molders' strike, see *Akron Beacon Journal,* July–September 1906. On the 1913 IWW strike, see Roy Wortman, "The IWW and the Akron Rubber Strike of 1913," in *At the Point of Production: The Local History of the I.W.W.,* ed. Joseph Conlin (Westport, Conn.: Greenwood, 1980), 49–60; Philip Foner, *A History of the Labor Movement in the United States,* vol. 4, *The Industrial Workers of the World, 1905–1917* (New York: International Publishers, 1965), 373–84; and Kevin Rosswurm, "A Strike in the Rubber City: Rubber Workers, Akron, and the IWW, 1913" (M.A. thesis, Kent State University, 1975). On the match girls' sympathy strike, see *Barberton News,* February 21 and 28, March 5, 1913. The use of the term *girls* here reflects reality considering the predominant number of female employees in the match shop under eighteen years old. See, for example, Ida M. Yost, "I Remember When," *Barberton Herald,* October 19, 1967. The election results

were derived from the *Barberton News,* 1909–19. The Barberton Socialist Party local was founded in 1908 and for a short time published a newspaper, the *Barberton Socialist.* Many sources report the election of a Socialist mayor in Barberton in 1911, but this was not the case. See also *Cleveland Citizen,* June 27, 1908; and Richard Judd, *Socialist Cities: Municipal Politics and the Grass Roots of American Socialism* (Albany: State University of New York Press, 1989), 54, 71. On Barberton's welfare capitalism, see clippings and pictures in the Utah Philips Scrapbook, Barberton Public Library; and extant issues of the Diamond Match Company's *Good Fellowship Bulletin* and Babcock and Wilcox's *Generator,* Barberton History Vertical Files, Barberton Public Library. See also Stuart D. Brandes, *American Welfare Capitalism, 1880–1920* (Chicago: University of Chicago Press, 1970); David Brody, *Workers in Industrial America,* chap. 2; Gerald Zahavi, *Managers, Workers, and Welfare Capitalism: The Shoeworkers of Endicott Johnson, 1890–1950* (Urbana: University of Illinois Press, 1988); and Sanford M. Jacoby, *Employing Bureaucracy: Managers, Unions, and the Transformation of Work in American Industry* (New York: Columbia University Press, 1985).

9. On the AFL's failure to organize the unskilled, see Montgomery, *The Fall of the House of Labor;* David Brody, *Labor in Crisis: The Steel Strike of 1919* (Urbana: University of Illinois Press, 1965); Walter Galenson, *The CIO Challenge to the AFL: A History of the American Labor Movement, 1935–1941* (Cambridge, Mass.: Harvard University Press, 1960); Mike Davis, *Prisoners of the American Dream: Politics and Economy in the History of the American Working Class* (London: Verso, 1986); Melvyn Dubofsky and Warren Van Tine, *John L. Lewis: A Biography* (New York: Quadrangle Books, 1977); and Craig Phelan, *William Green: Portrait of a Labor Leader* (Albany: State University of New York Press, 1989). On the ethnic churches and benefit societies, see Ohio Works Progress Administration Church Survey, Ohio Historical Society, Columbus, Ohio, which contains surveys from Barberton churches; Adella Rabith, interview with author, February 28, 1991 (quote); Vince Lauter, interview with author, June 13, 1989; and Joe Voros, interview with author, October 31, 1990. On African American churches, see "Black Churches in Barberton," Barberton History Vertical Files, Barberton Public Library; and William A. Johnston, "Colored Citizens" (typescript, [1940]), Barberton Public Library.

10. Roy C. Barnes, interview with author, March 28, 1991 (quote); Borsos, "Talking Union," 121–26. See also John Bodnar, *Immigration and Industrialization: Ethnicity in an American Mill Town, 1870–1940* (Pittsburgh: University of Pittsburgh Press, 1977); John Bodnar, *The Transplanted: A History of Immigrants in America* (Bloomington: Indiana University Press, 1985); Ewa Morawska, *For Bread with Butter: Life-Worlds of East European Immigrants in Johnstown, Pennsylvania, 1890–1940* (New York: Cambridge University Press, 1985); Robert Slayton, *Back of the Yards: The Making of a*

Local Democracy (Chicago: University of Chicago Press, 1986); Jacquelyn Dowd Hall, James Leloudis, Robert Korstad, Mary Murphy, LuAnn Jones, and Christopher B. Daly, *Like a Family: The Making of a Southern Cotton Mill World* (Chapel Hill: University of North Carolina Press, 1987); and Thomas Gobel, "Becoming American: Ethnic Workers and the Rise of the CIO," *Labor History* 29 (Spring 1988), 173–98. For a more extended investigation that considers the influence of mass culture, see Lizabeth Cohen, *Making a New Deal: Industrial Workers in Chicago, 1919–1939* (New York: Cambridge University Press, 1990). On the breakdown of ethnicity in the 1920s, see Gobel, "Becoming American"; Olivier Zunz, *The Changing Face of Inequality: Urbanization, Industrial Development, and Immigrants in Detroit, 1880–1920* (Chicago: University of Chicago Press, 1982); and, especially, Cohen, *Making a New Deal.*

11. Borsos, "Talking Union," 121–26; George Marinich, interviews with author, March 16 and June 10, 1989.

12. Borsos, "Talking Union," 139–45; Ray interview. On men selling apples, see *Barberton Herald,* December 9 and 12, 1930, January 20, 1931.

13. On the effect of the NIRA on labor relations, see James Gross, *The Making of the National Labor Relations Board, 1933–1937* (Albany: State University of New York Press, 1974); Howell John Harris, *The Right to Manage: Industrial Relation Policies and American Business in the 1940s* (Madison: University of Wisconsin Press, 1982); Christopher Tomlins, *The State and the Unions: Labor Relations, Law, and the Organized Labor Movement in America, 1880–1960* (New York: Cambridge University Press, 1986); James Hodges, *New Deal Labor Policy and the Southern Cotton Textile Industry, 1933–1941* (Knoxville: University of Tennessee Press, 1986); and Mike Davis, *Prisoners of the American Dream.* Harris provides the best overview of management's policies during the 1930s.

14. On the organization of rubber in the 1930s, see John Borsos, "Ironing Out Chaos: The CIO-ization of the United Rubber Workers, 1933–1941" (1992 manuscript, in author's possession).

15. For historians who consider the role of the AFL in this period, see Robert Zieger, *Madison's Battery Workers: A History of Federal Labor Union 19587* (Ithaca: New York State School of Industrial Relations, 1977); Robert Zieger, *Rebuilding the Pulp and Paper Workers' Union, 1933–1941* (Knoxville: University of Tennessee Press, 1984); Philip Taft, *The AF of L from the Death of Gompers to the Merger* (New York: Harper and Brothers, 1959); Christopher Tomlins, "The AFL Unions in the 1930s: Their Performance in Historical Perspective," *Journal of American History* 65 (March 1979), 1021–42; and Daryl Holter, "Sources of CIO Success: The New Deal Years in Milwaukee," *Labor History* 29 (Spring 1988), 199–224.

16. C. Ellis Bundy to Frank Morrison, January 2, 1934, Barberton Central Labor Union Charter Record, AFL-CIO Papers, George Meany Memori-

al Archives, Silver Spring, Maryland. On organization, see Daniel Nelson, *American Rubber Workers and Organized Labor,* 117–42; and Gerald "Joe" Palmer interview. The FLUs among rubber workers included 18491 at the Seiberling Latex plant, 18616 at the Seiberling Tire plant, and 18857 at the Sun Rubber plant. Strikes and Agreements file, American Federation of Labor Papers, Papers of FLU 18616, State Historical Society of Wisconsin, Madison. Hereafter, the various FLU papers in this collection will be identified as the Papers of FLU with the respective union number. On the match workers, see William Green to Carl Graham, December 7, 1933, Papers of FLU 18928; Report to AFL, June 2, 1936, Papers of FLU 19019; and *Summit County Labor News,* November 24, 1933. On the pottery workers, see vol. 1, box 170, National Brotherhood of Operative Potters Papers (hereafter NBOP), Kent State University, Kent, Ohio; and *Summit County Labor News,* November 24, 1933. On the Central Labor Union, see *Barberton Herald,* January 18, 1934; and *Summit County Labor News,* November 24 and December 1, 1933, January 12, 1934.

17. *Summit County Labor News,* November 24, 1933, January 12, 1934.

18. On ethnicity and unionization in general, see Friedlander, *The Emergence of a UAW Local;* Gobel, "Becoming American"; John Bodnar, *Workers' World: Kinship, Community, and Protest in an Industrial Society, 1900–1940* (Baltimore: Johns Hopkins University Press, 1982); and Walter Licht and Hal Seth Baron, "Labor's Men: A Collective Biography of Union Officialdom during the New Deal Years," *Labor History* 19 (Fall 1979), 532–45. In many ways Barberton union leaders seemed to be a combination of the older crafts model, detailed by Licht and Baron in "Labor's Men" and Ronald Schatz, "Union Pioneers: The Founders of Local Unions at General Electric and Westinghouse," *Journal of American History* 66 (December 1979), 586–602, and the younger more rural-based rubber workers, as outlined by Daniel Nelson in "The Leadership of the United Rubberworkers, 1933–1942," *Detroit in Perspective* 5 (Spring 1981), 21–30. Specific background for Barberton local leaders was derived from the Gerald "Joe" Palmer interview; "Labor in Barberton," Barberton History Workshop, in author's possession; Jack Palmer, interview with author, May 27, 1989; Marinich interviews; *Barberton Herald,* August 10, 1934; and William B. Sherman to William Green, April 20, 1934, Papers of FLU 19019.

19. The quotes about Gerhart are from *Summit County Labor News,* April 13, 1934. On Gerhart and Lee, see ibid.; *Daily Worker,* December 11, 1935; and Richard W. Shrake III, "Working-Class Politics in Akron, Ohio, 1936: The United Rubber Workers and the Failure of the Farmer-Labor Party" (M.A. thesis, University of Akron, 1974). John Williamson, the head of the Ohio CP, notes that Gerhart was willing to work with the CP, even though he was not a member. John Williamson, *Dangerous Scot: The Life of an American "Undesirable"* (New York: International Publishers, 1969), 132.

20. For the unions as social institutions, see, for example, *Summit County Labor News*, December 1, 15, 22, and 29, 1933, January 5, February 23, and March 30, 1934. Buffington's quote appears in ibid., February 23, 1934. Such festivities continued to flourish through the period, including the CLU's sponsorship of a workers' theater production, *The World's All Right*, starring, among others, Francis Gerhart and George B. Roberts, the rubber workers' organizer. Ibid., October 26, 1934. For the importance of such activities in building a labor movement culture, see Elizabeth Fones-Wolf, "Industrial Unionism and Labor Movement Culture in Depression-Era Philadelphia," *Pennsylvania Magazine of History and Biography* 109 (January 1985), 3–26.

21. For a parallel historical example in railroads, see Shelton Stromquist, *A Generation of Boomers: The Pattern of Railroad Conflict in Nineteenth-Century America* (Urbana: University of Illinois Press, 1987), 48–99.

22. Both groups formed national councils in 1934. They were among only a handful of unions to create such organizations in early 1935. See Leo Wolman, *Ebb and Flow in Trade Unionism* (New York: National Bureau of Economic Research, 1936), 70. At the time Wolman did his research, only eight such councils had formed.

23. Richard Lowry, interview with author, February 21, 1991. For a similar phenomenon in the Pennsylvania steel mills, see Thomas Bell, *Out of This Furnace* (1941; reprint, Pittsburgh: University of Pittsburgh Press, 1977). For contrasting accounts exploring the difficulties of getting immigrant workers to join, see Friedlander, *The Emergence of a UAW Local*; Bodnar, *Immigration and Industrialization*, 150–55; Gobel, "Becoming American"; Cohen, *Making a New Deal*; and Gerstle, *Working-Class Americanism*.

24. Rabith interview (first quote); Mike Matozel, interview with author, May 15, 1991 (second quote); Steve Stock, interview with author, September 11, 1990 (third quote).

25. Voros interview (first quote); Marie Starn, telephone interview with author, March 3, 1991 (second quote); Gerald "Joe" Palmer interview (third quote).

26. Marinich interviews. Biographical data on Barberton priests in the 1930s were furnished in a letter to the author from Christine Krossel, archivist for the Cleveland diocese, March 31, 1990. Additional data were derived from the Lauter interview. The Barberton parishes were located in a diocese that was rather receptive to working-class mobilization. See Henry B. Leonard, "Ethnic Tensions, Episcopal Leadership and the Emergence of the Twentieth-Century Catholic Church: The Cleveland Experience," *Catholic Historical Review* 71 (July 1985), 394–412. On Catholic thought and its relation to organized labor in this period, see Marc Karson, "The Catholic Church and the Political Development of American Trade Unionism (1900–1918)," *Industrial and Labor Relations Review* 4 (July 1951), 527–42; and Ronald Schatz, "American Labor and the Catholic Church, 1919–1950," *International La-*

bor and Working-Class History 20 (Fall 1981), 46–53. On the stance of the bishop of the Cleveland diocese, which encompassed Barberton, see David O'Brien, "American Catholics and Organized Labor in the 1930s," *Catholic Historical Review* 52 (October 1966), 323–49.

27. Gerald "Joe" Palmer interview; Papers of FLU 18616; *Rubber Age*, January 1935. On the NRA codes for matches and rubber, see *American Federationist*, March and April 1934; Match Code, Boiler Code, Rubber Code, National Recovery Administration Papers, Record Group 9, National Archives, Washington, D.C.; and Case No. 93, Cleveland Regional National Labor Board, Record Group 25, National Archives, Suitland Records Branch, Suitland, Maryland. The Seiberling Company outlined its rather benign labor policy to the La Follette Committee, a summary that won the approval of the plant's union leadership. See U.S. Senate, *Hearings before Subcommittee of the Committee on Education and Labor*, 74th Congress, 2d Session, April 1936, exhibits 2300 to 2303, 5806–8 (hereafter cited as the La Follette Committee Report). On Diamond Match's policy, see C. F. C. Taylor to Fred Marvin, October 10, 1936, Municipal Papers, Barberton Historical Society, Barberton, Ohio.

28. Ray interview.

29. Ruth McKenney, *Industrial Valley* (New York: Harcourt Brace, 1939), 111; *Summit County Labor News*, February 9, 1934; *B&W Boilermaker*, February and March 1947; Federal Mediation and Conciliation Service files, File #176-1330, Record Group 280, National Archives, Suitland Records Branch, Suitland, Maryland (hereafter referred to as FMCS).

30. *Summit County Labor News*, January 5 and 12, 1934.

31. Ibid., March 9 and June 22, 1934; *B&W Boilermaker*, February and March 1947; FMCS #176-1330.

32. According to Wilmer Tate, the Columbia Chemical "management has been the most vicious toward our efforts to organize than the management of any other plant in this vicinity." Wilmer Tate to William Green, April 20, 1934, Papers of FLU 19019. See also Case No. 93, Cleveland Regional National Labor Board. Local 149's minute book is in vol. 1, box 170, NBOP Papers. The quote is from Bill Hammer, interview with author, September 20, 1990. For a historical parallel, see Philip Foner's description of the rituals of the Knights of Labor in his *History of the Labor Movement in the United States*, vol. 1, *From Colonial Times to the Founding of the American Federation of Labor* (New York: International Publishers, 1947), 434–35.

33. Gerald "Joe" Palmer interview. For discussions of the course of meetings, see, for example, Local 149 minute book, November 15, 1933, April 6, 1934.

34. Jennie Lentol quoted in *Summit County Labor News*, April 13, 1934. Other leaders' names are derived from Francis Gerhart to William Green, March 17, 1934, Papers of FLU 18928. Similarly, the first secretary of Seiberling FLU 18616 was also a woman. Officers of Seiberling Local to

William Green, December 17, 1934, Papers of FLU 18616. Lilah Emrick discussed her involvement in the union beginning in the 1930s and women's roles in the movement in an interview with the author, August 22, 1990. For memories of participation in the Women's Auxiliary, see Sarah Street, interview with author, February 25, 1991. On the traditional role of women in the labor movement, feminism, and unionism, see Nancy F. Gabin, *Feminism in the Labor Movement: Women and the United Auto Workers, 1935–1975* (Ithaca, N.Y.: Cornell University Press, 1990); Julia Kirk Blackwelder, *Women of the Depression: Caste and Class in San Antonio, 1929–1939* (College Station: Texas A&M Press, 1984); Dolores Janiewski, *Sisterhood Denied: Race, Gender, and Class in a New South Community* (Philadelphia: Temple University Press, 1985); and Vicki Ruiz, *Cannery Women, Cannery Lives: Mexican Women, Unionization, and the California Food Processing Industry, 1930–1950* (Albuquerque: University of New Mexico Press, 1987).

35. Francis Gerhart to William Green, April 25, 1934 (first quote); telegram, Coleman Claherty to William Green, April 25, 1935, both in Papers of FLU 18928; *Akron Times-Press*, April 25, 1934 (second quote). Coverage of the strike can be found in the *Akron Beacon Journal* and *Akron Times-Press*, March–April 1934; McKenney, *Industrial Valley*, 142–44; and correspondence between FLU 18928 and the AFL in Papers of FLU 18928. In early 1934 unionists of Diamond Match actually created the Joint Committee of Engineering Machinists, Maintenance Mechanics, and Match Workers, which coordinated negotiations; see *Summit County Labor News*, January 5, March 23, and September 28, 1934.

36. For coverage of the strike, see the *Akron Beacon Journal* and *Akron Times-Press*, April 20–24, 1934, especially April 21; McKenney, *Industrial Valley*, 147–52; and correspondence between the local and AFL in Papers of FLU 19019.

37. The interpretation on the effect of the transformation of Barberton workers' consciousness is partially derived from oral history sources that not only vividly recall the Columbia Chemical strike and what it stood for but also have very little memory of the preceding Diamond Match strike. See Gerald "Joe" Palmer interview; Marinich interviews; "Labor in Barberton"; Earl Davis interview; Stan and Mary Valenchek, interview with author, March 20, 1991 (first and second quotes); and La Follette Committee Report, part 3, 1655–56 (third quote).

38. On the Columbia Chemical National Labor Board decision, see *Akron Beacon Journal*, May 12, 23, 28, and 30, 1934; *Summit County Labor News*, May 11, 18, and 25, 1934; and Case No. 93, Cleveland Regional National Labor Board.

39. C. J. Francis to Francis Biddle, January 10, 1935, FMCS #170-1252.

40. Don Williams, Joanne Williams, and Jeanne La Polla, interview with author, March 11, 1990 (quote); Gerald "Joe" Palmer interview.

41. Marinich interviews. During the Ohio Insulator strike Ray Potts, the ex-sheriff, came out directly in support of the strikers. Other middle-class support for the strikers can be found in *Akron Beacon Journal*, November 24, 1935; and "Labor in Barberton." Besides shop owners, Barberton lacked much of a middle-class presence since many of the factory managers lived in nearby Akron. See Hsiao Fang Li, "The Geographic Structure of Barberton's Industry" (M.A. thesis, Kent State University, 1948); and *Akron Beacon Journal*, March 24, 1974.

42. Daniel Nelson, *American Rubber Workers and Organized Labor*, 159–60. On labor-management relations in this period, see Harris, *The Right to Manage*; Mike Davis, *Prisoners of the American Dream*; and Daniel Nelson, "Managers and Non-Union Workers in the Rubber Industry: Union Avoidance Strategies in the 1930s," *Industrial and Labor Relations* 43 (October 1989), 41–52.

43. Voros interview. On interunion relations at Diamond Match see also George Roberts to William Green, December 17, 1934, Papers of FLU 18616; Francis Gerhart to William Green, January 13, 193[5], Papers of FLU 18928. Activities of the National Match Workers' Council are covered in the *Summit County Labor News*, which for approximately two years (1935–37) included the *National Match Worker* as an appendage. See also Wolman, *Ebb and Flow in Trade Unionism*, 70.

44. Buffington and Norman Tiffin both resigned from the Barberton CLU in August 1934. By 1936 all the members or officers of the central labor body were industrial unionists headed by Francis Gerhart. *Summit County Labor News*, August 24, 1934, January 8, 1937.

45. On rubber worker support for industrial unionization, see George Roberts to William Green, December 17, 1934, Papers of FLU 18616. Both FLU 18616 and FLU 19019 introduced resolutions at the 1935 AFL convention calling for organization along industrial lines. American Federation of Labor, *Proceedings of Conventions, 1935* (Washington, D.C.: American Federation of Labor, 1936), 75, 198 (quote), 724–29; Harold Roberts, *The Rubber Workers*, 141. For an eyewitness account of the Lewis-Hutcheson incident and FLU 18616's role, see John House, "Birth of a Union" (manuscript), 183–86, Ohio Historical Society, Columbus, Ohio.

46. John McNamara, interview with author, August 28, 1990; Earl Davis interview. In June 1934 the Barberton CLU had formed a committee to attend city council meetings "to make sure things ran properly." *Barberton Herald*, June 9, 1934; *Summit County Labor News*, June 8, 1934 (quote). By 1935 this impulse had turned to running their own candidates. *Barberton Herald*, November 8, 1935.

47. McKenney, *Industrial Valley*, 227–42; Jack Palmer, interview (first quote); *Akron Beacon Journal*, November 15 and 21, 1935; *Akron Times-*

Press, November 20, 21 (second quote), and 25, 1935; Local 149 minute book, October, November, December, NBOP Papers.

48. On Colonel Joseph Johnston, see Daniel Nelson, *American Rubber Workers and Organized Labor,* 155; Leo Huberman, *The Labor Spy Racket* (New York: Modern Age Books, 1937), 153–54; Clinch Calkins, *Spy Overhead: The Story of Industrial Espionage* (1937; reprint, New York: Arno, 1971); and "Testimony of A. S. Ailes," La Follette Committee Report, 394–95, 571–72, 602–3.

49. *Akron Times-Press,* November 21, 1935; Jack Palmer interview. See also sources in note 47.

50. *Akron Times-Press,* November 21, 1935 (Gerhart, Lee, and Evans quotes); *Akron Beacon Journal,* November 21, 1935 (pottery worker quote).

51. *Akron Times-Press,* November 23, 1935 (Brackett quote); *Akron Beacon Journal,* November 22 (Gerhart quote) and 24, 1935.

52. *Akron Times-Press,* November 25, 1935.

53. *Akron Beacon Journal,* November 25, 1935.

54. Marinich interviews.

55. *Akron Beacon Journal,* November 22–25, 1935; *Akron Times-Press,* November 22–25 (quotes on November 25), 1935. On the conclusion of the strike, see Local 149 minute book, NBOP Papers; *Akron Beacon Journal,* December 23, 1935; *Daily Worker,* December 11, 1935; and *Akron Times-Press,* December 23, 1935.

56. Mike Davis, *Prisoners of the American Dream,* 58.

57. Staughton Lynd, "Introduction," herein.

58. *Akron Beacon Journal,* January 20, 1936; *Akron Times-Press,* January 20, 1936; Sherman Dalrymple to Fred Marvin, January 13, 1936, Municipal Papers, Barberton Historical Society.

59. *Barberton Herald,* May 17, July 19, and October 25, 1935, January 31 and March 20, 1936. On the Workers' Alliance nationally, see Harvey Klehr, *The Heyday of American Communism: The Depression Decade* (New York: Basic Books, 1984), 294–304; Frances Fox Piven and Richard A. Cloward, *Poor People's Movements: Why They Succeed, How They Fail* (New York: Pantheon, 1977); Selden Rodman, "Lasser and the Workers' Alliance," *Nation,* September 10, 1938, 242–44; and Franklin Folsom, *Impatient Armies of the Poor: The Story of Collective Action of the Unemployed, 1808–1942* (Niwot: University Press of Colorado, 1991), 170–233, 340–46, 414–31.

60. On the early days of the Columbia Chemical sit-down, see *Akron Beacon Journal,* February 19, 20, and 21, 1936; and *Akron Times-Press,* February 19, 20, and 21, 1936. Internal details of the strike are provided in H. A. Bradley to William Green, February 25, 1936; H. A. Bradley to William Green, March 12, 1936; Coleman Claherty to William Green, March 30, 1936, all in Papers of FLU 19019; and Larry Miller, interview with author, January 8,

1991 (quote). On the great Goodyear strike, see Daniel Nelson, "Origins of the Sit-Down Era: Worker Militancy and Innovation in the Rubber Industry, 1934–1938," *Labor History* 23 (Fall 1982), 198–225; and Daniel Nelson, "The Great Goodyear Strike of 1936," *Ohio History* 92 (Autumn 1983), 6–36.

61. A. P. Lee to William Green, March 28, 1936 (quote); H. A. Bradley to William Green, March 12, 1936; William J. McGee to William Green, March 12, 1936, all in Papers of FLU 19019; *Akron Beacon Journal,* March 23–25, 1936.

62. A. P. Lee to William Green, May 23, 1936, Papers of FLU 19019. Chemical manufacturing required full-time operation of the plant. On FLU 19019's realization that this could be used on its behalf in a labor struggle, see William B. Sherman to William Green, April 20, 1934, Papers of FLU 19019.

63. Coleman Claherty to William Green, March 30, 1936; M. R. Ford to William Green, September 28, 1936; R. Lee Guard to William Green, September 30, 1936; Glen McCabe to William Green, October 1, 1936; Coleman Claherty to William Green, October 14, 1936, all in Relations with the CIO, William Green Papers, 1935–41, Office of the President, AFL Papers, State Historical Society of Wisconsin, Madison. Green responded to FLU 19019 by citing its "base ingratitude" in the light of the strike benefits given by the AFL in the strike in the spring. William Green to A. P. Lee, October 6, 1936, Green Papers. Two months later Green instructed one of his organizers to "call on the chemical workers and see if they are satisfied." William Green to W. H. Wilson, December 16, 1936, Green Papers. On the role of FLU 19019 in the Flat Glass Workers dispute with the AFL, see Lowell Galloway, "The Origin of the Early Years of the Federation of Flat Glass Workers of America," *Labor History* 3 (Winter 1962), 92–102; Trevor Bain, "Internal Union Conflict: The Flat Glass Workers, 1936–1937," *Labor History* 9 (Winter 1968), 106–9; and Trevor Bain, "The Impact of Technological Change on the Flat Glass Industry and the Unions' Reactions to Change: Colonial Period to the Present" (Ph.D. diss, University of California, Berkeley, 1964), 215–18.

64. *Akron Beacon Journal,* June 17, 1936; I. A. Hurley to E. S. Cowdrick, June 15, 1936, exhibit 1075, La Follette Committee Report, part 7, 3207. See also Borsos, "Ironing Out Chaos."

65. Paul Stanley to William Green, June 17, 1936; telegram, FLU 20186 to William Green, July 6, 1936, both in Papers of FLU 20186.

66. Report to AFL, W. H. Wilson to Frank Morrison, May 29, 1936; H. D. Hanna to William Green, July 22, 1936; H. A. Bradley to William Green, August 20, 1936; H. W. Brown to William Green, June 18, 1936; Coleman Claherty to William Green, July 6, 1936, all in Papers of FLU 20183.

67. John Knight and H. D. Hanna to Organized Labor, July 27, 1936, FMCS #182-1481 (first quote); H. D. Hanna to William Green, July 22, 1936,

Papers of FLU 20183 (second quote); AFL, *Proceedings of Convention, 1936,* 38; H. D. Hanna to William Green, August 3, 1936, Papers of FLU 20183.

68. FMCS #182-1481 (first quote); H. A. Bradley to William Green, August 20, 1936, Papers of FLU 20183 (second quote). For a copy of the contract, see Papers of FLU 20183.

69. *National Match Worker,* February 26, 1937. On the pursuit of shop-floor rights, see Coleman Claherty to William Green, July 13, 1936, Papers of FLU 18928.

70. H. A. Bradley to William Green, August 15, 1936, Papers of FLU 20183 (quote); Francis Gerhart to William Green, February 12, 1937, Papers of FLU 18928; H. A. Bradley to William Green, August 15, 1936, Papers of FLU 20183. On FLU 18928's lack of interest in the CIO, see FMCS #196-7847; and Charles A. Cockwell to James P. McWeeny, October 30, 1941, Papers of FLU 18928.

71. In 1956 both the Boilermakers and the Steelworkers bargained for the affiliation of FLU 20186, which chose the Boilermakers, becoming Local 900. In 1969 the workers at Pittsburgh Valve and Fittings (then Rockwell) affiliated with the Boilermakers, becoming Local 909. On the background of that affiliation, see George Sepelak and Jack Nelson, interview with author, August 27, 1989. Some CIO unions later became interested in the federal labor unions. On the Flat Glass Workers' interest in Local 19019, see Glen McCabe to William Green, October 1, 1936, Green Papers; AFL, *Proceedings of Convention, 1936,* 27; and Glen McCabe, "Address to United Rubber Workers Convention," in United Rubber Workers, *Proceedings of Convention, 1936,* 58–59.

72. H. A. Bradley to William Green, August 20, 1936, Papers of FLU 20183. On local manipulation of the CIO split, see, for example, Francis Gerhart to William Green, July 1, 1937; Joseph E. Duffy to William Green, July 19, 1937; Charles A. Cockwell to James P. McWeeny, October 29, 1941; James McWeeny to William Green, November 17, 1941; and Francis Gerhart to William Green, December 17, 1941, all in Papers of FLU 18928. On Green's reaction to the CIO, see Phelan, *William Green;* Dubofsky and Van Tine, *John L. Lewis;* and Taft, *The AF of L from the Death of Gompers to the Merger.* On "Labor's Civil War," see Mike Davis, *Prisoners of the American Dream;* Mary Heaton Vorse, *Labor's New Millions* (New York: Modern Age Books, 1938); and Bernstein, *The Turbulent Years.*

73. Gerald "Joe" Palmer interview.

74. In addition to Gerhart's and Wells's participation, Potters' Local 149 sent delegates to the Farmer-Labor convention in June, and FLU 20186 of the Babcock and Wilcox was the first group to make a substantial contribution ($100) to the party's effort to get reinstated on the ballot. *Akron Beacon Journal,* June 8 and September 10, 1936; Local 149 minute book, NBOP, May 29, 1936. See also Shrake, "Working-Class Politics in Akron." Daniel Nelson gives

especially short shrift to the Summit County Farmer-Labor Party, focusing on its failure in the 1937 mayoral election, while discounting the potential support the movement had among unionists in the summer of 1936. See his "The CIO at Bay: Labor Militancy and Politics in Akron, 1936–1938," *Journal of American History* 71 (December 1984), 565–86. For a differing account of the movement closer to my own interpretation, see Eric Leif Davin, "The Very Last Hurrah?" herein. On the nucleus of a labor party, see *Summit County Labor News*, February 5 and 26, 1937.

75. *Barberton Herald,* January 21, 1938, March 24, 1939.

76. Local 149 minute book, October 29 and December 10, 1937, April 29, 1938 (quote), NBOP Papers.

77. Paul E. Smoyer to John Brophy, April 27, 1937, Barberton Central Labor Union Charter Record, AFL-CIO Papers, George Meany Memorial Archives, Silver Spring, Maryland.

78. *Barberton Herald,* December 25, 1936, April 16 and 23 and October 8, 1937, July 15, 1938; *Summit County Labor News,* November 6, 1936, January 29 and July 9 and 16, 1937. See also Elizabeth Fones-Wolf, "Industrial Recreation, the Second World War and the Revival of Welfare Capitalism, 1934–1960," *Business History Review* 60 (Summer 1986), 232–57. On the summer holiday, see Fred Marvin to City Industries (form letter), June 25, 1937, Municipal Papers, Barberton Historical Society; and *Summit County Labor News,* July 9, 1937.

79. Sarah Street discusses the Barberton Women's Auxiliary in her interview with the author, February 25, 1991. Historians in other fields have posited convincing arguments that the presence of women in protest movements intensifies the nature of the struggle, making them more than simply economic. I, too, found this to be the case in Barberton. See June Nash, "Resistance as Protest: Women in Struggle of the Bolivia Tin Mines," in *Women Cross Culturally,* ed. Ruby Rohrich Leavitt (The Hague: Monton, 1973), 261–71; Temma Kaplan, "Female Consciousness and Collective Action: The Case of Barcelona, 1900–1918," *Signs* 7 (Spring 1982), 545–65; and Jacquelyn Dowd Hall, "Disorderly Women: Gender and Labor Militancy in the Appalachian South," *Journal of American History* 73 (September 1986), 354–82.

80. On family ties, see Williams, Williams, and La Polla interview; William Oyler, interview with author, October 24, 1990; and *Summit County Labor News,* December 14, 1934, December 10, 1937. George Sepelak especially emphasized these family bonds in the Sepelak and Nelson interview. See also *Summit County Labor News,* February 5, 1937.

81. Mary Randolph, interview with author, March 12, 1990; Rabith interview; Mary Smith, interview with author, September 22, 1990; Starn interview. On the implications of women's failure to develop a feminist ideology in the period, see Sharon Hartman Strom, "Challenging 'Woman's Place':

Feminism, the Left, and Industrial Unionism in the 1930's," *Feminist Studies* 9 (Summer 1983), 359–86.

82. *UE News,* January 25, 1941.

83. See for example, Francis Gerhart to William Green, January 15, 1936; and Francis Gerhart to A. C. Wharton, August 19, 1936, both in Papers of FLU 18928.

84. Evidence of the organizing drives can be seen in Local 149 minute book, NBOP Papers; H. D. Hanna to William Green, July 20, 1936, Papers of FLU 20183; Papers of FLU 20246; Papers of FLU 22153; and *Summit County Labor News,* January 15, 1937 (quote).

85. See Local 149 minute book, October 9 and 16, 1936, December 29, 1939, NBOP Papers,; Glenn Street to Dear Sir, December 2, 1940, and Glenn Street to Julius Emspak, February 24, 1941, Local 747 files, FF649, United Electrical Workers Papers, University of Pittsburgh, Pittsburgh, Pennsylvania; and *Summit County Labor News,* June 18, 1937. On the significance of women's roles as consumers in the building of a social movement, see Dana Frank, "At the Point of Consumption: Seattle Labor and the Politics of Consumption, 1919–1927" (Ph.D. diss., Yale University, 1988), 568, 571.

86. Edward M. Eloian, "The Transformation of Credit Unions in the United States" (Ph.D. diss., Michigan State University, 1987), 4–5, 60, 74.

87. *Barberton Herald,* January 21, 1938; *Summit County Labor News,* April 14, 1938 (quote).

88. *Akron Beacon Journal,* June 26, 1936; on Gerhart's firing, see *National Match Worker,* December 31, 1936.

89. See, for example, Local 149 minute book, NBOP Papers; and Minutes of Executive Board of FLU 20186, 1937–1939, Papers of Boilermakers Local 900, Local 900 Union Hall, Barberton, Ohio.

90. *Akron Beacon Journal,* September 24, 1936 (first quote); *Barberton Herald,* July 21, 1939 (second quote).

91. *Summit County Labor News,* July 21, 1939; *Barberton Herald,* July 30, 1937 (quote), March 17, 1939.

92. *Summit County Labor News,* September 15, 1939, July 12, 1940, January 10, 1941, February 14 and 21, 1941; *Barberton Herald,* January 10, 1941; FMCS #196-3902-1 (quote).

93. Local 149 minute book, July 16 and December 3, 1937, NBOP Papers; FMCS #182-1793, #199-3355.

94. Local 149 minute book, May 2, 1938, NBOP Papers; *UE News,* February 25 and April 22, 1939. For a sympathetic overview of the National Brotherhood of Operative Potters that contains some of the activity of the Barberton local, see Don A. Shotliff, "The History of the Labor Movement in the American Pottery Industry: The National Brotherhood of Operative Potters" (Ph.D. diss, Kent State University, 1977); *Labor Relations Reference*

Manual, vol. 4 (Washington, D.C.: Bureau of National Affairs, 1939), UE Local 747 Case No. R-1226, June 3, 1939 (13 NLRB No. 10), 271; *Labor Relations Reference Manual,* vol. 5 (September 1, 1939–February 29, 1940), Ohio Brass Case No. C-949, September 12, 1939 (15 NLRB 210), 120–21.

95. E. S. Fout to Julius Emspak, June 3, 1941, Local 747 files, FF 648, UE Papers, University of Pittsburgh (first quote); FMCS #199-6738 (second and third quotes).

96. Richard Niebur to James J. Matles, August 16, 1941, Richard Niebur Papers, UE Papers; *UE News,* August 16, 23, and 30, 1941.

97. *Akron Beacon Journal,* September 4, 1941 (Fout estimated that over 250 local merchants had made donations to the strike fund); *UE News,* July 5, 1941 (first quote); E. S. Fout to Dear Brothers, July 9, 1941, Local 747 files, FF 648, UE Papers (second quote); *OB Striker,* August 22, 1941, in Local 747 files, FF 648, UE Papers (third quote); telegram, Ralph T. Seward to James J. Matles, August 1, 1941, Local 747 files, FF 652, UE Papers.

98. *Summit County Labor News,* December 10, 1937 (Being Red quote), May 13, 1938 (property rights quote); *National Match Worker,* February 26, 1937 (commonwealth quote), June 11, 1937 (orchids quote).

99. *Summit County Labor News,* December 10, 1937, September 8, 1939 (Palmer quote), December 1, 1939 (war quote), March 15 and 22 and June 7, 1940. For Woonsocket's unionists need to soft-peddle their radicalism, see Gerstle, *Working-Class Americanism.* The comparison here between Joseph Schmetz of Woonsocket and Francis Gerhart of Barberton should be obvious and suggests the potential richness of a more systematic investigation of labor leaders at this level.

100. *National Match Worker,* January 22, 1937. For additional articles and editorials written in this vein, see, for example, ibid., February 26 and April 23, 1937; and *Summit County Labor News,* September 10, 1937, April 22, May 13, and December 23, 1938.

101. Barnes interview; Lowry interview. Kenneth West, after interviewing Flint sit-downers, summarized that the principle aim of strikers was not more money but respect. Kenneth B. West, "'On the Line': Rank and File Remembrances of Working Conditions and the General Motors Sit-Down Strike of 1936–37," *Michigan Historical Review* 12 (Spring 1986), 57–82.

102. Gutman's idea of the community basis of resistance is best expressed in Herbert Gutman, "The Workers' Search for Power: Labor in the Gilded Age," in his *Power and Culture: Essays on the American Working Class,* ed. Ira Berlin (New York: Pantheon, 1987), 70–92. Ira Katznelson develops his argument on community in *City Trenches: Urban Politics and the Patterning of Class in the United States* (Chicago: University of Chicago Press, 1981). See also Rick Fantasia, *Cultures of Solidarity: Consciousness, Action, and Contemporary American Workers* (Berkeley: University of California Press, 1988).

103. On these developments, see Borsos, "Talking Union," chap. 3.

104. Ibid., chap. 4, 5, 6.

105. A copy of the program of the first Labor Day Parade program can be found in the Papers of Boilermakers Local 900, Local 900 Union Hall, Barberton, Ohio. Knight's quote can be found in United Electrical Workers, *Proceedings of Convention, 1951* (New York: United Electrical Workers, 1952), 232–33.

106. Marinich interviews.

9

Unions with Leaders Who Stay on the Job

Stan Weir

It was noon, an hour and twenty minutes before the scheduled sailing time of the freighter SS *Hanapepe,* September 28, 1943. I went to the crowded mess room and took the seat left vacant for me. My arrival meant that all eleven members of the Deck Gang were present. We did not order lunch. The on-ship delegates or representatives of both the Marine Firemen, Oilers, Watertenders and Wipers union (MFOW&W) and the Marine Cooks and Stewards union (MC&S) looked at me, the delegate of the Deck Gang and the Sailors' Union of the Pacific (SUP), and nodded.

I put on my white cap. With that signal we of the Deck Gang got up, walked to the gangway and down off the ship. In doing so, we all made eye-to-eye contact with the men of the Black Gang (Engine Department), and with all the messmen and cooks of the Stewards' Department about to serve the crew members, who would for a time remain seated. The barely noticeable smile and nod from each of them, and from each of us in return, was a reaffirmation of the pledge we had all made, an unrehearsed and emotional admission of camaraderie.

Once on the dock we walked to an imaginary line parallel with the ship's side and about fifty feet from it, just far enough away so that we wouldn't have to look up at too sharp an angle during the exchange we were about to have with the ship's officers. Facing the ship in a line, we waited, a bosun, a ship's carpenter, six able bodied seamen (ABs), and three ordinary seamen.[1] Each of the three sea watches was made up of two ABs and an ordinary.

With the exception of Blackie Soromengo, the bosun, and Chips Costello, the carpenter, we were a little jumpy. They were twenty years or more older than the rest of us and veterans of the 1934 "Big Strike" that had stopped West Coast marine cargo movement for eighty-three days and had won recognition for all maritime unions on the West Coast.[2] But the term *'34 man* meant much more than strike veteran; it identified a member of what had been a very real movement that became clearly visible three years before the 1934 strike. These men did not wear buttons for identification, but a mark of honor was on them all. The instruction they gave to the younger men who entered the industry during the war revealed what they had learned: the power and hilarity of overcoming long years of submission and their terror of losing hold of that power. The strength and the anxiety of the '34 men were with us that day on the dock.

The bosun and carpenter well understood that we wanted to be able to tell others our own stories of direct action. We were anxious to establish our generation's reputation in the union and the industry. But they also knew the seriousness of what we were doing and the weaknesses as well as strengths of our eagerness. They gave us room and seldom used their authority to showcase themselves. We were forging an open alliance between the two generations standing there together on the dock.

The Background

The war and the shortage of seamen had given us "young men" our first union jobs and full-time work. We had never before been able to stand up and fight back openly. Such terms as *direct action* or *job action* were new to our vocabularies.

In the fall of 1943 the only unemployed were people between jobs or en route to military induction centers. Mobilization for total war production was increasingly a part of daily routine. Movie theaters, markets, and cafes in industrial areas were open around the clock. Workers in factories and shipyards were being pinned with "E for Efficiency" buttons after breaking all production records in competition with themselves. The young men of their families were the main source of both draft and volunteer recruitment for the armed forces. At the same time employers receiving "costs plus ten per cent profit" from government defense contracts were using advertising agency forms of patriotism to eliminate the protective work rules won by employees in the decade before the war.

Because of the unconditional no-strike pledge union leaders had declared and negotiated in union contracts, strikers were commonly dealt with as if their needs were unworthy of respect. The Roosevelt administration had early on hired scores of lawyers and professors to arbitrate all labor conflicts. Yet more strikers would go on strike in 1943 than during any year in the 1930s.[3] A big contradiction in what has been called "the good war"—though never mentioned in the media—was that during the so-called war for democracy neither employers nor union officials showed concern for the democratic rights of working people in the United States.

During the first year of the war there were still enough old-timers among West Coast seamen for them to pass on to new seamen the need to enforce both the formal and informal work rules won in the 1930s. In 1943 the number of U.S. merchant ships tripled. At the same time the mortality rate among merchant seamen in the war was proportionately higher than in any of the armed services.[4] Veterans of the 1930s maritime strikes came to be vastly outnumbered by new shipmates not long parted from high school and part-time jobs. In an attempt to overcome their disadvantage the older men sometimes sought to instruct by more formal methods than the usual bull sessions. Teaching their history of conflict with both the shipowners and official union leaders came easily; they had lived it. But most of all, the instructors sought to teach by involvement with their younger shipmates in job actions.

On the Dock

The appearance on deck of the chief mate interrupted my thoughts.[5] He stood above the main deck, where the men of the Engine Room, Stewards' Department, and Navy Armed Guard who manned the ship's guns were gathering. He was big, lean, and in his fifties. After a harrumph he yelled to the bosun, "Why is your gang on the dock?" He continued before the bosun could answer: "I want the appropriate helmsman from the 12 to 4 watch to come to the flying bridge at one o'clock sharp and stand by ready to take the wheel the moment the pilot comes aboard. And bosun, you and the men off watch must be standing by at the same time ready to haul up and make fast the gangway, then send three men to the bow and three to the stern to slack off, and then haul in the mooring lines when the longshore linesmen on the dock let them go. There will be steam in the windlasses."

"The appropriate helmsman"? "There will be steam"? Had they gotten this guy from central casting? We were all choking back laughter, yet none of us moved. The bosun broke the silence: "You've got it wrong, Mate. You've been going to sea long enough to know better. When you see us out here like this you have to deal with our elected delegate, Red, who is standing right here. Until you do that anything you want to discuss must wait."

(A delegate performs the same function that a shop steward does in union workplaces ashore. But because all ships have stewards' departments, whose members prepare and serve three meals and a light lunch a day, in addition to making the officers' beds and cleaning their rooms, a second use of the term would create confusion.)

I took two steps toward the ship ready to speak. At the same time the mate turned and walked quickly into the midship house. The captain came out onto the wing of the bridge moments later. He glared down at us from beneath a navy officer's hat with all the trimmings, "scrambled eggs" included, on the bill. "As master of this ship I order you to come aboard immediately and go to your assigned stations ready to work as directed."

I heard grunts of anger behind me. Louder noises came from other members of the crew standing two decks below the captain, just out of his line of vision. His head jerked with the realization that almost the entire crew was witness. The audience had given me what I needed. "No, Captain, there are questions of health that have to be taken care of here and now."

"Do you think you are running this ship?"

"Captain, do I have to explain to you what our roles are supposed to be as Deck delegate and captain? Your regular authority established for the operation of this ship is one thing. During any bargaining process it is suspended, and we are equals. If you are asking me to go over the history since crews like this one began to revive the unions ten years ago, then you will soon see the Black Gang out here on the dock, too. If there is any trouble after that, the room steward who makes your bed and the cooks and messmen who feed us will follow."

The captain went white in the face, then recovered to ask, "All right, Weir, why aren't you at your assigned duties instead of out here on this dock?"

He had quit stammering when using my name and so had taken a step toward admission that each of us was a representative. "A reminder, Captain. The delegates from all three departments came to you with complaints almost two weeks ago. You put us off then and three times more. The responsibility for the problem you now have is not ours. And, we are all on lunch hour."

"Is this the bedbug thing again?"

"Only in part. Bedbugs have been found in several of the mattresses of the unlicensed personnel and the Navy Armed Guard. All of the mattresses are very old, soiled and lumpy. Remember that we live three men to a fo'c'sle in a space half the size of your room. Remember, too, that unlike those used by you who live topside, the mattresses were two feet wide, six feet long and two inches thick when they came aboard many trips ago. Now they are longer and thinner. They have to be replaced."

"Have you appointed yourself delegate for all three departments and the navy men?"

"I can get two other delegates out here right now if you like."

"But we're about to sail."

"You have a telephone that's strung from the dock to your room. There are ships' chandlers in the East Bay just like there are in San Francisco along the Embarcadero. You can get all the items we need from any one of them in less than an hour."

With head tilted to one side and sugary voice, the captain went for what he probably thought was his biggest weapon: "There's a war on, you know."

A "fuck yoohoo" delivered slowly in a near-singing voice wafted aloft from the main deck gallery. Then, short, hard, and square-built Chips, who had been on two ships sunk by U-boats in the Caribbean, broke in, "The ship you are standing on is your first since you took an office job with this company when the war started."

The blows to the captain's credibility showed on his face. But even if I had wanted to, I couldn't afford to let his cheap shot go with only two responses. A document citing the articles of war was attached to the ship's articles we had signed two days earlier. We had discussed what to do if this came up.

"Yes, Captain, we know, and because of the war there is the War Shipping Administration [WSA] which pays this company and others for all costs connected with operating ships for the war effort. Your company has one of the many 'costs plus ten percent profit' contracts. You know, having worked in the office, that for every dollar your outfit spends on food and the other needs of the crew it gets back at least a dollar and a dime. If you have outfitted this ship as it should be, and have reported to the WSA as required, why is it that we lack so many needed food and sanitation items?"

The captain took too long to respond. Laughter exploded from the gathering on the main deck and ceased momentarily only when the identifiable, rough voice of Matt, the lanky and multitattooed deck engineer from Gulfport, Mississippi, drawled, "Okaaay, it's time for all of us y'alls to go out on the dock!"

"No, tell him that won't be necessary, uh, will it Red?"

Red? Was he giving in, using my nickname to bait me, or just out of control? Could it be that our ship's accounts at some ship supply house would show we had full stores of good grade food aboard? The fink probably had a deal going to supplement his salary. "No, it won't be necessary as long as you get the things I'm ready to list."

"You want more than mattresses?"

"Yes. Get fresh milk and good coffee aboard. Fresh vegetables besides cabbage." The purser had appeared at the captain's side and was making a list. "Add plenty of citrus fruit and fresh meat besides mutton to the list." He looked at the captain, got a nod, and went back to writing.

"Good, is that it?"

"No. You are aware that the showers need simple repairs. It is hard to get more than a trickle out of them. A lizard could piss a bigger stream than they put out now. This means we have to stand in line in the passageways waiting turns. Get four new shower heads, some good bar soap, a strong lye soap, five cases of Clorox in gallons, and two five-gallon cans of kerosene."

"What's the kerosene for?"

There was a chorus of guffaws from the main deck. "Is he going to tell us he's never had a dose of crabs?"

I said, "If you haven't got them up on your deck yet, you will during the trip if we don't get kerosene aboard. We bought some kerosene with our own money the first thing when we came aboard. We washed down all the toilets. There's no guarantee we got all the eggs. They may make a comeback. Just in case, order six dozen of the small jars of McKesson's A200 Pyrinate, at least one for every man. The chandlers will have it. It comes in jars, just like Vicks."

"Is that it?"

"Yes, except for a matter that can't be fixed by a purchase. It has to do only with the Deck Gang. We would have taken it up with the chief mate directly, but he didn't stay long enough for me to mention it. He is to stop watching us like some kind of gumshoe when we're working on deck. We think you will understand that it can slow down the work."

"I understand. I will take the matter up with the chief mate, and the purser will order the items you have listed. And so, while he's doing that, you can all come back aboard and go to work."

I hadn't expected that he would again try to get us to refuse a direct order to go to work, even though it was lunch time. I was out of patience, afraid my anger would show if I had to offer still another explanation for our refusal to go aboard. I moved back into the line of men behind me. Several of them began to talk to me out of the sides of their mouths at once. They wanted to bring it all to a halt, right then.

I looked at the bosun and Chips, who hadn't spoken. They smiled. We all turned as a group and walked toward the Dock Cafe just outside the piershed on the Embarcadero. All its windows had a view of the dock road.

The captain was yelling. We continued on our way until we heard him wail, "Where are you going now?"

The bosun didn't turn his head but bumped my shoulder with his: "You mind if I take this one?" I deferred to him without any show of my touch of resentment. As bosun, he was officially in charge of all work assignments for the entire Deck Gang when the ship was in port. We all stopped. The bosun and I turned around together, and he yelled back at the still figure on the ship's bridge, "It still isn't one o'clock, Gilchrist, our lunch hour isn't over. We're going to the cafe for a decent cup of coffee. And remember, there's nothing to do until a ship chandler's truck arrives." The bosun and I did another turnaround and rejoined the gang. The open piershed door just ahead drew us.

At the Dock Cafe

Once inside, our attention turned to the problems ahead. The captain had suffered a defeat, but official power was still on his side.

The three ordinaries had volunteered to run ahead and grab the cafe's big table for us. As first trippers, they felt the isolation of the noninitiated and were dependent on each other for support. If we all got to make this trip together, they would by natural process develop a new identity. Each of them would live in an eight-by-ten-foot room, which by tradition was still called a "fo'c'sle" (forecastle), with two ABs. Four hours on and eight hours off, eight to twelve, twelve to four, and four to eight, seven days a week, they would come to know the ship's routine. They would learn from us who to wake up for the next watch, when it was their turn to make coffee, and how to stand lookout and steer the ship. Days on deck, the bosun and Chips would lead the instruction about lines, knots and splices, chipping rust and red leading.

We already liked the ordinaries. Berto's father had come to Oakland from Portugal via the Hawaiian Islands, as the bosun had. Anthony and Bruno were from San Francisco's Italian neighborhood in North Beach. They were physically bigger than their fathers, who were commercial fishermen, but also were thickset from "helping out on the boat." Hard work didn't bother them.

By the time we arrived at the entrance of the cafe they had eleven chairs and cups of coffee at the table. We paused just inside the door. They were so involved in replay and laughter about what we had all just done together that they didn't notice our arrival.

"Did you see the look on the captain's face when someone sang, 'Fuck yoohoo'? He had a good voice, for god's sake."

"Yeah, but the best was when the captain went dirty. It was like he was singing it, 'There's a war on. . . .' What shit!"

"But Jesus, we just walked off and left him, and he wails, 'Where are you going?' Just like he was a little kid."

It was contagious. They were acting out what we felt. They went silent as soon as they heard our laughter. Together and still standing, we reached for our coffees and all drank at once.

The bosun did not sit down with the rest of us until he took a hard look all around the cafe. "Good job out there today. Good job. But remember, you didn't do it, not alone you didn't. We were the guys who got to do the grandstanding. What we did was a hell of a lot easier than what those men back aboard the ship are having to live through right now. Always keep in mind that in actions like this the Deck Gang gets the spotlight because our jobs are out on deck. At sailing time, we are the ones who have direct contact with the longshoremen, the tugboatmen, and that special bunch of older longshoremen called linesmen. They let go the mooring lines of ships that are about to sail, take them off the bollards on the dock. Deckhands like us then haul the lines aboard using the power windlasses. They do the reverse operation when ships arrive at the dock, take ships' lines from us deckhands and put the eye splices of the lines over the bollards."

Blackie Soromengo was no longer speaking to us as bosun. All the detailed instruction on tying up and letting go of the lines was for the benefit of the ordinaries. The rest of us already knew what he had just gone over. He wanted to show them respect, to pull them into the group, show them they were needed, here and now, in this action. But then he leaned further over the table to signal that he was about to address us all.

"See the two old-timers at the bar? They happen to be the linesmen for our ship. They came onto the dock a little after eleven. I know the short one. When they saw us walk out onto the dock all in a line, they got out of sight. Here, they will not look at us. The same from us, to them, for the time being. They will go out on the dock and stand by fore and aft only if they see us go aboard. But, when that rust bucket that we just left gets out into the stream with us on it, we will take off our hats both to them and the gentlemen on the tugs. And if you ever see any of them ashore, you pay for the drinks.

"You see, the men in the other departments of the crew don't get to do these kinds of things very often. This is one of the commonest kinds of direct action. Their work can only be performed inside the ship. We are all on deck at sailing times. To ask that the oiler fireman and watertenders shut down the ship's engine, when they are down below with two engineer officers at sailing time, is asking a lot. And think what it's like to sail down below in hundred-degree heat spending a third of your life getting your air through a windscoop and not able to look out at the ocean.

"It's harder yet for the people in the Stewards' Department. They are the cooks, bakers, waiters, and janitors for the rest of us, the lowest paid and the takers of the most crap. In '34 they were some of the hardest fighters we had. Now it's headed back toward the way it was before. When the officers are around, too often it's shut up and make no eye contact. Or worse, make a smile. Notice anything different about them? See any people on the deck or in the engine room whose ancestors came from Africa or Asia? No, only in that part of a ship's crew that does what too many of us think of as menial labor."

Like many southerners, Chips had good timing. He interrupted the bosun without it being a discourtesy. "Okay, there are a couple of things we have to get out of the way right now. Okay? All of you on that side of the table can see a half-mile of dock road in either direction. About forty minutes to an hour from now a truck from a ship chandler's may come into sight. Talk all you want, but keep your eyes on that road, starting now! Whenever it comes, we want to stop it here before it gets down the dock in sight of the ship. Got it?

"That brings up another thing." Chips's wiry frame was an advantage. You could tell what he had to say was serious by the veins pumping at the sides of his neck. "The first time you're in on something like this, your asshole can get awful goddamned tight. Relax just a little. They need to get that ship there away from the dock and out to sea, soon! To fire us now they'd have to hire a whole 'nother crew. The time for them to make their move against us will most probably be at the end of the trip. We'll get boarded by a couple of men dressed in U.S. Coast Guard uniforms, not regular military servicemen, more like FBI men in costume. They'll go to the captain and ask if he had any 'troublemakers' this trip. All he has to do is mention the names of the men he wants to hurt. Then the shipowner will hold all the money you made this trip, and the boys in blue will hold up your seaman's papers until you've gone to a military-style hearing up in some fucking federal building. If you screw up and give 'em the opportunity, they will really go after you, but if we are all real careful and look out for each other, they will cite only a couple of us that they think are leaders. Probably there won't be any charges mentioned. It'll just be that a couple of gold braids will hint around for about half an hour that you are probably some kind of communist. Their favorite question is 'Do you ever let your union activity go beyond union activity?' They'll finally let you go. You can usually cut the visit short by demanding the charges, again and again. Remember, even if you ask the union to represent you, there won't anyone come. That means that those of us who are not cited stay in town to make sure nothing worse happens to the guys they think are the leaders. In fact, we'll reserve a table in the federal building cafeteria. Anyone who doesn't show is a fuckup or has shit in his blood."

Seeing Chips was finished, Blackie looked into each of our faces. "There will be plenty of time for us to go over this later. I agree with Chips that the captain probably won't make his move against us now. It seems we have the captain at some kind of disadvantage, like Chips and I suspected we could when we first came aboard and did our own private inspection. Not one of us can afford to make a mistake. No coming aboard drunk, ever, not this trip. Work hard, work good, and mind what you say when you're standing wheel watch at night with only the mate on your watch up there to talk with. If the captain can get something on only two or three of us, he will give them to the 'three letter boys.' With hostages they will seek revenge against all of us for what we did today.

"We are going to clean up this ship and its gear, make it truly shipshape. We will lead careful lives for ourselves and all those in it with us. Red here and his partner, Big John from the Bronx, sailed with Chips and me early last year. Young Finns Waino and Paavo, I knew your fathers, Finn Waino and Finn Walter from the Finnish Brotherhood Hall in Berkeley. There were two halls, yours was the one just a little up the hill east of San Pablo Avenue, the one that had the IWW and some Trotskys, right? They let me flop there several nights during the 1935 tanker strike. We were helping out up in Richmond. I sailed with both of them on the lumber schooners. Walter was in the Centralia strike, a man who read everything he could get his hands on."

Blackie spoke in the same way to Nils and Carl, who he said were "from stump ranches somewhere around Coos Bay," and to the three ordinaries. "Berto, from our talk on deck the other day I know your folks are Portuguese from the Cape Verde Islands, the same as me, and that we all came to the States about the same time. Anthony and Bruno, you were both altar boys at Peter and Paul Cathedral across from Washington Square in North Beach. The definition of sin when out at sea is complicated. You may find some nonbelievers among us, yet I'm sure they try to live by what amounts to the Golden Rule. I know your dad and mom, Bruno, they have that fine old style Italian grocery and deli with the Ensalada Tea on the window in big enameled letters. It's across from the bakery that's in the basement on Grant Avenue at Green Street. That reminds me, let's eat our sandwiches."

Someone at the bar said "amen," and the laughter returned.

Only days ago we had had our election for Deck Gang delegate, and the bosun was for the moment so caught up in what we were doing that he had lost sight of what we were trying to accomplish in the long run. Besides, there was a little matter of pride. I was elected Deck delegate, I felt sure, because the gang knew that by electing me they were getting two people, me plus Big John. We already had a modest reputation. On a ship where a chief mate had ordered the Deck Gang to break out the cargo booms in a rough sea just before coming into the San Francisco harbor, we shut off all the steam on deck, and no gear got rigged until the ship was tied up at the dock. When we signed off, the captain turned us in to the Coast Guard. The matter never came up at a union meeting, but word had gotten around. The bosun and Chips had to realize that while they were our mentors and the thirties established their identity, the war period was creating ours. Because we were doing the same work and represented each other's hopes, we had to treat each other as allies.

Nils raised his hand. "Blackie, only you and Chips have done any of the talking. This is a meeting. Every one has to have a chance to speak."

Nils looked straight at me. I had become the chairman. The instant I nodded in his direction, he began to speak: "Suppose no truck shows, then what? We can't just play this by ear."

Blackie opened his mouth to speak and would have done so, but I waved him off. Finn Waino took the floor.

"We need for one of us to keep an eye on the ship in case something goes wrong there. For an instance, if something happens, we might need all hands again. Blackie, you said you knew one of these linesmen. Could you get him to scout the ship for us?"

All eyes moved to Blackie. He got up without a word, went to the bar, ordered a beer and spoke to the linesman. The man listened to Blackie without looking at him, then got up and left the cafe.

Blackie returned to his table without his beer to announce, "It's a risk for him, but he'll do it carefully and be back in a few minutes."

I took the floor. "Let's assume that the captain gets one or two suits and ties down here. We can't go over the whole thing right now, but we have to have the beginnings of a plan. If authority comes, in suits or uniforms, as delegate I have to talk to them. I need witnesses with me. I move that Big John, Blackie, and Chips be the ones. Again, if authority comes, they will probably drive right to the gangway and try to go directly to the captain. He should not get first crack at them. We should stop them here in the shed. The other seven of you go out the little door behind the bar and right down the apron of the dock. Once you're aboard, get all hands on deck. Then we . . ."

"Yeah, but Red, wait a minute. You, me, and Blackie and Chips should come aboard at the same time as the rest. Every time we make an appearance out there we should do everything to make them see us as a group." It was Big John. Somewhere in his New York upbringing he had developed a sixth sense about the powers of a crowd, even a small one.

All heads were nodding, and smiles were beginning to return.

"Okay, instead of talking, you want a full show of strength to be what speaks most for our case?"

"Right!" was sung in chorus.

"Good. Then let's go on. John, anything else?"

"Yeah. Remember, if a ship chandler's truck arrives, we stop it right here and see what it has aboard. That leaves one more thing to consider. What if it turns out that somehow they pull a power play, and it looks like it's going to be what Cade the Night Cook and Baker calls our 'natural asses'?"

We were under time pressure. I didn't wait for an answer. "It will then be up to all of you who can to round up as many men as you can from all three unions, Marine Cooks, Marine Firemen, and the Sailors' Union." I was looking at Blackie and Chips. "The more '34 men the better. Get them to the Alaska Fishermen's Building and march them through the offices of the officials of all three unions. Make them know that if they don't save whoever's arse is at stake, the news will spread to the memberships of every port on the coast."

"Red, that's a big job."

"That's right, and it can be done with you and Chips in action."

Blackie raised his hand to say, "We'll do everything we can, everything."

Paavo put up his hand. "We know you and Chips will do all you can, Blackie, but don't forget the ordinaries. Enough of this shit from the union that you have to be a full book member of the union before it can protect you."

Bert, Bruno, and Anthony were again laughing with this show of respect from what they felt were two older generations.

"Wait a minute, Red! In that case you don't want Blackie and Chips with you out there. They should stay back in case they have to cop a sneak off the dock to organize a delegation that will pack our great leaders' offices. And another thing. You're right, there should be four men to speak for us, but it ought to be you and the delegates from the other two departments on the ship, not just the Deck Gang."

Waino's hand went up, and he spoke without knowing if Paavo had finished. "Hey partner, we are all forgetting about what John said. It would be a hell of a lot more effective if any suits or uniforms that come aboard get surrounded by the whole crew, then one by one, five or ten of us tell them, no rough stuff, how we feel."

"The power of an intelligent crowd!"

I didn't get to see who made the remark and did not recognize the voice.

"Red." It was Carl, and he was laughing. "The crowd can handle it!"

Blackie was laughing quietly to himself. I looked around. No sign of anyone who wanted to speak. Carl had his arms wrapped around his head in mock submission. Several short guffaws broke the tension, and I took the opening. "Hey Carl, short haul, what you did just now is not easy for me to take. But you're not only saving me some sweat down the line, you're doing a favor for an idea that can make life easier for us all."

There were no laughs. Every face in the house was straight, and still no one wanted the floor.

We all rose from our chairs. Carl came to the bar with John and me. We bought preassembled roast beef sandwiches. I took one and laid it by my place at the table, then headed for the restroom.

Anthony came in while I was drying my hands and followed me back out into the cafe. "Red, wait up. Let's stand over here for a minute. Listen, how come you guys didn't even mention getting someone from the union out here to do something about all this?"

"That's what we are forced to try to avoid, Anthony."

"But you pay dues."

"I know. But if we got a patrolman [business agent] out here from the union hall, he would have to tell us that if we took any kind of direct action we would be violating the contract, that we would have to hang on and make the best of it till we got to Honolulu or back here at the end of the trip. Keep in mind the bosun and Chips picked this ship in the first place because it's in East Oakland at a seldom-used dock."

"You mean you guys had this all . . . ?"

"Don't say it. See you in a few minutes."

"No, wait, who are these guys, the bosun and Chips?"

"Two of the men who actually rebuilt the Sailors' Union in '32 and '33 before the Big Strike, two of them anyway. They were both organizing hit-and-run job actions whenever they could, particularly when guys who had been quiet for years began to dare to speak. Hey, we'll be talking more about this. Right now we're under the gun. Let me go eat my sandwich."

"No, Red, one more thing, how could Chips know that the captain had taken an office job in the company office as soon as the war started?"

"Were you ever in one of those cheap waterfront hotel rooms where most of the old-timers stay between trips? When they were our ages, they never made enough to have a home and a marriage. Most of those rooms are lit by a single light bulb hanging down from the ceiling with no shade on it. The dinginess drives the renters down to the lobbies, where they exchange stories, particularly about the ships they just came off of. Now we eat."

Anthony agreed. I got my sandwich and moved to one of the small tables. Others were doing the same. Paavo walked down the aisle behind me and stopped to press hard on my shoulder, then kept going. He came back a couple of minutes later and sat down across from me to say that Shorty the linesman had come back. The ship had looked peaceful. He couldn't get too close, but half of the Black Gang were sitting out on Number 4 Hatch shooting the breeze with two messmen and the deck engineer.

It was ten minutes to one. A half hour to go before we were all supposed to be back aboard and working. Waino saw me look at my watch.

"Red, fuck it, don't try to carry it all. We all got into this with our eyes open. Take it all too seriously and you lose your sense of humor."

"I didn't know it was showing on me that much. But yes, we've got a lot riding on this one. If we lose this one, the ordinaries may never get another ship."

"We'll find a way. Don't try to take all the responsibility; it's not good for any of us, them included."

We both smiled and waved each other free. I was beginning to understand that my overconcern got in the way of full participation in our decision-making process.

"Hey, all hands out here, now!" It was Paavo, who had just come through the cafe door yelling. "Yeah, all of you, a chandler's truck is coming, now. Arise and shine!"

We Win a Battle

I went out the door with the others at a full run. The back doors of the truck were already open. The driver was reading to Bruno the list of items to be delivered. Nils and Carl had not been able to wait. They were opening cases and yelling out the contents to anyone who might be listening. "Good," came the announcement from Nils. "They got All-Bran and Wheaties instead of Grapenuts, and it's all here: milk, vegetables, coffee, the kerosene, ahah, A200 Pyrinate, tested on the inmates at San Quentin before release for public consumption. We owe those guys, and it's no laughing matter."

Then I noticed Big John. He was grabbing whomever he could get his hands on, then throwing them into the truck. It was the adrenalin of the small crowd. He was smiling, without trying to hide the legacy of a lifetime without going to a dentist. His excitement was catching, and his leadership was easy to accept. After he had thrown four or five of the gang aboard the truck, he made known his plan: "Don't ever turn down a free ride in a Trojan horse!"

The rest of us jumped in. John yelled, "Now!" The driver started his truck and took off. When he made the turn out of the shed onto the apron of the dock, we all fell over one another. Upon arrival at the gangway he hit the brakes hard, and we were on the floor again. We came to a full stop, and he made no move to get out, just sat there looking straight ahead and cracking up.

The crew on the ship had seen us coming. About a dozen of them surrounded the truck. By the time they opened the doors, John had us jump down to the skin of the dock, all with bright new blue-and-white-striped mattresses over our heads, half hanging down our fronts and half down our backs. Cheers went up!

We didn't talk, not then. The members of our greeting committee each took a piece of the truck's cargo and ran up the gangway single file. The cargo was all aboard after two more trips down and up the gangway. The driver got the chief steward's signature, looked up to give us a quick wink, and drove away.

The tug's whistle blew. It was John's turn at the helm. The rest of us split up to go to the bow and stern. It was time for us to slack off the lines so that the linesmen on the dock could take our mooring lines off the bollards. Paavo stretched his arm out to show me his wrist watch; it was almost one-thirty.

I looked up at the inshore wing of the flying bridge from where I was standing on the stern. The captain caught my look, then smiled and waved as if returning a greeting initiated by me. I looked away, wondering what it must do to those among us who have jobs demanding that they wrong those they supervise or govern, all the while knowing that when they go home to their mates and children, they cannot let them see their full identities.

Paavo motioned me over to the rail. The linesmen had just dropped our lines into the water. We waved our appreciation to them with our hands close to our chests and our backs to the bridge. The third mate saw it all in a glance but looked the other way. We hauled in the lines by windlass and flaked them out neatly on deck by hand so that they would dry without "assholes" (tight kinks).

The tugmen and their boat pulled us away from the dock. Once we were out into the estuary between Oakland and Alameda, the tug whistle blew. Anthony went to the offshore side and let go of the tugboat's line. It was his first opportunity to display his new skill in action. He did not look at us, but he was smiling. I let the warmth of the moment register as I positioned myself beside him at the rail. Anthony yelled at the two men on the tug's stern as it moved toward the open bay. When they looked up, we took off our white canvas "stetsons," faking sweaty foreheads to deliver our respects. They made no eye contact as they hand-signaled that what they had done was nothing special.

An hour later we ducked under the Golden Gate Bridge and out into view of the Farallon ("Far and Alone") Islands. Our connection with official life ashore was all but severed. We were no longer full citizens of the United States. By signing the ship's articles when the man from the shipping commissioner's office came aboard, we had lost much of the protection of the U.S. Constitution. We were now, and until we returned to the port of voyage termination in the States, governed by the nation's special maritime laws as interpreted by the smiling man whose name was on the framed master's license that hung in the wheelhouse. This was more than compensated for by our certainty that on this trip there was little likelihood of any friction among the unlicensed crew. In a matter of days we had begun to learn the need to respect each other across the long-established boundaries that divide seamen of each ship into three parts: those who prepare and serve the food and maintain the living quarters; those who keep the ship's engine, electricity, and water supply running; and those who steer the ship, rig its gear, and keep its decks fit for sea.

Classrooms Aboard Ship

At no point during the entire trip to the Southwest Pacific and Australia did the captain or any other deck or engine room officer mention our "walk-off." We had demonstrated that we saw ourselves as an independent decision-making unit on all matters of safety and working and living conditions. Not one of the captain's pretended attempts at a conciliation with us met with success. We were polite to him in a way that kept the official reality of our relationship with him out in the open.

Unposted but almost regularly scheduled gatherings took place during the entire voyage. There was informal instruction in ship safety, seamanship, and union history and organization (both official and unofficial), sometimes in the presence of two or three Navy Armed Guardsmen, all out on deck as weather permitted. At no time did the presence of an officer create an interruption. The enthusiasm, especially among the young first trippers, was noticeable. They had seen that we were introducing them to more than a unionism by which they could protect themselves on the job. We were also passing on a life-style in which they could carry themselves with more dignity and power.

The sense of self-improvement was not limited to the new seamen. The interdependence of the three departments demonstrated during the walk-off brought different rewards to each of the age-based groups in the crew. Cade, the night cook and baker from one of the sea islands off the coast of Georgia, and Londos, the four-to-eight oiler who had come from Greece as a young man, were '34 strike men like the bosun and Chips. They all rediscovered each other and became one of the tightest social groups on the ship. It was a small-scale reenactment of the formation in 1934 of the Maritime Federation of the Pacific, when the MFOW&W, the MC&S, and the SUP led all the offshore maritime unions on the coast in the preformation of an industrial union.

The oiler, night cook and baker, bosun, and Chips the carpenter determined the subjects they thought would be most valuable to all crew members younger than they and discussed their choices informally with the rest of us. Each of them then began meeting the men in his department two or three at a time for instruction and discussion.

John, Anthony, and I met with the bosun and Chips as a watch. We were in their room for a little over two hours. The bosun began by going over what he considered the three primary rules of conduct.

"Learn your trade. Work good and work hard. Particularly when lifting or carrying at sea, give one hand to the ship but keep one for yourself.

"I've already told you the following things, I think, but I want to go through them now systematically. Never, but never, walk away from a beef. For example, do not pay off from a ship in the middle of a fight with an officer or captain. If you do, you leave it for the next crew that comes aboard. It will catch them off guard, as a surprise, and they will be at a double disadvantage because topside will know the history of the beef and they won't.

"But worst of all, if you walk away, you contribute to the breakdown of solidarity where it counts most, among the people on the job. They see that you didn't look out for them, and that makes it easier for them to do the same to others. The big breakdown in morale began when we let our leader Harry Lundeberg negotiate contracts that gave our port patrolmen or business agents control over grievance settlements. If this task gets left to people who don't do the same work we do, it's not going to get done right, if at all. If on each ship, each trip we solve our beefs by ourselves, solidarity, our primary weapon, remains within reach.

"The next and last reminder of standard rules for now is that when a trip begins to get old, and the night wheel watches up there on the bridge get long and lonely, keep a distance between yourself and the mate on watch. Be thrifty with your words, stories, and the content of the ideas that you express. You and that man are each witness to the other's boredom and sense of aloneness. That is not the stuff of brotherhood or comradeship, even though you both belong to unions. No matter how decent or well-meaning that other also needy man may be, he will almost certainly do what he has to do to keep his job. Part of that job is to supervise or keep watch on you. It is not unusual to learn, often too late, that the biggest advantage the ruler of the ship has in getting at those he looks upon as troublemakers is from information obtained by officers who got it earlier from helmsmen on their watch who unburdened themselves of shipboard or personal problems. Those guilty of this stoolpigeonry are often reluctant betrayers.

"One more thing. You too have a responsibility in all this. Don't go putting out on the open table any of the personal-private things you were told in confidence by a ship's officer. If you do, you lose your ability to be indignant at injustice. 'Nuff said."

Passing on the Lessons of the 1934 Strike

"The importance of the strikes of the 1930s, including the seamen's strikes, has been exaggerated," Blackie went on.

"All through the 1920s we were held down. The lack of dignity we experienced on the job, plus the pitiful wages that denied us homes or families, kept us from achieving what we were capable of. At first we blamed it on each other. We talked worse about those laboring alongside us than about anyone else.

"Later we recognized that it was the condition of our industry. In the early twenties the government was giving away or taking ships out of service. Our small merchant marine was shrinking and our jobs along with it. We lived with that idea for several years.

"Then came the 1929 crash of the stock market. We were already on the bottom when it hit. The thing about the Big Depression that followed was that no matter what direction you looked, there was a failure of leadership of all the nation's institutions. That went for the people who headed our unions as well as those in political parties and the government. We began to notice that the main message from our union leaders was that 'nothing can be done, the entire government is on the employers' side, all we can do is go along and hope that by causing no trouble some concessions will be thrown our way.' Somehow we believed them.

"We'd had Wobblies with us in maritime since 1905. A few old ones are still around. They're members of the Industrial Workers of the World. They were the only bold and independent idea bunch among us. There weren't many Communists around in the late 1920s. They looked pretty good for a while. Yet, neither group was enough to make a big difference. No noticeable change began to take place in us until the depression showed that none of the nation's established political leaders had any ideas on how to stop the suffering.

"You went to coffee with the regular guys who had been close-mouthed for as long as anyone could remember, and they were complaining about why the leaders 'don't do this and never do that.' By 1932 we could feel just from the change in attitudes of our own people that something big was happening. Regular guys were becoming more radical than the radicals, talking about the need for a different kind of union. In the early spring of 1934 you didn't need inside dopesters to know that there was going to be a big strike. It was only then that the radicals began to see the size of their audiences increase significantly. We gave them the chance to grow. And we made them listen, for a while.

"When the longshoremen went on strike that spring, they knew that it was going to be easier for them to pull off a strike than it was for us seamen, because they were ashore all the time and had better communication with each other. Still, they knew we were going to be out there with them, that it was as much our battle as theirs.

"A problem for us was that our seamen's unions were affiliated with the International Seamen's Union, or ISU. The main leader of the Sailors' Union of the Pacific at that time, Andrew Furuseth, was also an official in the ISU. He had a good reputation, had lobbied in Washington, D.C., for years, and had gotten new laws replacing those that made seamen an outright part of the ship's property while you were signed on. It's still partly that way, but believe me, it's a lot better now than it was then. Anyway, the national union officials of the ISU refused to let us go on strike with the longshoremen, and Furuseth agreed with them. That meant we had to take things directly into our own hands.

"We formed 'meet and greet committees' without the union's consent. Ships, mainly steam schooners from the lumber ports up north, would come into San Francisco and San Pedro and be boarded by committees. The crews would then pack up and go down their gangways with the members of their boarding parties. Let me tell you it was like some special holiday, even though times were tough. Some guys would hear about it and form a committee of their own.

"The union lost control and had no way of stopping us. Harry Lundeberg is now head of our union, but around that time he sailed as an unlicensed or 'waivered' third mate on the steam schooner *James Griffiths*. I went to San Pedro for a couple of weeks, and the next thing I heard he was a leading meeter and greeter. Charlie Cates, who was an SUP patrolman in Frisco not so long ago, was on a committee, too.

"Within a couple of weeks the California ports were full of tied-up ships without crews. Ships stopped loading lumber up north and were paying off crews. We were all out on strike. It was one of the best times to be alive; we were getting back at them for all the insults we'd taken to our minds and our bodies through hard work, long hours, bad food, loss of sleep, and filthy fo'c'sles, in addition to spoken and sometimes physical abuse."

At this point the bosun paused, as if he planned to stop for discussion. This is what we had wanted until he got onto the subject of the "meet and greet committees." Now Big John broke our silence: "No, no, keep on going as long as you're into describing this action, for god's sake; discussion later."

"Good, I understand. It was our strike. The entire power structure felt threatened, maybe not by revolution like the newspapers were saying, at least not at first. But then in addition to the police and scabs they brought out the National Guard, Legionnaires with tear gas guns, and armed vigilantes. Strikers were getting shot.

"You hear most about the two who were killed in San Francisco on 'Bloody Thursday,' July 5, 1934. Four days later there was a funeral procession up Market Street from the corner of Mission and Spear, where the guys were shot. I was affected more by that than by any other single day of the strike.

"The official strike leaders had little to do with organizing it. We were the ones who planned everything. Guys were doing things to make the march work right, and no one assigned them. I met a lot of people in the formation area who didn't have jobs or union cards. During the entire procession none of the thousands of marchers said a word. I didn't know whether to growl or cry. All the way up Market Street total silence divided a major American city.

"The waterfront strike in San Francisco became general five days after the funeral. Nobody really called it that I can remember. It was just that working people all over town were out joining us. There was a machine shop on the Embarcadero near Mission Street. A SUP sailor got shot out on the sidewalk in front of its door. He was saved because some machinist ran out and pulled him inside by his legs. I've always believed that the machinists in that shop were among the people who joined us.

"It was in those weeks that men and boys shining shoes and selling papers on the corner formed their own unions and stopped work. One of them is a good member of the SUP today. His name is Bill.

"When our strike in San Francisco became general, strange as it may hit you at first, in part it hurt us. By the wonderful act of joining us, the uptown working class of people unknowingly gave their union officials— and there was nothing bold about most of them—the chance to take control of the entire strike, including the maritime part of it. That we needed to build an alternative organization to the city's AFL Central Labor Council, in addition to all the other things we were doing, never occurred to us.

"The general strike ended on July 19, and it was fast downhill from there. Harry Bridges, the longshoremen's leader, began making speeches about how tired his rank and file was getting. We couldn't see why he was doing this. There were some among the longshoremen we talked to every day who you could tell were ready to go back to work, but they were a minority. But who knows? The guys I was picketing with thought Bridges made the guys feel they'd lost their leader. Within days the longshoremen voted to go back to work and arbitrate all unsettled issues.

"We seamen didn't like what the vote meant, but we went back to work with them. We didn't want to see our unions go back to doing things separately again. The ISU officials had been against us striking from the start, and we did it anyway. Then after Bridges's speeches and the longshore vote they got a second wind, and Andrew Furuseth, who had done so many good things as a leader of the Sailors, was acting like a regular ISU stiff. *Our* strike ended on July 31.

"The longshoremen wound up getting joint fifty-fifty control over hiring along with the employers, union recognition, better wages, and more. By comparison we seamen wound up with no contract, but with direct action control over hiring."

After 1934

"Take it easy, I've only got one more part to finish, and you'll have the whole 1934 to 1936 panorama before you. This is the vital piece of the failure we are a living part of today. It's all but impossible to discuss this bit by bit. Indulge me. This is the first time I've ever presented it this way, the way Chips and I and others have had to live with it. I have to get it all out."

I looked at Anthony and then at John. They looked like they felt as bad as Chips looked sitting there in his silence. I broke in on the bosun: "I have a suggestion. If either of you don't feel right about it, let's forget it and go on like we have. How would it be if Chips did the last part of the story?" Anthony and John nodded agreement. The bosun's face fell, and he looked at his partner for the first time during the session. Chips cut him off before he got a chance to speak to my suggestion.

"No, no, it's already arranged that I'll cover this same history for the other two watches tomorrow. You're just about finished, partner, and we have to get this hunk of it completed now. Okay you guys?"

I looked at John and Anthony again. They shrugged that it was all right with them, and the bosun continued.

"Forgive me, partner. . . . Like I said, the longshoremen got an arbitration award from Franklin D. Roosevelt's National Longshoremen's Board. It gave them full recognition on the Coast as the exclusive bargaining representative for all members of the longshoremen's union, improved grievance and collective bargaining procedures, joint control of hiring. For this they gave up their fight against labor-saving devices like the jitney or power-pulled, four-wheel carts. There was more to it, but that's it in a nutshell for now.

"The problem for seamen was that compared to the longshoremen the seamen were getting only the salt that comes from sweat. There were no more fink books, and we had our own halls in the Alaska Fishermen's Building between Clay and Commercial streets, 150 feet from the Embarcadero. We felt we could make it so that those halls were the only places the employers could get crews. If they tried anything else, we'd shut their halls and throw scab crews off any ship they boarded. And that's what we did, even though it took us about two more years.

"The government and the shipowners were smart. By offering the longshoremen official recognition, they began to cause a split between us. By comparison, Harry Lundeberg looked great in that period. For us to get anything like the longshoremen got, we were going to have to continue our fight, and the only way we could do that was to go outside the channels created by the government bureaucrats and the law itself. Lundeberg accepted that reality and was willing to lead the way we wanted him to, until after we won. (Then we went to living in the new channels the shipowners and government had dug for us.)

"We seamen were different from longshoremen, even though there were many ex-seamen among them. Compared to them, few of us had homes and families to care for. More important, we weren't involved in regular politics, but we were radical in the kind of politics that grows out of the job. We live where we work, on one ship at a time out at sea. We brought the kind of politics ashore that you learn in dealing with the people topside. Up to the time of the strike we'd been taking it without the power to fight back openly and under full steam. Somewhere along the line in the years before the Big Strike we decided we weren't going to live like that anymore. Shit! We surprised a lot of people; some of them didn't even know we could read.

"Yes, back then Lundeberg had the guts and ability to do what was necessary according to the time, no matter the risks. Just like us. Christ, he didn't even get his citizen papers until '34. Again, it was his willingness to lead the way we wanted him to lead that brought us the real excitement.

"As reports of the locations of ships with scab crews came in, guys taking their turns as dispatchers sent groups of us to the sites. We went up gangways with professional scabs waiting for us on the top landing. We weren't tough guys. We were young, and we knew what we were doing was right.

"The ISU officials went crazy. They wanted to stop us as much as the shipowners did. Nothing we did was official until we won. We got rid of the ISU piecards [paid union officials]. Old Furuseth got voted down and, with tears running down his cheeks, left the meeting and our hall forever. We were glad to see him go because we knew it was necessary. Lundeberg became holder of the SUP's top office, secretary-treasurer.

"No presidents in our union. The two or three unions on the West Coast before ours had some radical ideas, and then came the Industrial Workers of the World. The two of us paid dues to them until 1936.

"During the almost two years that we were fighting for our own hiring halls by job actions the Maritime Federation of the Pacific was being formed. Bridges and Lundeberg worked good together at first. It was going to be one big industrial union for us on this coast. But at the same time that we were throwing scabs off ships and stopping the ships, Bridges was beginning to discipline his guys if they did the same as us. In my opinion this is the main thing that brought bad blood between him and Lundeberg and broke up the federation.

"We got our 100 percent control over our own hiring halls put into writing in the contracts that ended the 1936 strike. At no time during the fight did the leadership of the longshoremen get in with us and go for 100 percent control of *their* hiring. They got that indirectly in '39, I think it was, when they won the right to elect their own job dispatchers. But still, you go into their hall right now and you'll see employer suits come in and look over the dispatchers' shoulders from time to time. Those Waterfront Employers' Association people wouldn't dare to come up the stairs in our hall. It's all ours.

"And I don't blame the regular working longshoremen. Study their situation long enough and you can understand the fix they're in. They have many of the same problems regular shoreside people have to contend with. They don't eat in cafes and live in cheap hotels. A lot of them sit down to meals with their families. Besides, the situation in our seamen's unions is just as bad, for a reason that is the same as in their unions and is the hardest to change: our unions are all led by bureaucrats.

"Now maybe you can see why we emphasize direct action. We know it's what you need in order to keep the new bureaucrats from taking the unions to their offices."

We'd listened all we could. At this point we didn't want to do anything but get off to ourselves and sort out for ourselves what the bosun had told us. We thanked him and Chips, set up a time for our next meeting, and left to go wash up for lunch, feeling somewhat guilty about Chips not getting to speak.

Talking It Over

The next morning John and I were both awake early. He noticed that
Anthony was hard asleep and motioned that we get up and out of the
fo'c'sle without any talk. The eight-to-twelve watchman with last relief
below had just done his duty and made a fresh urn of coffee. I drew two
cups and handed one to John. He didn't want to sit in the messroom. I
followed him out of the midship house. We sat, drank, and smoked. I
waited for whatever it was that he obviously wanted to talk about.

"You know what the bosun said yesterday about the separation between
us and officers?" He waited for my nod and went on. "I think that's why
Joseph Conrad's books are usually centered on the life going on *inside* his
characters. I've read only five of his books. But I didn't get the feeling that
there were a couple or three dozen people present on his ships. As I recall,
most all of them were officers, and they were loners."

"Why do you think that is?"

"I had never thought about it before last night. England being a country with colonies, the officers in British ships probably never got to sail in
the fo'c'sle. They went to an officers' school, and then when they got assigned to a ship, the unlicensed crews were from their colonies. Maybe it's
the separation. The bosun's right, but what limited lives are led by both
sides! On our ships the officers are at least from where we're from in most
cases, and they're some kind of company, even if we can't afford to get too
familiar with them. There's a sadness to all this, Red. Do you think I'm
right about Conrad?"

"I've only read three books by him, but yes, I don't remember anything
about crew life. There was none of the life like on our ships, but maybe
ours were more like theirs before real unions were organized. He was a
genius in ways. I could feel the thick heat of the flat summer Red Sea in
Lord Jim, and the feeling has stayed with me. He didn't pull me back to
read much more of his writing, though."

"The same with me and also about his description of the Red Sea. To
think of the labor of the ship's screw trying to cut its way through that
hot salt soup almost brings a sweat. Do you think he was saying that the
alienation of life aboard ship caused a strange unhappiness that carried
over into all his experiences?"

"That could be. It didn't hit me then. I'd have to go back and read him
again to say, and I'd probably read him differently now than I did on my
first ship."

"Yeah, that's right. But listen, do you think we've got a chance to accomplish what these '34 men have set out for us?"

"I don't know, but I like trying."

"Me too, Red. Don't get me wrong, life's been more interesting since we sailed with Bosun and Chips last year. But listen to me better. No matter what we try to do, we can only do it if the opportunities that make it possible have already developed. There would have to be more opportunities than there are right now."

"You're probably right, but there may be some big changes at the end of the war."

"But that's only a hope."

"Right, but should you and I be doing something else?"

"No, but still you're not listening. I could do much, much more, if I thought our chances of winning were really good. I think what we're doing is right, and I don't think it's dumb. I'm talking about something entirely different, like I told you. People like us right here on this ship and on all the others, for example, can do big things to make life better, but to get into doing it full ahead, they have to see with their own eyes and no one else's, growing evidence that there is a chance to win."

"But what if things just get worse and worse and all we can see ahead is still fewer chances?"

"Good point. But that means we have to find better ways to talk to the people around us. What can we say to people that will make them feel better about themselves? Every buck they make is an honest one, yet they don't give themselves any credit."

"But every time the strike men talk to us you can see that the experiences they had gave them more self-respect than the people they were before the strikes."

"Yeah, but that's just what I'm talking about. Look how long it took them. What are the chances that another period of change for the good will arrive when the war is over?"

"Are you asking me?"

"No."

"Then we had better get something to eat before we go on watch. You and Anthony are on deck with the bosun, I've got first wheel?"

"Right."

John and I didn't talk anymore to each other about the bosun and Chips's presentation for about five days. We were too busy talking with the men of the other two watches who had heard the same lecture we did. Then there were the men of the Black Gang, including the deck engineer, who had had their class with Londos, the oiler, and the Stewards' Department had sat down with the baker for a couple of hours.

We were trying to learn how different or alike our responses were to the ideas put before us, regardless of the departments we worked in. We lived on one ship but in three departments, which we had till then looked upon as separate units. Now we had all gotten essentially the same history lesson on nearly the same day. All at once we involved ourselves in individual and group discussions that crossed departmental lines. We had broken into open discovery of ourselves as a group and as individuals.

Up to that time we had been so focused on the accomplishments of the older generation that we could not see ourselves in our new world of work; we were invisible in its history. Then that all changed. The older men had given us their history not only to use as weaponry but also to show us that the world we had recently entered belonged to both the generations represented on board.

By the time we began the run for home from Brisbane, our last Australian port, the normal routine of shipboard social life had reestablished itself. There was a change from the first part of the trip: the constant interchange of members in the self-selected social groups of the unlicensed crew members. This was visible in the combinations that went ashore while in Melbourne, Sydney, and Brisbane.

One night in Melbourne John, Anthony, and I of the twelve-to-four watch all returned to the ship separately but at about the same time. Anthony had bought himself a bottle of whiskey. He had it stuck in his belt still unopened. We shared it with him. Soon we were comparing impressions of the still-new mix of members of the deck, engine, and steward departments. We had each overheard conversations comparing the three departments, which was the best to sail in and the different relationships with officers in each.

The second meeting of what turned out to be a series of three classes led to leaving our student status behind. The instructors did a lot of listening. I talked with the bosun about it later when he had just come from a get-together with the baker and Londos, the oiler. They had been a little hurt when we briefly took the classes away from them after the first session. At first they had not understood, but then the baker had pulled them aside to talk about "the need for autonomy in us all." The bosun ended by saying, "I think the baker's been to college," and broke out laughing.

Coming Home

Two days out of San Francisco I was working on deck close to where Matt, the deck engineer, was repairing the cylinder of a steam winch.

"Red, the young guys in that Deck Gang of yours are suffering from the worst case of 'channel fever' I've ever seen."

He was talking about the extremely painful need of every crew member to get ashore near the end of a voyage. We all had it, regardless of department or age. I already knew from talks with Anthony and then Bruno and Bert that they couldn't wait to get back among their families and close friends to reveal what they felt were their new strengths and selves. They were expressing feelings shared by all of us, including the men who had spent lifetimes making sea voyages. Each homecoming to families or friends in some way provided another chance at a better life.

The Farallons were now at our stern. We went under the Golden Gate Bridge and just after lunch came into sight of one of the main landmarks for Bay navigation, the Campanile on the University of California in Berkeley. By three o'clock we were moored north of the Ferry Building on the south side of Embarcadero Pier 23. The longshore linesmen who had helped us tie up were walking down the pier away from us, still wondering why we had given them such a big greeting. As soon as the cargo gear was rigged, we all went ashore, cleaned up for eating at such places as Tadich's Grill or the Tivoli, New Joe's, and Big Ben's Fish Grotto in nearby North Beach.

We were all back aboard two days later at two o'clock sharp. A strange silence came over us. It was more than just the knowledge that we would soon be visited by a Coast Guard team and then have to say our "so longs." We were no longer interdependent on a ship at sea. Many of us would see each other again in the union hiring hall, and some of us might again sail together so we would have the witnesses that help preserve memory.

Yet we were breaking up a winning combination. In some ways it would have been better if we had all stayed with the ship and for a while longer remained a steady crew. But seamen's jobs were plentiful during the war. Until the war once seamen got jobs, many of them made homes aboard particular ships to obtain security. This often required demeaning concessions to shipboard authorities. The seamen who avoided this trap felt revulsion for the victims, although they understood why it occurred. In times of full employment, to "homestead" brought ridicule and isolation.

The opportunity to demonstrate our collective independence from the shipowners and their officers was irresistible. It meant that they had to go to the trouble of getting another crew and developing working relationships with all of its members. It also meant that for a time we would be ashore free of their authority.

Two Coast Guard petty officers walked down the dock and up our gangway an hour before payoff time. We were all at the rail, expressionless, but stared at them until they disappeared into the officers' dining room. Their refusal to glance in our direction indicated their discomfort. Fifteen minutes later they went down the gangway and to their government car under the same tension. An hour later the shipping commissioner had us sign off the ship's articles. All hands were then paid off in full. For reasons we would never really know the captain had not reported our work stoppage, and the chief mate had not disputed payment of a single hour of the overtime hours we had worked. The two of them stood side by side to say their goodbyes to us with toothy smiles.

Less than three minutes after we left the Officers' Dining Salon we made our "suitcase parade" down the gangway and along the dock to the Pier 23 Inn on the Embarcadero. There was no longer any reason to have a meeting of the group we had formed in case any of us were cited by the Coast Guard. There were no ships at the adjoining piers, and longshore gangs had not yet been assigned to the *Hanapepe*. The entire barroom was ours. We had decided beforehand that we would not order any drinks until after the three speeches we had decided upon were ended. The bosun went first.

"Remember that the job ahead is to make it possible for us union members who are working seamen to protect ourselves from both the shipowners and the union officials. We have to have unions, but not like we've got now. That can't be done if the only place where we can go to participate in the power life of the union is the local union meeting. The union halls are on *their* turf. Up on these ships is where we have the foundation for authority over them. If we establish that, then we can take our power to the meetings with us. Even better if we choose the place to meet, like at a central pier. Our goal has to be to win respect. The goal of our officials has become to win respectability, uptown."

Londos was next. I introduced him as Oiler—of bearings on "three legged" engines.[6]

"I was a seaman for the old country. We held a meeting of the crew. They accused us of mutiny. I had to leave my country and family."

I introduced the night cook and baker as Gabriel Cade, as he had requested.

"On this ship we have eliminated a corruption, at least for a time. I am proud to be part of that, but it is not enough. The kind of contracts that are being signed have built a different kind of union that can't be ours. By design it eliminates our control."

It was time to wrap it all up. We all began drinking to one another, this time with fairly good whiskey instead of coffee from Oakland's Dock Cafe. The thoughtful frowns after Cade's speech were gone.

Minutes later I was standing between Bruno and Bert facing out into the large room. I could see Big John and the baker toasting three of the seven Navy Armed Guard sailors who had come in. They hadn't felt free to talk with us since we had entered home port. Now they took the chance because we no longer had any official attachment to the *Hanapepe*. There was a group around Londos listening, at that point, to one of the wipers. It was beginning to get dark outside and booze was becoming a substitute for food as the discussion groups got smaller. The bosun and the baker had moved to one side, and the baker was calling the bosun "Hector."

Someone noticed that the street lights had come on. The fast drinking ceased. Personal goodbyes were in progress. Big John was filling a third taxicab with our guys and their gear. The bosun was with him telling a group that no ship ever came into port cleaner or more shipshape. Minutes later Chips got the bosun into a booth and pushed John and me in with him. Then Anthony arrived to reprimand us.

"Hey, you guys have been saying goodbyes with only a 'so long' and that's it. How do you know if you'll ever see any of us again?"

"It all stays with you longer when you don't talk it out, Anthony."

Anthony took about three steps back and with Bruno and Bert said "so long," and they left.

Chips opened our discussion. "Blackie and I aren't going to get another ship for a while, maybe three months or so. We have a woman friend who is a doctor in East Los Angeles. She runs a small clinic. We're going to let her give us a 90,000-mile checkup. We'll do some repairs on her place and use it as a 'snug harbor' for a while."

"Chips, you know we have to get a ship within a month."

"Yeah, John. So when you guys get back from your next trip, check the Toscani or the Galileo Hotel in North Beach."

"When you talked us into taking that ship, you told us you were building something for the long-term. We may not be able to get a couple of '34 men to crew with us."

"Then do it by yourselves whatever way you can, but do it, long-term."

"How much longer have we got?"

"Who can say, Red? There may come a time when the smart thing to do will be to lay low for a while to prepare for the next chance. You'll know if it comes to that. For maybe another year it will be possible to pull off these kinds of actions, longer if the breaks come our way. You'll do it differently than when we're with you. Maybe you'll find better ways. But listen, before we all pile out of here there's something else."

"What?"

"Cape Verde Islands. I saw both of you go a little pop-eyed when I mentioned my home. It means that I'm Portuguese by culture, but by blood I'm part African. Ten years ago when we were building new unions on the waterfronts up and down this coast, the regular guys got more open-minded on a lot of things. Like so many others, I didn't grab the opportunity of that time. I suppose many of the men I sailed and walked picket lines with figured I was a Mexican because of my straight hair. I let it slide. My name isn't Soromengo, it's Soromenho—Portuguese, not Spanish.

"That's enough about that. Another thing: The piecards took the hiring hall away from us by putting goons like 'Johnny Loudmouth' in control of job dispatching. His specialty is to intimidate the guys up in age. It's a way of destroying memory. We don't write our history. Those guys are it.

"Notice that more and more the union leaves the job when the patrolman goes down the gangway, if indeed it came aboard with him. At union meetings our job is to sit and listen. But as long as we take control like we did on this one, even if only briefly on one ship in twenty, we keep them from having it all. The word's out that Lundeberg is beginning to hang out with Republicans, for god's sake. Enough, we have to get out of here. Be careful, Red, be careful, John."

"Hold it, Chips, you too, Bosun, John and I are going to tell you a couple of things that have been on our minds. When John and I first came into the SUP, it was like getting a new look at what our lives could be. Before the war neither of us were ever able to talk back to a boss without getting fired. We both still carry this around with us. We can see the strength that comes from job action, but it's hard to give up on Lundeberg completely. And it's the same for some of the longshoremen who are critical of Bridges."

"That's right." John was chuckling to cover his tension. "Me and Red didn't ourselves live those times before the war. We've lived them through you. Since we first got into the union is the best job security we've ever known. Maybe when the war is over, guys like Lundeberg will get better again."

Chips was pulling on Blackie's coat so hard that he slid him out of the booth and on to his feet. "All right, both of you, test what I'm saying goodbye to you with. Bureaucrats can never undo what's happened to them. They can't go back to being who they were. The reason bureaucracies get built is to avoid making the good fight. This changes everything about them. You don't have the same job protection now as when you first joined, and you now have full membership books in the union, not trip cards or probationary books. What do you think it means that the union doesn't provide representation when its members get called in by the Coast Guard? The Coast Guard's supposed to protect us from subversives, saboteurs. Bullshit! Actually, they're the government's trial run at a labor police force. The National Maritime Union has given them an office right in the headquarters' union hall in New York, and there's no campaign against them by the leadership of our West Coast unions. Double bullshit!"

Chips Costello and Hector Soromenho looked at us and saw that finally we were ready to break it up, too. They came toward John and me with good smiles. We all knew we couldn't do any more by talking. We shook hands, and they were out the door. We waited long enough for them to get a cab and then went out to get one for ourselves.

The Oakland General Strike

John and I missed the support and ideas that were ever present when Chips and the bosun were close at hand. At the same time we were glad for our independence from them.

Never again did we get so good a chance at winning as the one they found for us by preliminary exploration of several ships and then the discovery of the *Hanapepe*. Nevertheless, John and I helped to seed changes that improved the lives of crews, ourselves among them, on several more ships. These modest victories became harder to achieve as the war got older.

We never did get into more than what at the time seemed only a little trouble. Only when John and I were not sailing partners did I wind up appearing at Coast Guard tribunals. There was the time I was temporarily taken off my ship by Scotland Yard and British Naval Intelligence just before the ship went through the locks at Liverpool. Another time came when our crew on a coffee ship mustered to be silently stared at by twelve Americans in civilian clothes while at anchor on the Panama City side of the Panama Canal. But charges were never pressed against anyone in the crews. Nor were my seaman's papers or the papers of any of my crew mates ever confiscated.

A little over a year after we left the *Hanapepe*, Chips wrote us that the bosun had died of cancer. He said our letters had given them big kicks, made them proud. Chips was at home in Azusa, California, and said his seagoing toolbox had gotten a lot heavier. He had a new '34 partner, Henry Woods, a Native American from Sutter's Mill. Chips did not write again, and there were no return addresses on the two letters he sent us.

In late 1945 John and I began sailing up and down the coast on the steam schooners that brought lumber from the Northwest to build the new cities that came with the Gold Rush. On our first trip to Coos Bay, Oregon, the Empire Mill quit sending out wood. We deckhands were the longshoremen. The mate ordered all hands to chip rust and paint the ship's side because there was no lumber. We all went to Empire's one bar and stayed there for three hours until the mate apologized and canceled his "request." John and I did not lead the action. We were greenhorns on the schooners.

It was the end of the schooners' long lives. War surplus LST boats with a single 300-foot open hatch forward of the superstructure on the stern allowed stowage by bundles instead of by the piece, the first step toward automation on the West Coast.

John went home after a schooner run to Central America for a load of rare wood. The talk we had before he left revealed we both wanted to quit going to sea for a while. The main reason? The restrictions that life at sea put on our social lives. We were each beginning our serious search for a wife.

I moved from an apartment in San Francisco's North Beach to a duplex near the Southern Pacific tracks in West Berkeley and got a job at the Chevrolet assembly plant in East Oakland. During my first months working there I used public transportation. A bus and a streetcar took me to downtown Oakland, where I would transfer to the Oakland bus that would drop me in front of the plant at 73rd Avenue and Foothill Boulevard.

Morale in this industrial area of the city was high during the strike wave in spring 1946. Then it became clear that Walter Reuther, vice president of the United Automobile Workers (UAW), had not been serious about his "GM Program," with its slogans of "wage increases and no price increases" and "open the corporation's books and prove you can't afford to pay us a decent wage." Life in the plant became boring as well as hard. I had become an assembly line spray painter and active in Local 76, UAW. We had to get to work at least half an hour before the line started at 7:12 A.M., earlier if we wanted to get the pushcart man with his donuts and coffee.

One Monday morning I arrived downtown on the streetcar, and our motorman and conductor got off. They were standing in the still-dark street talking to other car men, local bus drivers, the drivers of big trucks, and San Francisco Bridge trainmen. I got down off the streetcar with several other passengers to figure out what was happening.

It was unbelievable. The Oakland police had been escorting scabs and merchandise into Oakland for delivery at Kahns and Hastings, the two department stores where retail clerks had been on strike for many weeks. The union drivers of streetcars, buses, and trucks refused to watch two strikes being broken. By stranding thousands of work-bound people in the heart of the city, they had called the Oakland general strike. It was December 2, 1946. No officials had announced or were leading it. It was just that we were all unable to get to work.

Our block began to organize within the next hour. The same was happening in other blocks we could see across Telegraph Avenue. Bars could stay open if they served only beer and turned up their jukeboxes. The prescription counters inside drugstores were open. Hamburger stands and coffee shops would remain open, but large restaurants were encouraged to close. Dancing in the streets started slowly because there were more men than women standing around. It was in full swing a short while later as women convinced the men that they knew how to dance.

By nine o'clock there were still no union leaders in sight. We were laughing about a comment from somewhere in the crowd on the sidewalk: "If some of you don't get serious, some of them are going to come and get us." I called Harry Lundeberg from a pay phone and told him what was happening. Within an hour a carload of Hawaiian SUP members found me, said "Hello Red Weir," and gave me a paper bag with several hundred large buttons that read "SIU-SUP Brotherhood of the Sea." They drove off laughing. I knew only one of them and never saw any of them again. The buttons were gone in minutes, used on hats as decorations and as badges of authority when downtown was cordoned off before noon. Anyone could leave town, but an active union card was needed to get in.

Later in the day I saw a Chevy worker called "Cousin Bill," an ex-SUP friend. He said he was going to sleep downtown and had already found a place. I told Bill I would go to work the next morning because our plant would probably be shut down, and a lot of us could then come back downtown. At 7:12 A.M. I was spray painting hoods and fenders again. No committeeman came near our department or, I later found out, any other. Nor did our Local 76 president make contact with the plant.

I was back in downtown Oakland by 5:00 P.M. Word was out that the officials of several unions planned to put out a strike call and that there might be a mass meeting that night at the Oakland Auditorium. Laughter spread with receipt of the news. No one had yet seen any of the official leaders. Their absence no longer created uneasiness. At the same time everyone was planning to attend the meeting.

Some of us bought tacos from a street vendor that we ate as we walked toward the meeting. We arrived to find the Oakland Auditorium surrounded by thousands of strikers. All the seats inside had been filled for over an hour. A public address system piped the speeches being made out to the crowd surrounding the auditorium.

All but one of the speakers had trouble addressing the audience. Harry Lundeberg alone spoke with the anger and boldness befitting a general strike. He called the city councilmen "super finks," who had ordered the use of the city police as "scab herders." In a heavy Norwegian accent he said they had been "taking lessons from Stalin and Hitler." Lundeberg ended by promising that the three ships at the army base would not get crews to sail them while the strike was on. (He didn't mention that long-shoremen in the International Longshoremen's and Warehousemen's Union had walked off those ships the night before only to find that their union immediately sent new gangs to replace them.)

But none of the officials, including Lundeberg, had any plan of action that would use the power of the general strike to improve the conditions of employment of the people represented in the audience or to win the long strike of the women at the Kahns and Hastings department stores.

The mass meeting was adjourned, and the strikers left without instructions for protecting themselves and their occupation of Oakland's core area. The radio commentator Gabriel Heater had said twenty-four hours earlier, "Well, Oakland's a ghost town tonight." We knew that all official authority wanted us to quit the downtown area. If union officers had honestly offered to lead us, they would have lost their bit of sovereignty in their "working relationship with the employers." But they knew that if they did not lead us, they would lose our respect. Because of their dilemma, they did not tell us either to leave or to stay.

Ideas about what to do passed among us. The process was at work during the walk back to our midtown blocks. Some would spend the night, and others would relieve them the following morning on Wednesday, the third day of the strike.

Puzzlement was the condition of the people downtown on Wednesday. The number of strikers was down. There was nothing real to do. The fun of Monday was gone. The 300 bus and streetcar men wearing their Eisenhower jackets as work uniforms who had marched on city hall in close-order drill, demanding to speak with the mayor, were still present but as individuals.[7]

Somewhere the union officials were meeting with the employers and city government. Representatives from several blocks regularly went to Kahns and Hastings department stores throughout the day to talk with the striking retail clerks. The clerks were still being told that they had to be patient.

Late Thursday morning a sound truck hired by the AFL Central Labor Council of Oakland drove up and down our blocks telling everyone to go back to work. "The strike is officially over," it blared. We heard that Oakland's city council and mayor had agreed that there would be no more scab herding by the Oakland police. There was an agreement to arbitrate the differences in the retail clerks' long strike.

I got to Kahns early that evening. The picket line was still going. Demonstrators, many truck drivers among them, continued to march with the betrayed women. I was told that many of the women wept at the morning's announcement. I listened to one woman while she sat on a folding chair to put on clean sweat socks and air her white tennis shoes. She told a handful of us nonclerks that if the unions' leaders couldn't get a good contract for them with a general strike, then what they had gotten to end the strike wasn't any good either. There were almost a dozen clerks, standing nearby, who nodded their heads before she finished.

The woman with the white tennis shoes was right. She, her friends, and all the other retail clerks of Local 1265 had to stay out another five months, until May 13, 1947. Even then they did not win but went back out of exhaustion and demoralization. The contract negotiated for them had a grievance procedure so weak that it was useless. The AFL officials of Oakland, Alameda County, and the entire Bay Area were embarrassed by their failure in the retail clerks' strike.

Looking back, I must also note that at no point during the strike did any of us downtown Oakland strikers—radical politicals included—climb up on a parked car and express the ideas that were already kicking around among us: "We can lead this strike ourselves." "Let's send out a dozen committees from one block to the other blocks to say this out in the open." "Our leadership will be the representative committees from every central downtown block." "Their meetings will be out in the open for all of us to see and hear, and clap or boo, as we agree or disagree in reaction to their ideas."

Eighteen years later, students at the University of California at Berkeley embraced versions of these ideas adapted to their time and circumstances. Mario Savio, who became the best-known of the student leaders, was part of the crowd that held captive a police car containing a student under arrest, Jack Weinberg. When Savio jumped up onto the car's roof and called for a strike organization independent of absent student body officers, the free speech movement was born. It spread to campuses across the nation and remains an inspiration for initiatives from below.

The shame of the CIO unions was just as great. Not long after the general strike I was an elected delegate from UAW Local 76 to the state CIO convention in Santa Cruz. On the last day of the gathering I took the floor and identified myself by name and local union, explaining that the Chevrolet–Fisher Body units of my local represented the largest single group of industrial workers in the East Bay, over 3,000 persons. There was also a Ford assembly plant in Richmond, an International Harvester plant in Emeryville, and many more, none of them over a half-hour drive from downtown Oakland.

I asked, "Where were you during the Oakland general strike?" There was a quick silence. Chairperson Dick Linden recognized Paul Schlipf, secretary of the state CIO and director of its Political Action Committee. Schlipf, who was a delegate from the Fisher Body section of Local 76, answered, "It wasn't a general strike. We weren't in it." Dave Jenkins, the majority whip, gave the signal, and there was applause. Linden hit the podium with his gavel to close discussion and go to the next matter on the agenda.

The union bureaucracies have put a good deal of effort into writing about the Oakland general strike. Time has been on their side. The rank and file of their unions do not often write books. Students and professors have difficulty finding rank-and-file participants in the strike and tend to rely on union officials and people to whom the officials direct them.

Paul Schlipf himself has written about the strike.[8] He stresses the Oakland Voters' League formed by the AFL and CIO in the immediate post-strike period. He states correctly that four out of five labor candidates of the League were elected to the nine-member Oakland City Council. What he does not say is that the successful candidates were no more bold or effective in community politics than the union officials who selected them had been as strike leaders and collective bargainers.

Union officials seek to hide the evidence of the intelligence, organizational skills, and solidarity shown by regular hourly working people in the Oakland general strike. The officials of business unions find it necessary to believe that their members are meek at heart and incapable of thinking through anything other than simple problems. This belief justifies union representatives when they lie to and manipulate the members who pay their bills.

One of the most bitter aspects of this mythmaking is to be found in the claim that the Oakland general strike began not on December 2, 1946, the Monday morning when all transportation halted without instruction from union officials, but on December 3. In 1991 the Labor Studies Program of Laney College in Oakland held a celebration of the 1946 Oakland general strike. A proclamation by Oakland's Mayor Elihu M. Harris on that occasion declared that the strike took place "from December 3 to 5, 1946" and was "called by the American Federation of Labor Central Labor Council," with support from other organizations, including the CIO.

Unions with Leaders Who Stay on the Job

I phoned Big John a few weeks after the Oakland general strike ended. He was thinking of moving to Florida for a job painting bridges. No one I ever knew was better working high in the air. I told him some of my thoughts about the strike, and the discussion that followed took us back to the SS *Hanapepe*. We recalled that the bosun, Chips, and the baker blamed union officials themselves for becoming bureaucrats. But now, because of what we were seeing on jobs ashore, John and I were starting to blame the vertical form of union structure the AFL and CIO introduced. Rank-and-file workers like us were electing union officials who were then taken out of the workplace and put in offices where they had little contact with us. They were more often around employers, government bureaucrats, and lawyers. John told me it was the same or worse in the building trades.

Big John is now dead. I never got to tell him what I learned from the historian Lorin Lee Cary: that in 1936 General Motors rank and filers wanted to build a semiautonomous stewards' council and then got pressured out of it by Adolph Germer, John L. Lewis's lieutenant in the UAW.[9] The papers Germer left to the Wisconsin State Historical Society show that the new CIO leaders fought all rank-and-file attempts to build new industrial unions on a horizontal rather than the old vertical model, in which local unions had to go to top officials for permission even on many routine matters.

John and I knew differently. We experienced it on the SS *Hanapepe* in 1943 and on several more ships during the next three years. I experienced it again in the Oakland general strike; again in 1982, when I attended the Sixth Congress of the rebel European Harbor Workers in Aarhus, Denmark, and encountered the Spanish longshoremen's new union, La Coordinadora;[10] and yet again in the formation of rank-and-file "coordinations" during the Air France strike of 1993 by union and nonunion workers acting together.[11] There can be unions run by regular working people on the job. There have to be.

There have to be unions with leaders who stay on the job because the scandal of the Oakland general strike has been repeated too many times. Union members use their power to develop a victory over employers, but union officials refuse to accept or act on the victory. Instead, they give away what was never theirs. Once in office full-time, officials are no longer a living part of the industry.

There have to be unions run by hourly-paid people on the job because Hector Soromenho and Chips Costello were right in believing that union bureaucrats cannot go back. Top union officers build cliques among their members and keep themselves in office by means of favors. They give concessions to employers and get help from the corporations in return. They build first-name relationships with politicians. All bridges are thus burned. Any attempt at reform by the head of a bureaucratic union organization would be seen as a betrayal by his or her supporters inside and outside the union.

The isolated individuals at the top of union bureaucracies are attracted by the kind of personal peace to be bought by making deals. The deals are made in places where union members cannot go.

My own difficulty in accepting what the bosun said about union bureaucracy spotlights the problem. I and others had the advantage of a special education from older peers. Yet when I was stranded in downtown Oakland as the general strike began, my first thought was to get it an official leader. I phoned Harry Lundeberg and asked him to become involved. It may be that I was not the first one to call him, but excuses are beside the point. I made the call, risking possible injury to the strike, because I feared that "leaderless workers" downtown that early morning might be unable to handle the strike by themselves.

Experience proved otherwise. It is true that Lundeberg was the only leader with a ready rhetoric and the courage to use it standing before a crowd. But the result of his appearance was to leave the audience with the impression that at least there was someone among the officials capable of leading.

It was while watching the behavior of leaders of the California State CIO at the Santa Cruz convention shortly after the Oakland general strike that I found myself wanting to go to a phone and arrange a reunion of the crew of the SS *Hanapepe* at Pier 23 Inn. Blackie and Chips had explained why bureaucrats can't possibly clean up their bureaucracies. Unfortunately I had been unable to learn the lesson from them. A return to classrooms aboard ship would do no good. There was no point in hearing the instruction again. I had to learn this most important of the lessons Blackie and Chips taught us from my own experience.

Notes

1. *Bosun* is a commonly used contraction of *boatswain*. On West Coast ships of the common 4,000– to 10,000–ton class before the containerization (automation) of the 1970s, the bosun supervised all maintenance and repair

work done on the main deck and above, with the exception of work on the cargo winches, which was done by a nonlicensed crew member called a deck engineer. After the Big Strike of 1934 the bosuns no longer had full supervisory powers but instead were "first among equals" because they then got their jobs out of hiring halls owned and controlled by the Sailors' Union of the Pacific (SUP).

A ship's carpenter is seldom referred to by any other name than "Chips." Other than carpentry, his duties were to care for and operate the anchor windlass and to take the soundings in the ballast tanks. On liberty ships and other standard freight ships, the chips and the bosun shared the same room, or fo'c'sle. Neither of these men stood watches as the regular seamen did. They were often the older men of the Deck Gang.

Able bodied seamen (ABs) in the 1930s and 1940s carried either a blue AB certificate that required one year of seatime or a green certificate requiring three years of seatime. Additional certification of efficiency in the handling of lifeboats was also required.

Ordinary seamen, called "ordinaries," are seamen who have less than the required seatime needed to get AB papers. With the ABs they stand sea watches for eight hours, four hours at a time twice in every twenty-four hour period on one of the three watches: eight to twelve, twelve to four, and four to eight, A.M. and P.M. From the ABs and the bosun, the ordinaries learn deck duties, ship routine, how to steer a ship, and how to stand lookout. Those hands not at the wheel during daylight watches work on deck with the bosun. Ordinary seaman is an official rating listed on seamen's papers, like the others mentioned here.

2. In this writing all references are to the lives, work, and unionism of West Coast seamen. The vast majority of seamen who sailed out of Atlantic, Gulf, and Great Lakes ports were organized in different unions with different histories. San Francisco was this writer's home port.

3. Almost 2 million (1,981,279) workers struck in 1943. In 1942, the first full year of the war, 2.8 percent of the nation's labor force became strikers. In 1945 the figure climbed to 12.2 percent. "Work Stoppages Caused by Labor Management Disputes in 1945," *Monthly Labor Review* (May 1945), 720, cited in Martin Glaberman, *Wartime Strikes* (Detroit: Bewick Editions, 1980), 36.

4. "The hazards of sailing the merchant fleet were not so great in 1944 as in former years, because of better protection afforded convoys. The 1944 losses in personnel [brought] the total number to 725 killed, 4592 missing and 581 prisoners of war. Despite the lower rate of losses and a greater number of men, the ratio of casualties was 1 in 33, a rate proportionately higher than the armed services." Vice Admiral Howard L. Vickery, vice chairman, U.S. Maritime Commission, "The Merchant Marine in the War in 1944," *Proceedings of the American Merchant Marine Conference*, vol. 1 (New York: U.S. Propeller Club, 1945), 18–20.

5. The *chief mate* is the mate from four to eight A.M. and in the P.M. The chief mate is the executive officer right behind the captain and oversees the deck crew's work.

6. Reciprocating steam engines with three pistons.

7. For more on the march to city hall and the general strike, see Stan Weir, "The Informal Work Group," in *Rank and File: Personal Histories by Working-Class Organizers,* ed. Alice Lynd and Staughton Lynd (Boston: Beacon, 1973), 193–94.

8. Paul Schlipf, "Building the UAW and the CIO in Oakland: An Activist Remembers, 1933–1950," *New Labor Review,* no. 5 (Spring 1983), 139–40.

9. Lorin Lee Cary, "Institutionalized Conservatism in the Early C.I.O.: Adolph Germer, a Case Study," *Labor History* 13 (Fall 1972), 493, 495. According to Sidney Fine, it was suggested just before the UAW convention in April–May 1936 "that delegates from the GM plants should caucus and consider the establishment of a GM council, made up of representatives of the various GM locals, to present a united front to the organization." Fine concurs that it was on Germer's advice that GM delegates at the convention took no action on a resolution calling for the formation of a GM council. Sidney Fine, *Sitdown: The General Motors Strike of 1936–1937* (Ann Arbor: University of Michigan Press, 1969), 92, citing Germer Diary, April 28, 1936.

10. See Stan Weir, "Rank and File Networks: A Way to Fight Concessions, *Labor Notes* 48 (January 27, 1983), 13; Stan Weir, "Spanish Waterfront Workers Are Building a New Type of Union," *Labor Notes* 77 (July 1985), 5; Stan Weir, "Introduction to La Coordinadora," *Radical America* 22 (January–February 1988), 53–55; and Don Fitz, "La Coordinadora: A Union without Bureaucrats," in *Within the Shell of the Old,* ed. Don Fitz and David Roediger (Chicago: Charles H. Kerr, 1990), 88–96. La Coordinadora operates out of a building a few blocks from the Barcelona hiring hall. It has 8,000 members, representing 80 percent of the nation's longshoreworkers. Local *delegados* and national officers work on the docks and make the same pay as other longshoreworkers. There are only two full-time union staff people, who are not officers, have no other function than answering letters, and receive longshoreworkers' wages. Decisions are made by periodic assemblies, which can be attended by any member and at which any member can vote. Each local union is autonomous. "The only way a national port strike can occur is for each autonomous union to recognize that a threat to another port is a threat to itself." Fitz, "La Coordinadora," 93–94.

11. David Bucah, "France Grass Roots Shake the Union Tree," *Financial Times* (London), October 30, 1993, 3.

Contributors

JOHN BORSOS is field representative for Health Care Workers' Union Local 250, Service Employees International Union, in Oakland, California. He received his Ph.D. from Indiana University.

ERIC LEIF DAVIN is a graduate student at the University of Pittsburgh. He is currently writing his doctoral dissertation on the history of the political transformation of Pittsburgh from 1932 to 1993.

ELIZABETH FAUE is the author of *Community of Suffering and Struggle: Women, Men and the Labor Movement in Minneapolis, 1915–1945* and other works. She teaches history at Wayne State University and has for several years coordinated the annual North American Labor History Conference.

ROSEMARY FEURER holds a Ph.D. from Washington University in St. Louis and has published several essays on labor history. She organized Labor-Vision, a cable TV program produced by rank-and-file labor activists in St. Louis. She is also coordinator for St. Louis Bread and Roses, dedicated to the promotion of workers' history, art, and culture.

JANET IRONS teaches history at Lock Haven University in Pennsylvania. She received her Ph.D. from Duke University.

MICHAEL KOZURA was a lecturer in the Sociology Department at the University of Michigan. Previously he worked as an over-the-road trucker, a warehouse laborer, and a union organizer.

STAUGHTON LYND is an attorney for Northeast Ohio Legal Services in Youngstown, Ohio. Together with his wife, Alice Lynd, he edited *Rank and File: Personal Histories by Working-Class Organizers*.

MARK D. NAISON works as a community organizer in the Bronx, New York City. He has written extensively on the Communist Party and the African American community. He is author of *Communists in Harlem during the Depression* and coeditor of *The Tenant Movement in New York City, 1904–1984*.

PETER RACHLEFF teaches history at Macalester College in St. Paul, Minnesota. He is the author of *Black Labor in Richmond, 1865–1890* and *Hard-Pressed in the Heartland: The Hormel Strike and the Future of the Labor Movement*.

STAN WEIR was a member of the Sailors' Union of the Pacific from 1942 to 1951. He worked as a longshoreman from 1959 to 1963 and from 1984 to 1986. He has also been an automobile worker, a truck driver, a labor educator, and cofounder of a small publishing company, Singlejack Books.

Index

The Making of Western Labor Radicalism: Denver's Organized Workers, 1878–1905 *David Brundage*

In Search of the Working Class: Essays in American Labor History and Political Culture *Leon Fink*

Lawyers against Labor: From Individual Rights to Corporate Liberalism *Daniel R. Ernst*

"We Are All Leaders": The Alternative Unionism of the Early 1930s *Edited by Staughton Lynd*